HATED
WITHOUT
A CAUSE?

To Donalds and
Margaret
with Christian
love
from CWI
team 2000.

Alec Carrie

HATED WITHOUT A CAUSE?

A SURVEY OF ANTI-SEMITISM

FOREWORD BY
MARTIN GOLDSMITH

GRAHAM KEITH

paternoster
press

First published 1997 by Paternoster Press

03 02 01 00 99 98 97   7 6 5 4 3 2 1

Paternoster Press is an imprint of Paternoster Publishing,
P.O. Box 300, Carlisle, Cumbria CA3 0QS

British Library Cataloguing in Publication Data

A catalogue record for this book is available from the British Library.

ISBN 0-85364-783-6

This book is printed using Suffolk New Book paper which is 100% acid free.

Typeset by WestKey Ltd., Falmouth
Printed in Great Britain by Clays Ltd., Bungay, Suffolk

Contents

Foreword

Christian anti-Semitism! Emotive words! We cannot run away from the horrendous realities of our history, peppered not only with anti-Semitic attitudes but even with the most fearful oppression, pogroms and persecution in the name of Jesus Christ. We inherit the history of our Christian forefathers and its consequences.

The Jewish community and anti-evangelistic Christian movements constantly remind us of these dark stains on our past, urging us to acknowledge our guilt. But they fail to remind us also of the fundamental truths of the Christian faith — grace, cleansing, atonement and new life. An awareness of our sin and guilt should bring us to heartfelt repentance. And wonderfully, through Jesus Christ, repentance proves to be the gateway to forgiveness, salvation and new life. 'Old things are passed away' — we no longer need to live under the heavy burden of guilt. We are free to live for Christ and share his good news with all people, Jews and Gentiles alike.

But the cry of 'anti-Semitism' in accusation against us is aimed at paralysing the Christian church into a quiescent silence. It stifles the joyful freedom which overflows in vital witness as we share the glories of the gospel with our Jewish friends. And it is rightly pointed out that if Jews do not need to come to God through Jesus Christ, then surely Islam and all other faiths may also qualify as acceptable ways to God and his salvation. So the church's call to evangelism is relegated to the dustbin, and mission becomes merely a polite listening to one another with no assurance of any objective truth or revelation.

My heart sank when I first heard that another book was being written on the subject of anti-Semitism. I set out to read it without enthusiasm. But I soon realized that this book looks at the subject with a quiet and objective Christian spirit. I was particularly pleased to note the excellent study of the biblical passages which are often quoted as the foundations for the whole development of anti-Semitism. Every person with a concern for Jewish-Christian issues needs to read this book. It is well researched, scholarly in its objectivity. As a vice-president of the Anglican mission CMJ and a board member of the European Jews for Jesus I warmly welcome Graham Keith's excellent book.

Martin Goldsmith,
All Nations Christian College,
Ware.

Preface

In April 1991 Thames Television presented a series of three programmes entitled 'The Longest Hatred'. Their theme was anti-Semitism, a topic which had acquired a new relevance with the collapse of
the Iron Curtain. The demise of the Soviet empire with its satellite states
had unexpectedly seen the unleashing of violent anti-Semitic passions
in eastern Europe.

I remember being annoyed that the first of these programmes should
place the roots of anti-Semitism in the early centuries of the Christian
church. With some preliminary research I discovered that this thesis
was endorsed, explicitly or implicitly, by many contemporary Christian
writers. At the same time, however, these writers did not take pains to
distinguish Christian opposition to Judaism from a more general attitude to the Jewish people. This seemed to me an unfortunate confusion.
If I speak for a moment as a Scot, I would be most unwise to equate
criticism either of Scottish nationalism or of Scottish Presbyterianism
with an attack on the Scottish people. Why should it be different with
criticism of Judaism?

My own study has convinced me that there was more to the Christian
legacy of anti-Semitism than I had at first thought. Yet, this must be
unpacked in detail. If Christian churches are to repent of past attitudes
and conduct towards the Jews, they need to be clear of what exactly
they are to repent. If there are warnings to be heeded for the future,
where precisely are the danger points in the churches' proclamation?

I was pleased that the booklet accompanying the Thames TV series
and the scholarly work by Robert S. Wistrich, which was written for
the occasion, presented a more balanced picture of the problem than
did the TV programmes. Wistrich justified his book on the ground that
an overview was needed in a subject where many specialist studies had

already been carried out. To some extent I have tried to follow his example. In particular, I have sought to blend a historical with a theological approach. Chapters 2–4 are primarily theological, Chapters 5–11 are primarily historical, and in Chapters 1 and 12 the two approaches overlap to such a degree that it is impossible to place them in one category rather than the other. There is always a danger in such a treatment of falling between two stools. Yet an issue as persistent as anti-Semitism requires an analysis from varied intellectual disciplines.

I am aware that history and theology are not the only disciplines which can be brought to bear on this issue. A number of psychological studies, especially in the USA, have considered whether certain personality types are more disposed to anti-Semitic beliefs. This is a fruitful line of study; but I have not felt it within my competence to include it. The social sciences, for their part, will have useful insights to disclose. Perhaps we can anticipate their playing a more prominent part in future analyses of this issue.

When I began this book, I did so as a member of the Glasgow Theological Forum. Though the Forum is now defunct, I would like to record my gratitude to members of the Forum for their encouragement that I should write this book. My special thanks go to Dr David Graham and Rev Howard Taylor for their helpful comments on sections of this book.

Martin Goldsmith also assisted me with pertinent comments on the modern scene. Finally, my mother and sister deserve great credit for their encouragement and forbearance during the period when the book was being written.

Graham A. Keith
Ayr.

NOTE ON ABBREVIATIONS USED IN THE FOOTNOTES

Since in some chapters I have referred to two or more different works by the same author. I have for convenience used the following abbreviations —

Edwards **TJICE** for John Edwards, *The Jews in Christian Europe 1400–1700* (Routledge. London 1988)

Edwards **TJIWE**, for John Edwards, *The Jews in Western Europe 1400–1600* (Manchester U.P. 1994)

Langmuir **HRAS** for Gavin I. Langmuir, *History, Religion, and Antisemitism* (California U.P. 1990)

Langmuir **TDAS** for Gavin I. Langmuir, *Towards a Definition of Antisemitism* (California U.P. 1990)

Lewis **SAS** for Bernard Lewis, *Semites and Antisemites: an Inquiry into Conflict and Prejudice* (Weidenfeld and Nicolson, London 1986)

Lewis **TJOI** for Bernard Lewis, *The Jews of Islam* (Routledge and Kegan Paul, London 1984)

It will be clear that I owe a substantial debt to all of these writers, as well as to Léon Poliakov's three volume history of anti-Semitism and to Stephen Haynes' recent stimulating work — *Jews and the Christian Imagination.*

Titles which appear in the **SELECT BIBLIOGRAPHY** are quoted by a short title system in the footnotes: Surname of Author/Editor, *Short Title*, p or vol:p

Other titles in the footnotes are quoted as: Surname of Author/Editor (note x) p where 'note x' refers to the number of the footnote (in the same chapter) which contains the bibliographical information for the title quoted.

ET stands for English Translation.

Introduction

The issue of anti-Semitism has yet to receive the prominence it merits within the Christian church. Too readily it has become identified with the Nazi era. There has, therefore, been until recently a tendency to dismiss the phenomenon as one which has passed away with the demise of the Third Reich. But, while the Jews may generally have basked in the sunshine of international sympathy after 1945, soon new storm clouds have appeared on the horizon.[1] Anti-Semitism clearly remains a powerful force in Europe, especially in those countries struggling to establish new identities after the collapse of Communism.

Moreover, the state of Israel has disappointed the Zionist vision of a safe haven for Jews from the anti-Semitic persecution to which they were subjected in Europe. Instead, it has put Jews at the forefront of the international stage. The policies of the Israeli government are subjected to meticulous scrutiny. Criticism has come not only from neighbouring Arabs, from whom such might well be expected, but from wider afield. Why, we might ask, does Israel receive such intensive coverage? Is this altogether fair?[2]

Some Christians may unintentionally have encouraged this trend by interpreting the establishment of the state of Israel, and its unexpected military successes, in the light of biblical prophecies. Their enthusiasm has rarely done justice to the complexities of this issue. Indeed, it may distract from a more fundamental issue for the churches — our contribution to anti-Semitism. Arab nations have with some justification claimed that European support for a Jewish state of Israel has been an evasion of taking responsibility for the Holocaust. Europeans have

---

[1] Even in the immediate aftermath of the Second World War the scene was not uniformly favourable to the Jews. In Poland surviving or returning Jews suffered atrocities in the period 1944 to 1947 — Wistrich, *Anti-Semitism*, 160–1.

[2] Lewis, *SAS*, 13–14.

simply deposited their own problems at the door of another. Perhaps a similar criticism might be made of Christian support for the state of Israel. Is this a way by which churches can overlook or even make amends for their own legacy with regard to anti-Semitism?

I am aware that to generalize and to talk of the responsibility of Christians or churches for anti-Semitism can be dismissed as misleading and futile. After all, there are many different types of churches and of Christians. They have varied in their approach to the Jewish people. Yet, some general trends can be distinguished. Besides, it is impossible for any church to ignore the Jews. It has been observed that while a Jew may follow some branch of Judaism without taking cognizance of Christianity, the reverse is impossible.[3] By virtue of the nature of the gospel of Jesus Christ (a Jew in his humanity) and by virtue of the documents in which this gospel is enshrined, Christians must at least form an impression of the Jews.

I will be suggesting that certain forms of anti-Semitism are described in the Bible, though it would be very foolish to rely on the Bible alone to chart or to explain the differing attitudes to the Jewish people at different times and in different places. I will also suggest that the Apostle Paul was alert to the possibility of anti-Semitism within the church. In fact, he warns gentile churches against an incipient anti-Semitism. But before I can justify such remarks, I will need to explain how I use the word 'anti-Semitism', a word of recent coinage.

Problems of terminology

'Words are the counters of wise men; they do reckon by them; but they are the coinage of fools', said Thomas Hobbes.[4] The usage of the word 'anti-Semitism' is a case in point. There has been much discussion among scholars on a precise sense to be given to this word, and sometimes whether it is appropriate to use the word at all. Rather than becoming entangled in what can easily become a sterile controversy, I have opted to use the word of all opposition to Jews as a group, since that is how the word is most commonly employed today. In more detail Charles Glock and Rodney Stark have suggested this helpful definition of anti-Semitism — 'the hatred and persecution of Jews as a group; not the hatred of persons who

---

[3] Pinchas E. Lapide, *The Last Three Popes and the Jews* (Souvenir Press, London 1967), 13
[4] Thomas Hobbes, *Leviathan* (1651) pt 1 ch. 4.

happen to be Jews, but rather the hatred of persons *because* they are Jews'.[5]

Outside of scholarly circles few are aware of how recent is the coinage of this word. A relatively obscure German journalist, Wilhelm Marr, is credited with popularizing this term in a book, *The Victory of Judaism over Germanism*, published in 1879.[6] He was one of a group of radicals who wished to provide a new basis for traditional Jew-hatred.[7] They lived at a time when religious toleration had become politically correct, and it was no longer profitable to smear the Jews on religious grounds. Besides, many of these radicals like Marr himself were atheists and so did not adhere to Christian presuppositions. They, therefore, strove to make it clear that they were opposed to Jews on social, economic, political and, above all, racial grounds. Religion, by contrast, was irrelevant to their standpoint.

The term 'Semite' was supposed to define the racial group to which the Jews belonged. As such, it was a strange choice of word, since in its proper usage it referred to a cognate group of languages (including Hebrew, Aramaic, Arabic, Babylonian, Assyrian and Ethiopic) rather than a racial group.[8] Even if it were ascribed in a sort of secondary fashion to racial groups, there was never any concern among Marr or the other anti-Semites who followed him to use the term more widely than of the Jews. If an explanation is sought for the unjustified identification of the Jews with the Semites in the last quarter of the nineteenth century, this can be found in the respectability of certain pseudo-scientific theories of race and racial origins.

Today anti-Semitism is not used exclusively of contempt for Jews on racial grounds. Those who coined the term could hardly insist that this restricted and relatively recent ground of antagonism toward the Jews should predominate over other forms of hatred which lingered on from the more distant past.[9] Ironically, even Marr in his later years grew disillusioned with and distanced himself from the leaders of the anti-

---

[5] cited by Langmuir, *TDAS*, 317. Langmuir goes on to give a criticism of this as a definition. His own discussion of this topic is perceptive, but rather limited in value for public discourse since his proposed definition of antisemitism (which he insists should not be hyphenated) is not widely known, let alone accepted in common speech.

[6] *Der Sieg des Judenthums über das Germanenthum* (Bern 1879).

[7] For Marr and his background see the essays by Moshe Zimmermann and Jacob Katz in Almog, *Antisemitism* 241–54 and 279–89.

[8] Wistrich, *Anti-Semitism*, xv–xvi.

[9] Langmuir, *TDAS*, 311–4 believes that in its present use the word 'antisemitism' gives too much away to the Aryan Myth.

Semitic movement he had helped to set up. People can be opposed to
the Jews for different and sometimes incompatible reasons. These
reasons may be connected with observable characteristics of the Jews,
but equally they can be quite fanciful.[10]

There are, however, dangers in using anti-Semitism as an
umbrella term to denote Jew-hatred of whatever sort and from
whatever time. It should not be taken as implying that the
same factors have been at work on each occasion. I would
identify with those scholars who would see a continuum in the
hatred of the Jews over many centuries, but would wish to
analyse the different causes and sources of that hatred at
various junctures in history.[11] We dare not, for example,
assume that pagan anti-Semitism was simply taken over by the
early Christian church. We must consider to what extent the
anti-Semitism of the church marked a new beginning. Similarly with the racial anti-Semitism of the modern period.
Moreover, it would be unfair to describe Jewish history as a
catalogue of persecutions by outsiders. (It is also dangerous
for the Jews themselves to view their history in that light.)
There were periods of peace and prosperity. Periods too of a
grudging tolerance. Any study of anti-Semitism will be concerned to explain the subtle changes in the attitude of gentiles
which have led to the more violent outbursts of anti-Semitism.[12]

Anti-Semitism and anti-Judaism

There is a further terminological problem. Those with theological
interests have sometimes adopted the term anti-Judaism to mark a

---

[10] This distinction is important to Langmuir, *TDAS*, 351–2.

[11] e.g. Shmuel Ettinger in Almog, *Antisemitism*, 9–12; Wistrich, *Anti-Semitism*, xvii–
xxvi.

[12] David S. Katz even makes the interesting suggestion that philo-Semitism is the
normal condition which has degenerated over time — in Wood, *Christianity*, 360–1.

[13] This differs from the usage of Langmuir, *TDAS*, 57, where anti-Judaism is described as 'a total or partial opposition to Judaism — and to Jews as adherents of it —
by people who accept a competing system of beliefs and practices and consider certain
Judaic beliefs and practices as inferior.'

distinct category of anti-Semitism. Though its usage does vary, anti-Judaism is in my view most conveniently used when it denotes opposition to the Jewish religion.[13] This need not imply a hostility to the Jewish people.[14] The Apostle Paul, for example, was critical of Judaism, but retained a great love for his own people. Outside the pages of the Christian Scriptures we find a figure like the philosopher Spinoza who did not cease to call himself a Hebrew after he had departed from the Judaism of his day. It is worth keeping a separate term for those Jews and non-Jews who have severe criticisms to make of Judaism. But that raises another set of questions. What exactly is Judaism, especially if certain religiously-minded Jews are critical of it? And who decides what counts as true Judaism? Here I believe Susan Perlman offers a helpful insight when she points out that Judaism is a human creation. While the creation of the Jewish nation may be reasonably ascribed to God, it was Jews who created Judaism.[15] By this she means that for some time now there has been a rabbinic community or something similar which has taken on itself the authority to adjudicate on the authentic Jewish religion. Of course, there have been dissentients to these custodians of orthodoxy. That is why it is possible to have Jews who can be described as anti-Judaistic.

I will use the term anti-Judaism to denote opposition to the publicly recognized Jewish religion. Since such opposition has sometimes come from Jews who believe they have the best interests of their own people at heart, I would want to make a fundamental distinction between anti-Judaism and anti-Semitism. Such a distinction is not uniformly recognized among scholars or among lay people, but it seems inescapable unless we are arbitrarily to deny the sincerity of all those Jews who have protested against what is accepted as their own religious orthodoxy. This picture may be applied even today when there may be no precisely defined rabbinical orthodoxy and some Jews are happy to talk of Judaisms in the plural.[16] Yet these Judaisms are not infinite; nor can they embrace anything.

---

[14] Here I gloss over the difficulty of defining the Jewish people. For some recent remarks on this problem see Bernard Wasserstein, *Vanishing Diaspora — The Jews in Europe since 1945* (Hamish Hamilton, London 1996) x–xii.

[15] '*Coming Clean: Jewish or Christian?*' in *Mishkan* 19 (1993) 43–53. Perlman does, however, recognize that some people may use Judaism in a different way — to denote Jewish beliefs or Jewish identity. But she herself believes that 'the rabbinic community does have the authority to say what is meant by the religion of modern Judaism, since it is a structure they have appropriated and modified to the point of ownership.' This can be extended further back into the history of Judaism.

[16] e.g. Neusner, *Judaism*.

Of course, some Jews have opposed Judaism not because they think they have a more accurate understanding of the authentic Jewish faith, but for social or political reasons. They may feel, for example, that traditional Judaism is a barrier to progress, and that if Judaism is to persist at all, it should be secularized. Such Jews, in fact, may share certain presuppositions with some anti-Semites. Provided this complexity is recognized, I do think there is value in such a distinction between anti-Semitism and anti-Judaism.

I should, however, warn readers that the way I will use this distinction differs somewhat from that most commonly found among Christian theologians, where anti-Judaism normally describes theological disagreement with Judaism, while anti-Semitism refers to racial hatred of the Jews.[17] My difficulty with their distinction is that it may suggest that anti-Semitism is limited to the proponents of some racial theory. I prefer to employ the more general definition of anti-Semitism proposed by Glock and Stark because it leaves the question open as to why people should detest the Jews as a group. Even in the Nazi era opposition to the Jews did not necessarily entail acceptance of Nazi racial ideology. Moreover, before the nineteenth century it is difficult to find any time when racial theories played a significant part in ill-feeling toward the Jews.

---

[17] for an example of such a distinction see Donald A. Hagner in Evans and Hagner, *Anti-Semitism*, 128.

One

Anti-Semitism in the time before Christianity

Eternal anti-Semitism?

There is a superficial attraction about the thesis of an eternal anti-Semitism, according to which there has always been and will always be a backlash of gentile animosity against the very existence of a distinct Jewish race. After all, in the Old Testament Scriptures a special role was assigned to the Jewish race by God from its very inception. In the book of Genesis the scattering of mankind after the debacle of the Tower of Babel is closely followed by the selection of Abraham to be the founder of a great nation through which the other nations of the earth are to be blessed.[1] Moreover, it is shortly after Abraham's descendants cease to be a family and emerge as a nation in Egypt that they first encounter opposition and persecution. A unique destiny for Israel, claiming a special calling from God, is inseparable from its beginnings. We might expect sharp reactions to that claim from outsiders.

An early Jewish midrash goes further than the biblical account. This states that God offered the Torah to the various nations in the world, but each refused for some reason of its own. So, the Torah was given on Mount Sinai to the Jewish people, while at the same time hatred of the Jews was bequeathed to all the other nations.[2] This idea of an eternal anti-Semitism has found supporters in the twentieth century. Strange as it may seem, it has been favoured both by early Zionists and

---

[1] Gn. 12:1–3; 22:17–18. It is made clear that the blessing comes to Abraham's physical descendants and to outsiders only if they share Abraham's faith — Rom. 4.
[2] The midrash is recounted in Wistrich, *Anti-Semitism*, 4–5.

by anti-Semites.[3] The reason is not far to seek. It rationalizes the sort of rigid separation between Jews and other races that both of these groups have wanted, though for very different reasons.

But it does not do full justice to history. It fails to take account of those times when the Jews have flourished and even been welcomed in gentile environments.[4] It fails to take account of what might be called philo-Semitism — a phenomenon which existed before the time of Jesus as well as in more recent times. To talk of eternal anti-Semitism, therefore, gives an unbalanced picture of gentile attitudes as a whole. At the same time it is unrepresentative of Jewish perceptions, seeing that there have been Jews who have protested against a rigid separation from all other nations and have argued that a constructive Jewish contribution to other nations need not infringe their distinct religious and racial identity.[5]

The problem of sources

The search for the origins of anti-Semitism is complicated by the paucity of sources about the Jews from the ancient world. The only significant evidence we possess outside the pages of the Old Testament derives from Greek and Roman sources.[6] Even then, the Greek evidence is localized; it is heavily slanted by the experience of Greek and Jewish co-existence in Egypt, especially in the city of Alexandria.

Although an extensive ancient Greek literature survives, it is remarkable how late the Greeks were in showing any interest in, or indeed awareness of, the Jewish people and their distinctive way of life. This came only in the last two decades of the fourth century BC in the immediate aftermath of the conquests of Alexander the Great.[7] At first the Greeks commented favourably on the Jews; they saw them as

---

[3] *ibid.*, xvi–xvii. Adolf Hitler himself believed that anti-Semitism was as old as the Jewish race — *Testament*, 50–1.

[4] Shmuel Ettinger in Almog, *Antisemitism*, 9.

[5] cf. the varied reactions of the Sages (the Jewish spiritual leaders from the second century AD) to the phenomenon of anti-Semitism as recounted by Moshe David Herr in Almog, *Antisemitism*, 27–38. No less a person than Josephus devoted virtually his entire literary output to a more cosmopolitan view of Judaism than had characterized the leaders of the disastrous Jewish revolt of 66–74 — cf. Bilde, *Flavius*, 233–4.

[6] These are now usefully collected by Stern in his three-volume *Greek and Latin Authors on Jews and Judaism*.

[7] E. Gabba in Davies and Finkelstein, *History*, 2:614–8.

philosophers with a similar outlook on wisdom as themselves.[8] It is not until the second century that we find clear indications of anti-Semitic feeling.[9] The context was the cauldron of Alexandria where the relatively privileged position of the Jews under the Ptolemaic kings was resented by the Greeks who felt the Jews were benefiting from citizenship in the polis but being exempted from certain of the burdens.[10] As the Jews persisted in strength in Egypt, anti-Semitism began to acquire the status of a tradition, which gained a further impetus from a fusion with a parallel strand of anti-Semitism nurtured in the Seleucid Empire in the aftermath of the Maccabean revolt.[11]

In due course this filtered into the Roman world, where the Romans gave their own colour to this tradition.[12] They seized on accusations of misanthropy and unsociableness on the part of the Jews, and berated their impact on the society of Rome itself. The long-established, healthy ways of Roman society were being corrupted by these foreigners — still worse, by foreigners who had actually been conquered by the Romans. This Roman anti-Semitism flowered among some of its greatest writers — including Seneca, Quintilian, Tacitus and Juvenal — who worked in the latter part of the first and into the second century AD.[13] These were writers of distinction and as such were the pagan writers from antiquity who left the most significant legacy to later generations. Indeed, their remarks gave some pretext for the racial anti-Semitism distinctive of the nineteenth and early twentieth centuries.

It is true that the Graeco-Roman world showed little interest in race as a ground for attacking the Jews as long as race is understood in narrowly biological terms.[14] But where race denotes culture, the totality of national and social characteristics, it was quite a different story. For Roman writings about foreign nations are imbued with a strong sense of superiority engendered by pride in their own achievements and in their culture.[15] By contrast, contempt is often shown for others whose

---

[8] *ibid.*, 622–3.
[9] An Egyptian priest, Manetho who wrote in the third century BC, is sometimes said to be the earliest anti-Jewish writer of whose work something has survived. However, the original text of Manetho, which suffered from manipulation and distortion, probably did not mention the Jews at all — *ibid.*, 630–3.
[10] *ibid.*, 624–38.
[11] *ibid.*, 636. For the anti-Semitism within the Seleucid Empire see *ibid.*, 643–6.
[12] M. Stern in Almog, *Antisemitism*, 15–17.
[13] *ibid.*, 22–25.
[14] This is carefully argued by Sevenster, *Roots*, 36–56.
[15] *ibid.*, 40.

culture failed to match Roman norms. The Jews among others fell far short on this score. Images such as those of Tacitus, who described themas the 'basest of peoples' and of Cicero who included them with the Syrians as 'nations born for slavery' would provide fuel for the fires of those who wished to start a conflagration against the Jews on racial rather than religious grounds.[16]

We can, therefore, say with confidence that tensions between the Greek and Jewish populations in Egypt in the second or possibly the third century BC saw the start of a literary tradition of anti-Semitism which has persisted in varied forms until today. That is not to say that this period saw the first significant burgeoning of anti-Semitism. The possibility remains that anti-Semitism emerged in earlier contexts in Jewish history. If so (and I believe that to have been the case), then these outbursts of anti-Semitism left no direct legacy to subsequent generations of anti-Semites.

Opposition to Jews as a distinct nation state

It has been suggested by Moshe Herr that it was the exile of the Jews in 586 BC which occasioned the emergence of anti-Semitism.[17] Certainly, this brought the Jews into close contact with a number of nationalities which previously had no experience of them and who must have been amazed at the rigorous separation on which many of the Jews insisted. They would not intermarry or even eat with their gentile neighbours. Nor would they join in their festivals and religious rites, but insisted on maintaining their own practices as laid down in the Torah. Moreover, despite their exile and dispersion they claimed a unique destiny to which God had called them. The host country could not help but wonder about this strange minority which had appeared in their midst. We can readily see how the exile could have given rise to outbursts of anti-Semitism in the form of resentment or even fear about this alien group in the midst. This was exactly the line which was exploited by Haman in the Persian Empire according to the book of Esther.[18]

But it is imposing an unnecessary limit to instances of pagan anti-Semitism if we insist that it applies only to situations where the

---

[16] Tacitus, *Hist.* 5:8:2 — *taeterrima gens*; Cicero, *De prov. cons.*, 5:10 — *nationibus natis servituti.*
[17] quoted in the Thames Television booklet *The Longest Hatred* (1991) 3.
[18] Est. 3:8.

Jews were living in the lands of others. A similar criticism may be levelled at the three instances of 'Jew-hatred' cited by Louis Feldman for the period prior to the conquests of Alexander the Great — the persecution of the Pharaoh just before the Exodus, the attack of the Amalekites on the Jews as they wandered through the desert, and the plot to kill the Jews which was instigated by Haman in Persia.[19] These are undoubtedly serious early instances of exceptional hatred for the Jews. Nor were they confined to embittered individuals. The Egyptian Pharaoh did not act simply from some irrational fear of his own; his misgivings were evidently shared by many of the Egyptian people.[20] With the Amalekite tribe it is clear that their dastardly attack on the Jewish stragglers in the desert went well beyond an understandable suspicion about Jewish intentions as they approached their territory.[21] Other tribes were similarly threatened but did not act in the same way. As for Haman, his conspiracy against the Jews would have had sinister and far-reaching consequences because his anti-Jewish sentiments were shared by a number of people throughout the Persian Empire.[22]

But it would be wrong to preclude from consideration the period when the Jews had a settled state of their own. Of course, as one nation alongside other nations, the Jews were bound from time to time to encounter the hostility of their neighbours. Boundary disputes arose, while inevitably ambitious monarchs from foreign nations attempted to play power politics either alongside or more often against the Jewish leaders. This would in the Old Testament invite the judgment of God, but as far as human behaviour was concerned it was unremarkable. At the same time there is evidence from the Old Testament of a more intense and less rational hatred of the Jews which found its clearest expression when Jerusalem was destroyed by the Babylonians in 586 BC, but was by no means confined to that period.

The prophet Ezekiel, a contemporary of the sack of Jerusalem, catalogues and pronounces judgment on those nations which had

---

[19] Feldman, *Jew*, 84–6.
[20] Ex. 1:12, 13.
[21] Ex. 17:8–16; Dt. 25:17–19. The Edomites, who were not to be known for their friendship to the Jews, reacted with suspicion but stopped short of shedding blood — Nu. 21:14–21. The Ammonites and Moabites, however, were more hostile and their hiring of the prophet Balaam to curse Israel should probably be reckoned as an early incidence of anti-Semitism — Nu. 22–24; Dt. 23:3–6.
[22] Est. 8:13; 9:1, 5–10 and 16.

maliciously benefited in some way from this Jewish disaster.[23] In some cases, as with Tyre and possibly Sidon, they had seen the downfall of Jerusalem simply as an occasion for plunder.[24] But in other cases a more sinister motive is alleged. This is understandable, given that as recently as 594/3 the kings of five of the nations listed by Ezekiel (Edom, Moab, Ammon, Tyre and Sidon) had convened in Jerusalem in a concerted effort to rid themselves of the Babylonian yoke.[25] The subsequent capitulation of Jerusalem can hardly have been in their interest. With any modicum of foresight they should have seen that it simply brought their own doom closer.

But the Ammonites, Philistines and Edomites, amongst other nations, preferred to rejoice and show their contempt at the misery of the land of Judah — a contempt which Ezekiel interprets as such contempt for God himself that he is bound to act in vengeance for the honour of his own name.[26] Two nations — Edom and Philistia — are accused of an 'eternal hatred' which had inevitably manifested itself in the hour of Jerusalem's supreme disaster.[27] With the Moabites too, it is evident that their malicious glee and contempt had been a longstanding feature in their outlook on the Jewish people.[28] In 586, Ezekiel comments, the Moabites had thought to themselves that Judah had become like one of the other nations, thereby losing any claim to a special status under its God.[29] Presumably it had irked the Moabites that they had on their boundaries a nation whose history did for the most part bear out their claim to be God's chosen people.

I suggest, therefore, that any account of anti-Semitism before Christianity would be incomplete without consideration of the time when

---

[23]   Ezk. 25–32. The one exception is Egypt which is condemned for its pride, manifested not least in its foolish confidence that it could save the Jews from the impending disaster. Ezekiel reverts to this theme, with special concentration on the judgment of Edom in Ch. 35 — cf. 36:5.

[24]   Ezk. 26:2.

[25]   Je. 27:3.

[26]   for details see the account of Ralph W. Klein *Ezekiel — The Prophet and his Message* (University of South Carolina 1988) 129–143.

[27]   Ezk. 25:15 for Philistia and 35:5 for Edom. The reference to the Philistines is the more difficult to explain seeing that the rest of Scripture mentions frequent border wars between the Jews and Philistines but does not probe further into the Philistine attitude toward the Jews or their religion.

[28]   Thus Jeremiah could speak of Moab shaking her head in scorn whenever she spoke of Israel — Je. 48:27 cf. Zp. 2:8–11.

[29]   Ezk. 25:8–11.

the Jews did possess an independent nation or nations of their own and were faced with an unnatural hatred from some of their immediate neighbours.

The Edomites and other hostile neighbours

The antagonism of the Edomites assumes special prominence among Israel's neighbours. This is not because Edom was one of Israel's strongest opponents. In fact, the contrary is true. Over most of its history it was 'a small, remote and unsuccessful nation'.[30] But Edom's opposition was particularly virulent and unnatural. It was virulent because it was unremitting and because on occasions it issued in the pitiless destruction of innocent life in Israel.[31] This climaxed in its behaviour in 586 BC when at first the Edomites merely observed the destruction of Jerusalem then began to get involved in mockery and in looting. As a final straw, they cut off a way of escape for certain Jewish survivors.[32]

At the same time this hatred was unnatural because the Jews were taught to treat the Edomites as their brothers.[33] This was firmly enshrined in their own Scriptures beginning with the story of the brothers Esau and Jacob, from whom the Edomite and Jewish peoples derived.[34] Moreover, the story did not present Jacob in the best of lights, and was at pains to describe how Jacob in later life was ready to compensate his brother for his earlier deceit.[35] Later generations of Jews were taught to respect Edom's boundaries.[36] Generous terms were offered whereby an Edomite of the third generation could enter the assembly of the Lord.[37] Nor is any complaint made in Scripture about Edomite religion, as it is about the idolatrous worship of their neighbours, the

---

[30] Bartlett, *Edom,* 186.
[31] Ezk. 35:5, 6; Am. 1:11, 12; Joel 3:19
[32] Ob. 10–14 cf. Ps. 137:7.
[33] Nu. 20:14; Dt. 2:4 and 23:7; Am. 1:11; Ob. 10; Mal. 1:2.
[34] cf. the oracle given to Rebekah at Gn. 25:23 — 'Two nations are in your womb, and two peoples from within you will be separated; one people will be stronger than the other, and the older will serve the younger.'
[35] Gn. 32–33 esp. 33:4–11. Is there a hint of the origin of the later hatred of the Edomites at Gn. 25:41, where Esau is said to hate his brother because of the blessing his father Isaac had pronounced upon him? Did the Edomites resent their lesser destiny?
[36] Nu. 20:14–21; Dt. 2:1–8.
[37] Dt. 23:7.

Moabites and the Ammonites. Possibly the Edomites did worship the Lord but after a fashion of their own.[38]

Nor did the Jews obviously behave in a way which would have given any pretext for the animosity of the Edomites. They do seem to have respected the boundaries of Edom. It is true that King David did subdue the Edomites and place garrisons there, but in this he simply extended the policy of his predecessor Saul, who was concerned to eliminate raids into Israel from its various neighbours.[39] Only David among the kings succeeded in bringing the Edomites within his control.[40] The remaining history of Jewish dealings with Edom is punctuated by revolts until the Edomites broke free altogether.

The Edomites, for their part, signally failed to treat the Jews as their brothers. It was their sustained malice which, according to the prophets, brought a judgment from God which involved their complete destruction as a nation.[41] This probably refers to a defeat inflicted by Nabonidus of Babylon in the mid-sixth century when the Edomites drop out of history.[42] Later inhabitants of the geographical region known as Edom (the Nabataeans) have no certain connection with the biblical Edomites.[43] In subsequent Jewish thinking Edom began to take on symbolic importance; it was used of corporate gentile opposition to the Jews. Within the Roman Empire, for example, it was used to signify Rome itself.[44]

Thus Edom has played an important part in Jewish thinking about their own role among the nations. It has fostered the idea of an irrational and irreversible hatred among those who ought to be their brothers. Sometimes Jews have been guilty of the sort of over-generalization which accompanies a persecution mentality. Not all the nations which Israel has encountered have proved as bad in their outlook as the Edomites.

It would be more accurate to see Edom as typical of the exceptional hatred which has flared up from time to time against Israel among its neighbours or at least among some of them. In the Old Testament

---

[38] see Bartlett, *Edom*, 187–207 for detailed comment on our present evidence for religion in Edom.

[39] David — 2 Sa. 8:14 cf. 1 Ki. 11:15f. Saul — 1 Sa. 14:47.

[40] Alec Motyer, *The Prophecy of Isaiah*, (IVP, Leicester 1993) 269.

[41] Is. 34:8–17; Je. 49:7–22; La. 4:21, 22; Ezk. 35:1–9; Ob. 16.

[42] Bartlett, *Edom*, 161.

[43] *ibid.*, 163–74.

[44] *ibid.*, 186.

Edom is sometimes used as a prize example of a relentless, incorrigible enemy of God.[45] Such exceptional hatred manifested itself at times in the desire to eradicate Israel's distinct national identity when that identity was virtually co-extensive with her special religious calling. Thus, in Psalm 83 a conspiracy to obliterate Israel's memory is ascribed to the enemies of God himself.[46] In the period from the conquest of Canaan to the sack of Jerusalem an attack by outsiders on Israel is uniformly seen as an attack on God himself, even where the attacking nations may be God's chastening instruments for the sins of his people. Though these attacking nations themselves invite the judgment of God, they are not absolutely excluded from the possibility of future blessing. Edom, however, seems to be an exception.[47] By its persistent and unremitting hatred of Israel, it had put itself beyond the pale of divine forgiveness.

Thus, among the nations which bordered on Israel Edom stood in a class of its own. Only the Moabites and Ammonites (the children of Lot) came remotely near it, their attitude being characterized by contempt rather than by hatred. There were even times when individual neighbours might be friendly to the Jews, as with King Hiram of Tyre, who had an alliance first with King David and then with his son Solomon.[48] But alliances of Jewish kings with foreign nations rarely met with prophetic approval; they undermined the nation's trust in God. In any case they did not last. The prevailing outlook of the surrounding nations was one of hostility, though that hostility could vary greatly in intensity and though individual foreigners could successfully identify their own interests with those of the Jews. The same comment could be made for the period immediately after the return from exile in Persia. As long as the Jewish cause in the land of Israel remained in a depressed condition and as long as the city of Jerusalem was dilapidated, the neighbouring nations were content; but as soon as firm progress was made to re-establish a Jewish state and to rebuild Jerusalem, their attitude altered. 'They were very much disturbed that someone had come to promote the welfare of the Israelites.'[49]

---

[45] e.g. Ps. 60:9 (=Ps. 108:10); Is. 34:1 - 34; Ezk. 36:5.

[46] The precise historical context of this psalm is unknown though the reigns of Saul (1 Sa. 14:47, 48) and of Jehoshaphat have both been suggested.

[47] I have in mind such passages as Ps. 87, where even Babylonians are said to be future citizens of the city of God.

[48] 2 Sa. 5:11, 12; 1 Ki. 5.

[49] Ne. 2:10 cf. Ezr. 4:4, 5.

It is interesting that the most violent opponents of Israel — Edom and to a lesser extent Ammon and Moab — were not those which could pose the biggest political threats. Internationally they did not rate highly. Those superpowers which did bring devastation to the land of Israel — Assyria and Babylon — do not appear to have been motivated by anything more than a desire to increase their power and their plunder. The kingdom of Judah with its wealthy temple in Jerusalem was inevitably a prime target. In subsequent history too the main impetus to the most extreme outbursts of anti-Semitism has not come from the most powerful of nations or groups, but from those who have felt that their own power is challenged by the very presence of Jews. Such was the case with the Pharaoh in Exodus and with King Barak of Moab; and the pattern has often been repeated.

Instances of anti-Semitism can, therefore, be identified from the period when the Jews had an independent state of their own. At the same time it must be recognized that such anti-Jewish feeling varied greatly from time to time and from nation to nation. This variation in response indicates how unhelpful is the notion of an eternal anti-Semitism.

A further observation should be made about the reaction of outsiders to the Jewish people at this juncture. Whatever the failings of the Jews individually and collectively, the treatment of the Jews by outsiders could almost invariably be construed as a reaction to God himself. Thus, the collapse of Jerusalem in 586 BC and the exile of the remnant of the Jewish people were events of international proportions. The reactions of surrounding nations betrayed their attitude to the God of Israel. Even if the Jewish people had wished to be considered as in no way different from other nations, God had not allowed this scenario to materialize.[50] Hence, some of the prophets, notably Ezekiel and to a lesser extent Jeremiah, were given a platform by the sack of Jerusalem to set forth God's judgment of the nations as a whole. The note struck by Ezekiel is reflected in this prophecy to the mountains of Israel —

> *Because they ravaged and hounded you from every side so that you became the possession of the rest of the nations and the object of people's malicious talk and slander, therefore, O mountains of Israel, hear the word of the Sovereign LORD: This is what the Sovereign LORD says to the mountains and hills, to the ravines and valleys, to the desolate ruins and the deserted towns that have been plundered and ridiculed by the rest of the nations around you — this is what the Sovereign LORD*

---

[50]   Ezk. 20:32. cf. 1 Sa. 8:19, 20.

says: In my burning zeal I have spoken against the rest of the nations, and against all Edom, for with glee and with malice in their hearts they made my land their own possession so that they might plunder its pastureland [51]

It seems that this sort of malicious gossip against the Jews was not confined to the neighbouring nations, but was found even in these countries to which the Jews were dispersed. There too God's name was being profaned, according to Ezekiel, because it was said of the Jews, 'These are the LORD's people, and yet they have had to leave his land.'[52] God was bound, said the prophet, to bring restoration in his own time and manner to the Jewish people, if he was to vindicate his own name among all the nations which had associations with the Jewish people.[53]

Thereafter, even with the return of many Jews to their ancestral land, there would always be a Jewish Dispersion, while even within Palestine the Jews until recent times would not enjoy the same political freedom as they did before 586 BC. This means that it becomes more complex to unravel the attitudes of outsiders to the Jews. Within the Dispersion the Jews constituted a cohesive ethnic group. They were, therefore, capable of exercising economic or political influence as well as being a living witness (for good or for ill) to Judaism. Theoretically a hostile reaction to the Jews might be prompted by economic or political as well as religious reasons. Similarly, with restricted liberty within Palestine the Jews there were bound to interact at various levels with their overlords. There were many possible areas of tension.

Antiochus Epiphanes — a landmark in anti-Judaism

One of the most notorious of these overlords was the Seleucid King Antiochus IV Epiphanes. At first sight his career would seem a clear instance of anti-Semitism. He has become notorious as that 'contempt-ible person' whose sinister appearance in Daniel 11:21f. in some way prefigures the work of the Antichrist at the end of the age.[54] His track

---

[51]   Ezk. 36:3–5.
[52]   Ezk. 36:20.
[53]   Ezk. 36:21–38.
[54]   The precise meaning of Daniel 11 has been vigorously disputed. It was Jerome's detailed commentary on this book which first established the idea that Antiochus was a type of the Antichrist. Such an idea has, however, not been universally accepted — see J.A. Montgomery, *International Critical Commentary: The Book of Daniel* (1927) 468–70.

record is formidable. He was virtually unique among the Seleucid kings who had dealings with the Jews in his policy of eradicating the Jewish religion and of forcibly replacing it with Greek institutions and practices.[55] Not only did he loot the Temple in Jerusalem and fill the city with blood, but he published a law which outlawed on pain of death the key elements of Judaism — circumcision, observance of the sabbath and other religious festivals, the ritual sacrifices as prescribed in the Torah, and even the scrolls of the Torah themselves.[56] At the same time he took steps to establish idolatry. Numerous shrines were established in Judaea at which unclean animals like pigs were to be offered in sacrifice. The temple at Jerusalem was renamed after Zeus Olympius in a deliberate attempt to merge Jewish religious traditions with paganism. The great altar of burnt offerings was itself covered by a pagan altar.[57] To further the policy of Hellenization Jerusalem was repopulated with numerous gentile inhabitants and soldiers.[58] So extensive and comprehensive was this attempt at a cultural and religious change that some historians would identify it as a landmark in human history — the first attempt at the annihilation of a religion through a cultural revolution.

It does not, however, follow that all this was inspired solely or primarily by the ingenuity or malevolence of Antiochus. His policy was prompted by divisions among the Jewish ruling classes, whose factions used the extent to which they were prepared to hellenize as a way of boosting their claims to power against their rivals.[59] Even the two books of the Maccabees, which are not slow to portray Antiochus as a villain, have to admit in their distinctive ways that it was Jewish renegades who initiated Antiochus' violent suppression of Judaism. Thus, in 1 Maccabees we read of Jews who incited the people, 'Let us enter a covenant with the Gentiles round about because disaster after disaster has overtaken us since we segregated ourselves from them.'[60] This argument then was made the basis for an appeal to Antiochus for appropriate legislation. In 2 Maccabees more specific accusations are levelled — first against the high priest Jason, who obtained his office by bribing the king and then used it to promote Hellenism, and later

---

55 Feldman, *Jew*, 91.
56 Hengel, *Judaism*, 1:292–3.
57 *ibid.*, 1:294–7.
58 1 Macc. 1:34, 38.
59 Feldman, *Jew*, 92 and in more detail Hengel, *Judaism*, 304–6.
60 1 Macc. 1:11–15. For the ideological background see Hengel, *Judaism*, 1:299–303.

against another high priest Menelaus, who assisted Antiochus in pillaging the temple in Jerusalem.[61]

Of course, Antiochus, himself a master of intrigue and diplomacy, would not have consented to this anti-Judaistic policy had he not been sympathetic to it. This, however, does not necessarily mean that he was anti-Semitic. There is, for example, no evidence that he persecuted the sizeable number of Jews in his realm outside of Judaea.[62] His motives may well have been primarily political.[63] Antiochus will have had a watchful eye on the Ptolemaic kingdom in Egypt which retained an interest in Judaea, where until recently it had been predominant. The tolerance of a dissenting group in Judaea could have given the Ptolemies the prospect of regaining their influence. Significantly, Antiochus first took violent action in Jerusalem immediately after an unsuccessful campaign in Egypt where he was humbled by the Romans.[64] He might have hoped to eliminate a potential source of rebellion by insisting on religious uniformity among the Jews of Judaea. If this were his motive, he did in fact seriously miscalculate. He incited the Maccabean revolt which was to gain unexpected success and so to exercise a considerable influence on the future destiny of the Jewish religion.

At the same time Antiochus was interested in money, and was following a family tradition in looking to a temple as a lucrative source of revenue.[65] We read that his death was popularly thought to be a divine judgment when it followed shortly after an attempt at a similar act of pillage in the sanctuary of Artemis at Elymais.[66] Motives of security and of greed may provide the major part of the explanation for Antiochus' ruthless attack on Judaism and its central institutions. I would not, however, wish to dismiss altogether an antagonism toward the Jewish religion. Why else should he adopt the risky strategy of departing from his father's policy of allowing the Jews complete religious freedom and of favouring an extremist group among the Jewish ruling classes? Surely with a basic understanding of the Jewish mind he

---

[61] 2 Macc. 4:7–17; 5:15.
[62] Feldman, *Jew*, 91.
[63] John R. Bartlett, *The Cambridge Bible Commentary: The First and Second Books of the Maccabees* (CUP, 1973), 29–30.
[64] cf. Dn. 11:30.
[65] Bartlett, (note 63), 24–5. Porphyry highlighted Antiochus' greed, as indicated by Jerome in his *Commentary on Daniel*, 11:31ff.
[66] Polybius 31:9.

would have realized that this policy would inevitably foster revolt. I can only assume he underestimated this danger because he was so contemptuous of the traditional Jewish religion that he thought that with concerted pressure its support would quickly crumble.[67]

It is unwise, however, to speak of Antiochus Epiphanes as an anti-Semite since there is no evidence that he wished to obliterate the Jewish people or had any animosity toward the Jews as a racial group. He clearly was opposed to the Jewish religion, an opposition which cannot be entirely blamed on misinformation, since he had personal acquaintance with the Jews and their religious institutions. But in the context of his day, when leading Jews were eager to abandon their distinctive religion, anti-Judaism did not imply anti-Semitism.

Whatever Antiochus' personal motives, he soon became a model for a future political anti-Semitism.[68] When one of his successors, Antiochus Sidetes, was besieging Jerusalem in 135/4 BC, he was urged by certain friends to put a complete end to the Jewish race or, failing that, to abolish their laws and force them to change their ways. These friends appealed to the tradition of Jewish misanthropy. Their ancestors had been refugees from Egypt who 'had occupied the territory round about Jerusalem, and having organized the nation of the Jews had made their hatred of mankind into a tradition, and on this account had introduced utterly outlandish laws: not to break bread with any other race, nor to show them any good will at all.' They claimed it was the discovery of the xenophobic nature of the Jewish laws and religion which had prompted Antiochus Epiphanes systematically to desecrate everything associated with the Temple in Jerusalem. Despite the powerful case they adduced, they were unable to persuade Antiochus Sidetes to take the draconian measures they proposed.[69] But the fact remains that Antiochus Epiphanes had set a precedent for what might be described as a distinctly anti-Semitic political programme. Curiously, it was assumed that the destruction of the key city of Jerusalem would put an end to the distinctive Jewish race and religion. It would not be the last time the resilience of the Jewish religion would be underestimated.

---

[67] A distaste for the Jewish religion ties in well with Dn. 11:28 where his heart is described as 'set against the holy covenant' — cf. verse 30. A different approach which plays down any religious motivation in Antiochus may be found in Otto Morkholm's contribution to Davies and Finkelstein, *History*, 2:278–91.

[68] Hengel, *Judaism*, 1:306–7.

[69] The story is recounted in Diodorus Siculus 34:1:1–5.

It may also be significant that the earliest known charge of ritual murder against the Jews was associated with Antiochus' entry into the Temple at Jerusalem. There he was said to have discovered a Greek who had been seized by the Jews and was being fattened up for sacrifice. This unfortunate Greek claimed that he had ascertained this was an annual practice. In due course he would be taken to a wood where he would be killed. The Jews would offer the body in sacrifice and themselves partake of the entrails of the victim. In the process it was their practice to swear an oath of hostility against the Greeks and then throw the remains of the dead man into a pit. After such a gruesome tale the Greek captive was duly freed by Antiochus.[70] Presumably the story was devised to emphasize the entrenched hatred of the Jews for outsiders, and perhaps to excuse Antiochus Epiphanes from a charge of sacrilege for his treatment of the Jewish Temple.[71] It may have gained currency in the immediate aftermath of Antiochus' action, though the earliest version of the story now available to us dates from Apion early in the first century AD.[72]

Here is a further reason for considering Antiochus an important landmark in the history of anti-Jewish attitudes, though our present evidence does not allow us to say how far the king himself instigated or even knew of the anti-Jewish propaganda. The complex political circumstances of his reign reveal a strong undercurrent of anti-Judaism among both gentiles and Jews. The later stories also show how easy it was for anti-Judaism to turn into anti-Semitism proper. True anti-Semites, from whatever period, have cared little for any distinction between observant and non-observant Jews.

Jewish economic and political influence

Antiochus Epiphanes' interest in Judaea had been prompted not least by the revenue he hoped to draw from it in one way or another. On a wider scale much interest has been shown by scholars in the economic power of the Jews in this period and the extent to which it may have

---

[70]   Apion in Josephus, *Against Apion*, 2:91–96. A slightly different version is found in an obscure historian Damocritus, who claims that the sacrifice happened only once in every seven years. Damocritus also mentioned another anti-Judaistic legend, the worship by the Jews of an ass's head — cf. Stern, *Greek*, 1:531.
[71]   Emilio Gabba in Davies and Finkelstein, *History*, 2:644.
[72]   Tcherikover, *Hellenistic*, 366–7 dates the story to the Roman period.

inspired hatred against them.[73] This is not a straightforward question since ancient writers were not attuned to the recognition of economic factors.[74] Nor do economic factors ever operate in a vacuum. In ancient societies wealth was almost invariably accompanied by political influence.

We do find suggestions that in certain parts of the Roman Empire Jewish economic activity did rouse suspicions, especially in the light of the close ties the Jews had with one another and in the light of the imperial sympathy they enjoyed. From the time of Julius Caesar, whom the Jews had supported in his civil war with Pompey, it had been regular Roman government policy 'not merely to tolerate Judaism but positively to promote it, so long as it posed no threat, through attempts at proselytism, to the state cult or to the social and political order.'[75] The Jews were virtually unique in being allowed to form corporate groups; they enjoyed full freedom to organize and administer their own synagogues. In other cases such action was normally prohibited as a first step on the road to sedition.[76] But because of their unusual privilege the Jews will have seemed to many to be a sinister power group.

Jealousy at the privileges of the Jews, including their wealth, lay behind the most furious pogrom of the Graeco-Roman era in 38 AD in the city of Alexandria, which contained the largest Jewish community in the world at that time. It has been estimated at 180,000 — some 30–40 per cent of the total population. Louis Feldman aptly describes it as the New York of its day.[77] According to Philo, the violence which flared that year was not sudden or unexpected but had been smouldering for some time among the masses.[78] Josephus, in fact, speaks of incessant strife as far back as the time of Alexander the Great who had given the Jews a favoured position in his new city.[79] The Ptolemaic dynasty, which followed Alexander, preferred to cultivate the support of the Jews rather than to trust the native Egyptians. Consequently, the Jews were often found as tax-collectors or as bureaucrats. Though such

---

[73] Sevenster, *Roots*, 57–66 gives an interesting account of how the personal prejudices of scholars have influenced their judgments, and how we are restricted in our conclusions by the nature of the ancient evidence available to us.

[74] Feldman, *Jew*, 107.

[75] *ibid.*, 101.

[76] *ibid.*, 93.

[77] *ibid.*, 108.

[78] Philo, *Legatio ad Gaium*, 120.

[79] Josephus, *War*, 2:487–9.

opportunities were restricted under Roman rule, which began about 31 BC, the Jews enjoyed greater opportunities for commerce than under the Ptolemies, who had managed a state-run economy.[80] Moreover, effectively from the time of the Emperor Augustus the Jews had in certain respects superior rights to the Greek citizens of Alexandria. The latter, who had formed the ruling class under the Ptolemies, were reduced to what amounted to subject status without even a council of their own, while the Jews had their own ruling body (*gerousia*), an ethnarch and even their own judicial system.[81] Needless to say, Jewish privilege, and the very size of their population, fanned resentment, which flared into open hostility in the uncertain period following the death of the Emperor Tiberius.

Then the anti-Jewish elements in the city were able to take advantage of the worries of the governor, Flaccus, about his position before the new Emperor. The immediate cause of the anti-Jewish outburst was the visit to the city of the Jewish King Agrippa I.[82] When the Jews honoured this eminent member of their own race, the Greek mob insinuated that the Jews were being intrinsically disloyal to the Roman government. Flaccus endorsed the charge and deprived the Jews of all civic rights. He herded the Jews into one area of the city, effectively creating the first ghetto. He did nothing to stop the Greek mob looting Jewish homes and shops, attacking their synagogues, and burning alive those Jews whom they could capture. After a desperate period of confinement in their own unhealthy ghetto, the Jews were able to restore the situation only by means of desperate appeals to the Emperor Caligula, who had Flaccus recalled in disgrace and exiled.[83] Jewish influence was further underlined when Agrippa I was largely responsible for the accession of Claudius to power after the assassination of Caligula.[84]

Clearly, the Jews were a cohesive group within Alexandria who from time to time could bring vital pressure to bear on the Emperor. It is little wonder that the Greeks in the city were resentful, not least because the Jews were clamouring for more rights in the city. In fact, Claudius had to intervene urging both Greeks and Jews to abide by the *status*

---

[80]   Feldman, *Jew*, 109.
[81]   Ernest L. Abel, *The Roots of Anti-Semitism* (Associated University Presses 1975) 104–6.
[82]   for details see Feldman, *Jew*, 115–7.
[83]   *ibid.*, 95–6.
[84]   Josephus, *Ant.* 19:236–8.

quo which had persisted before the violence of 38. The Jews were not
to aspire after greater privileges.[85] As it was, they were a powerful and
wealthy enough group within the city.

However early the anti-Jewish violence of 38 AD in the history of
anti-Semitism, it does reveal certain features of concerted anti-Jewish
activity which will recur frequently in later history. The hatred was
entertained by the masses, though it must at least have had some
support in upper-class Greek circles. The Jewish element in the city
for its part was powerful and enjoyed many privileges. And yet it was
allowed to opt out of certain burdens, like military service, imposed
on the rest of society. This gave a pretext for the accusation that the
Jews were unpatriotic, though the root cause of the annoyance was
presumably the feeling that the Jews were being encouraged to enjoy
many privileges, but without any attendant responsibilities. A weak
governor sought to bolster his own position (in the end, unsuccess-
fully) by making capital out of the popular anti-Jewish sentiment.

Clearly, Roman indulgence and patronage of Judaism both roused
resentment against the Jews and protected them from the worst manifestations of that resentment. Thus, when that patronage was with-
drawn at the outbreak of the Jewish revolt in 66, this proved the cue
for violent outbursts against the Jews not only in Alexandria but in the
cities of Syria and Israel. Josephus mentions hatred, fear and greed for
plunder as three major factors behind the action against the Jews.[86]
Jewish strength and prosperity were widely recognized.[87] Interestingly,
in those cities in Syria where there were no massacres (Antioch, Sidon
and Apamea) Josephus comments that there was a substantial non-
Jewish population.[88] Presumably they did not feel threatened by Jewish
expansion and numbers.[89]

While both Philo and Josephus highlight anti-Jewish feeling among
the lower classes at Alexandria, this may reflect their aristocratic

---

[85]   Claudius *Pap. Lond.* 1912:73–105. This is conveniently included in English translation in Whittaker, *Jews*, 99–100.
[86]   Josephus, *War*, 2:464, 478.
[87]   for a detailed study on Jewish wealth in the east at this time see Feldman, *Jew*,
110–13.
[88]   *ibid.*, 479.
[89]   It has been estimated that by the middle of the first century AD the Jews numbered
8 million and constituted about one-eighth of the population of the Roman Empire —
Salo W. Baron, *A Social and Religious History of the Jews*, 2nd ed. (New York:
Columbia University Press 1952) 1:170 and 370–2. The proportion of Jewish inhabitants would, of course, have been considerably greater in the east.

prejudices.[90] Upper-class Greeks probably shared the sentiments of the masses. But we do have indications from Rome itself of suspicions among the intelligentsia of Jewish economic power. This is all the more interesting in that the city of Rome saw no armed Jewish uprising and no anti-Jewish pogrom.[91] But there was concern about the Jewish right to levy an annual half-shekel tax from all members of their religion over the age of twenty and send it to the Temple in Jerusalem, not least because Jewish organization and community spirit enabled them to manage this operation most efficiently. Thus, Cicero in his *Pro Flacco* could assume that the Roman jury would sympathize with any act restraining the export of the requisite gold, because it seemed inappropriate to siphon off wealth from Roman provinces to serve the interests of Jewish superstition.[92] A similar concern was expressed over a century later by Tacitus when he commented on the opulence of the Temple and criticized the wasteful practice of converts to Judaism in sending their wealth to swell the Jewish coffers.[93] (This was part of a wider anxiety he felt about the inroads of Judaism on society in Rome.) Josephus records a similar complaint from the Roman general Titus to the leaders of the Jewish revolt in Jerusalem. He could even speak of the Jews growing rich at the expense of the Romans.[94]

The complaint, then, of these Romans concerned the sending of money to Jerusalem and the consequent denuding of other areas of the Roman Empire. It did not necessarily entail the enrichment of individual Jews. Indeed, Roman satirists who were roughly contemporary with Tacitus would mock Jewish beggars associated with particular areas of the city of Rome.[95]

The charge of misanthropy

Whatever irritations were caused by Jewish political or economic influence, these did not constitute the main cause for complaint by outsiders against the Jews. This turned rather on their aloofness from other races and their close bond with others of their own race — a phenomenon which was often identified with misanthropy. Thus,

---

90   Sevenster, *Roots*, 169.
91   Menahem Stern in Almog, *AntiSemitism*, 19.
92   Cicero, *Pro Flacco*, 66–7 cf. *De prov. cons.*, 5:10.
93   Tacitus, *Hist.*, 5:5:1 and 5:8:1.
94   Josephus, *War*, 6:335–6.
95   Martial, *Epigrams*, 12:57:1–14; Juvenal, *Sat.*, 3:10–16, 296; 6:542–7.

about 300 BC one of the earliest Greek writers to deal at any length with the Jews, Hecataeus of Abdera, speaks of Moses establishing for his people a way of life which was 'somewhat unsocial' and 'hostile to foreigners'.[96] This observation is all the more remarkable in that Hecataeus' account is generally sympathetic toward the Jews. Indeed, he admires the Jews for showing such enthusiasm toward their law that they were prepared to suffer torture rather than disobey it.[97] Moreover, he tries to explain Moses' approach as an understandable reaction to the hostility and banishment the Jews had experienced as foreigners in Egypt. Thus, when he is faced with the apparently anti-social aspects of the Mosaic Law, his tone is that of a dispassionate ethnographer who is concerned to describe rather than criticize the strange customs of other nations.[98]

Hecataeus was not alone among Greeks of his time who were prepared to make favourable comments about the Jews.[99] But this phase did not last. The emigration of Jews in substantial numbers to Egypt under the Ptolemaic dynasty brought them into close contact with both native Egyptians and Greek settlers. Jewish aloofness became more of a practical issue and so was seen in a more sinister light.[100] At some point, probably in the late third century BC, an addition was made to the history of the Egyptian priest Manetho which linked the Jews to a group of lepers and other diseased persons whom King Amenophis had banished from his land in order to purify it from all contagion.[101] The band of exiles were said to have found a leader in a priest from Heliopolis called Osarseph, who was identified with Moses. This leader adopted a deliberate policy of ridiculing and defiling all that was sacred to the Egyptians — 'He made it a law that they should neither worship the gods nor refrain from any of the animals prescribed as especially sacred in Egypt, but should sacrifice and consume all alike, and that they should have intercourse with none save those of their own confederacy.'[102]

This account of Jewish origins is found with considerable variation

[96] cited in Diodorus Siculus 40:3:4. The translation of the key words ἀπανθρωπον τινα και μισοξενον βιον is that of Feldman, *Jew*, 126.
[97] cited in Josephus, *Against Apion*, 1:190–1.
[98] Stern, *Greek*, 1:30.
[99] *ibid.*, 24.
[100] Abel (note 81) 40–2.
[101] for Manetho's significance see Stern, *Greek*, 1:62.
[102] cited in Josephus, *Against Apion*, 239 cf. 249–50.

in several other sources.[103] Indeed, an earlier version had been known to Hecataeus.[104] The accusation of deliberate contempt for all that others held holy was also common and even more significant.[105] Perhaps it reached its fullest expression in the Roman historian Tacitus, who could write — 'Moses introduced new religious practices, quite opposed to those of all other religions. The Jews regard as profane all that we hold sacred; on the other hand, they permit all that we abhor.'[106] Tacitus is prepared to grant that the Jews were extremely loyal and compassionate to one another, but toward outsiders 'they feel only hate and enmity.' He then indicates that in his mind it is their common practice which justifies this conclusion — 'They sit apart at meals and they sleep apart, and, although as a race they are prone to lust, they abstain from intercourse with foreign women; yet among themselves nothing is unlawful.'[107] He continues in the same distorted vein by claiming that circumcision was introduced to facilitate this segregation, even though he must have known that circumcision was by no means confined to the Jews.[108] Nor does Tacitus have much time for Jewish proselytes — 'the earliest lesson they receive is to despise the gods, to disown their country, and to regard their parents, children, and brothers as of little account.'

Though not in the extreme form represented by Tacitus, the idea that the Jews thought of themselves as somehow distinct from the rest of the human race was to have a long history. It can be found as late as the early fifth century AD.[109] Its importance can be gauged from the fact that a number of Jewish writers endeavour to rebut the charge of hatred for the rest of mankind.[110] These include the famous Josephus, who not only devotes his essay *Against Apion* to this topic, but has this in the back of his mind in his more substantial work *The Jewish Antiquities*.[111] In the process Jewish history undergoes some interesting adjustments. In Josephus' version, for example, one prime motive for Abraham to visit Egypt is his desire to study matters of theology under

---

[103] Stern, *Greek*, 1:63–5.
[104] Diodorus Siculus 40:3:1–2.
[105] Feldman, *Jew*, 128–9.
[106] Tacitus, *Hist.*, 5:4:1.
[107] *ibid.*, 5:5:1–2.
[108] Sevenster, *Roots*, 134–5.
[109] Feldman, *Jew*, 129–30.
[110] *ibid.*, 131–3.
[111] *ibid.*, 133–49.

the Egyptian priests. He is even said to have been prepared to accept the priests' doctrines should he find them superior to his own; while if he should win the debate, he would try to win over the priests to his own stance.[112] By thus rewriting history to make Abraham look like a Greek philosopher, Josephus reveals his sensitivity to the charge that Jews were not open to viewpoints other than their own. Many other aspects of Jewish law and incidents in their history which emphasize their separation are similarly toned down.

In the light of this it is basically correct to say with Ruether that pagan anti-Semitism was rooted 'in the special social consequences of the Jewish religious law'.[113] Pagans were little disturbed by distinctive Jewish theology; some of the more learned could even find sympathy for an aniconic approach to the deity.[114] Others could find a place for the Jewish God among the pantheon of international deities.[115] Nor is there any indignation among Graeco-Roman sources about the Jewish claim to be an elect nation set apart by the supreme God for himself.[116] It was, after all, expected that each nation would have its own God or gods; to this extent the Jews were no different from other nations.[117] Even their pretensions to a special divine calling could be paralleled elsewhere, not least among the Romans, some of whom believed that Rome's greatness could be attributed to her piety toward the gods.[118] Moreover, recent Jewish history seemed to pour scorn on the claim that Israel was a favourite of the supreme God. 'How dear it was to the immortal gods is shown by the fact that it has been conquered, let out for taxes, made a slave', mocks Cicero.[119] If, then, the Jews trumpeted a special relationship with their God, such a boast was more likely to prompt ridicule than hatred or jealousy.

The Jews were disliked because they would not participate in civic or local religious rites, which they of course considered idolatrous. This

---

[112]   Josephus, *Ant.*, 1:161.
[113]   Ruether, *Faith*, 24.
[114]   Feldman, *Jew*, 149–50.
[115]   *ibid.*, 50–1.
[116]   In Stern's three-volume collection *Greek and Latin Authors* I can find only one significant allusion to this theme, and that comes from the knowledgeable Emperor Julian — 2:516–7. Julian does not object to the notion, but finds fault with Moses for saying nothing as to how the other nations of the earth are governed.
[117]   cf. Cicero, *Pro Flacco*, 69 —'*sua cuique civitati religio*'.
[118]   Feldman, *Jew*, 102–3.
[119]   Cicero, *Pro Flacco*, 69. cf. Apion's remark in Josephus, *Against Apion*, 2:125.

was regarded as a lack of patriotism rather than an insult to the gods themselves.[120] In fact, the Jews sometimes went further. Not content with a refusal to participate, they showed outright contempt for the religious practices of others. Even the Emperor Claudius, whose accession to power owed much to a Jew, Agrippa I, in a pro-Jewish edict saw fit to warn the Jews not to be contemptuous of the religions of others, while they enjoyed freedom to observe their own religious practices.[121] It is surely a mark of the strong feelings of the elder Pliny that he can launch a swipe at the Jews as 'a race remarkable for their contempt for the divine powers' in the unlikely context of a description of a type of date.[122] It is, no doubt, this characteristic which prompted the charges among some pagans of the Jews as atheistic and impious.[123] But, to put this in perspective, our sources from the Graeco-Roman period do not give this the same emphasis that they do with the accusation that the Jews are misanthropes. Interestingly, this will tie in with evidence from the Apostle Paul, who takes up the charge of misanthropy and develops it in a new vein.[124] At the heart, therefore, of tensions and divisions between Jew and gentile in the Graeco-Roman world lay Jewish conduct and attitudes rather than the peculiarities of the Jewish view of God.

The Jews defaming God's name

The Apostle Paul declares that the conduct of his fellow-Jews reflected seriously on the character of their God. They had brought God's name into disrepute by their arrogance and inconsistency. Though they claimed to adhere to the Law of Moses and so to be teachers of the nations in righteousness, yet they had failed to abide by the very laws they advocated. Since Paul was quoting from Isaiah, he cannot simply have had Jews of his own day in mind.[125] He was speaking of the legacy of the Jews over a much longer period of time.

---

[120] Feldman, *Jew*, 151.
[121] Josephus, *Ant.*, 19:29. — cf. *Corpus Papyrorum Judaicarum* no. 153.
[122] Pliny, *Nat. Hist.*, 13:46 — '*gens contumelia numinum insignis*'.
[123] Sevenster, *Roots*, 96–102.
[124] 1 Thes. 2:14–16 cf. Rom. 2:17–29.
[125] Paul quoted from the Septuagint version of Is. 52:5, simply rendering the direct speech of the original into indirect speech. Paul's remarks, however, fall short of the assertion of Ezekiel that the Jerusalem of his day had actually gone further against God's laws than the surrounding nations — Ezk. 5:5f.

Paul's testimony can claim some support from non-Christian sources. It can claim support from the pagan charge of misanthropy. It can also claim indirect support from Josephus, the Jewish apologist and historian of the great Jewish revolt of 66–74 AD. In his account of this war Josephus blames internal strife among the Jews. This dissension, he suggests, became inevitable when some Jews ceased to observe God's law.[126] Thus, Josephus can enumerate several crimes by the Jewish rebels which distressed the Jewish moderates and to his mind made divine judgment inevitable.[127] But most frequently he berates the rebels for a whole range of sins —

> What have you done that is blessed by the lawgiver (i.e. Moses), what deed that he has cursed have you left undone? How much more impious are you than those who have been defeated in the past! Secret sins — I mean, thefts, treacheries, adulteries — are not beneath your disdain, while in rapine and murder you vie with each other in opening up new and unheard of paths of vice; aye, and the temple has become the receptacle for all, and native hands have polluted those divine precincts.[128]

Significantly, two of the secret sins, theft and adultery, mentioned by Josephus correspond exactly to those with which Paul arraigns his fellow-Jews in Romans 2:21–22.[129]

Seeing himself as something of a Jeremiah, Josephus goes on to argue that the disaster befalling Jerusalem and the Jewish people marked God's judgment on them for their sins. But the parallel between Josephus and Paul does not extend to every detail. The sins Josephus has in mind include not only violations of the Torah, but the failure to recognize God's providential hand at work through the Romans.[130]

---

[126] Bilde, *Flavius*, 74–5. Dissension or stasis was an important criterion in Josephus' thinking — Feldman, *Jew*, 147–8.

[127] Josephus, *War*, 2:454–6; 4:314–8, and 383–8.

[128] Josephus, *War*, 5:401–2 cf. 5:442–3. (The translation is that of the Loeb Classical Library.) Josephus' own speech to the rebels in Jerusalem is unlikely to be authentic; but it does represent his mature reflection on the conduct of these rebels.

[129] Paul's other charge, that of temple robbery, may perhaps be echoed in a passage included in Josephus, *Ant*, 4:10 where Moses is said to have exhorted the people — 'Let none blaspheme the gods which other cities revere, nor rob foreign temples, nor take treasure that has been dedicated in the name of any god.' Moreover, one anti-Jewish writer Lysimachus could claim that because the name Jerusalem in its Greek form sounded like temple-robbery that was why the city was given that name — Josephus, *Against Apion*, 1:311. Does Paul intend a similar pun with his use of the word ἱεροσυλεῖς in Rom. 2:22?

[130] Bilde, *Flavius*, 75 and 186–7.

Even more significantly, these sins are committed by a minority of Jews. Josephus represents the Jewish war-party at the time of the revolt as able to enforce their own outlook in spite of a lack of support both among the common people and among the upper classes, of which Josephus himself was a member. He makes out that the rebels were an unrepresentative group. But his picture is far-fetched. A marginalized group would not have been able so to dictate Jewish politics as to force the majority of the nation into a bitter and lengthy conflict against its will. If Josephus wants to say that the revolt was caused or at least preceded by violations of the Jewish law, these violations will have been more widespread than he cares to admit. Moreover, he puts into the mouth of the Roman general Titus the suggestion that from the beginnings of Roman rule in Judaea in 63 BC the Jews had adopted a rebellious and unjust outlook toward Rome.[131]

Josephus is far from being anti-Jewish or anti-Judaistic. Indeed, his largest work, *The Jewish Antiquities*, is designed to present Judaism as a distinguished and attractive religion based on a sublime concept of the divine and on moral capability and virtue.[132] At the same time Josephus insists that the Jewish religion turned on the careful observance of the laws of Moses.[133] He is convinced that these laws were wholesome and therein lay the best answer to pagan charges of Jewish misanthropy. In particular, he illustrates that the Mosaic Law was designed to promote humanity and not hatred toward the world at large. The people, for instance, were taught to share with others. A Jew had to furnish supplies not only to gentile friends and neighbours who asked for them, but even to avowed enemies.[134] While Josephus does exonerate the Law from a misanthropic tendency, he does not in either *The Jewish Antiquities* or *Against Apion* explore the possibility that the Jews may have been responsible for a misconception of the Mosaic Law through their own disobedience or through a distorted emphasis which gave pride of place to those precepts which kept them aloof from outsiders — e.g. the dietary laws and circumcision. Josephus in effect is sanguine about the question of Jewish observance of the Law.[135]

---

[131]　Josephus, *War*, 6:328ff.

[132]　Bilde, *Flavius*, 99–101.

[133]　Sevenster, *Roots*, 114–6.

[134]　Josephus, *Against Apion*, 2:211–3 cf. 2:146 and 291.

[135]　It is notable that Josephus finds difficulty in dealing with the story of Jonah which represents the Jewish prophet as far more reluctant than his God to see divine blessing on the gentile Ninevites — *Ant.*, 9:206–14 and Feldman's comments at *Jew*, 139–40.

According to the tenor of *The Jewish War* those who discredited the Law were an unrepresentative minority. The Christian Apostle Paul would have disagreed; the problem was more widespread among the Jews than Josephus cares to imagine.

A few pagan writers indicate that later Jewish authorities had distorted the Law of Moses, but they were exceptional.[136] Most commonly all the traditional practices of the Jews were ascribed by gentiles to Moses. If, then, the Jews seemed misanthropic and antisocial, it was Moses who was regularly blamed.[137] I have no doubt that this is at least in part what Paul had in mind when he quoted Isaiah to the effect that 'God's name is blasphemed among the Gentiles because of you.'

Conclusion

In the post-exilic period other nations had the opportunity to encounter at first hand what they would often term the misanthropy of the Jews. In many ways the exclusivist tendency among the Jews was accentuated by the struggles of the Maccabean period when the separatist element in the Jewish community began to predominate over the Hellenizers. By the first century AD the voice of Josephus seems to have been crying in the wilderness when he supported a less rigorous form of Judaism; for it was Josephus' fate to be ignored by his fellow-countrymen for many centuries.[138] Since Josephus advocated a sort of Judaism which would have been acceptable beyond the bounds of the Jewish people and since his type of Jewish universalism was very different from Christianity, the church cannot be blamed for subsequent Jewish isolation. The tendency to aloofness and to total contempt for gentile practices was already well established among the Jewish people before the church ever attained the sort of position where it might begin to hound the Jews.[139]

Since Jewish communities were so close-knit and almost self-sufficient, it is difficult to ascertain the precise motives for hostility toward the Jews. The separatist tendency could often be construed as a political danger. It was this point that the Pharaoh in Exodus made to his

---

[136]   Notably Strabo at, *Geographica*, 16:2:49, and possibly Hecataeus as cited by Diodorus Siculus at 40:3:9.

[137]   That is not to deny that there were those gentiles who had a high regard for Moses — cf. Feldman, *Jew*, 233–87.

[138]   Bilde, *Flavius*, 15–16.

[139]   cf. Wright, *New Testament*, 230–2 and 237–41.

retainers and his people. Haman, too, was to argue from political expediency to win King Ahasuerus over to his policy of eliminating the Jews. But this need not mean that the real motives of either of these men had much to do with politics.

Jewish separatism could also be construed economically. Jewish cohesion meant that all Jews potentially might profit from their corporate wealth. When the Temple in Jerusalem was rebuilt on a grand scale by Herod the Great, it seemed to stand as a symbol of Jewish prosperity.[140] Even back in the time of the exile Haman had promised that his massacre of the Jews would be accompanied by substantial gains to the king's coffers; presumably most of these revenues were to come from the wealth of the murdered Jews.[141]

This does not mean that ancient anti-Semitism was provoked primarily by envy of Jewish wealth or by fear of the Jews' political influence. But anti-Semitism could be cloaked behind these rational considerations.

The basic reason for that uniqueness of the Jews which prevented their assimilation was their religious identity. This would be recognized by outsiders, seeing that Moses was preached in every city from the earliest days of the Diaspora and was read in the synagogues every sabbath.[142] Besides, the Jewish Scriptures make it plain that God had set the Jewish nation apart.[143] It could never be absolutely like one of the other nations, however much some generations of Jews might desire this or outsiders try to eliminate Jewish identity. Probably the more intense outbursts of anti-Jewish activity, such as the persecution of the Egyptian Pharaoh, were directed against these religious claims. But this anti-Semitism was a sporadic phenomenon, to be differentiated from (say) the sneering contempt of the Romans at a nation whose value system could be so different. In the ancient world, as in more recent times, there was a wide range of attitudes toward the Jews.

---

[140] cf. the references quoted by William Lane, *The Gospel of Mark*, (Marshall, Morgan and Scott, London 1974) 451.

[141] Est. 3:9. For the extent of the riches involved see Carey Moore, *Esther — The Anchor Bible* (Doubleday and Company, New York 1971) 39–40.

[142] cf. Acts 15:23.

[143] cf.Nu. 23:9.

Two

Anti-Semitism in the New Testament — the Gospels and Acts

Since the ending of the Nazi Holocaust the Christian church has been buffeted by two distinct storms of criticism about its responsibility for generations of anti-Semitism.[1] The first storm was stimulated by Jules Isaac, a Jewish historian from France who had lost most of his family through Nazi atrocities in the 1940s. Isaac insisted that the Christian church was primarily responsible for the anti-Semitic legacy on which the Nazis capitalized. But he did so without impugning the New Testament itself. Instead, he claimed the church had misunderstood its own Scriptures and its own founder.[2]

The second storm was initiated by a Roman Catholic theologian, Rosemary Radford Ruether, who argued (surprisingly perhaps for a Christian) that the New Testament could not be exonerated from the charge of inherent anti-Semitism. More precisely, she believed that anti-Judaism is so fundamental to the earliest Christian position that nothing short of a new Christology is required if anti-Judaism is to be rejected.[3] Alongside this, she made a more controversial claim that anti-Judaism, an essentially theological attitude, constantly finds social expression in anti-Semitism.[4] Clearly, this view posed a more radical challenge than that of Isaac. Though by no means all scholars have accepted Ruether's position, her contribution has considerably influenced subsequent debate.[5]

---

[1] There is a useful summary of this phase of scholarship in Gager, Origins, 13–23. Langmuir, HRAS, 18–41 goes even further back into the history of writing on anti-Semitism.

[2] Isaac's views are contained in *Jesus and Israel* and *The Teaching of Contempt*.

[3] Ruether, *Faith*, 246–51.

[4] *ibid.*, 116.

[5] For an acceptance of Ruether's analysis of the anti-Judaic element in early Christianity but a denial of the anti-Semitic consequences see Donald A. Hagner in Evans and Hagner, *Anti-Semitism*, 128–150 esp. 129 note 5 and 149 note 67.

It is at first sight extraordinary that the New Testament should be seen as the seedbed of anti-Semitism when its leading figure, Jesus of Nazareth, is unmistakably identified as a Jew in terms of his human origins and culture.[6] Moreover, most of the writers of the New Testament were themselves Jews, and would hardly be disposed to inculcate animosity against their own race. But Ruether adduces the sociological concept of 'sibling rivalry' to explain the virulence (as she sees it) of the New Testament attack upon the Jews.[7] By this she implies that bitterness is often at its most intense between groups which pose rival claims to exclusive truth within the same religious symbol system. From its outset Christianity, growing up as it did within a Jewish matrix, was bound to clash with the Jewish religious establishment because they, above all, understood the peculiar claims of Christianity and were uniquely placed to be able to refute them. Yet Ruether's analysis must be questioned in the light of growing consensus among scholars that Judaism at the time of Jesus was pluralist.[8] Thus, if the New Testament attacks expressions of religion among the Jews, this can be paralleled from other Jewish writings of the time which have no association with Christianity.[9] James Dunn, therefore, queries whether a claim that the New Testament is anti-Jewish or anti-Judaistic makes much sense. It does, however, fit the historical context to see the New Testament affirming the religion of Jesus as the true Judaism, in contradistinction to several other claimants.

This is the line I wish to follow in what amounts to a reversion to the earlier stage of the debate as initiated by Jules Isaac. It is crucial to distinguish what the New Testament actually says from how the church throughout its history has interpreted this. Such a distinction will involve identifying the precise nature of New Testament anti-Judaism and distinguishing it from the social or political phenomenon of anti-Semitism. I will be arguing that the church has directly or indirectly promoted anti-Semitism when it has only partially understood the Bible's testimony on the Jews. The New Testament does have some harsh words about Jews. But at the same time it has harsh words about all mankind. Since the wider context has to be appreciated, some attention must be given to these vital passages of the New Testament.

---

[6] Rom. 9:5.
[7] Ruether, *Faith*, 30.
[8] Dunn, *Partings*, 18–9.
[9] *ibid.*, 143.

Historical criticism of the gospels and anti-Semitism

The examination of the New Testament evidence is not as straightforward as it might once have been. The historicity of the gospels and of
Acts is now openly questioned by Christian as well as Jewish scholars.
Before the rise of modern critical scholarship, the gospels would have
been seen by Christians as largely objective accounts of the ministry
and teaching of Jesus, with Acts giving a similar perspective on some
of the leading events within the early church. A certain theological
colouring would have been accepted as long as this was not understood
to have distorted the underlying facts. The inspiration of the Holy Spirit
behind the human authors of Scripture would have kept their accounts
free of error.

But such presuppositions are generally rejected or at least ignored
in much of modern New Testament scholarship, which tends to see
the gospels as the responses of the early church to the problems and
challenges it faced. In other words, the gospels are designed as much
to provide a justification for the stance of a particular Christian
community as they are to spread good news to outsiders. At first sight
this outlook on the gospels would promise a cure for any anti-Semitism which has become embedded in society from biblical sources.
Surely, it will be argued, we can identify exaggerated or unfortunate
responses to early challenges posed by certain Jews. Once these
passages are seen in their true perspective, we can eliminate them
from the authentic Christian position. One American scholar, Norman Beck, has even proposed making a new translation in which he
will eliminate or modify such passages of the New Testament as are
'damaging to the Jewish people, dehumanizing to Christians and
detrimental to Christianity'.[10]

Such hopes for the elimination of the seeds of anti-Semitism, however, have proved over-optimistic. Critical scholarship has not reached
agreement on the original teaching and mission of Jesus as distinct from
later accretions.[11] Samuel Sandmel, a Jewish scholar who argues that
the New Testament contains some anti-Semitism, has pointed out that
some of the earliest German critical scholars proved even more anti-
Semitic than the New Testament itself. For they denied a divine Christ
and represented him as a human being whose wondrous virtues stood

---

[10]   Beck, *Mature*, 13.
[11]   Gager, *Origins*, 27.

out all the more prominently in contrast to the abominations inherent in Judaism and in Jews.[12] In other words they reflected their own anti-Jewish or anti-Semitic prejudices in their scholarship. Since the Second World War, by contrast, the tendency has been to stress the Jewishness of Jesus, sometimes to the extent of losing sight of any uniqueness Jesus may have possessed.[13] No doubt, this reflects a more sympathetic mood towards the Jews among scholars, not least in the light of the Holocaust experience. But we might well ask if such scholarship is not as subjective as that of the earlier German scholarship which was more hostile to the Jews.

A similar criticism may be levelled at the influential work of Ruether, whose picture of Christian origins is drawn from a critical and distinctly subjective reading of the New Testament. According to her view, Jesus did not claim to be the Messiah.[14] More probably, he saw himself as a messianic prophet calling Israel to repentance in the light of the imminent advent of a messianic figure whom he called 'the Son of Man'. He believed that response to his message of repentance was vital if Israel was to accept the One who was to come. Thus, Jesus was a loyal son of Israel who was prepared to criticize Jewish religious attitudes from within. His own teaching contained no anti-Judaism. He was, however, perceived as a threat for different reasons by the Roman authorities and by the Jewish religious leaders who conspired to do away with him. Even his disciples believed Jesus had failed and so deserted him at the time of his arrest and crucifixion. Later they came to regret this, and in their desire to cover up their own unbelief and desertion of Jesus they tried to fasten the blame for this crucifixion on the Jewish authorities. Hence anti-Judaism was a central part of their stance from the beginning.

Somehow the disciples managed to transcend their rejection of Jesus and to see in his crucifixion a paradoxical triumph over all the powers of evil. When they began to proclaim this message to their fellow-Jews, they were met largely with disbelief and hostility. Thus, the early Christians were a messianic sect who happened to be particularly bold and persistent in pressing their claims despite the anomaly of a crucified Messiah.

---

[12] Sandmel, *Anti-Semitism*, 158.

[13] Dunn, *Partings*, 142.

[14] Ruether's view is set out in *Faith*, 64–95 and clarified in her essay in Davies, *Anti-Semitism*, 230–256.

Ruether's reconstruction of events may be ingenious, but it remains highly speculative. Certainly, it diverges widely from orthodox Christianity which has not only claimed Jesus as the Messiah and the Son of God, but has affirmed that Jesus' ministry in this world is inexplicable unless he understood himself to be the Messiah. But in Ruether's view Jesus looks more like a failed version of John the Baptist. Gavin Langmuir has appositely remarked that Ruether and those who have followed her are endeavouring to defend the Christian faith in the aftermath of Hitler by changing it.[15] This, however, cannot help with the historical question of the relationship between Christianity, theological anti-Judaism and social anti-Semitism. Given that this is a historical question, we have to concentrate on the historical expressions of the Christian faith, which will include the authority given to the New Testament canon. However well-intentioned the project, to rewrite or selectively to re-edit the New Testament in the interests of better relations between Christians and Jews can do little to alter the legacy from the past.

Again, Ruether's claim that invariably anti-Judaism will find social expression in anti-Semitism runs into considerable difficulty in the case of the Apostle Paul, a vital figure by any estimation in emerging Christianity. As she acknowledges, Paul is anti-Judaistic (though that does raise the question of what sort of Judaism Paul opposes).[16] Yet, that opposition is held alongside great sadness and an earnest desire for the correction and salvation of the Jewish people.[17] Nor is such an outlook peculiar to Paul. In the gospel of Luke, which probably has a non-Jewish author, Jesus weeps over the Jerusalem which is about to reject him and consequently face horrendous judgment.[18] In both Paul and Luke religious polemic against certain Jews, if that is not too strong an expression, cannot be a form of self-justification, designed to gloss over weak points in their stance. On the contrary, it is sufficiently assured to express sadness over the fate of those who should have shared their convictions but refuse to do so. There is thus a simple answer to Ruether's key question — 'Is it possible to say *Jesus is Messiah* without, implicitly or explicitly, saying at the same time *and the Jews be damned?*'[19] Paul and Luke, at least, would have answered with an emphatic 'yes'.

---

[15]   Langmuir, *HRAS*, 40.
[16]   Ruether, *Faith*, 104.
[17]   Rom. 9:1–3; 10:1; 11:14.
[18]   Lk. 19:41–4, cf. Mt. 23:37–9.
[19]   Ruether, *Faith*, 246.

I have concentrated on Ruether's views on the development of early Christianity, not because they seem persuasive but because they have had such an impact on the contemporary debate. Moreover, her approach illustrates the uncertainties which arise from the modern critical approach to the gospels and to Acts. Ironically, attempts to look behind the gospel accounts and to speculate on the immediate motives or circumstances of the gospel writers may divert attention from the actual gospel accounts. Thus, vital questions like who exactly was responsible for the death of Jesus take second place to more speculative issues like what motives could the early church have had for disseminating anti-Jewish propaganda. In the process it may be too easily assumed that the gospels themselves justify the traditional view that the Jews were solely responsible in human terms for Jesus' crucifixion. Yet, I believe that a careful study of the New Testament text will show that this assumption is unwarranted. The possibility remains that it is distortions or misunderstandings of the New Testament which have promoted anti-Semitic attitudes.

Certainly, there is much to be gained in a historical approach to anti-Semitism from considering the New Testament books according to a largely pre-critical perspective, since this was the view which prevailed in the churches until about a century ago and still commands the respect of the ordinary Christian in the pew. Anti-Semitism in history, after all, cannot be described as the prerogative of intellectuals, though it has certainly won the affection of some. Undoubtedly, it has been at its most powerful and its most sinister when it has fashioned the attitudes of ordinary men and women. It will, therefore, be opportune to try to piece together from the New Testament books a consistent picture of the Jewish question.[20] We can then ask whether such a picture would inevitably be anti-Semitic or at least contain anti-Semitic tendencies. Then, the further question could be broached as to how accurately the church has reflected the New Testament picture.

Anti-Semitism in the New Testament — the leading issues

Scholars like Sandmel, from the Jewish side, and Beck, from the Christian side, have comprehensively listed those sections of the New Testament which they believe to be relevant to the questions of anti-Judaism and of anti-Semitism. Those readers who wish to see the full

---

[20] Interestingly, Ruether, *Faith*, 232 advocates a radical reappraisal of the canonical Scriptures.

range of passages would do well to consult their works.[21] I will take a more selective approach, concentrating on the particular charges against the Jews which are said to derive from the New Testament and so to have encouraged the social expression of anti-Semitism.

These charges may be grouped as follows —

(1) The Jews were guilty of a unique crime — deicide, that is, the murder of God. In the process the Jews brought on their own heads an irrevocable curse. Often Matthew 27:25 is put forward as the basis for this idea.

(2) Because of this crime or more generally because of their persistent unbelief the Jews have not only been deprived of the special privileges they enjoyed in the years before the Common Era, but have no hope of further corporate blessing as a nation. This theme is most commonly located in the gospel of Matthew and in the work of Luke, especially the Acts of the Apostles. Clearly, too, the testimony of Paul is vital. But since it is complex, I will reserve it for treatment in a separate chapter.

(3) The Jews have by their treatment of the Messiah turned into the epitome of all that is evil and opposed to the truth. Clearly this is a stage worse than the above. It is claimed that this standpoint is included in John's gospel.

1) *Matthew 27:25 and the charge of deicide*

The cry of the crowd, 'His blood be upon us and our children', recorded in Mt. 27:25, has formed the main basis for the charge of deicide which has been brought against the Jewish people as a whole over the centuries. Haim Cohen has commented aptly, 'None of the many other charges levelled at the Jews . . . has been held so obdurately against them as unassailable proof of guilt and responsibility for the crucifixion as has this exclamation of theirs.'[22] The reason is not far to seek. It has often been understood that this cry entails the self-condemnation of the Jewish people for all time. This interpretation can be found in figures as influential as Tertullian in the early Latin church and Origen in the early Greek church.[23] It is still endorsed today by some eminent Christian expositors.[24] Within Roman Catholic circles the proposal to move

---

[21]   Sandmel, *Anti-Semitism*, and Beck, *Mature*,.

[22]   Haim H. Cohen, *The Trial and Death of Jesus of Nazareth* (New York, Harper and Row, 1971) 22. cf. B. Przybylski in Richardson and Granskou, *Anti-Judaism*, 182.

[23]   Tertullian, *Adv. Iud.*, 8; Origen, *c. Cels.*, 4:22.

[24]   Michael Rydelnik, 'His Blood Be Upon Us', from *Mishkan* 6/7 (1988) 2–3.

away from the traditional interpretation of this passage roused heated debate about the time of the Second Vatican Council.[25]

Such have been the passions engendered in Jewish–Christian relations by this section of Scripture that some scholars have argued that the whole scene, with Pontius Pilate washing his hands before the Jewish crowd, is unhistorical, a deliberate creation of the early church in its polemic with the Jews. Even if Matthew is the only gospel writer to record this scene, we ought not to dismiss it lightly.[26] A more profitable approach would be closely to examine the context to ascertain whether the traditional Christian interpretation is correct. In fact, it meets with considerable difficulty.

Most significantly, there is no verb in the original Greek version of the cry of the people.[27] When most English translations insert the verb 'be', they make a wish or even a prayer out of a simple acceptance of their own responsibility for Jesus' execution. They endorse Pilate's wish to exonerate himself and place the responsibility entirely on themselves. It is clear from various Old Testament parallels that to talk of someone's blood being on one's own or another's head was a common Jewish way of ascribing responsibility.[28] While it was serious language, the cry of the crowd can hardly be construed as an unnatural and almost devilish appeal to God to reckon Jesus' blood to their own account. It is fully consistent with other New Testament evidence that the Jewish participants, priests and people alike, acted in ignorance of Jesus' true identity and so of the significance of what they were doing.

Although Matthew does employ the word *laos* in verse 25 for all the people and he does elsewhere use this as a technical term for the whole nation of Israel, he need not here be implicating the whole Jewish people. As he does not always use this word in a technical sense, here it is probably no more than a variant for *ochlos* used of the mob in verse 20.[29] Responsibility was thus being claimed by the whole of a particular crowd, who had no authority to involve the entire Jewish people.

Perhaps the most difficult aspect of this passage is the reference to the children of the crowd who are said to be involved in the responsibility for

---

[25] Beck, *Mature*, 160.
[26] Its historicity is ably defended by Joseph Blinzler, *The Trial of Jesus* (ET, Cork: Mercier Press 1959) 215–8.
[27] R. T. France, *Matthew, Tyndale New Testament Commentaries* (IVP, Leicester 1985) 392.
[28] cf. Nu. 35:33; Dt. 19:10; Jos. 2:19; 2 Sa. 1:16; 3:28, 29; 14:9.
[29] Rydelnik (note 24) 3

the crucifixion. The most probable explanation would see this as implicating the next generation of the inhabitants of Jerusalem, whose future had already been threatened by Jesus because of a long history of unbelief.[30] The cry of the Jerusalem crowd did not in itself occasion the coming judgment. The conduct of the Jerusalemites had virtually determined it. The cry was a further stage in a persistent rejection of God's way of blessing.[31] More outrages would follow in the form of mistreatment and murder of those messengers (like Stephen) whom Jesus would be sending to the people of Jerusalem; but within a generation decisive judgment would fall on Jerusalem and its Temple.[32]

Given that Matthew is claiming to describe a historical situation, we must not assume that all the actors achieved their desires.[33] It would be foolish to suppose that Pontius Pilate was absolved of guilt merely by going through the hand-washing ceremony. So, too, the Jerusalem crowd had no authority to implicate their own children by their declaration; for the prophet Ezekiel had made it plain that the iniquity of the fathers could be visited on their children only if they consented to and repeated their fathers' misdeeds.[34] Even when Jesus had earlier spoken of the impending judgment on Jerusalem, he had at the same time indicated a way of escape for all who believed his words.[35]

The significance of Mt. 27:25 is restricted to a particular mob in Jerusalem.[36] It is not Matthew's way of placing permanent guilt at the door of all the Jews for the death of Jesus. Neither here nor at any other part of his gospel does Matthew contradict the possibility of the offer of forgiveness of sins to those very Jews who had clamoured for Jesus' crucifixion, as we find in the Acts of the Apostles.[37] Thus, the traditional view which sees Mt. 27:25 as an act of self-execration on the part of the whole Jewish people not only fails to do justice to Matthew's context, but runs counter to the analogy of faith.[38]

---

[30] France (note 27) 392. Jesus' threats are recorded at Mt. 23:34–24:2.
[31] Rydelnik (note 24) 8.
[32] Mt. 23:34–6.
[33] Rydelnik (note 24) 4.
[34] Ezk. 18.
[35] Mt. 24:15, 16. cf. Mk. 13:14; Lk. 21:20, 21.
[36] for a more detailed discussion see H. Kosmala, *Annual of the Swedish Theological Institute*, 7 (1968/9) 94–126 — cf. the comments of Scot McKnight in Evans and Hagner, *Anti-Semitism*, 72 note 64.
[37] Dunn, *Partings*, 155.
[38] That is, the principle by which Scripture interprets Scripture.

2)   Does Matthew despair of the Jews?

Some New Testament scholars believe that Matthew shows an unrelieved pessimism toward the Jews.[39] Douglas Hare, for example, not only concurs with the general view that Matthew is the most critical of the Synoptic writers about the Jews, but sees this as a theological difference rather than one of perspective. Matthew, in his view, 'concludes that Israel is not worthy of the gospel, and that it is God's will, communicated to the Church by the risen Jesus, that the gospel should henceforth be offered to gentiles only'.[40] Surprisingly, Hare does not adduce Mt. 27:25 in support of his radical view, but he does point to other passages where Matthew goes significantly further than either Mark or Luke in the threats made against the Jewish nation. All these passages occur in the section from Chapters 21 to 23 where Jesus is engaged in immediate controversy with the Jewish religious leaders in Jerusalem.

Hare points first to Mt. 21:43, which adds to the version of the parable of the wicked tenants as found in Mark and Luke this sentence — 'Therefore I tell you, the kingdom of God will be taken away from you and given to a nation producing the fruits of it.'[41] Hare is surely correct in his observation that this widens the reference of the parable to the nation as a whole. The Jews are to be displaced from their privileged status as the special people of God, and some new group is to take their place.

Hare's next passage is Mt. 22:7 which makes the surprising addition to the parable of the king who arranged the wedding feast for his son — 'The king was angry, and he sent his troops and destroyed those murderers and burned their city'. This seems to be pointing toward the destruction of Jerusalem as a divine punishment for the rejection of Christ's own missionaries. In consequence, the gospel invitation is to go out to a totally new group of people who must in this context be gentiles.

Hare's final passage, Mt. 23:37–9, gives a novel twist to a theme also found in Luke's gospel.[42] He again sees this as broadening the attack earlier in the chapter on the religious leaders in Jerusalem to include the whole of Israel. Jesus uses Jerusalem as a symbol to assert that God is about to abandon the Jewish nation.

---

[39]   see the list cited by A. Saldarini in (ed) D. Balch, *Social History of the Matthean Community* (Fortress Press, Minneapolis 1991) 42 note 12.
[40]   Douglas R.A. Hare in Davies, *Anti-Semitism*, 40.
[41]   The parallel passages occur at Mk. 12:1–12 and Lk. 20:9–18.
[42]   cf. Lk. 13:34–6.

Thus, Hare believes, Matthew has created a framework where the
risen Jesus can tell his disciples to go and make disciples of 'all gentiles'.[43] Hare interprets this parting command as specifically excluding
any future mission to the Jews.

This is a remarkable conclusion, given that it would effectively contradict the picture in the Acts of the Apostles of the gospel being first preached
to Jews in Jerusalem and elsewhere before it was announced to gentiles.
There are other reasons why Hare's conclusion is not persuasive. Notably,
Matthew has already declared that first Jesus and then the disciples
engaged in exclusively Jewish missionary activity.[44] If that were to cease,
we would expect some definite indication of this. Otherwise it is preferable
to see the injunctions of Mt. 28:19 as extending the bounds of the previous
commission given to the disciples.[45]

But, if Hare's conclusion of an abandonment of all interest in Jewish
evangelism is unjustified, we can happily accept some of his other
points. Jewish rejection and execution of their Messiah did eventually
necessitate a divine judgment, especially the removal of the distinct
religious privileges of the Jewish people. This was symbolized most
powerfully in the destruction of the Temple, which gave the city of
Jerusalem its prestige within the Jewish world.[46] Israel's loss was to
pave the way for a new people of God.

If Jews were to be excluded from this new people of God, they would
suffer this fate through their own unbelief, crystallized in their failure
to recognize the Messiah of whom their prophets spoke. But there was
no reason in principle why individual Jews were to be excluded. Indeed,
Matthew gives clear indications that Jesus' disciples were to form the
basis of the new Israel.[47] And, of course, they were all Jews. At the same
time Matthew foreshadows the inclusion of gentile believers in the
church of Christ.[48] Scot McKnight suggests that it is more faithful to
Matthew's perspective if we interpret his gospel as elevating all people
to the level of the potential people of God than as consigning the Jewish
nation to the lowest rung of the theological ladder.[49]

---

[43]   Hare's translation of Mt. 28:19 in Davies, *Anti-Semitism*, 40.
[44]   Mt. 10:5, 6, 23; 15:24.
[45]   France (note 27) 413–4; cf. Saldarini (note 39) 42 note 14 and McKnight in Evans
and Hagner, *Anti-Semitism*, 76 note 83.
[46]   France (note 27) 332.
[47]   *ibid.*, 53–4, though Matthew never uses the term 'new Israel' as such.
[48]   *ibid.*, 55.
[49]   McKnight, in Evans and Hagner, *Anti-Semitism*, 75.

Matthew is undoubtedly gloomy about the prospects of the nation of Israel as distinct from individual Jews. But as many of his remarks are directed toward that particular generation of Jews, Matthew can have little to say on the more long-term prospects for Israel.[50] Indeed, a good case can be made that Matthew's own gospel was intended as a contribution to a persistent mission to the Jews.[51] The virulence of his attacks on the Jewish religious leadership may well reflect his anxiety that the spiritual successors of the Pharisees were becoming rather too successful in defining Judaism in their own terms.[52] By contrast, Matthew expounded an understanding of the Torah which he represented as more authentic than that of the scribes and Pharisees.[53] Above all, he set forth Jesus as the fulfilment of the messianic promises in the Jewish prophets. If Matthew does not appear to have given up on his fellow-Jews, his gospel could hardly be teaching that God has permanently abandoned the Jewish people.

3) *Does Luke despair of the Jews?*

At one time it was commonly acknowledged that Matthew was the most scathing of the Synoptic writers in his treatment of contemporary Jewish piety, but in a recent work Norman Beck has made the surprising suggestion that the Acts of the Apostles contains 'anti-Jewish polemic . . . which is the most devastating and destructive of Judaism in all of the New Testament documents'.[54] This is a bold assertion, considering that the theological perspective of the Acts (and its companion work, Luke's gospel) seems limited in comparison with the depths of Paul.[55] Interestingly, Beck reveals his reason, 'For the writer of Acts it was the Jews who became followers of Jesus who were truly Israel, the people of God, whereas those Jews who refused to follow Jesus thereby forfeited their membership in the people of God.' And

---

[50]   cf. Mt. 23:36 and 24:34. Here the key word γενεα must mean 'generation', though various alternatives have been proposed — cf. France (note 27) 346. The same applies for the parallel passages in Mk. 13:30 and Lk. 21:32.

[51]   Saldarini (note 39) 141–4.

[52]   Dunn, *Partings*, 151–2.

[53]   cf. Mt. 5:17–20.

[54]   Beck, *Mature*, 207. cf. Sandmel, *Anti-Semitism*, 73 — 'there is to be found in Luke a frequent, subtle, genteel, anti-Semitism'.

[55]   cf. the comments of Donald Guthrie, *New Testament Introduction* (IVP, Leicester 1970) 337–8.

he is undoubtedly correct to observe that Luke assigns no validity to any form of Jewish religion which does not accept Jesus as the Messiah, since this is for him the true fulfilment of the Old Testament prophecies. But it is a moot point whether Luke's standpoint is really anti-Jewish.[56] In emphasizing faith rather than birth as the criterion by which Jews belonged to the people of God, he was following the same line of thought as John the Baptist, Jesus and Paul.[57] There is nothing unusual or exceptional in Luke's presentation.

In fact, various positive remarks by Luke about the Jews deserve to be highlighted. While he does affirm the guilt of those Jews who were responsible for handing Jesus over to the Romans, he does not do so to the extent of exonerating the gentile participants.[58] Moreover, he makes it clear that the Jewish people and even their leaders were acting in ignorance when they demanded the death of their Messiah.[59] Thus, Jesus' prayer 'Father, forgive them, for they do not know what they are doing' is to be understood much more widely than of his Roman executioners.[60] Evidently, Luke believes that though the action of the Jewish religious leaders and crowd was culpable, they failed to see Jesus' true glory.[61] Hence their sin was not unpardonable. Indeed, in the very same sermons in which the apostles lay the guilt of Jesus' death firmly at the door of the Jewish perpetrators, they hold out to them the offer of forgiveness and the gift of the Holy Spirit if they repent and believe in Jesus as Messiah.[62] With Luke, therefore, the execution of Jesus did not in itself entail the rejection by God of the Jewish people. The same would be true for Paul, who had himself for a time persecuted

---

[56]　for a positive perspective on the attitude of Acts toward the Jews see Jacob Jervell, *Luke and the People of God: A New Look at Luke–Acts* (ET Minneapolis 1972) 41–74.

[57]　John the Baptist — Mt. 3:9; Lk. 3:8. Jesus — Jn. 8:9–40. Paul — Rom. 2:28–9 and 4:16.

[58]　It is commonly the Jews of Jerusalem, both their rulers and the people, who are blamed — e.g. Acts 2:22, 23; 3:13–17; 4:30; 5:30; 7:52; and 13:27 — cf. S. G. Wilson in Richardson and Granskou, *Anti-Judaism*, 1:157. This is in keeping with the quote at Lk. 13:33 that the Messiah had to die in Jerusalem. At the same time Acts 4:27 (and cf. 2:24) recognizes the complicity of Herod, Pontius Pilate and the gentiles generally.

[59]　Acts 3:17; 13:27.

[60]　It is interesting that Luke is the only gospel writer to record this — at Lk. 23:34.

[61]　Perhaps the fullest treatment of this theme in the New Testament occurs at 1 Cor. 2:8. It is also significant that in his gospel Luke should highlight how little Jesus' true disciples understood of him and of his work before the resurrection — cf. Lk. 24:25–7 and 44–8.

[62]　e.g. Acts 2:38, 39; 3:19–21.

the early church, but believed he had been given the opportunity of forgiveness because he had acted ignorantly in unbelief.[63]

There is another way in which Luke balances the Jewish and indeed the general human responsibility for the death of Jesus. That is by his insistence that the human agents were unwittingly fulfilling a plan of God — a plan which had certainly been set out in the earlier Scriptures but whose meaning had not been recognized until now.[64] Through this plan God was bringing blessing first to the Jewish people and then more widely. Perhaps Luke intended his readers to see a parallel with the story of Joseph in Genesis, where Joseph interprets his brothers' wicked act in selling him into slavery as a wise provision by God for the well-being of the family in the future famine. By appealing to a hidden strategy on God's part Joseph was able to assure his brothers that he would not use his own power against them.[65] The highlighting of a divine strategy behind Jesus's crucifixion serves a similar purpose. The human perpetrators need not fear some terrible judgment as long as they repent of the sin they committed in ignorance.

Ruether has pointed out that most references to 'the Jews' in the Acts are hostile.[66] It is also true that Acts does threaten sinister consequences for those Jews who persistently reject the evidence both of their Scriptures and of recent history that God has made Jesus both Lord and Christ by his resurrection from the dead.[67] On three separate occasions, in fact, the Apostle Paul tells groups of Jewish people that their unbelief is incorrigible, and since they have rejected the gospel, he must turn to gentiles who will listen.[68] Since one of these occurs in the very last chapter of Acts, this has sometimes been taken as Luke's last word on the situation, as though he were saying that all hope of further Jewish conversions was ended.[69]

But such a conclusion would be too sweeping.[70] The events of Acts 28

---

[63] Paul's own testimony at 1 Tim. 1:13.

[64] Acts 2:23; 3:18–26; 4:27, 28; 7:52.

[65] Gn. 45:4–8; 50:19–21.

[66] Ruether, *Faith*, 89 claims that in Acts the term 'the Jews' is used in a hostile sense about 45 times, while the terms 'a Jew', 'Jews', or 'Jewish' are used in a descriptive sense for the background of Christians less than 10 times.

[67] e.g. Acts 3:23; 13:40, 41.

[68] Acts 13:46 (Pisidian Antioch); 18:6 (Corinth); and 28:28 (Rome).

[69] J.T. Sanders, *The Jews in Luke-Acts* (Fortress Press, Philadelphia 1987) 80–3, 297–9. Lloyd Gaston in Richardson and Granskou, *Anti-Judaism*, 1:139 musters a formidable array of scholars who think Luke believes God has rejected the Jews for all time. As he recognizes (p 140) this would put Luke in direct contradiction with Paul.

[70] cf. the detailed criticisms of Dunn, *Partings*, 150–1.

refer only to the city of Rome; there is no suggestion that if Paul or any other evangelist arrived in a new city where the Jewish community had yet to hear about Jesus, they would have diverged from their normal practice of taking the gospel first to the Jews.[71] Such an outlook was thoroughly consistent with the practice of Paul who still prayed for the conversion of the Jews and sought to rouse the Jews to a healthy spiritual envy at the very time when he recognized that the Jews had in the main stumbled over the gospel.[72] Moreover, it is quite astonishing that if Luke had wanted to assert the end of God's dealings with the Jewish people, he should have failed to mention the destruction of the Temple in Jerusalem, especially as this prediction figures prominently in his gospel.[73]

In short, it is foreign to Luke's purpose to suggest God had given up on the Jews. He is concerned to set forth the drastic consequences of Jewish unbelief, but that is a very different matter. He cannot ignore the contemporary reality of widespread Jewish unbelief; hence the number of seemingly hostile references to the Jews. At the same time he speaks enthusiastically of Jewish Christians, and at no time suggests that they should give up their distinctively Jewish practices because they have become Christians.[74] All the leading Christian evangelists or spokesmen in Acts (Peter, Stephen, Philip, Paul and Barnabas) are Jews. In these respects the tone of Acts is far from being anti-Jewish, while Luke's gospel insists that in his sufferings and in the deliverance he wrought in Jerusalem Jesus was fulfilling the Jewish Scriptures.[75]

4)   Does John make out the Jews are demonic?

Many scholars hold that John's gospel contains one of the most pronounced forms of anti-Judaism in early Christianity.[76] They appeal to John's frequent use of the term 'the Jews' in a hostile sense. These Jews are those who most actively oppose Jesus, who fail to understand how he fulfils their Scriptures, and who take the initiative in forming the plot to get rid of Jesus. Ruether concludes,

---

[71]   cf. I. Howard Marshall, *Luke: Historian and Theologian* (Paternoster, Exeter 1970) 182.
[72]   Rom. 10:1; 11:13, 14.
[73]   I. Howard Marshall, *Acts, Tyndale New Testament Commentaries* (IVP, Leicester, 1980) 32.
[74]   see especially Acts 21:20. Marshall (note 71) 187 suggests on the basis of Lk. 21:24 and Acts 1:6 that Luke may have shared Paul's view of a future conversion of Israel.
[75]   Marshall (note 71) 105–6.
[76]   e.g. Ruether, *Faith*, 111–6; Sandmel, *Anti-Semitism*, 101–119.

The Jews, for John, are the very incarnation of the false, apostate principle of the fallen world, alienated from its true being in God. They are the type of the carnal man, who knows nothing spiritually. They are the type of the perishing man who belongs to the "time" of the world, but, unlike the spiritual brethren of Jesus, can never recognize the kairos of the eternal event.'[77]

If John had been content, she continues, with a general distinction between man-in-God and man-alienated-from-God, all would have been well. But John in fact equates this distinction with that between the disciples of Jesus and the Jews.[78] Inevitably this casts a slur on the name 'Jew'. In time it would lead to the diabolization of the Jews.[79]

This argument, however, contains several overstatements. It ignores the diversity of uses in John's gospel of the term 'Jews'.[80] (Sometimes the term is used in a purely geographical sense, at others it is confined to the Jewish leaders, especially those of Jerusalem and Judaea.) It ignores that some of these uses are favourable; Jesus, for example, is described as a Jew and salvation is said to be of the Jews.[81] It ignores the references in John's gospel to Jewish believers.[82] It makes out that the Jews were exceptionally perverse in the rejection of the Messiah, who is also in some sense their Creator.

John's position on the latter issue is important, but not exactly as Ruether represents it. He makes out that the Jews were typical rather than exceptional examples of the world in its rejection of its Creator.[83] Jewish unbelievers are naturally emphasized by John since Jesus' earthly ministry concentrated on them. But unbelief is not an exclusively Jewish prerogative. It is ironic that the gentile Pontius Pilate, who otherwise detested the Jews, should align himself with Jewish unbelief when he refuses to accept Jesus's insistence that he has come to bear witness to the truth.[84] He illustrates the preference

---

[77] Ruether, *Faith*, 113. She alludes to Jn. 7:6 in the last sentence of the quoted section.

[78] No less a person than the famous liberal Protestant scholar, Rudolf Bultmann, makes this mistake — cf. his *The Gospel of John: A Commentary* (Westminster Press, Philadelphia 1971) 86–7.

[79] Ruether, *Faith*, 116.

[80] D.A. Carson *The Gospel According to John* (IVP, Leicester 1991) 141–2; J.D.G. Dunn in ed. J.D.G. Dunn *Jews and Christians — The Parting of the Ways A.D. 70 to 135* (J.C.B. Mohr, Tubingen 1992) 182–7.

[81] Jn. 4:9, 22.

[82] Jn. 7:43; 9:16; 10:19; 11:45.

[83] D. Granskou in Richardson and Granskou, *Anti-Judaism*, 1:203–9.

[84] Carson (note 80) 593.

for darkness over light which characterizes every unregenerate heart, whether of Jew or of gentile.[85]

If we turn to the later Johannine epistles, we find the same distinction between those 'who are of God' and 'those who are of the world' being applied in new contexts. Those who have left the Christian community to follow some new teaching, particularly teaching about a docetic Christ, have thereby shown their true spiritual allegiance as belonging to the world.[86] It does not seem to matter whether they were originally Jews or gentiles; it is their attitude to Christ which is vital. Again, if it be permitted to take Revelation among the writings of John or at least a Johannine community, its polemic has remarkably little that is anti-Jewish; it is primarily anti-Roman.[87] It is reasonable, therefore, to suppose that the anti-Jewish features in John's gospel arise from the context of Jesus' life as a ministry to the Jewish people; they do not indicate some underlying anti-Semitism.

Moreover, it is clear from this gospel that even Jesus' true disciples at one time belonged to the world.[88] Once they had been in darkness like everyone else.[89] The power of God, however, had been decisively at work in their lives to ensure that their allegiance had been changed.[90] They are informed of this by Jesus so that they should not arrogantly assume for themselves some high spiritual standing which was not theirs at birth. At the same time the demonic character of the world, meaning humanity as a whole, never becomes in John's gospel an argument to write off a particular group of people, be they Jews or anyone else. Rather, it is treated as the vital backcloth for the demonstration of the love of God, as in the famous verse, 'God so loved the world that he gave his one and only Son, that whoever believes in him should not perish but have eternal life.'[91]

---

[85] cf. Jn.3:19, 20.

[86] 1 Jn. 2:18–19 and 4:1–6.

[87] Beck, *Mature* 276. The only overtly anti-Jewish references in Revelation are at 2:9 and 3:9, both of which describe a group of professing Jews as a synagogue of Satan. Though some have seen this as a reflection of an intra-Christian conflict, I doubt if it is possible to exclude a reference to non-messianic Jews. The question of the Jewish background to this book is explored in an interesting article by Peder Borgen in Evans and Hagner, *Anti-Semitism*, 199–211.

[88] Jn. 15:15–19 cf. 6:70.

[89] cf. Jn. 9:39–41.

[90] This change is succinctly summarized by Carson (note 80) 354 — 'What was necessary was that the Father draw them (6:44), that they be given to the Son (6:37), that they be taught by God (6:45) and chosen by Jesus (6:70).'

[91] Jn. 3:16.

It has still been argued that John's gospel contains anti-Judaism, even if it is not anti-Semitic in the racial sense. This would be the case if there were clear indications that Jesus attacked Jewish institutions or even Jewish leaders in their official role. John's gospel does contain many references, even subtle allusions, to ways in which Jesus fulfilled traditional Jewish institutions or expanded on the role of earlier Jewish leaders. He could claim, for example, to be the true Son of God, the genuine vine or the good shepherd; he also improved on Moses by being the true bread from heaven.[92] One passage which sets out Jesus' role particularly clearly is his conversation with the woman of Samaria. While endorsing the Jewish religious tradition and the appropriateness of the Temple at Jerusalem, Jesus indicates that a new age is dawning when many of the vital symbols of the old Jewish religion will become obsolete.[93] The true worshippers will henceforth be distinguished by their worship of the Father in spirit and in truth; racial background will cease to have any relevance. This hardly amounts to an attack on Judaism as such; it is concerned to recognize the proper place and limits of its institutions.

While John's gospel does not attack the institutions of Judaism, the same cannot be said of the religious leaders of his own day. In fact, the section of the gospel from Chapters five to ten contains an extended controversy between Jesus and the Jewish leaders in Jerusalem. Superficially this might suggest a fundamental difference on the structures of the Jewish religion. But whatever may have been the immediate occasion for these disputes, it is a basic moral flaw that Jesus pinpoints. The religious leaders are too concerned with receiving praise from one another to seek the praise that comes from the true God; hence they neither understand their Scriptures correctly nor are able to discern the basis of Jesus' own ministry.[94] In this way, John poses the question as to whether these leaders can honestly reflect Judaism; he is far from attacking Judaism itself.

It is fair to say that John's gospel may not always or indeed often be read with due attention to the significance of its main themes, let alone its finer nuances. David Granskou has observed that the association between the world and the Jews in John's gospel could work in different ways — 'It could spread the hostility toward Jesus out beyond the Jews, thereby

---

[92] Carson (note 80) 98.
[93] Jn. 4: esp 19–24.
[94] Jn. 5:41–4; 12:42, 43. Similar themes can be found in the Synoptics at Mt. 6:1–18; 23:5–12; and in Paul at Rom. 2:29.

diluting the gospel's anti-Judaism. Or it could heighten the anti-Judaism by suggesting that the quintessence of the world's unbelief can be seen in Judaism.[95] I am convinced that a correct reading of John's gospel should entail the former consequence, but in practice, with our penchant for seeing the faults of others long before our own, the latter may be the actual result. Contemporary preachers and expositors should be alert to such possible misunderstandings and do all they can to obviate them.

Perhaps the danger is at its most acute in connection with the passage in John 8 about which Jews are particularly (and understandably) sensitive, since they see it as the heart of the anti-Jewish polemic in the book. Often verse 44 is quoted in full where Jesus is addressing some Jews in Jerusalem who pride themselves on being Abraham's children — 'You belong to your father, the devil, and you want to carry out your father's desire. He was a murderer from the beginning, not holding to the truth, for there is no truth in him. When he lies, he speaks his native language, for he is a liar and the father of lies.'[96] From this it might seem but a short step to the medieval view of the Jews as incarnations of Satan. But this would be to emphasize one aspect of this chapter at the expense of others. It is clear, for example, from the wider context that these Jews are not beyond hope. Jesus has earlier offered them a way of escape from Satan's bondage.[97] If he does use strong language, this is to sound an urgent warning against presumption and unbelief. Besides, such strong language can be paralleled elsewhere both in the New Testament and in contemporary Jewish writings more generally. James Dunn is justified in concluding that even John 8 'is still in the realm of intra-Jewish polemic'.[98] Again, a passage like this requires very careful handling in the context of the general Christian public. I agree that this has considerable potential for anti-Semitic misuse, but at the same time deny that this would be a fair reflection of John's intention.[99] He did not make out a special case that

---

[95] in Richardson and Granskou, *Anti-Judaism*, 1:204–5. I would have preferred Granskou to speak of the Jews here rather than Judaism, since talk of Judaism does beg the vital question as to whether there is a single carefully defined entity which can be described by this term.
[96] quoted by Sandmel, *Anti-Semitism*, 109; Cohn-Sherbok, *Crucified*, 24; cf. Ruether, *Faith*, 113.
[97] Jn. 8:31, 32.
[98] Dunn *Partings*, 160.
[99] It is clear that this passage was used, alongside other non-biblical items, to convince German schoolchildren in the Nazi era of the totally evil character of the Jews — cf. the composition included in Gutman and Schatzer, *Holocaust*, 40–1.

the Jews were demonic, whatever later Christians may have done with his gospel.

Conclusion

Since Jesus is the key figure in the gospels and in Acts, inevitably these books bring into sharp focus the differing attitudes among the Jews to Jesus. We encounter some of the passions which were roused when Jesus' claims were rejected — whether by Jesus' own townsfolk at Nazareth, by the Jewish religious establishment at Jerusalem or by Jewish communities in the Diaspora. The accounts are so vivid that it is tempting to imagine we are dealing here with something new and unexpected.

But if we examine the three main features of the New Testament which are supposed to embody its anti-Semitic potential, we will discover that all have extensive Old Testament parallels. The murder of Jesus is represented as an extension of a Jewish practice whereby God's true prophets were regularly killed by their own countrymen.[100] (Nor, as we have seen, was Jesus' death to be the last such incident.) This pattern is certainly found in the Old Testament Scriptures. No less a figure than Moses twice came very close to being stoned by the very people whom he had helped to rescue from Egypt.[101] Elijah, another of the great Jewish heroes, complained that his own people and not simply the heathen Queen Jezebel, were seeking to kill him.[102]

The Old Testament Scriptures also indicated that unbelief by the Jews would entail forfeiture of their blessings. In the book of Ezekiel God was so provoked by the idolatry of the people that he withdrew his presence from the Temple. In the forthcoming Babylonian Exile Jewish national identity and covenant privileges were effectively put into cold storage. Around the same time Jeremiah declared that God was about to make a distinction between those Jews currently in exile in Babylon and those in Judaea and Egypt.[103] The latter were to be written off and made a byword on the earth. Clearly they had lost their status as God's people who were under his care and direction. Only those already in exile would remain within the terms of God's covenant

---

[100]   e.g. Lk. 6:22, 23; 11:49; 13:34; Acts 7:52; 1 Thes. 2:15; Heb. 11:36–8.
[101]   Ex. 17:4, Nu. 14:10.
[102]   1 Ki. 19:10, 14. Other Old Testament allusions to the death of prophets are found at Ne. 9:26; Je. 26:20–4.
[103]   Je. 24.

blessing. These older Scriptures left the Jews in no doubt that persistent unbelief would rob them of God's blessing. Thus, when Jesus said to the chief priests and Pharisees that the kingdom of God would be taken away from them and would be given to a nation which would produce the fruits of it, he was not saying anything intrinsically new.[104]

The criticism of the Jews as a nation also has a long pedigree in the Old Testament. Moses criticized the Jews as stiff-necked and rebellious from their very beginnings as an independent nation.[105] The time of their greatest blessing — the receiving of the covenant at Mount Sinai — turned out also to be an occasion of exceptional provocation in their worship of the golden calf.[106] Their subsequent performance in history could be described by Ezekiel as surpassing that of the Sodomites in wickedness.[107] Of course, there were times when Israel did attain more closely to her calling as a holy nation, but the Old Testament record is replete with Israel's failings. This goes well beyond an understandable self-criticism.[108] What other nation would include among its hymns the long psalms 78 and 106 which seem to find infinite variations on the theme of the unbelief and sin of the Jewish people? By comparison the criticism of the Jews in John's gospel appears tame.

In the history of the Christian church sections of the New Testament have been more commonly turned to anti-Semitic ends than have portions of the Old Testament. The reason, however, for this lies not in their tone or content, but in the fact that there has been more general knowledge of the New than of the Old Testament. Indeed, had the church been better acquainted with the Old Testament, it would have had a proper context to elucidate the clash over what represented the true Judaism, which underlies the pages of the New Testament. Nor would this have been of merely antiquarian interest. The church in the present age has to face the challenge as to what is authentic Christianity. In themselves the labels 'church' or 'Christian' are not guarantees of the genuine article.

It is also worth remembering that the Old Testament prophetic tradition clearly represents a sort of in-house criticism of the Jewish

---

[104] Mt. 21:43 — cf. Craig A. Evans in, Evans and Hagner, *Anti-Semitism*, 5–6.

[105] e.g. Ex. 33:3; Dt. 9:7.

[106] Dt. 9:7–29.

[107] Ezk. 16.

[108] Hare in Davies, *Anti-Semitism*, 29 recognizes this with his category of 'prophetic anti-Judaism', but in my view does not go far enough with what he proposes to include under this head. Mary C. Callaway does more justice to this theme in her article in, Evans and Hagner, *Anti-Semitism*, 21–38.

people. A critique from an insider is normally made with good intent and so is more generally acceptable than criticism that is directed entirely toward outsiders.[109] The status of the New Testament in this regard is hard to judge, seeing that the disjunction of the church from the mainstream of Jewish life was a complex phenomenon.

However severe the Old Testament prophetic techniques may be toward Israel, it is going too far to argue with Mary Callaway that they should not be read as accurate historical descriptions of Israel.[110] She is rightly concerned that these descriptions might be used by non-Jews, as they were later by John Chrysostom, for example, to point the finger at the Jewish people as though these failings were exclusive to them. That would indeed be an improper exegetical technique. But the lessons from the Jews as representatives of the church in the Old Testament era are applied directly to the New Testament church of Jew and gentile alike.[111] They have an abiding place as both warnings and encouragements to the church throughout its history in this world.

I am unconvinced by Ruether, Sandmel and their followers that there is anti-Semitism in those sections of the Christian Scriptures at which we have looked. There is much more justification for Jules Isaac's thesis that anti-Semitism in Christian circles has resulted from misunderstandings of their own Scriptures. Too readily gentile churches have brushed off unbelief as a uniquely Jewish problem, simply because unbelief was manifested historically by the Jewish contemporaries of Jesus. This will become even clearer when we consider the Apostle Paul.

---

[109] cf. Evans in Evans and Hagner, *Anti-semitism* 8–11.

[110] Callaway in Evans and Hagner, *Anti-Semitism*, 38. Of course, prophetic statements do not fit the canons of contemporary historical writing because of their direct references to the outlook of God; but that is not the issue in question.

[111] e.g. at 1 Cor. 10:1–11 Paul draws lessons for a predominantly gentile church from the history of the Jewish people who experienced the Exodus.

Three

The Testimony of the Apostle Paul

The Apostle Paul plays a vital role in the history of the relationship between Christianity and Judaism. Much of the New Testament centres on him. As an indication of his importance, the Acts of the Apostles describes on no less than three separate occasions his conversion from Saul the Pharisee and determined persecutor of the church to Paul the apostle of Jesus Christ among the gentiles.[1] In fact, the latter half of this book turns the spotlight continuously on Paul as the other apostles and evangelists fade into the background. Moreover, within the New Testament canon no less than thirteen letters are attributed to Paul, which makes for a significant proportion of the whole.[2]

The story of Paul in Acts is vivid and colourful; his letters are profound in doctrine and intricately revealing of Paul's own mindset. Paul, however, remains a complex figure who was variously understood in his own day as now.[3] He claimed his missionary activity was determined by his hope in the promises made by God to the Jewish patriarchs, and yet he could be represented at Jerusalem as teaching the Jews of the Dispersion to jettison the Law of Moses.[4] Today, the same

---

[1] Once in the third person at Acts 9:1–19, with accounts put into Paul's own lips at Acts 22:3–16 and 26:9–23. Paul also refers directly to this experience at Gal. 1:13–7 and 1 Tim. 1:12–17. The description of Paul as an apostle to the gentiles must not be construed as tantamount to a suggestion that Paul felt no responsibility to the Jewish people — cf. Acts 9:15; 26:16–18; Rom. 11:13–14; 1 Cor. 9:20.

[2] Several letters are now considered by many scholars as Deutero-Pauline, including Ephesians, Colossians, 2 Thessalonians and the Pastorals. For our purposes their precise authorship does not matter. The point remains that for most of Christian history they have been regarded as Pauline.

[3] cf Rom. 3:8; 2 Pet. 3:16.

[4] Compare Acts 26:6–7 with Acts 21:21.

accusation is brought against Paul. One Jewish scholar, Samuel Sandmel, declares that he showed contempt for the Torah, while another (Dan Cohn-Sherbok) holds that in Paul's view the reign of the Torah was synonymous with the domination of demonic powers.[5] Christian commentators for their part keenly debate what Paul meant when he described Christ as the end of the law.[6]

Even among those who have been most enthusiastic to find the roots of anti-Semitism in the New Testament it is encouraging to find a distinction between Paul's opposition to Judaism and any hostility to Jews as such. Undeniably Paul launches a determined polemic against Judaism, though it will be important to clarify what Judaism he has in mind.[7] This does not, however, entail enmity against his fellow-Jews. In fact, the contrary is true as we shall see. Sandmel points out that the only charge which Paul makes against the Jews is spiritual blindness, which falls some way short of the charges found in the gospels themselves.[8] Ruether, for her part, recognizes that Paul affirms that God has not cast off the Jewish people, but has a plan eventually to remove their blindness and thereby bring them into the blessings of the covenant with Abraham.[9] In short, Paul leaves little room for negative stereotypes of the Jews, and does hold out the prospect of a better future for them.

Since Paul's complexity has been widely acknowledged and uncertainty has remained over important exegetical questions, Paul's letters have probably had limited influence over Christian attitudes toward the Jews. In the popular mind, they may simply have reinforced the impression from the gospel accounts of the scribes and Pharisees that the official Jewish religion was imbued with a legalistic self-righteousness. To that extent they may have increased contempt for Judaism and its adherents. At best, that would be a one-sided legacy from Paul which would ignore his evident sorrow about the attitudes among his fellow-countrymen. And even that legacy, whereby Judaism has been dubbed with the image of a thoroughgoing legalism, has been challenged in recent scholarship.

---

[5] Sandmel, *Anti-Semitism*, 8; Cohn-Sherbok, *Crucified*, 21.
[6] cf. Rom. 10:4.
[7] cf. Donald A. Hagner in Evans and Hagner, *Anti-Semitism*, 128–150.
[8] Sandmel, *Anti-Semitism*, 17–18.
[9] Ruether, *Faith*, 104–7.

Did Paul distort contemporary Judaism?

Since 1977 the publication of *Paul and Palestinian Judaism* by E.P. Sanders has left a profound impact on the world of Christian scholarship. Through a detailed analysis of the relevant rabbinic literature, he contended that the common perception among Christians of Paul's Jewish contemporaries as nit-picking legalists was completely mistaken. In this he endorsed the complaints of earlier Jewish writers.[10] Sanders declared that the main form of Judaism of the time was centred on God's special and gracious covenant with Israel, which embraced not only God's election of Israel and Israel's duty to be faithful to God's instructions, but his provision of atonement for transgression, especially through repentance. A Jew was in this covenant relationship to God by virtue of his birth, and could continue in it provided he used the means God had generously supplied to enable this. 'The conception is that God acts, that Israel accepts the action as being for them, that God gives commandments, that Israel agrees to obey the commandments, and that continuing to accept the commandments demonstrates that one is *in*, while refusing to obey indicates that one is *out*.'[11] Sanders insisted that election and ultimately salvation in this system are through God's mercy rather than human achievements. Sanders gave the name of 'covenantal nomism' to his perception of Judaism.

If Sanders is right, drastic consequences may follow. Perhaps Paul misunderstood or more likely distorted the Judaism of his own time. And some scholars, like H. Räsänen, have taken this line.[12] Then, the conclusion would be unavoidable that Christians have in varying degrees perpetuated a caricature of Jewish religion as peddled by one of its more disillusioned exponents. Paul would thus have to bear considerable responsibility for inculcating an anti-Jewish outlook among many Christians.[13]

Alternatively, Paul may have been misinterpreted by generations of Christian exegetes. This is by far the more common response, but there is no general agreement on what the correct interpretation should be.

---

[10] e.g. C.G. Montefiore in *Judaism and St. Paul. Two Essays* (London 1914) and H.J. Schoeps in *Paul: The Theology of the Apostle in the Light of Jewish Religious History* (London 1961).

[11] Sanders, *Paul*, 237.

[12] cf. his *Paul and the Law* (Tübingen, J.C.B. Mohr 1983).

[13] *ibid.*, 268.

Sanders, for example, who opts for this approach, sees Paul as criticizing his fellow-Jews not for legalism, but for their failure to see that salvation is available only in Christ. 'This is what Paul finds wrong with Judaism: it is not Christianity'; Paul's rejection of Judaism follows straightforwardly from his insistence on the exclusivity of Christianity.[14] Another approach is to say that Paul is concerned exclusively with the relationship of the gentiles to the Torah; he does not broach the question of Jewish observance of the law because it is irrelevant to his purpose.[15] Most plausibly of all, it has been proposed that Paul's opposition was directed against Jewish nationalism rather than Jewish legalism. The Jews may have overemphasized those laws — i.e. regarding circumcision, sabbath, food — which made them distinct and kept them apart from other nations. Their pride in these laws made them unduly restrictive toward the gentiles. As James Dunn puts it, Paul was attacking neither the law nor the covenant but 'a covenantal nomism which insisted on treating the law as a boundary round Israel, marking off Jew from gentile, with only those inside as heirs of God's promise to Abraham'.[16]

There is no doubt that Jewish identity was closely bound up with her distinctive religious institutions. No doubt, too, that many Jews recognized this and were proud of the fact.[17] But that it itself need not mean that Jews grudged the gentiles a share in their religious inheritance. Indeed, in Romans 2 Paul criticized the typical Jew for being eager to teach outsiders about his law when he did not keep it himself. The passage is worth quoting in full —

> Now you, if you call yourself a Jew; if you rely on the law and brag about your relationship to God; if you know his will and approve of what is superior because you are instructed by the law; if you are convinced that you are a guide for the blind, a light for those who are in the dark, an instructor of the foolish, a teacher of infants, because you have in the law the embodiment of knowledge and truth — you, then, who teach others, do you not teach yourself? You who preach against stealing, do you steal? You who say that people should not commit adultery, do you commit adultery? You who say that people should not commit adultery, do you commit adultery? You who abhor idols, do you rob temples? You who brag about the law, do you dishonour God by breaking the law? As it is written: "God's name is blasphemed among the gentiles because of you."[18]

---

[14] Sanders, *Paul*, 552. Parallel to this, Sanders holds that in Paul's mind the only thing wrong with doing the law was that 'it is not faith'– 550.
[15] e.g Lloyd Gaston, *Paul and the Torah*, in Davies, *Anti-Semitism*, 66.
[16] Dunn, *Partings*, 138.
[17] Dunn, *Jesus*, 216–9.
[18] Rom. 2:17–24.

Here we do find a nationalistic pride which is all too ready to teach others of superior Jewish ways. It is based on an assured self-righteousness, which in Paul's mind is quite unjustified. He believes that not only Jews but God himself have thereby acquired a bad name among the gentiles.

The same impression emerges from Paul's reflections in Phillippians. 3:2–11 on his background in Judaism prior to his conversion.[19] He begins with his Jewish pedigree, citing his being circumcised on the eighth day, his Jewish birth and his belonging to the tribe of Benjamin. But he does not confine himself to matters of national pride. He moves on from there to personal achievements — his membership of the Pharisees (as evidence of his strict adherence to the Law), his zeal which led him to persecute the church, and his blamelessness in terms of public standards of righteousness. At one time, when he was still an adherent of Judaism, this combination of privileges and attainments would have given him great 'confidence in the flesh', but now he counts them as refuse in comparison with the knowledge of Christ. Plainly Paul sees his Judaistic past as vitiated by pride. But it is not simply the pride of a nationalist in his country's religious traditions. It also involves the pride which comes from a sense of outstanding self-achievement.[20] Such pride was for Paul not only wrong in itself, but it formed a barrier to accepting God's true way of righteousness, which involves believing that God justifies the ungodly through the cross of Jesus Christ.[21]

So, we have to turn back to the traditional interpretation of Paul's complaint against the Judaism which he himself at one time embodied. This highlighted the self-righteous sense of achievement engendered in anyone who thought he was successfully following God's law. Paul had come as a Christian to see this as a misuse of the law. In Romans 10:2, 3 there are two elements he identified in the Jewish rejection of Jesus — 'I can testify about them (the Israelites) that they are zealous for God, but their zeal is not based on knowledge. Since they did not know the righteousness that comes from God and sought to establish their own, they did not submit to God's righteousness.'[22] It was not simply

---

[19] It is true that Paul does not use the term 'Judaism' here as he does at Gal. 1:13–14; but it is clear that the two passages give overlapping perspectives on Saul's exceptional progress in Judaism.

[20] cf. the analysis of R.H. Gundry, '*Grace, Works and Staying Saved*', Biblica, 66 (1985), 13–14.

[21] cf. Rom. 4:5.

[22] This general analysis of Jewish unbelief is paralleled by his description of his own earlier ignorance and unbelief in 1 Tim. 1:13.

that the Jews failed to see Jesus and his work outlined in their Scriptures, as Sanders seems to be suggesting. That was true, but the Jewish error went further. They could not understand God's way of righteousness because they misread these Scriptures as setting forth a way of life for those who sought to obey them out of their own resources. The law, however, was intended first and foremost to bring the knowledge of sin and so to point to the work of a Saviour.[23] For it was impossible for anyone to fulfil the righteous requirements of the law out of his own resources and without the direction of the Holy Spirit, Christ's gift to all who would believe in him.[24]

But what of the supposed contradiction between Paul's view of Judaism and the Rabbis' covenantal nomism? It would be unwise to reject Paul's view as a misrepresentation without very good reason. He is much nearer to the mindset of first-century religious Jews than any twentieth-century scholar.[25] That is an important consideration since abstract religious treatises from any period are limited in the information they can pass on about the practice of contemporary piety. They are unlikely, for example, to explore the questions of sincerity or of parading one's piety before others — considerations which loom large in Jesus' criticism of the Jewish religious leaders. Besides, apart from Josephus, Paul is the only Pharisee from this period who provides us with biographical details.[26] These details cannot be dismissed as a jaundiced account of his background in Judaism since he did feel great sorrow for the misguided religiosity of his fellow-countrymen, and was evidently prepared to suffer at their hand in the process of evangelizing them.

Besides, Sanders' own conclusions about contemporary Judaism may require modification. He has shown that Judaism did not consist in a crude form of works-righteousness as though the Jews believed that God weighed up their good deeds, and only if the balance came down in their favour, would they either enter or remain in God's favour.[27] But Sanders has not disproved that legalism might exist in more subtle forms — particularly in a form which combined faith in God's grace with one's own works.[28] If God had made a gracious covenant with Israel and so given it

---

23 Rom. 3:20; 7:7–13.
24 Rom. 8:3, 4.
25 Gundry (note 20) 36.
26 Dunn, *Jesus*, 67–9.
27 This is accepted by the critical Gundry (note 20) 19.
28 D.A. Carson, *Divine Sovereignty and Human Responsibility* (Marshall, Morgan and Scott 1981) 86–95 and 120–1 gives a useful summary of the strengths and weaknesses in Sanders' approach.

a privilege above other nations, this might be easily construed as making the Jews into a sort of élite.[29] Then they might begin to boast of their privileges in comparison with others.[30] And this is exactly what Paul claims at Rom. 2:17. This picture is further confirmed at Eph. 2:11 with Paul's allusion to the scathing way in which the Jews described the gentiles as 'the uncircumcision', as though this automatically made them highly inferior to the Jews, the 'circumcision'.[31] Besides, the identification of gentiles with 'sinners', made instinctively in many contexts, unmasks a measure of self-righteousness on the part of many Jews.[32] Such self-righteousness, Paul inferred, would have been justified only if the Jews had fulfilled the demands of their law, but here they had in fact failed.[33] They had falsely assumed that mere possession of the law or at least listening to it was tantamount to practising it.[34]

The term 'sinners' was not confined to the gentiles. By extension, the term was commonly used by various Jewish groups of other Jews whose lives seemed to them to be unworthy of the covenant.[35] By contrast these groups would describe their own adherents as 'the righteous'. Much of this language was sectarian in origin. It could be used of one group against another (e.g. the Qumran Community against the Pharisees), or it could simply be applied against folk like the tax-collectors who seemed to have abandoned any pretence of following the Jewish religion. Such language, along with the rampant sectarianism of Judaism in this period, would promote the ideas both of a group-righteousness and of self-righteousness for any individual who successfully attained the standards of his group. Presumably that is what Paul had in mind when he could use the description 'as for legalistic righteousness, faultless' of his pre-Christian days.[36] If we may press Paul's testimony further, the sectarian mentality even instilled a competitive streak in the Judaism of his time; for Paul could claim that he had progressed in Judaism 'beyond many Jews of my own age'.[37]

---

[29] Dunn, *Partings*, 27–8.
[30] Carson (note 28), 104–6.
[31] cf. the implicit criticism on reliance on circumcision at 1 Cor. 7:19; Gal. 5:6; 6:5.
[32] Dunn, *Jesus,* 73–4.
[33] Rom. 2:25.
[34] Rom. 2:13. Similar points are made elsewhere in the New Testament — e.g. Mt. 7:21; Jas. 1:22, 25; 1 Jn. 3:7.
[35] Dunn, *Jesus*, 74–7.
[36] Phil. 3:6.
[37] Gal. 1:14.

Certainly, as Sanders points out, Judaism did make provision for repentance and forgiveness. But this need not mean that Jews renounced their own works altogether in their hope of attaining salvation. It is the role or goal of forgiveness in Judaism that is all-important as Ridderbos points out — 'Judaism knew no other way of salvation than that of the law, and it saw even the mercy and the forgiving love of God as lying precisely in the fact that they enable the sinner once more to build for his eternal future on the ground of the law.'[38] There is no suggestion that man should have to look elsewhere then the law itself for the resources to be able to adhere to it. The Rabbis were more sanguine about human nature than Paul came to be.[39] It is here that Paul conducted his main assault on Judaism — 'If a law had been given that could impart life, then righteousness would certainly have come by the law.'[40]

Moreover, good works in the thinking of the Rabbis were more than a proof that a person was in a right standing with God; they made up a righteousness necessary at least to actuate God's grace for the forgiveness of sins. In effect, this represents a synergistic approach to salvation.[41] They did believe that it was possible to fall out of the covenant. Continuing in the covenant was dependent to some degree on obedience to the law. This was perfectly consistent with the view that the making of the covenant initially was all of God's favour. But it led to a system where God's grace did only so much; it had to be complemented by works of the law. It is a very different religious outlook from the *sola gratia* and the *sola fide* of the Protestant Reformers, as they (I believe correctly) interpreted Paul.

This lay at the heart of Paul's concern for the Galatian Christians who had entered upon the Christian life through faith in Jesus, but had somehow been convinced that their continuance as true Christians depended on their performing certain works of the law. He had to point out that their staying in the Christian path depended as much on faith (and faith alone) as at the very beginning.[42] Their acceptance before God never depended on their performance of certain works of the law. Or if they insisted that it did, then they would be under obligation to fulfil the whole Law.[43] And since they could not do

---

[38] Ridderbos, *Paul*, 133.
[39] Gundry (note 20) 36–7; Carson (note 28) 93.
[40] Gal. 3:21.
[41] Gundry (note 20) 6–7, 19, 35–6.
[42] Gal. 3:1–5.
[43] Gal. 5:3.

that, they would effectively be under God's curse.[44]

Behind Sanders' thesis of the essentially gracious character of Palestinian Judaism lies a bold presupposition — 'it may be doubted that the notion of "legalism" — an attitudinal sin which consists in self-assertion — goes back to the first century.'[45] It may be true that Paul had no single word for 'legalism'.[46] But the idea is surely current both in the gospels and in Paul's letters. Indeed, Sanders has been justifiably criticized for failing to detect a development in Paul's thought whereby the tension between faith and works is widened from works of the Mosaic Law to embrace any sort of works.[47] This tendency is particularly noteworthy in the so-called Deutero-Pauline literature though it is by no means confined to this. Thus the letter to the Ephesians, addressed primarily to gentiles, can say, 'For it is by grace you have been saved, through faith — and this not from yourselves, it is the gift of God — not by works, so that no one can boast. For we are God's workmanship, created in Christ Jesus to do good works, which God prepared in advance for us to do.'[48] Paul thus provides a basis for the adaptation of his insistence on the incompatibility of faith and works to religious systems other than that of contemporary Judaism. He seems to have seen boasting in human privilege or human achievements as a universal temptation.

This may go part of the way toward explaining one significant difference between Paul and the Synoptic writers in their approach to contemporary Judaism. In many other respects they draw a similar picture from their very different perspectives. For instance, they bear witness to the importance of a reputation for piety before men, the disparagement of those who do not meet the mark, and the competitive element in Jewish piety. But whereas Jesus in the gospels of both Matthew and Mark attacks the religious leaders of his day for elevating human traditions to the level of God's commandments and at the same time circumventing some of God's true ordinances, we find in Paul little concern for the actual content of the Law in contemporary Judaism.[49] His interests lie in the correct use and in the limitations of that law; and

---

[44] Gal. 3:10.
[45] Sanders in Richardson and Granskou, *Anti-Judaism*, 1:78–9.
[46] C.E.B. Cranfield, *St Paul and the Law, Scottish Journal of Theology*, 17 (1964), 55.
[47] J.M.G. Barclay, *Paul and the Law: Observations on some recent Debates, Themelios*, 12 (1986), 11.
[48] Eph. 2:8–10. Other relevant passages are 1 Tim. 1:7 and Tit.3:4–7.
[49] Jesus' criticism — Mt. 15:1–11; Mk. 7:1–23.

his comments would apply to any sort of approximation to that law found in gentile communities. Clearly he felt that the same type of legalistic pride and self-justification as had characterized his own days in Judaism might rear their ugly heads within a gentile Christian church. Where believers are chosen of God and that election is entirely of God's grace, then they had no cause whatsoever to boast in works of their own. If the church had maintained this insight and regarded it as a warning, there would have been no inclination to see Judaism as the exclusive target for Paul's polemic. At least one potential source of anti-Semitism within the church would have been eliminated.

The Jews in the purposes of God

Two sections of the Pauline corpus concentrate on the place of the Jews and the gentiles in the purposes of God — Romans 9–11 and Ephesians 2–3. The two complement one another perfectly. The Romans passage majors on the place of the Jews; the Ephesians passage on the inclusion of the gentiles.

Both passages confirm the central place of Israel in God's plan of redemption. The Jews possess a whole series of special privileges from God, culminating in the human ancestry of Christ.[50] They are the people whom God foreknew; that is, he showed them his special covenant love.[51] Even now in the days of their disobedience, there exists a faithful remnant in accordance with God's electing grace.[52] Their privileges and the calling of God toward them are irrevocable.[53]

The essentially Jewish character of the church is recognized when Israel is viewed as the natural olive tree from which some branches have been broken off (through unbelief) while branches from a wild olive (the believing gentiles) have been grafted in. The gentile Christians are warned not to draw the wrong conclusion — 'Do not boast over those branches (that have been broken off). If you do, consider this: You do

---

[50] Rom. 9:4, 5.
[51] Rom. 11:2. The word for 'foreknew' is the same as that used at 8:29. John Murray helpfully notes that it means those whom God set regard upon or whom he knew from eternity with distinguishing affection and delight and is virtually equivalent to whom he foreloved — *The Epistle to the Romans, New London Commentaries* (London 1967), 1:317.
[52] Rom. 11:2–7.
[53] Rom. 11:29.

not support the root, but the root supports you.'[54] Neither here nor in
Ephesians is there any suggestion that Israel has been totally displaced
from its claims to the covenant favour of God. In Ephesians Paul
speaks of extended, not redirected blessings when he can marvel at the
recent revelation that the gentiles, who at one time were outside the
covenants of promise and were without hope and without God in the
world, have been given access to God in the one Spirit through the work
of Christ on the cross.[55] This meant that now the gentiles are 'fellow-
citizens with God's people and members of God's household.'[56] Or in
further language which indicates that the gentiles are sharing in Israel's
inheritance rather than displacing her, Paul describes the gentiles as
'heirs together with Israel, members together of one body, and sharers
together in the promise in Christ Jesus.'[57]

Paul will not have a complete rejection of Israel by God; instead, the
hardening of the Jews is partial and temporary.[58] It will last only until
it has fulfilled its specific purpose in God's economy of salvation. The
disobedience of the Jews has given the opportunity for the gathering in
of the gentiles. Paul looks forward to a time when God will have mercy
on the Jews whom he has currently consigned to disobedience. He
foresees a day when in accordance with Old Testament prophecies
much more than the present remnant of Jewish believers will be enjoy-
ing God's favour.[59] This is not based on favouritism toward the Jews,
but reflects a pattern of God's work whereby both gentiles and Jews
have been consigned to disobedience for a time in order that both might
be the recipients of his mercy.

The interpretation that Paul is setting out a better future for the
Jewish people has often proved controversial within the church. On the
whole, however, it has been the majority view where the passage has
not in practice been ignored. There are those who doubt that Paul did
have the Jewish race in mind in the key verse 26 ('and so all Israel shall
be saved'); they prefer to think he was referring to the mixed church of
Jew and gentile as a new Israel after the analogy of Gal. 6:16. But this

---

[54] Rom. 11:17–18.
[55] Eph. 2:12–13.
[56] Eph. 2:19.
[57] Eph. 3:6.
[58] Rom. 11:25. At the beginning of the chapter, with an allusion to 1 Sa. 12:22 and
Ps. 94:14, Paul has already rejected the very idea that God could forsake the Jewish
people.
[59] At Rom. 11:26, 27 where Paul alludes to Is. 59:20, 21 and 27:9.

would hardly suit the context of Romans 11 where Paul has in the first verse set out his key question — 'Did God reject his people?' — and made it clear in the next verse he means ethnic Israel, of which he is a member. Throughout the chapter there is a sustained contrast between Israel and the gentiles. That contrast is evidently in view in verse 25, and it would be quite remarkable if Paul were to attempt a redefinition of Israel at the beginning of verse 26.[60]

Others have denied that there is any future reference in the passage, but contend that it reflects Paul's missionary strategy in the present.[61] They point out that Paul was praying for the salvation of the Jews in his own day and was magnifying his ministry among the gentiles so that some Jews would be stirred to a healthy envy and so would be saved when they saw gentiles being blessed with those very privileges they had themselves once enjoyed. This process was already going on in Paul's time.[62] So, it is argued, Paul envisaged nothing more than a steady flow of Jewish believers into the church both in his own day and in days to come. By this view everything in the passage can be satisfactorily explained without reference to some future change in the attitude of the Jews to the gospel.

This view, however, overlooks certain temporal considerations. The word until (*achri hou*) in verse 25 denotes distinct phases in God's own missionary plans. First, 'the fullness of the gentiles' is to come in, then it will be the turn of 'the fullness of Israel'.[63] The latter phrase is best understood as a contrast term to the remnant of believers who existed in Paul's day. Again, when Paul refers to a period of gentile disobedience in the past prior to their coming to faith and receiving the mercy of God, he suggests there is a direct parallel with the Jews.[64] They are now going through their period of disobedience so that they too might become recipients of God's mercy. This could only be at some time in the future since it is impossible for any individual or group to continue in disobedience and at the same time be recipients of God's mercy.

Moreover, without some expectation of future blessing on the Jews, it

---

[60] cf. Murray (note 51) 2:96.
[61] see recently Wright, *Climax*, 246–51.
[62] The inclusion of 'now' in the phrase 'in order that they too may *now* receive mercy . . .' in verse 31 is reasonably stressed in this viewpoint. Not all English translations include this second 'now'. Some manuscripts also omit it; but the balance of probability is in favour of retaining it — cf. Motyer, *Israel*, 155–6.
[63] 'All Israel' in verse 26 presumably has the same reference as 'their fulness' in verse 12.
[64] Rom. 11:30–2.

is difficult to see the force of Paul's *a fortiori* arguments in verses 12 and 15. In verse 12 he comments, 'if their fall is the riches of the world, and their loss the riches of the gentiles; how much more their fullness?' The thrust of verse 15 is very similar — 'If the casting away of them is the reconciling of the world, what shall the receiving of them be, but life from the dead?'[65] Seeing that the fall or the casting away of Israel are clearly historical events which caused Paul much pain, it is natural to look for a similar historical basis for the fullness and the receiving of Israel.

If it is still felt that Paul's own missionary outlook toward his fellow-Jews sufficiently explains the reception of Israel, it is worth noting that in verse 14 Paul speaks modestly of saving 'some'.[66] There is no claim here that the fullness of Israel, mentioned as recently as verse 12, is being reached.

I would conclude that Paul's discussion in Romans 11, especially at verses 12, 15 and 26, does entail a future blessing on the Jews out of all proportion to anything Paul saw in his own day, a blessing that would have beneficial repercussions for the whole church of Jews and gentiles alike.[67] If this teaching were allowed its full effect, it would impress gentile Christians with a sense of loss as long as these hopes are unfulfilled. André Charue has expressed this poignantly, 'So long as the Chosen Nation has not been integrated into the Church, the Church remains mutilated, as though one of its best limbs had been cut off.'[68] Sadly such feelings seem to have been attained only by a few individuals rather than by churches as a whole.

Certain safeguards, however, need to be applied to this picture of future blessing. Paul does not say anything about when the re-entry of Israel to covenant blessing is to take place other than that it must be preceded by a time of hardening for Israel and a time of blessing for the gentiles. There is no need to postulate that the conversion of the bulk of the Jews will occur just on the eve of Christ's parousia.[69] It

---

[65] The translation here is that of the Revised Version. It is worth noting that in the original Greek of verse 15 no verb is included.

[66] Murray (note 51) 2:80.

[67] Probably it is this restoration of Israel to covenant blessings to which Ezekiel refers at 37:11–28. Significantly, God's name will then be honoured rather than profaned among other nations because of the Jews — cf. Ezk. 39:7.

[68] cited by Jocz, *Jewish*, 315.

[69] This idea may have gained currency because the phrase 'life from the dead' in verse 15 has been taken by some to refer to the resurrection. For comments on this view see Murray (note 51) 2:82–4. Others take the reference to the coming of the Redeemer in

would also be misleading to speculate about this resulting from some abnormal event (say, a special intervention by God).[70] The Apostle Paul indicates that it is to be the same gospel message as has brought blessing among the gentile believers and the tangible signs of that blessing which will ultimately bring the Jews to seek the mercy of God.[71]

Nor does this interpretation of Paul require that God show partiality towards the Jews. God may deal with Jew and gentile in a distinct temporal order. But that is not favouritism, since there is no suggestion that we are to think of the fullness of the Jews as superior to the fullness of the gentiles.[72] Besides, the future blessing which is mapped out for the Jews will benefit gentiles as well. The same preliminary strategy has been applied to bring blessing to both groups — 'God has bound all men (ie. Jews and gentiles) over to disobedience so that he may have mercy on them all.'[73] This is a far cry from condoning a privileged position for the Jews on account of their birth — a position to which Paul is adamantly opposed.[74]

Paul never allows the prevailing Jewish rejection of the gospel in his day to warp his judgment. He is well aware of the serious consequences of their unbelief; hence his astonishing *cri de coeur* — 'I could wish that I myself were cursed and cut off from Christ for the sake of my brothers, those of my own race.'[75] He does not doubt that their disobedience is culpable. Paul is at pains to establish that Israel had the knowledge of the gospel, but proved recalcitrant to God's gracious offers.[76] This is perfectly consistent with his earlier remarks about their acting in ignorance; for their recalcitrance consisted in their misreading their own Scriptures to imply that salvation would come from obedience to the law out of their own resources. As a result of their disobedience, they had alienated themselves from God's favour and blessing, and incurred his judgment.[77] That judgment had already come in the form

---

[69] *continued*   verse 26 to refer to the beginning of a special millennial age inaugurated by another appearance of Christ. But the 'and so' which introduces this quotation must not be taken as implying a sense of temporal progression — see Motyer, *Israel*, 152–3.

[70]   No less a person than Karl Barth toyed with this notion — *Church Dogmatics* 4:3 (ET, T. and T. Clark, Edinburgh 1962) 877–8.

[71]   Ridderbos, *Paul*, 358; Hagner in Evans and Hagner, *Anti-Semitism*, 146–9.

[72]   Paul sets his face firmly against any thought of partiality in God — cf. Rom.2:11; 10:12.

[73]   Rom. 11:32.

[74]   Wright is particularly strong on this point — *Climax*, 254–5.

[75]   Rom. 9:3.

[76]   Rom. 10:14–21.

[77]   The use of the word 'enemies' of the Jews in Rom. 11:28 indicates that they are alienated from God's favour and blessing — Murray (note 51) 2:100. The same word is used in Rom. 5:10.

of a spiritual hardening and blindness.[78] Paul does not specify anything beyond this essentially inward, spiritual form of judgment, except perhaps in the controversial passage in 1 Thes. 2:14–16 which I shall examine in due course separately. But we ought not to exclude the possibility that Paul would see a divine judgment on unbelieving Jews in certain external circumstances, since in Galatians he speaks of those who rely on works of the law as being under a curse and goes on to cite a passage from Deuteronomy, which itself introduces a most comprehensive list of judgments.[79]

There are, then, two sides to Paul's perception of his fellow-Jews. These are set side by side in the almost paradoxical statement in Rom. 11:28, where Paul declares that 'as far as the gospel is concerned they (the Jews) are enemies on your account; but as far as election is concerned, they are loved on account of patriarchs.'[80] In other words, Paul can affirm God's alienation from the Jewish people in their current state of unbelief, but still entertain hopes for the future of his people because God will not lay aside his covenant love which he promised to the physical seed of the Jewish patriarchs.

What place does 1 Thessalonians 2:14–16 have in Paul's work?

Undoubtedly the strongest remarks against the Jews in the Pauline corpus occur at 1 Thes. 2:14–16. Many scholars have found these inconsistent with what they take to be a more positive attitude toward Israel as shown in Romans 11. Some have sought to explain the inconsistency by a progression in Paul's thought whereby he gradually laid aside an original hostility toward non-Christian Jews.[81] Others have made the more radical proposal that this section is an interpolation by a later hand.[82]

But there is no need to postulate any inconsistency. The 1 Thessalonians passage applies to a particular situation; Paul's general observation in Rom. 11:28 that currently the Jews are enemies of the gospel for

---

[78]   Rom. 11:7–10, 25.

[79]   Gal. 3:10 citing Dt. 27:26. The context in Galatians, of course, would extend the curse to unbelieving gentiles as well as Jews. Gordon J. Wenham has argued that the similar curse in Lv. 26 will apply to unbelieving Israel — *The Book of Leviticus* (New International Commentary on the Old Testament 1979) 333.

[80]   For the meaning of 'loved' here see Ridderbos, *Paul*, 332.

[81]   e.g. Markus Barth, *Israel and the Church*, (Richmond, John Knox 1969) 43–78.

[82]   e.g. Beck, *Mature*, 40–44.

the sake of the gentiles. Here the immediate context is vital; for Paul believes that the persecution of the Thessalonian Christians by their fellow-countrymen mirrors the fate of Jewish Christians in Judaea at the hands of unbelieving Jews. Not only does Paul claim first-hand experience of this persecution in 1 Thessalonians, but he also alludes to this in Romans where he implores prayer for protection from unbelievers when he is shortly to visit Jerusalem.[83]

Paul's description of the Jews in 1 Thessalonians was not original. It blends earlier Christian and pagan elements. He draws on Christ's remarks that the Jewish religious teachers were filling up the measure of their fathers' sins in the killing first of the prophets and then of himself.[84] At the same time he highlights the pagan objection that the Jews were hostile to all other men.[85] Paul, however, develops this critique in a distinctively Christian way. The Jews show their hostility to other nations by their efforts to prevent Paul and the other apostles from preaching to them. Paul concludes his comments with an affirmation that they are certain of the full measure of God's wrath.[86]

This is further evidence that Paul's hopes for a future restoration of Israel do not blind him to the dire implications of Jewish unbelief. Jews must not presume from their status as God's special people that they are exempt from God's judgment on unbelief and ungodliness. On the contrary, condemnation will come first to the Jew who does evil and then to the gentile, just as glory, honour and peace come first to the Jew who does good and then to the gentile.[87]

A very pessimistic view of the contemporary Jewish condition was in Paul's mind perfectly compatible with a love for them as his own kinsmen and as God's specially chosen people. It was also consistent with an optimistic view of the outcome of God's covenant purposes toward the Jews. That is not to say that it is easy for all Christians to

---

[83] Rom. 15:30–2. Paul had every reason to anticipate this danger as Acts 21:17 to 23:35 makes plain.

[84] cf. Mt. 21:33–43; 23:29–36; Lk. 11:47–52.

[85] cf. Josephus, *Against Apion*, 2:121; Tacitus, *Hist.* 5:2.

[86] The meaning of 1 Thes. 2:16, especially the phrase εἰς τελος is difficult. I accept the view of L. Morris in *The New International Commentary on the New Testament — 1–2 Thessalonians* (Grand Rapids 1959). One advantage of this view is to tie in closely with Jesus' own words in Mt. 23:33 of the certainty of final judgment. A corollary to this would be the absence of any vindictive spirit since judgment is left entirely in God's hands. For some different approaches to this verse see C.A.Wanamaker in *The New International Greek Testament Commentary*, 117–8.

[87] Rom. 2:1–11.

attain such insights and the corresponding emotions. In fact, if the history of the church shows anything, it does indicate that it is very rare for every element in Paul's perspective to be held in the proper balance.

Moreover, we should not overlook the fact that in the context of 1 Thessalonians Paul was implicating a particular group of Jews — those in Judaea — and not every member of the race. His remarks should, therefore, not be applied universally to Jews of his own day. At the same time he was suggesting that the persecutors of the church in Thessalonica, who were mainly non-Jews, were in line for similar judgment from God.[88] Thus, Paul's diatribes against unbelief and its consequences were not restricted to Jewish unbelief. If God showed no partiality, as he argued in Romans 2, then gentile unbelief would come under God's final condemnation, especially where it manifested itself in unremitting persecution of the church of Christ.[89] Indeed, in Romans 11 Paul is at pains to point out the inappropriateness of boasting even from gentile Christians.[90] If they in time show the same unbelief as did the Jews, they will certainly find themselves cast off.[91] The gentiles are not to consider themselves free from the dangers of spiritual pride and complacency which characterized the Jews. In short, the gentiles are prone to the same range of religious attitudes as the Jews. Thus, God's dealings with the Jews are not to be considered some special case. Rather, they are paradigmatic for his dealings with the nations as a whole.

Some conclusions from Paul

No New Testament writer examines the Jewish question with the intensity and comprehensiveness of Paul. Not surprisingly, it has proved difficult for the church to hold together all the different facets in Paul's response. Who, for example, can match the strength of his emotions as set out in Romans 9:2, 3? Not only did he pray for

---

[88]   It emerges from Acts 17:5 that unbelieving Jews were the first to stir up persecution in Thessalonica, but it is clear that they secured support among non-Jewish elements in the city.

[89]   cf. 2 Thes. 1:4–10. Paul left no uncertainty that those who endeavoured to destroy the church by whatever means came under the threat of strict judgment from God — 1 Cor. 3:17. Whenever Paul cited his own earlier persecution of the church, it was to underline the extent of God's mercy to him, not to downplay this sin e.g. 1 Tim. 1:12–16.

[90]   Rom. 11:17–21, 25.

[91]   Rom. 11:21, 22.

unbelieving Jews, but he adopted a definite missionary agenda towards them. And in his attempts to help them, he himself suffered significantly.[92] Thus, Paul was far from being anti-Semitic. Indeed, there is every reason to describe him as a philo-Semite as long as that description is not understood exclusively in racial or nationalistic terms. His burden for the Jews sprang as much from his sense of their religious privileges (particularly the promises to the patriarchs, which had still to be fully realized) as from his ties of kinship with them.

This philo-Semitism, however, was combined with anti-Judaism. He had to oppose the prevailing Judaism as he saw it misrepresenting the true purpose of the Mosaic Law. Far from dismissing this Law as demonic, he was keen to stress both its validity and its provisional nature in the plan of God.[93] While its distinctive demands were abolished in Christ, Paul did recognize a sort of abiding moral law, though he nowhere detailed its contents.[94] That the Jews had proved unable to see the true glory of their Law was due to a hardening in their spiritual understanding.[95] Their failure to accept the gospel of Jesus was an act of disobedience which occasioned God's judgment. But Paul did not so aggravate their sin as to make out that it was the supreme act of apostasy from which no forgiveness was possible.[96] They had acted in ignorance; hence there was the possibility of their receiving mercy as he himself had done. Besides, the Old Testament prophets did give hope for better days to come.

Today the claim is often made that any attempt to evangelize Jews is an act of anti-Semitism. Paul is a standing witness against this both in his attitudes and in his practice. Indeed, he would turn the tables on these critics of Jewish evangelism. His own stance would suggest that to withhold the gospel from the Jews — whether because it is thought that rabbinic Judaism is an adequate alternative to Christianity or

---

[92] Compare the difficulties Paul faced in and after his visit to Jerusalem as recorded in Acts 21:17–27:44. Paul had also suffered the synagogue punishment of 39 lashes on five occasions — 2 Cor. 11:24.

[93] Wright, *Climax*, 241.

[94] Barclay (note 47) 12–13.

[95] 2 Cor. 3:14–16 cf. the exegesis of Wright, *Climax*, 176–84.

[96] Nowhere in the Pauline corpus do we find a reference to the unforgivable sin as at Heb. 6:4–6; 10:26–31; 1 Jn. 5:16–17. But such a concept would balance well with the idea of sins of ignorance which can be forgiven. For the Old Testament background see Wright, *Climax*, 223.

[97] Wright, *Climax*, 253 — cf. the words of a contemporary Jewish Christian — 'any effort on the part of Christians to exclude Jews from their evangelism is — however well-intentioned — a form of spiritual antisemitism' — Baruch Maoz, '*Ethics in Jewish Evangelism*', *Mishkan* 19 (1993), 4.

because Jews are considered so hardened that it is impossible for them to be converted — is itself a form of anti-Semitism.[97] Perhaps a more pressing question for the church is whether it has taken Paul's missionary agenda with sufficient seriousness. I fear that far from inciting the Jews to a healthy envy at the presence of evident spiritual blessings, gentile believers have often succumbed to the very arrogance against which Paul warns them, and have provoked revulsion among the Jews not only against the church but against the name of Jesus.[98]

Indeed, the tables have been fully turned. If Paul could accuse the Jews of his own day and before of profaning God's name among the gentiles, have not professed gentile believers been guilty of doing the same for Jesus' name among the Jews?[99]

---

[98] potential gentile arrogance — Rom. 11:19–22, 25 — cf. Eph 2:11–12.
[99] Jews profaning God's name among the gentiles — Rom. 2:24 quoting Is. 52:5.

Four

The Election of the Jewish People — Israel as God's Servant

The Hebrew Scriptures claim that God took special pains over the creation of the Jewish people. Not only was the Creator of the whole universe ultimately responsible for their distinct identity, but he intended this people as his own treasured possession, in some ways to be different from the other nations of the earth. Wherever the Hebrew Scriptures have been known directly or indirectly, this claim has been recognized. Even a largely secular society, like the west today, is not ignorant of this, however diverse the ways in which it tries to explain the phenomenon. In short, the claim to be God's special people does force attention on Jewish distinctiveness. And it is this, I suggest, which provokes extreme reactions both for and against the Jews.

For their own part the Jewish people have not always relished this special role. While many Jews have taken pride in their privileged position, others have been keen to dispense altogether with the idea of a divine election of Israel. In modern times this has corresponded roughly to a distinction between religious and secular Jews. Certainly it would seem impossible to maintain a separate Jewish religious identity without some claim to a unique election of the Jewish people by God.[1] That is not to deny that religious Jews would formulate this doctrine in significantly different ways to Christians.[2]

In the light of this it would be useful to explore what the Scriptures teach of this election and its implications. Here misunderstandings abound among non-Jews. Where these outsiders hold that divine elec-

---

[1] Jocz, *Jewish*, 296–7 argues that not only separate religious identity, but distinct national identity is at stake.

[2] *ibid.*, 307–12.

tion of the Jews is valid, then they may well incline to too high or too optimistic a view of the Jews; whereas there is a tendency to the opposite danger among those who believe that their election has been superseded or has always been a rationalization of Jewish separatist or misan- thropic tendencies.

The Hebrew Scriptures assert the election of Israel without flattering the Jewish people in any way. The New Testament Scriptures maintain the validity of Israel's election, but make no attempt to hide the dire consequences of unbelief among the majority of Jews. Both stress that Israel's election is to fulfil a purpose toward the other nations of the earth. Thus, they studiously avoid the pitfalls of insularity and of partisanship. The Jews are elect of God and called to special privileges, but they are never seen as an élite. These general principles call for greater elucidation.

The Jewish people in the Old Testament Scriptures

According to her own Scriptures Israel was chosen to be a paradigm for other nations.[3] Significantly, it was shortly after God had created the framework for different nations with the dispersal of the workers on the Tower of Babel that he issued a call to an individual called Abram and gave him promises including that of a land and a family.[4] This family was in due course to multiply into a nation through whom all nations of the earth would be blessed. The transformation of the family into a nation occurred amid the slavery of Egypt. God publicly acknowledged this nation as his own special people through the events of the Exodus and the subsequent covenant at Mount Sinai.[5]

There God declared his purpose for the Jewish people, 'If you obey me fully and keep my covenant, then out of all nations you will be my treasured possession. Although the whole earth is mine, you will be for me a kingdom of priests and a holy nation.'[6] As a holy nation, it was set apart from other nations, but not for a completely isolated existence. The Jews were to be a model for other nations; in other words, they

---

[3] e.g. Wright, *Living*, 40–5.
[4] In more detail Wright *Living*, 33–5.
[5] for an excellent brief summary of the terms and implications of Israel being an elect nation see J.I. Packer's article on Election in *The Illustrated Bible Dictionary*, (Inter Varsity Press, Leicester, 1980), 1:433–5.
[6] Ex. 19:5, 6.

would fulfil a priestly role of teaching other nations God's ways and praying for God's blessing upon them.[7] They would successfully discharge their privileged responsibility only as they proved faithful to God's covenant. That would entail distinctive standards of personal and social ethics as well as a unique cult. Israel would pray and look for God's blessing to come upon her that all the nations might praise the same God and experience his blessing.[8]

Though Israel may in her best days have done this to some degree, overall she proved a failure in her role. While she should have brought the nations to the Lord in humble submission, she achieved the very opposite.[9] She brought God's name into disrepute among the nations because of her failure to obey the Law. Thus, Paul could in Romans 2 expose the absurdity of Jewish claims in his own day to act as a teacher to the nations. The same idea had already been underlined in the prophecy of Isaiah. At one stage in that book a contrast is made between a servant of God who has failed because of spiritual blindness and deafness, and a servant who is to come and of whom it can be said that 'the will of the Lord will prosper in his hand'.[10] The former servant is clearly the Jewish nation, while the role of the latter is fulfilled in the New Testament by Jesus. Thus, Jesus is to be identified as the true servant of God who not only restores the tribes of Jacob but acts as a light to the gentiles.[11] Interestingly, this does not mean that the servant role of Israel is to be totally discarded. God still addresses Israel as his chosen servant in spite of frank recognition of her sin and failure.[12]

Israel as a paradigm in the New Testament

In the New Testament Israel also provides an object lesson for other nations, but in an unexpected way. For it transpires that in the rejection of her own Messiah and Saviour Israel is much nearer to the rest of the nations than might have appeared at first sight.

This theme figures prominently in the prologue of John's gospel

---

[7] for the priestly role see Wright *Living*, 40–1. To his remarks should be added Israel's role in praying for other nations — cf. Ps. 67.
[8] e.g. Ps. 47:1–4; 67; 98:1–4; 99:1–4; 117.
[9] J.A. Motyer, *The Prophecy of Isaiah* (IVP, Leicester 1993) 328.
[10] the blind servant — Is. 42:18–22; the faithful servant — Is. 42:1–7; 49:1–6; 50:4–11; 52:13–53:12.
[11] Is. 42:6; 49:6.
[12] e.g. Is. 41:8–10; 44:1–5, 21, 22.

where the reactions of the world and of the Jewish people to the Logos (the Word) are juxtaposed. John writes, 'He was in the world, and though the world was made through him, the world did not recognize him. He came to that which was his own, but his own did not receive him.'[13] Talk of 'that which was his own' or of 'his own home' probably refers to the Jewish people.[14] The Jewish people crystallize the general response of the whole of the world (used in John of the created order of human beings and their affairs in rebellion against its Maker) to Jesus. Certainly, as the gospel of John progresses, it is generally Jews of one group or another who typify the response of the world to Jesus.

Gentiles are also involved in the malice against Jesus. Pontius Pilate is implicated in Jesus' execution and thereby reveals that he has no love of the truth with which he is confronted in Jesus.[15] In Acts Herod Antipas, the tetrarch, is named alongside Pilate and the Jewish religious leaders as united in an unholy conspiracy against the Jesus as the Lord's anointed.[16] It seems that with a representative from the gentile world, representatives from the Jewish nation, and Herod acting as a sort of bridge between the gentile and Jewish worlds, almost every shade of religious colouring is represented in the final opposition to Jesus.[17] Ordinary people play their part too alongside the leaders. While the Sanhedrin may have taken the initiative in arresting Jesus and putting him on trial, the Jerusalem crowd yell insistently for Jesus' crucifixion. The Roman soldiers, for their part, take a perverse delight in mocking Jesus' claims to be a king.[18] The very presence of Jesus sets Jew and gentile side by side in their opposition to the true God. Indeed, the Jewish mob seems almost willing to take on gentile values when it declares, 'We have no king but Caesar.'[19]

----

[13] Jn. 1:10–11.
[14] D.A. Carson, *The Gospel According to John* (IVP, Leicester, 1991) 124–5.
[15] Jn. 18:37, 38.
[16] Acts 4:27.
[17] Josephus, *Ant.*, 14:403 refers to Herod the Great as a 'half-Jew' because he was an Idumaean. Many Jews would no doubt have taken a similar view of Herod Antipas, who was a son of Herod the Great.
[18] Jn. 19:1–5.
[19] Jn. 19:15–16. Though in connection with a different gospel David Gooding, *According to Luke* (IVP, Leicester 1987) 327 has some perceptive remarks on the extent to which Jerusalem had become imbued with gentile values, and so was to be judged by God by being given over to the gentiles.

The New Testament also affirms that while all the enemies of Jesus were culpable, both Jew and gentile acted in ignorance. Neither his Jewish nor his gentile enemies discerned the true glory of God. Neither, therefore, could discern the Lord of Glory.[20] It was natural for a Jew to think that the gentiles through the blindness of their idolatry would be unaware of the true God. Most Jews would have endorsed what Paul wrote about the gentiles — 'They are darkened in their understanding and separated from the life of God because of the ignorance that is in them due to the hardening of their hearts. Having lost all sensitivity, they have given themselves over to sensuality so as to indulge in every kind of impurity, with a continual lust for more.'[21] Paul, however, sees the majority of his own people as similarly darkened in their understanding and in their hearts.[22] Such a picture would have appalled most Jews, even though it had been foreshadowed by Isaiah as we have seen. It is true that the hardening of the heart manifested itself in a very different way in the Jewish world from the gentile world.[23] With the gentiles the result was blatant idolatry and all manner of shameful conduct, whereas with the Jews it was the attempt to establish their own righteousness by their own moral efforts. Both gentile and Jewish unbelievers were guilty of disobedience — a disobedience which sprang from the ignorance engendered by their blinded hearts.[24] The book of Acts particularly stresses the ignorance of the Jewish participants in Jesus' crucifixion. The same book at one point declares that gentile idolatry is characterized by ignorance.[25] It is a culpable ignorance if we may add Paul's analysis from Romans 1. J.H. Bavinck uses the psychological phenomenon of repression as a way of describing the pagan reaction to God —

> He (Paul) does not mean to say that these people have consciously and deliberately rejected the truth of God. It normally takes place unconsciously and unintentionally, but it happens nevertheless and humanity is guilty. The aerial of their hearts can no longer receive the wavelength of God's voice although his voice surrounds them on all sides. In his innermost being, every person has turned away from God and now God has vanished out of sight.[26]

---

20   1 Cor. 2:7, 8.
21   Eph. 4:18–19.
22   2 Cor. 3:14, 15 cf. Rom. 11:7, 8.
23   This point is well made by Ridderbos, *Paul*, 123–4.
24   For the emphasis on disobedience — cf. Rom. 10:16, 31 (the Jews); Eph. 2:2 (gentiles); Rom. 11:32 (both).
25   Acts 17:30.
26   J.H. Bavinck, *Human Religion in God's Eyes: A Study of Romans 1:18–32, Scottish Bulletin of Evangelical Theology*, Vol. 12, p 48.

Perhaps a similar unconscious repression went on in many Jewish hearts. Though Saul of Tarsus set out on his fateful journey to Damascus 'breathing out murderous threats' against the Christians, yet Christ could include in his words to him, 'It is hard for you to kick against the goads.'[27] The latter words indicate that there was more to Saul than the outwardly assured Pharisee that he seemed to be.

However the ignorance of Jew and gentile be explained, it is a vital aspect of the testimony of the New Testament, with important implications as we shall see for the church's attitude to the Jews. If we find similarities in the nature of the sin of both Jews and gentiles, it will come as no surprise that God follows a similar strategy in the salvation of both groups. Those who fall into the category of the saved do so because they are recipients of God's mercy.[28] But prior to receiving that mercy, all concerned — Jew and gentile alike — have been consigned to disobedience. Of course, that disobedience occurs at different times in history, but the same principle operates — first the disobedience, then the mercy. Moreover, Paul informs us that the salvation of Jews and gentiles is more intricately interconnected than might otherwise have been thought. Far from being an afterthought to or a direct consequence of the salvation of the Jews, the salvation of the gentiles has in the purposes of God flowed from the disobedience of the Jews. The gentile believers will in turn provoke Israel to jealousy so that they too may receive God's mercy and blessing. 'God grants no mercy to Israel without the gentiles, but neither does he do so to the gentiles without Israel.'[29] Paul concludes this section of Romans with a doxology emphasizing the inscrutability of God's ways.[30] It is indeed remarkable how God welds the wickedness of human disobedience into his own plan of salvation. Remarkable too how God should engineer the interdependence of Jew and gentile in that plan.

From the same section of Romans, Paul draws out important lessons for gentile churches. They are not to forget either the Jewish root of the church or that they stand by faith alone. Should they move from that position of faith, they will experience exactly the same severity from God as has Jewish unbelief.[31] Elsewhere Paul could use the history of the Exodus generation — the paradigm unbelievers of the Bible — to

---

27 Compare Acts 26:14 with 9:1.
28 Rom. 11:32 cf. 9:16.
29 Ridderbos, *Paul*, 360.
30 Rom. 11:33–6.
31 Rom. 11:17–24.

illustrate what would be the consequences of unbelief in its various forms for a gentile congregation.[32] Disobedience to the gospel in a gentile environment will lead inevitably to judgment, especially to a hardening of the heart.[33] The message is that perseverance in faith is vital to the gentile churches; they are not to imagine that God will be partial toward them. At the same time gentile believers were not to write off the Jews as beyond hope of forgiveness. Paul may have foreseen some of the first signs of anti-Semitism in the church and so taken steps to counteract this.[34] No doubt, that is why Paul reveals so intimately his own feelings about his countrymen and his efforts on their behalf. No doubt, that may also in large measure explain his strenuous denial that God has cast off the Jewish people once and for all.[35]

Why have Israel as a model nation if she was to prove a failure?

Jews and gentiles have both sinned in ignorance before God. In both groups that sin has been punished, primarily through a spiritual hardening. Again, both groups are similar in that those who have come to salvation from either side of that great divide have first been consigned to disobedience so that they might become recipients of mercy. Of course, there have been differences. The Jews have been privileged in many ways, including their being made repositories of the oracles of God. In that respect, their sin is more glaring and more reprehensible. But we might still ask why Israel should have this status as a special nation if from the first God knew it would prove a failure and indeed in some sense intended it that way?[36] Were they simply permitted to abuse their privileges in order to throw into greater relief the merits of Jesus?

It has been pointed out that the Jewish people mirror the whole of mankind in its relationship to God.[37] They are a sort of microcosm revealing how God deals with the whole human race (in both judgment and mercy) and at the same time how humans respond — with our natural blindness and antagonism to God which can, however,

---

[32] 1 Cor. 10:1–11. The letter to the Hebrews deals with a similar theme at 3:7–4:12.
[33] 2 Thes. 2:10–12.
[34] Wright, *Climax*, 248.
[35] Rom. 11:1.
[36] Israel's failure is already foreshadowed as early as the Song of Moses recorded in Dt. 31:15–32:43.
[37] David Torrance in *Witness*, Torrance, 7.

be removed by his grace. It is, therefore, misleading to talk of the Jew as a type of *homo religiosus* as though there was some subset of mankind with a peculiarly religious disposition.[38] On the contrary, the New Testament reveals the whole of mankind as inescapably religious in the sense that God has revealed something of himself to them all.[39] If the Jews have had a much fuller revelation of God than the gentiles, that in itself is not a ground for asserting a more fundamental religious instinct or a more promising initial response to God.[40]

Paradoxically, part of Israel's testimony to other nations was the confession of her own inadequacy to live up to her calling to glorify God and her own need of a King (or Messiah) who would save her from all her spiritual enemies.[41] This messianic hope was extended beyond the bounds of Israel — 'In that day the Root of Jesse will stand as a banner for the peoples; the nations will rally to him, and his place of rest will be glorious.'[42] Some outside of Israel evidently recognized this. In Matthew's gospel the Magi, a group of gentiles from the east, visited Palestine at the time of Jesus' birth not to see a great people with a wonderful spiritual life but to seek 'the one who has been born the King of the Jews'.[43] This was acknowledged too by the believing remnant in Israel. When the baby Jesus was brought to the Temple by his parents, the aged Simeon, who could beautifully describe Jesus as 'your salvation which you have prepared in the sight of all people, a light for revelation to the gentiles and for glory to your people Israel', then proceeded to warn Jesus' mother that his coming would provoke division and opposition in Israel.[44] So, Israel had a double-sided legacy for the nations — a legacy of failure in her role as the people of God and yet the glorious hope that from her midst would come one to deliver all mankind from its miseries. Hence the Jewish people illustrated the inadequacy of any human religious tradition which did not look to a special work of redemption from God himself.[45] If salvation could not

---

[38]   as E. Käsemann argues of the Jew in Romans 9–11 — *Commentary on Romans* (ET, Grand Rapids, Eerdmans 1980) 253ff.
[39]   Rom. 1:18–20.
[40]   cf. Dt. 7:7; 9:4–8.
[41]   This hope is well summarized in the Benedictus of Zechariah — Lk. 1:68–79.
[42]   Is. 11:10 quoted by Paul at Rom. 15:12 — cf. also Is. 42:1–4.
[43]   Mt. 2:1–2.
[44]   Lk. 2:28–35.
[45]   Torrance, *Witness*, 5.

come from the works of the Jewish Law, then it could only be by the grace of God.

The Jews as witnesses today

In an important recent work Stephen R. Haynes has highlighted the impact among Christians of what he calls the 'witness-people myth'.[46] By this he identifies a trend among Christians to view historic and contemporary Jews as a special index or witness to God's dealings with men and even as a proof of God's reality. In effect, the Jews become a key pillar in an edifice of natural theology. Haynes pinpoints Augustine of Hippo as the key figure in the origination of this myth, though he acknowledges that the seeds of this idea are present in the Christian Scriptures themselves. He also demonstrates that this approach to the Jews is prevalent today. More controversially, he argues that though this tradition is more friendly to Jews than outright anti-Semitism, its long-term effects may be equally detrimental to the Jews, largely because it encourages Christians to work with an imaginary picture of the Jewish people rather than with the reality. 'If the Jews are assumed to be witnesses and signs — regardless of what it is that they are thought to be witnessing to — they are likely also to be objects of unnatural expectations, religious projections, and irrational fantasies.'[47]

It is, therefore, appropriate to identify to what the Jews bear witness, if indeed it is correct to speak in these terms at all. The term 'witness' is not exactly the same as the biblical designation of servant, but it can reasonably be taken as an aspect of it. While the idea of witness is not uncommon in Scripture and is particularly prominent in John's gospel, its direct application to the Jewish people is rare.[48] It is confined to two related passages in Isaiah where the Jews are summoned to bear witness to the uniqueness and reality of their God.[49] (Interestingly, this is a role in which they prove a failure; they turn out to be witnesses who are blind and deaf!) But it would be too narrow an approach to Scripture to concentrate on the occurrence of the word 'witness' and the like. After all, there is a sense in which the Jews were bound to witness to

---

[46] Haynes, *Jews.*
[47] *ibid.*, 182.
[48] cf. James M. Boice, *Witness and Revelation in the Gospel of John* (Zondervan, Grand Rapids, 1970) 16–23.
[49] Is. 43:8–13 and 44:8. For useful commentary see A. Motyer (note 9) 333–5.

the reality and character of their God simply by virtue of their election. Often in the pages of the Old Testament outside nations are envisaged as watching the fate of this peculiar people. Whether the Jews desired it or not, they bore testimony to something about their God.

But does such a witness persist into the time after Christ? This is, in effect, the issue posed by Haynes. One strand of thinking within the Christian church has denied that the Jews (or the state of Israel for that matter) have any special significance today. Understandably the Jews figured prominently in both the Old and the New Testament because the gospel was first propagated among them. That day, however, is now past, and the Jews by their rejection of their Messiah have effectively made themselves into one of the peoples of the earth — no different in principle from any other. Thus the Jewish people may from time to time come under God's judgment or experience God's mercy. But so too do other peoples, because God remains King over all the earth. We are not to look for anything more significant in God's dealings with the Jewish people than with any other people. Besides, there is a danger that if the Jewish people are to be witnesses in some way to the rest of mankind, then they can only be witnesses to divine judgment. And that would provide justification for the Jews to be kept in a depressed condition or worse. The treatment of Jews under medieval Christendom is eloquent testimony to that danger. Then the supposed special judgment of God became a self-fulfilling prophecy.

A very different case would be made by those who believe that God has not abandoned his covenant promises toward the Jewish people. (Such is the stance made by nearly every mainstream Christian document on Christian-Jewish relations since the end of World War II.[50]) If the calling of God is irrevocable, it is argued, the Jews continue to be a special servant of God. Some Christian bodies have drawn from this the novel and daring conclusion that Judaism does have merit as a religious tradition in the eyes of God.[51] But this would be to make Jesus optional as an approach to God — something which goes contrary to the New Testament Scriptures and the mainstream Christian tradition. Besides, it begs the question of what form of Judaism is acceptable to God, seeing that contemporary Jews are not agreed on a uniform religious Judaism. This is a critical point since God's election

---

[50]   Haynes, *Jews*, 172.

[51]   cf. the comments of The World Council of Churches, *The Theology of the Churches and the Jewish People* (WCC Publications, Geneva 1988) 173–6.

embraces the Jews as a people, not some religious sub-group.

A much better approach is to suggest that even in their unbelief the Jews are unconscious or reluctant witnesses — witnesses to the Messiah and witnesses through their Scriptures to the blessings of which all believers partake, whatever their origin. Of course, unbelieving Jews can no longer directly bear witness to the Messiah. As John Reid puts it, 'The Church takes over the role of witness in a retrospective sense: the Messiah has come. The (Jewish) People's former witness: the Messiah will come, no longer has meaning and must change. The new role of the People can only be to witness to the condition of mankind without Christ.'[52] That, of course, entails judgment. But Reid is aware of the danger of divorcing the mercy of God from his judgment, of separating his goodness from his severity. These two aspects of God's dealings with men must be held together if we are to avoid holding up the Jews as prime targets of God's wrath and condemnation. The Jewish witness to the covenant mercy of God must be retained. In particular, there has been throughout history a believing Jewish remnant which testifies to the grace of God. Then there remains the hope set out in Scripture of a future restoration to spiritual blessings of the Jewish people.

Those who hold to the view of the Jews as unconscious witnesses would claim to find some evidence from the record of post-biblical history that the Jews are still special to God. No doubt, they would differ in the extent to which they would be prepared to interpret that history. It is here that Haynes' warnings carry their greatest weight. But most would point to the remarkable fact that the Jews have survived as a distinct race when for so many centuries they have had no homeland and been dispersed throughout the world, and have been subject to numerous attempts at destroying their separate identity.[53] This in itself might be dismissed as the result of an extraordinarily resilient tradition, were it not for God's promise in the book of Jeremiah that as long as the natural order of day and night persists, the Jewish people will remain a nation before him.[54] Thus, God ties his own reality and truthfulness to this promise in the Hebrew Scriptures that the Jews will somehow preserve a distinct identity. It does not matter if the Jews see their own identity in this light or not. It does not matter if the Jews are

---

[52] John K.S. Reid in Torrance, *Witness*, 53.

[53] Alan Richardson, *Christian Apologetics*, (SCM, London 1947) 141–2.

[54] Je. 31:35,36. Though this promise is not repeated in as many words in the New Testament, it may be implicit in Acts 1:6, 7 where Jesus seems to accept that a time will come when sovereignty is restored to Israel.

conscious of being guided and preserved by a divine hand. The Jews cannot avoid bearing witness to the God who gave special promises to Abraham and to his descendants.

It seems to me that the view I have outlined in the last two paragraphs carries greatest weight. It might be open to Haynes' criticism that it leads Christians to work with mythical rather than real concepts of the Jews, if too detailed an interpretation is attempted of Jewish history. I suggest this danger would be minimized if we stick to the New Testament emphasis that the judgment on unbelieving Jews consists essentially of a spiritual hardening while the mercy of God involves the removal of that hardness.[55] Often in practice this has been overlooked in preference for forms of outward judgment — the dispersal of the Jews until recently, their rejection in many areas of the world, and the many persecutions they have faced. Conversely, the unexpected military success of the state of Israel against all the odds has been seen as a sign of special blessing and mercy from God. Perhaps there is an instinctive urge in many of us to seek tangible outward signs of God's dealings, as though it was a straightforward thing to read the hand of God in the vicissitudes of history.[56] But the New Testament takes comparatively little interest in these things. It sees the greatest calamity in the spiritual and moral blindness which is engendered by rejection of gospel light and and which itself represents a divine punishment.[57] That must remain at the heart of the church's testimony to the Jews — the insistence that without the recognition of their Messiah they will remain spiritually blind. And while that would no doubt seem tame in comparison with former ecclesiastical statements about the Jews, concentration on this theme would serve to heighten its seriousness.

In other words the keynote of the New Testament picture of unbelieving Jews should be located in Paul's words — 'Their minds were made dull, for to this day the same veil remains when the old covenant

---

[55] I would be unhappy with the extreme form of this viewpoint which is to be found in some dispensationalist writers and which makes Israel or the Jewish people into the centre of God's purposes for the world. This usurps the role of Christ himself — cf. the comments of Motyer, *Israel*, 16–17 and 165–6.

[56] I do not mean to deny that in the historical books of the Bible we have an authorative account of God's dealings at certain historical junctures; but outside Scripture and the history of which it speaks we have no such record.

[57] The theme of Jewish spiritual blindness is also found in the Old Testament — e.g. at Dt. 29:4; Is. 6:9, 10; 29:10. It is clear spiritual blindness represents a punishment from God — cf. Rom. 1:18–32; 11:8–10; 2 Thes. 2:10–12.

is read. It has not been removed, because only in Christ is it taken away. Even to this day, when Moses is read, a veil covers their hearts.'[58] Here Paul exposes the root of Jewish unbelief. They have the Scriptures which contain God's message, but fail to see their true meaning. At the same time the passage is not without hope as it does give a prospect of better things. Moreover, it ties Jewish unbelievers very closely to gentile unbelievers since Paul can proceed to speak in general terms of those who fail to understand the message he proclaimed — 'Even if our gospel is veiled, it is veiled to those who are perishing. The god of this age has blinded the minds of unbelievers, so that they cannot see the light of the gospel of the glory of Christ, who is the image of God.'[59] Paul was convinced that basically Jewish and gentile unbelievers have the same problem of spiritual blindness.

What are the implications for anti-Semitism?

If the whole of the New Testament had been carefully considered, it would have provided an antidote to forms of anti-Semitism which have emerged in the church. It has tempered its anti-Judaism with the delineation of the Jewish people as spiritually blind. Their sin may be serious, but it does not mean that the Jews should be demonized. It certainly does not qualify them for the title of apostates. In fact, it places them on exactly the same plane as the rest of mankind. The Jews will not be able to profit from their own rich spiritual inheritance until they recognize their natural blindness. Jesus sometimes directly confronted his fellow-Jews with this blindness. On one occasion when the idea met with resistance from a group of Jews, he declared, 'If you were blind, you would not be guilty of sin; but now that you claim you can see, your guilt remains.'[60] These remarks could easily have been generalized to the majority of the Jewish people of that time. Indeed, they can also be applied to the gentile church at times when it has forgotten its natural blindness.[61]

The church has always found it difficult to grasp the teaching of the New Testament that the crucifixion was a sin of ignorance even among the Jews. If that had not been clearly stated and if it did not form the

---

[58] 2 Cor. 3:14–15.
[59] 2 Cor. 4:3, 4.
[60] Jn. 9:41.
[61] cf. Rev. 3:17.

basis for the apostolic preaching at the beginning of Acts, we could scarcely believe it. Even skilled exegetes like John Chrysostom have misunderstood this important point, with catastrophic results for the Jews. They have been made guilty of the unique crime of deicide — surely a most inappropriate charge if they were ignorant precisely at the point of Jesus' true identity. They have been written off as beyond hope of pardon. But their crucifying their own Messiah should have been regarded as the clearest evidence of their spiritual blindness. (The same would apply for the gentile participants.) Such blindness was not incurable. It should have provoked sorrow among gentile believers as well as prayer that the blindness be removed. Instead, it has often been used to justify arrogance among gentile Christians as though they could never be guilty of such spiritual blindness.

It is true that the New Testament does indicate a sin that cannot be forgiven. It is also true that this phenomenon is mentioned mostly in connection with Jews. Thus, Jesus had occasion to warn the Jewish religious experts of this when they accused him of carrying out his exorcisms by the power of Satan.[62] Again, the book with the most detailed warnings on this score — the letter to the Hebrews — seems to be addressed to a Christian congregation comprised largely of Jews. But no grounds are given for restricting these warnings to Jews. They apply to all who are enlightened and have tasted in some way of the powers of the age to come. And where gentiles have been given access to the full range of God's blessings, they must be embraced in these warnings.

The New Testament does not present anyone as a typical Jew. It does give details about a range of individuals with very different personalities like Simon Peter, Paul, Martha and Mary, Caiaphas and Judas Iscariot. Even to mention them is sufficient to give the lie to the notion that there is such a thing as a typical or representative Jew. Perhaps the most dangerous of these possibilities is Judas Iscariot because of his betrayal of Jesus and the description of him as 'the son of perdition'.[63] Undoubtedly, Judas was sinister, but he emerges in the gospels as an isolated figure. He was neither truly one of the twelve disciples though he belonged to them outwardly nor did he belong to the priests to whom he betrayed Jesus. There is no reason to accept the theory upheld by the Jewish scholar, Hyam Maccoby, that from a literary perspective the gospels require that Judas be identified with the

---

[62] Mt. 12:22–32; Mk. 3:22–30.
[63] Jn. 17:12.

Jewish people as a whole.[64] No doubt, this interpretation can be found in Jerome, who contended that 'the Jews take their name, not from Juda who was a holy man, but from the betrayer. From the former we (Christians) are spiritual Jews; from the traitor came the carnal Jews.'[65] Whatever Jerome's other contributions to biblical scholarship, this particular statement is exegetically monstrous. It may be going too far to suggest that Judas was unique in the history of mankind. But when the gospels talk of Satan entering into Judas, it would surely be inappropriate to draw conclusions about religious or racial background.[66] We are faced with a profound warning for the whole of humanity.

Paradoxically, the same portions of the New Testament which undermine any sense of Jewish religious superiority adequately refute any idea that the Jews are to be placed in some special category of sinners far more heinous than the rest of mankind.[67] The Jews are a mirror of the religious attitudes of the whole of mankind. We are not to romanticize about them as though by their own ingenuity they had brought wonderful religious insights (say, the idea of one God or an exceptional ethical code) to the whole of mankind.[68] But neither are we to demonize them as though they had so given themselves over to Satan that there was no crime or outrage of which they were not capable. It is vital for the church to grasp both elements in Paul's delineation of the Jews as 'As far as the gospel is concerned, they are enemies on your account; but as far as election is concerned, they are loved on account of the patriarchs.'[69] If the first part of this is ignored, Christians will begin to draw a rosy picture of the Jews which is very different from

---

[64]   Maccoby, *Judas*, 81–2. Sandmel, *Anti-Semitism*, 38 n 14 suggests a similar idea — that the name, Judas, which could refer either to Judaea or Jews, is intended as a personification of Jewish hatred.

[65]   Jerome, *Homily* 35 (on Psalm 109). I have used the translation of Sister Marie Liguori Ewald from *The Homilies of Saint Jerome* (Catholic University of America Press, Washington D.C. 1964). Interestingly from a later part of the very same homily Jerome affirms the debt of Christians to the Jews and their duty to pray for them. Hence with Jerome the identification of the Jews with Judas cannot be the worst possible type of description.

[66]   Lk. 22:3; Jn. 13:27.

[67]   On the other side of the coin many who have recognized among the Jews those of exceptional virtue have also been committed to the view that other Jews have proved people of exceptional treachery. Haynes, *Jews*, 1–4 illustrates this point both from Dante's *Inferno* and from certain Reformed Confessions.

[68]   Richardson (note 53). 143–4.

[69]   Rom. 11:28.

the reality. If it is the second part of Paul's statement which is ignored, the door will be open to all manner of suspicions about the Jews.[70]

The charge, therefore, that anti-Semitism is embedded in the New Testament is false. Certainly, if sections of the New Testament are read superficially or without due regard for the full context, they may well provide scope for those who come looking for additional fuel to fan the flames of an anti-Semitic prejudice which has already been started for very different reasons. Sadly, the church has been guilty of misreading its own Scriptures at this very point, and in the process has betrayed the same sort of blindness as has afflicted the Jews. Subsequent history has proved the appropriateness of the warning that Paul issued to the gentile church against the same religious arrogance as led the Jews to reject Jesus. Obviously we cannot blame the New Testament for this; the real culprit is gentile arrogance in ignoring the plain warning of Scripture.

It has sometimes been suggested that the (gentile) church's proud rejection of the Jewish people mirrors the Jews' own proud rejection of Jesus of Nazareth.[71] And in certain respects, I believe, such a parallel can be illuminating. The majority of Jews rejected Jesus because they resented the fact that he emerged as the true servant of God — a role in which they had failed. Many gentile churches, for their part, have despised the Jews because they have not wanted to see in the Jews a picture of themselves. They preferred a more flattering image by which they were spiritually superior, altogether above those sins committed by the Jews.

---

[70] Haynes, *Jews*, 6–8 would describe this statement of Paul as ambivalent, the sort of remark that has fuelled the witness-people myth. I would prefer to say that Paul's teaching can be easily misunderstood or distorted either for or against the Jewish people.

[71] I am grateful to the Rev Howard Taylor for this suggestion.

Five

The Early Church and the Jews

Pagans, Jews and Christians

One of the first tasks of the early church was to forge an identity distinct from its Jewish roots. This emerges clearly in the second century in the work of the Christian apologists who sought to commend the claims of Christianity to the Roman Emperors and to free Christians from the persecution to which they had been intermittently subjected since the time of Nero. They would often describe Christians as a 'third race' in contradistinction from both the pagans and the Jews.[1] To some extent this choice of expression was determined by the status of the Jews as the one group which had hitherto lived in the Roman Empire without assimilating to Roman ways, and was accepted as such. The apologists were trying to claim for Christians the same political rights as Jews, while asserting their differences from them; for Christians and Jews had sometimes been confused in early pagan polemic.[2] Until the fifth century and the emergence of coercive tactics against paganism, it remained the regular practice for the church to devise its apologetic on two fronts — against the challenges of pagan idolatry and against Judaism.[3]

Of the two, the challenge of Judaism was by far the more significant. As soon as the church claimed that the appearance of Jesus as Messiah had been predicted by the Jewish prophets, it had to justify its exegesis against Jewish alternatives. Even in their regular exposition of the

---

[1] Simon, *Israel*, 107–11.
[2] Dunn, *Partings*, 241.
[3] Wilken, *Judaism*, 22–4.

Scriptures to their own respective constituencies Christian and Jewish teachers had to keep a watchful eye on what line was being taken in the rival camp.[4] At the same time Christians had to explain to pagans why the Jewish people by and large did not believe in Jesus if the Jewish Scriptures upheld the Christian position.

The church's stance seemed even more remarkable to outsiders in that it did not try to observe the Jewish Law in anything like its entirety. The pagan Celsus put the challenge bluntly — 'Who is wrong? Moses or Jesus? Or when the Father sent Jesus had he forgotten what commands he gave to Moses? Or did he condemn his own laws and change his mind, and send his messenger for quite the opposite purpose?'[5] The Jews, therefore, did pose a problem for Christians seeing that they possessed those Scriptures which could (in theory at least) disprove the Christian position or at least make it look inconsistent. The situation was aggravated by the fact that, with the exception of Jerome, the early church was not equipped to tackle the original Hebrew text.[6] Indeed, it was commonly thought that the popular Greek translation, the Septuagint, was just as authoritative.[7] It was, after all, extensively quoted in the New Testament writings.

In their efforts to address these issues Christians were more anxious to win over interested pagans and to reassure confused members of their own flock than they were to persuade the Jews of the cogency of their arguments. In fact, a recent Jewish scholar has claimed that the last friendly literary venture to win over the Jews was Justin Martyr's *Dialogue with Trypho*, which dates from about the mid-second century.[8] The less friendly attitude may have been prompted in turn by a hardening among official Jewish attitudes, since the Sages (as the Jewish Rabbis were called by that time) had instructed Jews not to discuss their faith with Christians.[9] This did not, however, stop contacts at an informal level as the career of Origen, who took pride in his numerous Jewish consultants, makes plain.[10]

---

[4]   de Lange, *Origen*, 103.

[5]   Origen *c. Cels.*, 7:18. The translation is that of Henry Chadwick in the Cambridge University Press edition of 1953.

[6]   Wilken, *John*, 81–3.

[7]   de Lange, *Origen*, 50–1.

[8]   David Rokeah in Almog, *Antisemitism*, 55. Augustine's *Tract. adv. Jud.*, may be one exception.

[9]   ibid., 61.

[10]   de Lange, *Origen*, 23–8.

Thus, for the second century it may be correct to assume Ruether's perspective of anti-Judaism forming an integral part of the testimony and the self-identity of the Christian church. I would, however, dispute the appropriateness of this for an earlier period, since it was only around this time that Judaism ceased to be pluralistic, with the growing pre-eminence of the sort of rabbinic Judaism earlier associated with the Pharisees.[11] Before this, the church could have staked a claim to represent the true Judaism; the parting of the ways between Judaism and Christianity was not decided overnight.[12] Indeed, a small group of Jewish Christians who were orthodox in their faith did persist as we shall see; but their role from now on was marginal.

The problem of the Jewish legacy — the challenge of Marcion

Although direct contacts between the church and the synagogue may have diminished, the church could not forget its Jewish antecedents. Indeed, they were often raised by pagan opponents or by those considered heretical within the church. Among the latter group Marcion was to pose the most significant challenge.

From c. 140 Marcion, the son of the bishop in Sinope in Pontus, who was banished from the church by his father, began to develop a network of thriving churches around his heretical doctrines.[13] He raised issues which exposed a weakness in the church's thinking about the Jewish Law and elicited in the main a response which heightened the church's anti-Judaism. All this took place at the level of doctrine or ideology. It illustrates that with its possession of the Jewish Scriptures (and for that matter the New Testament Scriptures which spoke of the Jews) the church could develop or change its attitude towards the Jews without any immediate inspiration from the Jews themselves. Thus, the largest block of anti-Jewish material in Tertullian, one of the most outstanding North African Christian writers, is to be found in his work *Adversus Marcionem* rather than in his *Adversus Judaeos*.[14]

Marcion encountered a situation where the church was uneasily claiming to be a new faith and at the same time to be dependent on the antiquity of the Jewish Scriptures.[15] But he boldly went beyond this

---

[11] Dunn, *Partings*, 238–9.
[12] ibid., 230–43 gives a useful account of some of the complexities of this parting.
[13] Stephen G. Wilson in Wilson, *Anti-Judaism*, 2:45.
[14] David P. Efroymson in Davies, *Anti-Semitism*, 100
[15] for this and what follows *ibib.*, 100–5.

apparent inconsistency to explore the implications for the doctrine of God. It did not seem to him to be the mark of a wise God to give laws at one time and to rescind them at another. (Marcion had further objections to make about the wisdom of these laws.) Moreover, it was strange that God should send his Son to the Jewish people as their Messiah when they did not recognize him. This again smacked of incompetence. Marcion thought the only satisfactory way to deal with these problems was to remove all religious authority from the Jewish Scriptures, even if this meant rejecting the notion that Jesus had fulfilled these Scriptures. Instead, Marcion accepted Jewish claims for a Messiah who was yet to come; but such a Messiah would be relevant only to the Jews.[16] By contrast Jesus, in Marcion's view, came as the revelation of something new — of a previously unknown god, and of a new human situation free from the old Jewish Law and free from the God who created the world and the Law. This was a radical solution, but one which had the merit of consistency. Everything in the Jewish legacy could be disowned as far as the church was concerned. No longer did the church need to borrow from it in its seemingly selective and arbitrary way.

There is no reason to suggest Marcion had a special interest in the Jews.[17] The effect of his theology would have been to marginalize rather than denigrate them. The mainstream church, however, could not follow this path. In combating Marcion, it generally accentuated its anti-Judaism. Faced with Marcion's jibe of an unsatisfactory Law, the church in part accepted the criticism, but explained it in terms of an unsatisfactory people rather than an unsatisfactory God. It was because the Jews were particularly prone to sin that God had in his wisdom to make special arrangements for them. Tertullian, for example, argued that the food taboos and the requirement to offer sacrifices were God's way of thwarting the Jewish partiality to gluttony and idolatry.[18] Variations on this argument were found in Irenaeus and in Justin.[19]

A similarly heightened anti-Judaism is found in Tertullian's response to Marcion's remarks on the Jewish rejection of Jesus.[20] Not only had this been foretold by the prophets, but it was plain from much

[16]   Wilson article in Wilson, *Anti-Judaism*, 2:53–4.
[17]   *ibid.*, 2:53.
[18]   Tertullian, *adv. Marc.* 2:18:2–3.
[19]   Efroymson in Davies, *Anti-Semitism*, 105–6.
[20]   *ibid.*, 102–4.

of the language used in the Jewish Scriptures that God, Jesus' Father, had been antagonistic to the Jewish people for some time before. Thus, Tertullian made out, God had been opposed to Israel and had been determined to replace the old covenant with something better.

Christian apologetic against Marcion became an occasion for heightened hostility toward the Jews. But it cannot entirely be blamed for it. After all, in its initial uncertainties about the Jewish Law, it revealed presuppositions which were more anti-Judaistic than the New Testament. Nor did all Christians who were contemporary with Marcion react the same way. Melito of Sardis, for example, took a much more positive stance on the Law, as we shall see, but ironically this did not prevent him taking a strong line on the Jews, though for very different reasons.

The Christian trump card — the argument from history

Marcion was not the only figure to highlight the tensions inherent in the church's legacy from the Jews. Educated pagans did the same — from a different angle.[21] Unlike Marcion, they were impressed by claims to antiquity, but wondered how Christians could lay claim to Jewish traditions when the Jews in the main rejected this interpretation and most Christians were themselves of gentile origin. Naturally, the question was tied to the Jewish rejection of Jesus. Indeed, Christians made this the centrepiece of their argument, contending that the hand of God had been manifest in history since the time of Jesus in various calamities that had befallen the Jews and in the successes that had attended the Christian gospel in the gentile world. It was important to see these two processes as going on hand in hand. The truth of the Christian gospel was being attached to the discomfiture of the Jews.

Arguments from recent or contemporary history as evidence of divine favour or disfavour enjoyed almost universal currency at that time.[22] Even the Jews could not afford to neglect an explanation for the destruction of their Temple; they had no doubt it was because of some serious sin, though not because of their treatment of Jesus.[23] In probably the most comprehensive work of the early church to answer educated pagan criticisms of Christianity, the *contra Celsum*, Origen

---

[21]   *ibid.*, 108–13.
[22]   Wilken, *John*, 132–4.
[23]   *ibid.*, 135

adduced the history of Christianity as the most powerful evidence of its truth, above both miracles and Old Testament prophecy.[24] It is worth exploring why this should have been. Miracles were limited in apologetic value since they belonged to a past age and were unlikely to convince sceptics about the credentials of those who were supposed to have performed them.[25] Similar problems arose over the prophecies in the Jewish Scriptures. Not all outsiders found their meaning clear, while there remained the problem of the alternative interpretations given by the Jews who were guardians of these very Scriptures.[26] Historical evidence, by contrast, was considered much less ambivalent. Besides, it could be tied to a prophecy made by Jesus himself. The one firm prediction of Jesus, apart from his own parousia, involved the destruction of the Temple in Jerusalem before the passing of that generation, a calamity which he ascribed in general terms to the failure of the people of Jerusalem to acknowledge his true identity.[27] Christians eagerly pointed to its fulfilment within the time stated. By the third century Origen was able to comment, 'never before had there been a period when the Jews were ejected for so long a time from their ritual and worship.'[28] He believed that God had decisively intervened in history to terminate, once and for all, Jewish ritual and Jewish laws; for it was impossible for Jews to observe their religion without access to a Temple in Jerusalem.[29] In fact, it became standard Christian interpretation that God had foretold and brought to pass the destruction of Jewish ritual worship for all time. In addition to the words of Jesus, corroboration was sought from Dn. 9:27, which in the Septuagint reads, 'the sacrifice and offering will be destroyed.'[30]

This picture of the demise of old covenant religion was combined with the rejection of the Jews by God, which seemed to be evidenced in the series of disastrous revolts of the Jewish people, first in the war of 66–73 and then in the two revolts in the first half of the second century — revolts which were followed by harsh legislation from the Romans. At the same time the fortunes of the church in the gentile

---

[24] de Lange, *Origen*, 70
[25] *ibid.*, 70–2.
[26] Origen, *c. Cels.*, 1:50.
[27] Mt. 24:1, 2 and Lk. 19:41–4 were passages to which early Christian writers often turned in this connection.
[28] Origen, *c. Cels.*, 4:22.
[29] Wilken, *John, op. cit.* 134–5.
[30] *ibid.*, 137.

world were steadily, even spectacularly, advancing. Christian protagonists saw this as the two sides of the same coin. 'The providence which
. . . did not wish that the practices of the Jews should continue, and so
destroyed their city and temple . . . and the prescribed worship. Just as
providence did not want them to be performed, and destroyed them,
in the same way it increased the success of the Christians and added
daily to the multitude.'[31] God had not removed his blessing from the
Jews to create a void among men, but rather to open the way to blessing
for the gentile nations. Significantly, this was argued even in the
pre-Constantinian period.[32] Then, Christianity in the eyes of its apologists was proving its authenticity by its very success. Such triumphalist
theology was carried a stage further with Eusebius of Caesarea, who
saw virtually messianic fulfilment in the period of peace which Constantine brought to the Roman world after a series of harrowing civil
wars (as well as intense persecution of the church).[33] The way was being
paved for Christendom where all nations, in theory at least, professed
allegiance to Christ, with the Jews as the solitary exception.

The church was moving beyond all that it was strictly required to say
in its apologetic to the pagan world. This need have been no more than
that Christ had pronounced various woes on certain of the Jewish people,
particularly the people of Jerusalem, for rejecting him. These woes had in
due course been fulfilled, and the gospel was now opened up to the wider
nations. There was certainly good historical evidence for that. But the
church did, in fact, develop a broader case so that it began to have a vested
interest in keeping the Jews depressed. No doubt, one reason for this was
the continuing vitality of Jewish synagogues, which could be found
throughout the Roman world. They remained a challenge which could
not be ignored by the leaders of the church. They did attract some
Christians, not so much because of active proselytizing as through their
reputation as a worshipping centre hallowed by long tradition and by their
possession of religious symbols they shared with Christianity.[34]

Such a threat might be countered by arguing that it was impossible
to observe Judaism properly in a foreign land and that the Jewish
dispersion and attendant misery were destined to last for ever. Thus
Eusebius could juxtapose the political and religious destinies of the

---

[31] Origen, *c. Cels.*, 7:26.
[32] Ruether, *Faith*, 142.
[33] *ibid.*, 143.
[34] Wilken, *John*, 90–1 deals with the difficult question of Jewish proselytizing.

Jews by saying that it had been predicted by their own prophets that 'they themselves would be deprived of their ancient worship, robbed of the independence of their forefathers, and made slaves of their enemies instead of being free men.'[35] This miserable condition, he added, would last for all time, because 'they would be dispersed among the gentiles throughout the whole world with never a hope of any cessation of evil or breathing space from troubles.' It was frequently assumed that the dispersion of the Jews automatically entailed a divine judgment, as in the Old Testament. Passages like Is. 25:2 and Je. 19:10f. were understood to refer to a perpetual desolation of Jerusalem, with scant regard for their original context.[36] That many Jews in Jesus' time already lived in the Dispersion and so cannot have been punished in this way for rejecting their Messiah was conveniently overlooked.

Scriptural evidence was sought and duly found for the Jews being in subjection. The Apostle Paul, for example, had cited Ps. 69:22, 23 as an indication of the judicial hardening which had come upon the unbelieving Jews of his time.[37] Part of this spoke of 'bending their backs for ever', which was sometimes understood not simply to refer to a spiritual blindness or servitude but also to have a socio-political dimension.[38] Certainly, political servitude is much more readily recognized than is spiritual bondage!

Traditionally, the Jews had made much of the rivalry between the twin brothers Esau and Jacob, and had seen themselves in the character of Jacob in the context of the prediction at Gn. 25:23n that the elder brother Esau would serve the younger Jacob. The Jews had drawn comfort from the prediction that they would prevail over their enemies, here represented by Esau.[39] But Christian exegesis turned this on its head. Augustine could write that there was almost unanimous agreement among the Christians he knew that this meant that the 'older', the Jews, were destined to serve the 'younger', the Christians.[40]

One other favourite biblical analogy with Christian writers was to say that Cain who killed his shepherd brother Abel represented the Jews

---

[35]   Eusebius, *Dem. Ev.*, 1:1.
[36]   Isidore, *c. Iud.*, 2:12.
[37]   Rom. 11:9, 10.
[38]   This particular nuance is found only in the Septuagint. Ruether, *Faith*, 146 collects some appropriate evidence, though it is worth noting that Augustine consistently gives this passage a spiritual sense — *Tract. adv. Jud*, 5, 7; *de Civ. Dei*, 17:19; 18:46.
[39]   de Lange, *Origen*, 80.
[40]   Augustine, *de Civ. Dei*, 16:35.

who killed the good shepherd Jesus, who was also their brother.[41] Amongst other things this implied that the Jews were destined to wander the earth as a punishment for their murder. Their very homelessness and humiliation were clear signs that God was taking apposite vengeance. Even Augustine, who was more restrained than many of the early writers about seeing the outworking of God's hand in history, could speak of the Jews, like Cain, being in mourning for the loss of their kingdom and being in terrified subjection to the immensely superior number of Christians. And he did not hesitate to speak of this situation lasting until virtually the end of the age — 'to the end of the seven days of time, the continued preservation of the Jews will be a proof to believing Christians of the subjection merited by those who, in the pride of their kingdom, put the Lord to death.'[42]

The Christian church, therefore, had built up an extensive apologetic by which the credibility of its stance was thought to rest on the Jews remaining in a largely unbelieving and subservient condition. In the medieval period, with the emergence of Christendom, this would become a self-fulfilling prophecy. Although Augustine, who more than any one else was responsible for western Europe's endorsing the idea of the Jews as living proof of Christianity, understood the subjection of the Jews in a spiritual sense, this was often lost in later times.[43] The subjection of the Jews was generally construed as political subjection.[44] Certainly, this was one way in which theological anti-Judaism paved the way for social expressions of anti-Semitism. But this development went far beyond the New Testament. The credibility of the latter did involve the history of the Jews, but not beyond the generation of Jesus when judgment was forecast on Jerusalem and on the Jews of Judaea generally. It was not dependent on the condition of the Jews in the longer term. Indeed, the whole framework seriously discouraged evangelization of the Jews.

---

[41] Ruether, *Faith*, 134.

[42] Augustine, *Adv. Faust. Man.*, 12:12.

[43] Not only was Augustine fair to the context of Rom. 11:9, 10, but he could claim the further support of Gal. 4:25.

[44] I should not, however, overlook that Augustine did see the Dispersion of the Jews, which was part of their political condition, as a judgment of God. He based this not simply on the parallel with Cain, but on God's treatment of his enemies at Ps. 59:11 — 'Slay them (= the Jews) not, lest my people (= the Christians) forget; make them wander to and fro.'

Melito and a foreshadowing of Christendom

Melito of Sardis, widely renowned as a writer from the latter half of
the second century, provides a further insight as to why Christians of
a later period would insist on the humiliation or at least the inferiority
of the Jews in society. He was the first Christian to bring an unambi-
guous charge of deicide against the Jews.[45] In itself, this might appear
a relatively unimportant detail, especially as earlier writers had at least
assigned a large share of the blame for the death of Christ to the Jews.
Melito's charge might even appear less a reflection of his attitude
toward the Jews than an indication of his 'Christocentric monotheism',
which tended to obscure any distinction between Jesus and God the
Father.[46] All Christ's sufferings were thus to be attributed to God, and
Melito did not scruple to talk of God 'being murdered'.[47]

But Melito's Christology would only be part of the picture. There is
every reason to think that the Jewish people were of prime interest to
Melito from the space he devoted in his one complete surviving work
(*On Pascha*) to the twin issues of the status of Israel and the charge of
deicide.[48] Moreover, the rhetorical, almost dramatic, tone which he
adopted throughout this work set the crime of deicide in its most
hideous colours. Here is a sample —

> '*You (i.e. Jews) brought both scourges for his body*
> *and thorn for his head;*
> *and you bound his good hands,*
> *which formed you from earth;*
> *and that good mouth of his which fed you with life*
> *you fed with gall.*
> *And you killed your Lord at the great feast.*
> *And you were making merry,*
> *while he was starving;*
> *you had wine to drink and bread to eat,*
> *he had vinegar and gall;*
> *your face was bright,*

---

[45] S.G. Wilson in 'Melito and Israel' in Wilson 2:91. S.G. Hall, *Melito of Sardis —
On Pascha and Fragments* (OUP, 1979) xi–xvii gives useful summary of Melito's life
and writings.
[46] Hall (note 45) xliii.
[47] *ibid.*, *On Pascha* 715. For further theopaschite statements see lines 451–8 and
Fragment 13 line 31.
[48] S. Wilson estimates that about three quarters of the work are devoted to these
themes in his article in Wilson, *Anti-Judaism*, 2:82.

his was downcast;
you were triumphant,
he was afflicted;
you were making music,
he was being judged;
you were giving the beat,
he was being nailed up;
you were dancing,
he was being buried;
you were reclining on a soft couch,
he in grave and coffin. [49]

The contrast between the Jews and their Messiah could hardly be drawn more starkly!

Surprisingly, this anti-Jewish line was consistent with a high view of Old Testament Israel. Melito accepted that God not only made the human race as a whole, but was also responsible for the special status of Israel. He listed some of the benefits which Christ (or God) had brought to Israel, including the feeding with manna in the desert and the acquisition of the inheritance in Canaan. [50] This, however, was not something in which the Jews could take pride. Rather, it highlighted their ingratitude in rejecting the God who had brought them so many unique blessings. Melito brought his indictment of the Jews to this climax —

'*He who hung the earth is hanging;*
he who fixed the heavens has been fixed;
he who fastened the universe has been fastened to a tree;
the Sovereign Lord has been insulted;
the God has been murdered;
the King of Israel has been put to death by an Israelite right hand.'[51]

Thus, in the hands of Melito the privileges of the Jews had become an index to their ingratitude and their depravity. Far from being a crime committed in ignorance, this deicide was all the more heinous in that it was perpetrated by God's own special people. [52]

The responsibility of the Jews was not qualified in any way. [53] No

---

[49] *On Pascha* 559–581. The translation is that of Hall (note 45).
[50] *ibid.*, 582–633.
[51] *ibid.*, 711–6.
[52] It is true that Melito at *ibid.* 589f. imputes ignorance to the Jews, but ignorance in Melito has much more sinister undertones than that in the early sermons of the Acts or in Paul's testimony in 1 Timothy. It is ignorance of the basics of their own religious tradition.
[53] Wilson in Wilson, *Anti-Judaism*, 2:93.

attempt was made to restrict it to the Jewish leaders or to Palestinian Jews. Since Melito proceeded to make out that judgment had come on the Jews as a result of their act of deicide, we must conclude that Melito intended his remarks to apply to all Jews of his own day.[54] Melito even anticipated and rejected a Jewish plea that divine necessity dictated their crucifixion of the Messiah. It was simply written, Melito argued, that the Messiah had to suffer. The Jews, therefore, should have pleaded with God that the murder should have been at the hands of foreigners, but they had failed to do this.[55]

By contrast, Melito not only absolved the gentiles from any involvement in the crucifixion of Christ, but with a highly selective group of examples actually claimed that the gentiles had welcomed Christ.[56] A framework was thus created whereby the gentiles almost deserved to take the place of the Jews as God's people. Certainly, Melito held to a form of replacement theology which took a comparatively high view of the Jewish Law among the Christians of that age.[57] The Law had been like a sketch or a model of a design which had been useful in its time; but now that the actual building had been erected, it had become superfluous.[58] This does follow biblical guidelines like those in the letters to the Galatians and the Hebrews; but when Melito suggested that the role of the Jewish people had similarly been replaced by gentiles, he was going beyond what was warranted by the New Testament.

It is difficult to estimate Melito's legacy.[59] No doubt he had taken note of the thriving Jewish community in Sardis, and may have been influenced in his remarks above (on Jewish festivities at Passover) by the public Jewish celebrations in his city.[60] But we have no precise evidence as to how the Jewish and Christian communities in Sardis interacted, if at all.

In the short term, despite his reputation as a writer, Melito's influence in the wider church must have been limited on any question to do with Easter, since he was a Quartodeciman and so representative of a local tradition which was soon to be displaced by the alternative

---

54 (note 47) *On Pascha* 730–747.
55 *ibid.*, 525–547.
56 *ibid.*, 672–7.
57 Wilson, in Wilson, *Anti - Judaism*, 2:90.
58 (note 47) *On Pascha* 217–300.
59 Wilson, in Wilson, *Anti - Judaism*, 2:96–7.
60 *ibid.*, 97–8.

Roman approach. Besides, the early church (by contrast to the medieval church) does not seem greatly to have been interested in the charge of deicide. Ironically, that charge required more detailed reflection on the nature of Christ than the church was inclined to give before the great Trinitarian debates of the fourth century. In fact, the early church preferred to speak in general terms of the blindness of the Jews than to focus on the specific act of deicide — and in this respect it was nearer than the medieval church to the New Testament emphasis.

Though Melito wrote at a time when Christendom was hardly conceived, he did provide a framework in which such a concept would become very attractive. Then it would be assumed that the gentile world bit by bit had accepted God's Son, while the Jews had been left as a scattered people outside the church as a memorial of God's judgment on that unbelief which had culminated in their act of deicide. Significantly, Melito is the first recorded writer to advance the apologetic line that it was no accident that Christianity first emerged in the reign of the first Roman Emperor, Augustus, and continued to flourish under most Roman Emperors, with the exception of a few evil characters like Nero and Domitian.[61] This viewpoint was as historically misleading as Melito's insistence on exclusive Jewish responsibility for the crucifixion; for it greatly exaggerated the extent to which the gentile world had accepted Christianity. Indeed, the two errors may have been two different sides of the same coin.[62]

Other writers in the early church period exploited a contrast between believing gentiles and unbelieving Jews. Such a contrast had, of course, been foreshadowed in the Acts of the Apostles and in the letter to the Romans where the rejection of Jesus by the majority of Jews opens up the gospel to the gentiles. The New Testament documents, like Melito to some extent, present this as surprising and unnatural.[63] Some church fathers, however, thought that it had been foretold in the Old Testament and was therefore to be expected. They appealed, for example, to the prophecy which Rebekah was given that 'two nations' were in her womb.[64] The church, it was understood, was the younger nation who had appeared on the scene later and had attained rule over its elder brother, the Jewish nation. Thus, Old Testament predictions of blessing

---

[61] cf. Fragment 1 in Hall (note 45) 62–5.
[62] cf. Wilson in Wilson, *Anti-Judaism*, 2:100.
[63] Ruether, *Faith*, 131–44.
[64] Gen. 25:23 quoted by Augustine at *Tract. adv. Jud.*, 7.

never really applied to Jews who from the beginning were dismissed as persistent rebels against God. Promises of future blessings were in fact reserved for the gentiles. 'O nation (Jews), you were the guardians of the riches that were preserved for the nations (gentile church) . . . Its rightful owners have taken the trust, and you are concerned with the regulations,' declared Isaac of Antioch.[65] In other words, the Jews gained little benefit themselves from their religious traditions; it was all being kept in store for the gentiles. The thought that gentile believers were being grafted into a Jewish stock was being marginalized, if it was not forgotten altogether.

At first the beneficiaries were thought to be the gentile church (i.e. believing gentiles) rather than the gentile nations as a whole. Later, as the nations within the Roman Empire were considered more or less Christianized, any such distinction disappeared. Thus, the foundations were laid for a Christendom in which 'Christian' powers assumed a divine mandate for lording it over the Jews.

Increasing hostility to Christians who kept the Mosaic Law

Such developments as these were bound to leave their mark on Christian attitudes to converts from Judaism and to those Christians who seemed rather attached to either the Jewish synagogue or the Mosaic Law. In fact, an increasingly hostile tone can be detected from the leaders of the church. Whereas Justin Martyr had been prepared in the second century to recognize Christians who adhered to the Jewish law as true believers, provided they did not enforce their belief or practices on others, by the beginning of the fifth century this view had not only been forgotten but had been replaced by a virulent repudiation of distinctly Jewish practices in the church as anti-Christian.[66]

This emerges from a fascinating correspondence between two leading ecclesiastical figures, Jerome and Augustine. At the time of writing neither was probably aware of the lasting significance of what they were committing to personal correspondence. But they are symptomatic of a growing mood of intolerance to anything smacking of Judaism within the church. Moreover, the very stature both men were to acquire later in the western church meant that their own viewpoints gained a wide circulation.

---

[65] Isaac of Antioch, *Hom. c. Iud.*, cited by Ruether *Faith* 138–9.
[66] for Justin see *Dial.*, 46–7.

This correspondence was initiated by Augustine, who was dismayed that Jerome should have argued that Paul had only pretended for politic reasons to oppose Peter in the dispute recorded in Galatians 2. Augustine was concerned about the repercussions for the authority of Scripture if the view gained currency that scripture contained false-hoods for supposedly pious purposes.[67] But the debate inevitably took on a much wider dimension, and embraced the issue of whether Christians, including any converts from Judaism, could reasonably abide by Jewish ceremonies. Jerome emphatically denied that any believer in the era after Christ could behave in this way — 'I shall maintain, and, though the world were to protest against my view, I may boldly declare that the Jewish ceremonies are to Christians both hurtful and fatal; and that whoever observes them, whether he be Jew or Gentile originally, is cast into the pit of perdition.'[68] Jerome's rhetoric may suggest that he was taking a bold line. In point of fact, he was following a long line of Greek exegetes in his handling of Galatians 2.[69] Augustine, for his part, was happy to accept Jerome's view, with only one minor modifi-cation. He was prepared to allow for a gradual process whereby the first generation of Jewish Christians persisted in their old ceremonies until these lost all their significance.[70] But that day had long passed when Augustine wrote. For him the observance of Jewish rites invari-ably betrayed a legalism which ran counter to the gospel. Vividly he described any Christian who wished to revive Jewish ceremonies in his own day as acting as impiously as anyone who wilfully disturbed the ashes of those who were at rest in their graves.[71]

Effectively, the attitude of Jerome and Augustine eliminated any middle ground whereby Jewish converts to Christianity could retain a Jewish identity and at the same time practise Christianity. If they were to be accepted into the Christian church, they would have to cast aside all trappings of their Jewishness. The divide between the Jewish com-munity and the Christian church had now broadened into an unbridge-able gap. They were totally distinct religious and social communities. And this was the legacy which was passed on to the medieval church.

In fact, a recent study by Ray Pritz has enabled us to chart in more

---

[67] Augustine, *Epp.*, 28:3–6; 40:3–7; and 82:44–30. The frequency and length of Augustine's letters on this subject are an index of the importance he attached to it.
[68] Jerome, *Ep.*, 112:14.
[69] *ibid.*, 4–6.
[70] Augustine, *Epp.*, 82:18.
[71] *ibid.*, 16.

detail the history of Jewish-Christian congregations and the attitude of the wider church to them.[72]

The earliest church was, of course, Jewish. And the New Testament bears testimony to thriving but to relatively distinct churches first among the Jews and later among the gentiles. As these churches developed along separate paths, tensions arose as also did opportunities for mutual co-operation and edification. But no one ever thought to deny the validity of the Jewish church. In fact, the boot was on the other foot. The early church leaders had to contend with the Judaizers, those who insisted that gentile Christians adopt Jewish practices before they be accepted as full believers. Whereas in the first generation of the church it was the status of gentile believers which was questioned, by the beginning of the fifth century the pendulum had swung to the opposite extreme.[73] It was denied that any Jew who converted to Christianity had the right to persist in such Jewish rites as the Sabbath and circumcision. Should anyone do so, he was effectively declaring himself a Jew and not a Christian. In short, the term 'Jew' was now being defined in exclusively religious terms. It could not be taken simply as an ethnic description.

This hardline attitude was first spelt out by Epiphanius, Bishop of Salamis in Cyprus, who wrote the *Panarion* (Refutation of All Heresies) in 374–6.[74] He included among these heresies a group of Christians of Jewish origins called the Nazarenes who were said to be orthodox in every respect other than their observance of certain aspects of the Law of Moses. This might seem too trifling a difference to merit inclusion in a list of heresies, but for Epiphanius it was enough for them to be dismissed as Jews.[75] The same outlook was reflected by Epiphanius' younger contemporary, Jerome, and was later endorsed by Augustine. Indeed, the existence of this church was raised by Jerome in his correspondence mentioned above with Augustine.[76] And we have seen that

---

[72] Pritz, *Nazarene*.

[73] That is not to say that the only possible positions were extremes. Jack T. Sanders has illustrated that for the period from 70 to 135 it is appropriate to talk of a spectrum of opinion on these and related issues — *Schismatics, Sectarians, Dissidents, Deviants* (SCM, London 1993) 49–67.

[74] *ibid.*, 29–30. If Epiphanius is the first to us the name Nazarenes, it might suggest this was a recent group. Pritz, however, argues convincingly against this at *Nazarene*, 71–82.

[75] Epiphanius, *Pan.*, 29:7.

[76] For a wider angle on Jerome's comments on the Nazarenes see Pritz, *Nazarene*, 48–70.

both men were agreed that such a church could not be classed as a Christian church. They were to be regarded as Jews.

This dismissal of the Nazarenes was all the more remarkable for the fact that both Epiphanius and Jerome were aware that the Nazarenes were cursed in synagogues and hated by their fellow-Jews.[77] The Nazarenes thus fell increasingly between two stools. From an early stage they had been rejected among the Jewish religious authorities though this did not prevent them from keeping in touch with developments among the Rabbis and maintaining a spiritual interest in their fellow-Jews.[78] They may never have been close to the gentile churches, but in the fourth century they would hardly have benefited from the narrowing of Christian orthodoxy, which ironically resulted from the church's freedom from state persecution and the subsequent imperial protection of Christianity. As part of the subtle changes which occurred at this time a clearcut division between Jewish and Christian practices was considered essential — a tendency which became noticeable as early as the Council of Nicaea (325) where the Emperor Constantine insisted on uniform Easter practice for this very reason.[79] The Nazarenes may well have been one of the main casualties of this changing climate.

We cannot say precisely when this group, which is unlikely ever to have been a large body, disappeared. Most probably, it was in the latter half of the fourth century.[80] Pritz is no doubt right to suggest that it was the distinctive Nazarene outlook on the Law of Moses which sealed their doom. They did not accept the rabbinic expansions on it, but at the same time they could not endorse the church's virtual abandonment of the ceremonial law.[81] They found themselves in a world which no longer had room for such a mediating position or rather for such a bridgehead between the church and the synagogue. The world was certainly the poorer. A long tradition of distinctively Jewish Christians, perhaps reaching back to the first Jerusalem church which escaped to Pella during the fateful siege of Jerusalem, was thus terminated.[82] Once they were gone from the scene, their position could be misrepresented as though the only possible reason for retaining Jewish practices was that of justification by works. It may be no coincidence that

---

[77] Pritz has amassed the evidence for this from Epiphanius and Jerome and collated it with the talmudic tradition at *Nazarene*, 102–7.

[78] *ibid.*, 58–70.

[79] Eusebius, *Vita Constantini*, 3:18–19.

[80] Pritz, *Nazarene*, 81–2.

[81] *ibid.*, 110.

[82] So Epiphanius at *Pan.*, 29:7:7–8. This is accepted by Pritz, *Nazarene*, 10.

Epiphanius, the first writer to dub them as heretics, wrote at about the time the Nazarenes disappeared. They were no longer around to explain their distinctive stance.

In the process the wider church lost the witness of one group of Christians who had access to the Hebrew tongue and could engage on their own terms those who continued in Judaism. For they maintained an interest in the rabbinic traditions and did not lose hope for the restoration of Israel despite the fact that they were specifically cursed in synagogues. But from the fifth century on conversions from Judaism to Christianity would inevitably be more difficult. They had no community of Jewish believers into which such converts could be assimilated. Instead, they had to enter a distinctively gentile church. At the same time conversions would be more drastic in that those Jews who did become Christians were not infrequently those who had some axe to grind against the Jewish community. In other words, we may suspect that often their conversion had more to do with unfortunate events within the Jewish community than with the attractiveness of Jesus or the cogency of Christian arguments.

The polemic of John Chrysostom

The fourth century did prove something of a watershed for the church, with the emergence of Constantine, the first Christian Emperor. This did not, however, entail a Christian Empire overnight. Far from it. Christians of that century were only too aware that the change of political fortunes could easily be reversed.[83] They had to contend not only with several Emperors who effectively gave their support to the Arian heresy, but with Julian from the Constantinian dynasty, who threw off his Christian upbringing and vigorously championed a short-lived pagan revival. Christianity's place at the helm was for some time far from assured even though some of its protagonists did identify its predominance over both paganism and Judaism in the Roman Empire as a fulfilment of Old Testament prophecies.

This uncertain situation was the context for the sermons of John Chrysostom which Ruether has aptly described as 'easily the most violent and tasteless of the anti-Judaic literature' within the patristic era.[84] The limited context, however, of Chrysostom's outbursts must

---

[83] Wilken, *John*, 128–9.
[84] Ruether, *Faith*, 173.

be borne in mind. He was not directly addressing Jewish people. Nor was he interested in any violent action against them. Indeed, in the pluralistic setting of Antioch he would have been happy for the Jews to continue their rites quite independently of Christians.

But in 386 Chrysostom was alerted to the fact that many Christians in the congregation at Antioch, where he served as a presbyter, were participating in Jewish ceremonies, notably in the autumn when the Jewish New Year brought a series of special festivals and again in the spring at the time of Passover. Through eight homilies delivered between autumn of 386 and autumn of 387 Chrysostom aimed to warn his congregation against complacency over this problem and to do all in their power to bring back the Judaizers.[85] He wanted a clear division between the church and the synagogue in Antioch.

It was not that Chrysostom believed the church was losing members to the synagogue; for many of the Judaizers saw no incongruity in participating in the life of the church as well as in observing certain Jewish festivals and rituals. But their readiness to subscribe to the Jewish calendar as opposed to the ecclesiastical calendar, their resorting to Jews for magical charms and amulets when they needed healing, and even their willingness to take oaths in the synagogue was tantamount to a public declaration that they felt closer to the presence and power of the divine in the synagogue than in the church.[86] In other words, Judaism for them was no obsolete or bankrupt religion which had lost the authority it had had up to the time of Jesus Christ. It continued, in some measure at least, to be a repository of divine truth. While this sort of practice went on and attitudes like these prevailed, Chrysostom believed their actions were both divisive to the church and subversive of its ultimate authority. 'If the ceremonies of the Jews move you to admiration,' declared Chrysostom, 'what do you have in common with us? If the Jewish ceremonies are venerable and great, ours are lies. But if ours are true, as they are true, theirs are filled with deceit.'[87]

Probably the single most attractive feature of the Jewish way of life to the Christian Judaizers was the presence in the synagogue of the

---

[85] for the background see Wilken, *John*, 66–68.
[86] for more detail see *ibid.*, 73–94.
[87] Chrysostom, *Adversus Judaeos*, 1:6 (= *Patrologia Graeca* 48:852). The translation here, as with other extracts from this work of Chrysostom, is from Paul W. Harkins, *St John Chrysostom — Discourses against Judaising Christians* (The Catholic University of America Press 1979).

scrolls of the Law and the prophets. Irrespective of the specific Christian debt to the Jewish Scriptures, all books, especially ancient ones, exercised considerable mystique in the ancient world. The Jewish Scriptures were especially mysterious. Not only were they kept in old-fashioned scrolls in a holy place, but they were written in a strange script, backwards — a unique feature for the Mediterranean world. By contrast, Christian books suffered somewhat from undue familiarity. They were written in the vernacular and bound in codex form.[88] In a world which held that the more ancient a tradition the more revered it should be, Christianity by contrast was somewhat handicapped by its modernity.

Chrysostom revealingly disclosed that it was the Jewish possession of the Scriptures in their synagogues which particularly roused his ire. Addressing the Judaizers who revered the synagogue, he said, 'This is the reason above all others why I hate the synagogue and abhor it. They have the prophets and do not believe them; they read the sacred writings but reject their witness — and this is the mark of men guilty of the greatest outrage.'[89] Mere possession of holy prophets and holy writings did not automatically confer any sanctity upon the Jews; in fact, it made them the more guilty and the more detestable, if they did not interpret them correctly. Chrysostom was certainly echoing biblical teaching that those who have the truth but do not use it aright are more guilty than those who have never had it. He also believed that the rejection and crucifixion of Jesus was the greatest crime anyone could ever have committed. But I suspect that at the same time his irritation with the Jews reflected a weakness in contemporary Christianity in that it had to depend to some extent on the Jews as custodians of the ancient Scriptures.

Such a weakness was reinforced in Chrysostom's mind by the current idea that the Jewish Temple might be rebuilt in Jerusalem. The Christian teaching which insisted that the Temple in Jerusalem with its rituals no longer had any place in the purposes of God and would never be rebuilt was known to the Emperor Julian. During his short reign (361–3) this pagan Emperor gave the Jews permission to rebuild the Temple in Jerusalem with the specific purpose of disproving Christianity.[90] Though this scheme proved abortive, Christians were stung by

---

[88]   Wilken, *John*, 80.
[89]   Chrysostom (note 87) 1:5 (PG 48:850) cf. 6:6 (PG 48:914).
[90]   *ibid.*, 138–148.

the challenge Julian had posed and some like Chrysostom became aware of the vulnerability of Christianity at this point. The vigour of Chrysostom's reaction to the Judaizing Christians in Antioch is a measure of how keenly he felt this challenge and how amazed he was that there should actually be professing Christians who should fraternize with the Jews and be enthusiastic about a rebuilt Temple in Jerusalem. To him the truth of the predictions of Christ and so of the whole of Christianity were at stake.[91]

The problem of Judaizing Christians was much broader than the case highlighted by Chrysostom in Antioch, though Chrysostom was unusual in his vigorous denunciations and somewhat sensationalist approach. Wherever there emerged 'Judaizers', they did in various ways question ecclesiastical authority. They appealed directly to Jesus, who did observe the Jewish law, and insisted that they were simply following his example in this as in other respects.[92] If church authorities argued that many Jewish rites had become a dead letter, the presence of a lively Jewish community with its own traditions appeared to give the lie to that argument. Moreover, at this time many Jewish communities were happily integrated and indeed respected in wider society. There was no stigma attached to the Jews which would prevent Christians from associating with them for personal or for religious reasons.

In the short term Chrysostom's sermons were unsuccessful. Indeed, they backfired on him, raising questions among the wider congregation as to what was so fascinating about the practices of the Jews.[93] Interestingly, his remarks about the Jews in other contexts, especially from his Constantinople days, could be quite favourable.[94] But as Wilken points out, 'The meaning of religious texts is not exhausted by their original setting; what happens to them later is often more significant than their first life'.[95] Chrysostom's work proved popular enough to be very well represented in the manuscript tradition of his time. This means they had an effect on a whole range of contexts quite different from their original setting. And where Chrysostom contended that not only he hated the Jews but so did the prophets, the martyrs and even God himself, it is little wonder that his writings served as justification

---

[91]   *ibid.*, 153–8.
[92]   *ibid.*, 93–4.
[93]   *ibid.*, 74–5.
[94]   *ibid.*, 126 n 9.
[95]   *ibid.*, 162.

for more direct manifestations of violence against the Jews than Chrysostom had ever envisaged.[96] Their circulation proved especially unfortunate in a later age when Christianity became indisputably the dominant religion.[97]

Though the Antioch known to Chrysostom was pluralistic and the Jews had experienced a largely peaceable existence there for about 600 years, the days for such co-existence were numbered. Early in the fifth century the Jews became the targets of periodic attacks in Antioch; their great synagogues were destroyed. Communal violence against the Jews persisted into the sixth century with first an attempt at mass conversion, which failed, and then an outbreak of massacre, until the Jews were finally expelled from the city.[98] It would be an exaggeration to impute all the blame for this to Chrysostom. He could not have foreseen the upsurge of Christian triumphalism and intolerance, since in his day Christendom was far from being established. But in an unforeseen way Chrysostom had prepared the ground for the revolution in attitude toward the traditional Jewish community in Antioch.

Perhaps the most unfortunate part of Chrysostom's legacy was his abandonment of any idea that the Jews could be converted. Earlier Christian writings about the Jews may have highlighted the sinfulness of Israel's rejection of its Messiah and detailed some consequent divine judgments. But they gave at least lip service to the notion that individual Jews might be won over to their Messiah.[99] Chrysostom, however, effectively discarded such a notion. He held that the unforgivable sin had been committed when the Jews had crucified Christ.[100] He did not scruple to impute this sin to the Jews of his own day as well as those of Christ's time. While their sins in the Old Testament era may have been monstrous enough, they had never been sufficiently serious for God to despair altogether of them. The murder of Christ, however, was in a

---

[96] cf Ruether, *Faith*, 179. It is, however, only fair to add that Chrysostom used the language of hatred rarely. Commonly he preferred more neutral expressions like the description of the Jews as 'enemies of God'. He could even term the Jews as pitiable = Chrysostum (note 87) 1:2 (PG 48:845) and 4:1 (PG 48:871).

[97] Wilken, *John*, 162.

[98] C.F. Kraeling, 'The Jewish Community in Antioch', *Journal of Biblical Literature* 51 (1932), 158–60.

[99] see Harkins (note 87) intro. xxxiii–iv.

[100] Chrysostom's view had been taken by Hippolytus and by Eusebius of Caesarea — see Ruether, *Faith*, 128 and 144.

very different category —

> You did slay Christ, you did lift violent hands against the Master, you did spill his precious blood. That is why you have no chance for atonement, excuse or defence. In the old days your reckless deeds were aimed against his servants, against Moses, Isaiah, and Jeremiah. Even if there was ungodliness in your acts then, your boldness had not yet dared the crowning crime. But now you have put all the sins of your fathers into the shade. Your mad rage against Christ, the Anointed One, left no way for anyone to surpass your sin. That is why the penalty you now pay is greater than that paid by your fathers.[101]

This penalty consisted in an everlasting bondage.[102] Not only would the old ritual of Judaism never be restored with a rebuilt Temple in Jerusalem, but the Jews were destined to remain followers of religious rites which were quite fruitless and an abomination to God.

Chrysostom evidently overlooked the biblical teaching that the Jews had acted ignorantly in unbelief when they had Jesus crucified. There was, therefore, no place for mercy to be shown to the Jews of his own day. Moreover, if Chrysostom could say that he and God hated the Jews, clearly it was every Christian's duty to share this attitude. While Chrysostom understood this to imply in practice nothing more than the complete avoidance of the Jews, their synagogues and their homes, others in a different setting could easily draw more drastic political and social implications. In fact, the very time Chrysostom delivered his fateful sermons witnessed an upsurge elsewhere in the Roman Empire of activity by Christians against Jewish synagogues which saw their being confiscated or else burnt to the ground, even when this was technically illegal.[103]

Conclusion

The case of Chrysostom highlights the sensitivity of the early church in handling the Jewish Scriptures. As David Rokeah puts it, 'Since the origins of Christianity and the path to Christianity were intertwined with the Holy Scriptures of the Jews, the Jews' very existence, even without any action on their part, constituted a problem for the Church.'[104] Rokeah is right, I believe, to see dependence on these

---

[101] Chrysostom (note 87) 6:2 (PG 48:907).
[102] *ibid.*, 5:10 (PG 48:899) and 6:2 (PG 48:905f).
[103] Simon, *Israel*, 224–9.
[104] Rokeah in Almog, *Antisemitism*, 63.

Scriptures as at the heart of the church's attitude to Judaism. This far outweighed any threat ever posed by Jewish persecution or proselytizing. In its public stance the church had to explain Jewish history, and in the process it emphasized the spiritual blindness (and sometimes worse characteristics) of the Jews. Above all, the church had to defend its own credentials as the authentic interpreter of these Scriptures.

In time the church found its best response to the Jewish challenge in an appeal to recent history which had seen its own remarkable growth coupled with a marked decline in the fortunes of the Jews. These political changes could then be linked to the Scriptures through their assessment as fulfilment of the prophecies.

But until that historical process had seemingly decided in favour of Christianity, the church had to be wary in its approach to the Jews. It could not condemn them too vigorously as long as it was concerned to establish its own Jewish roots.[105] It is perhaps a mark of a new self-confidence at the beginning of the fifth century that Augustine should propound the idea that the unbelieving Jews fulfilled a vital role for the church in attesting the veracity of the Scriptures. Augustine held that when pagans asked for the authority on which the Christian revelation was based, Christians could simply point to those Scriptures guarded by a rival religion.[106] Clearly the Jews had ceased to be a threat to Christianity at the level of biblical exposition.

In fact, Augustine bequeathed to later generations the concept of the Jews as special witnesses of God, in effect a sort of object lesson to the rest of mankind.[107] Perhaps it would be unfair to Augustine personally if I were to suggest he viewed the Jews as objects rather than as people. His *Tractatus adversus Judaeos* does, after all, contain appeals for the conversion of Jews to Jesus — a feature which is rather unusual for that literary tradition.[108] But this was one of his minor works destined to have relatively little impact. Elsewhere he did repeat the idea that not only in their possession of the Scriptures but also in their exile and social inferiority they were living testimonies to the reality of their God — and to the reality of his judgment on those who would not believe the Scriptures. This had political

---

[105] Rokeah in Almog, *Antisemitism*, 56–62 points out that earlier Christian writers like Tertullian and Origen paint a much more favourable picture of the Jews in their works addressed to pagans than in their in-house writings.

[106] Augustine, *Comm Joannem*, 35:7 — cf., *Enarr. in Ps.*, 56:9.

[107] Haynes, *Jews*, 27–33.

[108] Augustine, *Tract. adv. Jud.*, 8–10.

ramifications. Christian leaders would tolerate Jews in a way they would hardly do for pagans and heretics.[109] It would not help their cause to aim at the eradication of the Jews.[110] But this toleration was combined with an insistence that the Jews be kept in a depressed condition. Thus, the legislative codes of the later Roman Empire are full of restrictions on the Jews. They are consigned to the bottom of the pile in political and social terms, with their economic activity severely hampered.[111] Every effort was made to ensure that their social standing accurately reflected their religious position as adherents of a *nefanda superstitio*.[112]

Even in its outward success the church could not ignore its Jewish roots. As a religion which took seriously the events of history, Christianity could not overlook those events which indicated the hand of God in judgment and in mercy on the destiny of nations. Unfortunately, it assumed a triumphalist spirit whereby judgment was reserved for the Jews and mercy for the gentile church. This was severely to distort the Apostle Paul's presentation in Romans 11 which allows both for the reincorporation of Jews into the church as their natural stock and for God to show the same severity toward gentile unbelief as he had done towards Jewish unbelief. It is true that the church did not officially lose all hope of a mass Jewish conversion, but it effectively downgraded it by tying it to events immediately preceding the end of the age.[113] Augustine, for example, tells us that believers of his time were even enthusiastic about this but connected it with a future reappearance of Elijah.[114] This would entail a loss of urgency in bearing witness to the Jews in the present. The Greek church, for its part, believed that in his words at Mt. 28:19 Jesus had restricted future missionary activity to the gentiles.[115] There was no longer any point in taking the gospel to the Jews; Chrysostom was

---

[109] Simon, *Israel*, 229–32 lists various theoretical and practical limitations on the church's anti-Jewish policy.

[110] The mark of Cain, who was said to be a model of the Jew, and the divine command at Ps 59:11 not to kill God's enemies were two biblical passages which ruled out the killing of the Jews. That is not to deny that localized pogroms did take place in which Jews were murdered; but these did not reflect official church policy. Augustine could adduce further reasons — Haynes, *Jews*, 30–32.

[111] Ruether, *Faith*, 186–90.

[112] *Codex Theodosianus*, 16:9:4.

[113] cf. Parkes, *Conflict*, 159.

[114] Augustine, *de Civ. Dei*, 20:29.

[115] D.R.A. Hare and D.J. Harrington, 'Make Disciples of All the Gentiles (Matthew 28:19), *Catholic Biblical Quarterly* 37 (1975), 367ff.

an extreme example of that tradition. This left the Jews in Augustine's words as *testes iniquitatis suae et veritatis nostrae* (witnesses to their own sin and to our truth); effectively, their role had become that of an object lesson to the wider world.[116]

---

[116]   Augustine, *Enarr. in Ps.*, 59:1:22.

Six

The Middle Ages — A Hardening of Attitudes Toward The Jews

The early medieval period — roughly between 430 and the First Crusade of 1096 — was characterized by relative tranquillity between Christians and Jews. The only serious exception was the short-lived Visigothic kingdom in Spain.[1] In northern Europe, in fact, especially the north of France, the Rhineland and England, Jewish life demonstrated great vitality and prosperity as late as the first part of the twelfth century.[2] But after this relations so deteriorated that the late medieval period can be described as the first period in history of socially significant anti-Semitism.[3] As a result, the Jews fell from a position of relative security and genuine, if grudging, toleration to a role where they became steadily impoverished and were treated as social outcasts.

Ironically but significantly, this corresponded to the emergence of Christendom — a self-consciously Christian civilization where, it was supposed, the reign of Christ had visibly triumphed and had been endorsed by the secular rulers of the day. But Christendom was not simply the culmination of various religious developments. It reflected a bureaucratic revolution in the twelfth and early thirteenth centuries which highlighted the skills of literacy, numeracy and legal sophistication and so brought power to the Christian 'clerks' who acquired these

---

[1] The Visigoths began to rule in the early 6th century. Up to 589 they were dominated by an Arian theology. Their rulers, however, converted to a Catholic form of Christianity, which persisted up to the Muslim conquest of Iberia in 711.
[2] R.I. Moore in Wood, *Christianity*, 33–57. Moore points out that the local Jewish communities survived the massacres of 1096 and even the atrocity at York in 1190.
[3] Langmuir, *HRAS*, 305.

skills.[4] Recently the Jews had greatly outstripped Christians in these fields, and had been recognized as talented counsellors at various European courts. But with increased importance now attached to their skills, they became the targets of envy among the clerks, who ensured that both the status and the reputation of the Jews were steadily demeaned. The clerks had achieved this by the thirteenth century when they built up as a stereotype of the Jew the sort of 'dirty, downtrodden, sinister but contemptible' figure who would seem anything but a rival for political power.[5] In fact, this was the time when drawings began to depict Jews as physically distinctive with long, hooked noses, while the influential Fourth Lateran Council of 1215 took a major step in segregating Jews from Christian society by insisting that they wore special clothing.[6] Before this the Jews had been relatively well integrated into wider society. Jewish exclusiveness, as it was later regarded, largely resulted from persecution, including the limitation of their rights.[7]

Besides benefiting from changes in society, the clerks posed as the guardians of the new Christian order which their skills had helped to fashion. That implied intolerance of either behaviour or belief which seemed to threaten that order. It was not enough for them to believe in the supernatural opposition of the devil; they sought to identify the devil's agents in such deviants as heretics, lepers and Jews.[8] These ideas did not originate with the ordinary people who for many centuries had lived alongside the Jews in comparative peace. They were disseminated by a ruling élite who ensured that their ideas were quickly transmitted to the popular level.[9]

Clearly, this endangered the security of the Jews. Their position as repositories of the biblical tradition and so as reluctant witnesses to Christian truth was jeopardized. They were now more likely to be seen

---

[4]   Moore in Wood, *Christianity* 50–57. For wider background to the changes in European society in the eleventh and twelfth centuries see Moore *Formation*, 102–4. Moore acknowledges that his thesis is weakened in detail by the fact that there is sparse evidence for Jewish involvement in government in northern Europe.
[5]   R.I. Moore, *Formation*, 147–8.
[6]   ibid., 44–5.
[7]   ibid., 84.
[8]   No doubt this was an example of what Adolf Hitler had in mind when he expressed admiration for the Catholic Church because 'it did not content itself with the Devil; it had to have visible enemies in order not to relax in the struggle' — Rauschning, *Hitler*, 234.
[9]   Moore, *Formation*, 113–123.

as threats to the Christian order because they blatantly denied central Christian beliefs or contaminated their Christian neighbours with their own false practices. Certainly, as we shall see, the old view of the Jews as silent witnesses to Christian truth and as a group who were to convert to Christ toward the end of the age was never entirely abandoned. It was enshrined in papal orthodoxy. But it now had to compete with a much more sinister concept of the Jew, which often led to violent measures against Jewish communities from their rulers or from the populace as a whole.

Around the same time wealthy Jews came to be regarded as rivals in the realm of trade.[10] For a long time the Christian church had maintained at best a suspicious outlook on merchants since it thought they must be motivated by greed. This attitude, however, was modified in the twelfth century which saw a period of rapid urban growth and consequent commercial expansion, involving Christians in ever increasing numbers. Jews, who had predominated as merchants while that profession had been despised, did not benefit from the relaxation of that contempt. Instead, they were seen as unwelcome competitors, and because of their religious isolation they could easily be squeezed out of the market economy. Thus, many Jews were compelled to transfer their energies to the even more obnoxious activity of money-lending.

The Jews may also have been affected indirectly as a result of intellectual undercurrents. The Christian church was being challenged from within by demands for rational, empirical proof. Traditional doctrines could no longer be justified on the ground of ecclesiastical authority alone. These had to be established or adjusted in the light of personal experience. Gavin Langmuir dates the change in perspective to the career of Beranger of Tours who in the 1040s expressed doubts about the Real Presence and effectively made the Eucharist a central element in the agenda of theologians.[11] Shortly Christians had to come to terms with some of the questions posed by the Jews, who constituted 'the only learned, the only uncompromising opponents of the whole idea of the Incarnation.'[12] Between 1070 and 1150, after a prolonged period of inactivity on this front at least seven major and several minor theological treatises were written to counter Jewish unbelief. Even *Cur Deus Homo* by Anselm of Aosta, the most important work of medieval

---

[10] Cohen, *Crescent*, 77–82.
[11] Langmuir, *TDAS*, 116–124.
[12] Richard W. Southern, *St Anselm and his Biographer* (Cambridge 1966) 88.

theology before Aquinas, was written with Jewish objections in view, even though such was not the outward form of the treatise.[13]

These early Christian treatises were moderate in tone, betraying little animosity against the Jews. In time, however, this was to change. Where rational argument was felt to be weak, it was replaced by vituperation or by insinuations about the irrationality, even the sub-humanity of the Jews. Thus, some Christians helped to repress their own religious doubts by creating an increasingly fanciful and grotesque picture of the Jews.[14]

Papal orthodoxy

The position of the Jews in the later medieval period deteriorated in spite of a relatively consistent line pursued by the popes of the period. The basic framework for papal policy had been set by Gregory the Great (590–604), who is generally credited with the creation of the medieval papacy. He wrote, 'Just as one ought not to grant any freedom to the Jews in their synagogues beyond what is decreed by law, so should the Jews in no way suffer in those things already conceded to them.'[15] Gregory followed closely the terms of earlier Roman codes, but he was at the same time a disciple of Augustine.[16]. And it was Augustine's general understanding of the Jews which remained uppermost in papal policy.

According to this Judaism retained no spiritual value. The Jews who persisted in it were guilty of carnality and of such spiritual blindness that they could no longer understand their own Scriptures. Undeniably they were enemies of God and of the Christian faith. Though they were being punished for this and of course for their part in the death of Jesus, their punishment resembled that of Cain. They were to be kept in a degraded condition, but not killed. Indirectly, their preservation benefited the church in two ways. They bore witness to the truth of their own Scriptures. They also kept before the church the hope of Christ's return since their conversion was commonly expected to occur just before the end of the age.[17]

---

[13] Langmuir, *TDAS*, 127–131.
[14] Langmuir, *TDAS*, 131–3 and 197–208 attaches great importance to the work of Peter the Venerable, Abbot of Cluny from 1122 to 1156, in this connection.
[15] cf. Shlomo Simonsohn, *The Apostolic See and the Jews — Documents: 492–1404* (Pontifical Institute of Mediaeval Studies, Toronto 1988) 15 (Document 19).
[16] Kenneth R. Stow in Almog, *Antisemitism*, 74–5.
[17] for more details see *ibid.*, 73 — i.e. what Stow calls the second school of Christian thought.

At first the Jews held rights in society without preconditions, but Pope Alexander II (1061–1073) was responsible for a small but significant shift of emphasis. He tied Jewish rights to their remaining in subservience to the Christians in what might loosely be described as a sort of contractual arrangement.[18] A political dimension had thus been added to the Apostle Paul's concept of the Jew in spiritual bondage by contrast to the Christian who had been set free in Christ.[19] Hence we read in a letter from 1208 of Pope Innocent III, who has been described as 'the incarnation of the medieval papacy at its zenith', to the Count of Nevers this relatively detailed rationale for ecclesiastical and so for state policy toward the Jews —

> So that Cain might be a wanderer and a fugitive over the earth, and yet not be killed by anyone, the Lord set a mark on him by making his head to shake. Thus, the Jews, against whom the blood of Christ calls out, although they ought not to be killed (in case Christian people should forget the divine law), yet they had to be scattered over the earth as wanderers until their countenance be filled with shame and they seek the name of the Lord Jesus Christ. For blasphemers against the name of Christ ought not to be patronized to the extent that they oppress the servants of God, but they should be repressed with the slavery of which they rendered themselves worthy when they laid profane hands on the one who had come to bestow on them true liberty, and they shouted that his blood should be on them and their children.[20]

Clearly this policy required a delicate balancing act. The Jews were to be kept in a subservient condition with a distinctly limited toleration. But such privileges as they had were not to be taken away. Inevitably the policy was somewhat imprecise and abstract.[21] Nonetheless, it had some influence. In the Papal states, for example, the Jews tended to fare better than in most other realms. They never suffered from wholesale expulsions. They were also protected from pogroms, with rare exceptions, both by papal authority and a generally humane attitude on the part of the Italian people.[22] But its influence was restricted, not least in that it could do little to stem the tide of accusations of ritual murder,

---

[18] *ibid.*, 77–8. Stow proceeds to go into further details on pages 78–81 of what the contract involved.

[19] cf. Gal. 4:21–31.

[20] Simonsohn (note 15) 92–3. The quote about Innocent III is derived from Synan, *Popes*, 83. Synan gives a useful summary of his pontificate on pages 83–102. For this Pope's contribution to the idea and reality of Christendom — see Cohen, *Friars*, 248–51.

[21] Gavin I. Langmuir in Wood, *Christianity*, 81–2.

[22] Hay, *Europe*, 162–3.

profaning the host and well-poisoning which were to be levelled against the Jews.

No doubt, Innocent III could detail the privileges to which he believed subservient Jews were entitled. They were not to be forced to accept baptism, not to be wilfully wounded, killed or deprived of their property, not to be disturbed in the performance of their own religious rites and not to be compelled to render services other than those they had provided in the past. In addition, they were assured that Jewish cemeteries would not be disturbed and bodies would not be disinterred.[23] But even to list these Jewish rights is to highlight the limitations of papal policy. At no time did the Popes ever ensure that Jews or their children were free from the risk of forcible baptism.[24] Though popes deprecated such a procedure, they held such a high view of the sacrament that they had to declare all such infant baptisms valid even though they were technically illicit. Moreover, the same Innocent III was prepared to engage in casuistry when adjudging what constituted a forcible baptism — 'Anyone who is drawn to Christianity by violence, through fear and torture, and who receives the sacrament of baptism in order to avoid incurring harm . . . must be forced to observe the Christian faith, as one who expressed a conditional willingness, though in a strict sense he was not willing.'[25] This was of the utmost practical importance to the Jews since any Jew who was baptized forcibly — whether as an adult or as a child — and then reverted to Judaism became guilty of apostasy, a serious charge equal to that of heresy in the eyes of the Inquisition.[26]

Strains on the toleration of the Jews

Pope Innocent III made it clear that he envisaged a modest degree of toleration only for those 'who shall have presumed no plotting for the subversion of the Christian faith.'[27] Superficially this might appear a

---

[23]   Simonsohn (note 15) 74–5. The terms of this Papal letter were incorporated into Decretal X: 5,6,9. For some comments on the background see Stow in Almog, *Antisemitism*, 79–80.

[24]   Hay, *Europe*, 73–4.

[25]   Simonsohn (note *15*) 80.

[26]   Edwards, *TJIWE*, 32–3 where he cites evidence from the 14th century *Le manuel de l'Inquisiteur* by Nicolau Eymerich.

[27]   *qui nichil machinari presumpserint in subversionem fidei Christiane* — reference as for note 20.

restricted and reasonable proviso. And so it would be, if it had been confined to the Pope's objections to exhibitions of derision by the Jews when Christians were engaged in Good Friday celebrations and to their public blasphemies against Jesus.[28] But in fact his concern went much deeper. Wherever the Jews seemed to lord it over Christians or simply failed to be in subservience to them, Innocent held that they had broken the terms of the contract whereby they were allowed peaceful co-existence in Christendom. Thus, he disapproved of Jews being wealthy enough to own Christian wet-nurses or servants, or of their earning a living by lending money to Christians. He even objected to the erection of a new synagogue in Sens (France) next to an old church, since the synagogue was the loftier building and the Jewish worship was sufficiently noisy to disturb the church service.[29]

Innocent's motives included a concern for God's honour and a desire to preserve the church from contamination and to protect Christian society from a fifth column in the midst. Talking of the contempt which Jews who owned Christian servants or wet-nurses were able to bring on the Christian faith, Innocent commented, 'For as soon as they begin to gnaw in the manner of a mouse and to bite in the manner of a serpent, one may fear lest the fire that one keeps in his bosom burn up the gnawed parts.'[30] Significantly, it was under Innocent that the Fourth Lateran Council insisted on separate clothing for Jews and Saracens from their Christian neighbours in order to prevent unintended mixing on the part of Christians.[31]

In fact, it was vital for the Jews to recognize their submission as a just punishment for their ancestors' treatment of Jesus. They should be grateful to their Christian hosts for allowing them to live alongside them — a privilege which Christian rulers were by no means obliged to give them. Presumably, Innocent failed to see the inconsistency in expecting gratitude from the Jews for this reason when they were supposed to be spiritually blind. Perhaps he thought that it was only through subservience that the Jews might eventually be induced to acknowledge their mistakes.

Be that as it may, Innocent III's attitude was to prove influential. A similar outlook emerges from Spain at the end of the fifteenth century

---

[28] They referred to Jesus as *rusticum quendam suspensum a populo Iudeorum*.
[29] Simonsohn (note 15) 82–3 (document 79) and 86–7 (document 82). There are general comments in Stow in Almog, *Antisemitism*, 81–2.
[30] Simonsohn (note 15) 87.
[31] Canon 68. It was around this time that the rouelle, the yellow star on Jewish clothing, originated — cf. Poliakov, *History*, 1:64–7.

when the monarchs Ferdinand and Isabella decreed the expulsion of all Jews. A dictionary for Inquisitors published around that time makes these justificatory comments —

> Up to now, Jews subjected to perpetual captivity, through their own fault, have benefited from Christian mercy, which has welcomed and nourished them. Up until our days, they have lived together with Christians. But today the most Christian rulers of Castile, Aragon, Sicily and Granada have taken measure of their ingratitude. The Jews respond to the generosity of the Christians by seeking conflict with them, by imposing usury on them, by subverting numerous Christian faithful, whom they instruct in the Law of Moses and whom they initiate into their rights and ceremonies.

The treatise proceeds to say that the Jews had many centuries in a Christian society to change their ways but did not. The Christian rulers of Spain would have been fully justified if they had ordered the execution of all Jews; instead, they had shown further clemency in doing no more than having them banished.[32] By this point attitudes to the Jews may have hardened since the time of Innocent III, who had remained confident that the Jews could be accommodated within Christian Europe. But a similarity of concept is apparent. The Jews are guests in the domain of another. Their stay is dependent on their good behaviour, and through time more and more will be demanded in this respect.

Shortly after Innocent's papacy the Jews began to be seen in a further damaging light. They could be viewed as heretics. This perception was largely induced by the discovery of the Talmud.[33] This book was brought to the attention of Pope Gregory IX in 1236 by a Jewish convert to Christianity, Nicholas Donin, from La Rochelle in France. The timing of this request is unlikely to have been accidental. This Pope was known to have something of a personal obsession about heresy; he had done much to promote the Inquisition.[34] In his concern for the dissemination of orthodoxy, as such was perceived by the papacy, he was anxious to eradicate any threatening influences or obstacles to true faith. Donin alleged that the Talmud and related Jewish books were

---

[32]   cited by Edwards, *TJIWE*, 39 from *Le dictionnaire des inquisiteurs* (1494) ed. L. Sala-Molins.

[33]   The idea of a distinction between orthodox and heretical forms of Judaism may have been initiated even earlier when the Inquisition was invited to intervene by the anti-Maimonidean faction in an internal Jewish dispute — Poliakov, *History*, 1:68–9. Moore, *Formation*, 27 points out that Roman law had already placed Jews under the same disabilities as heretics.

[34]   ed. Hubert Jedin and John Dolan, *History of the Church Vol 4* (ET, Burns and Oates, London 1980) 214–6.

such obstacles; Jews who honoured them would have nothing but contempt for Christianity. For they were no extension of Old Testament religion, but the source of a very different faith.[35]

The Pope did not respond immediately to Donin's charges. Commissions comprising ecclesiastics and academics first gave the matter careful consideration. The friars (the Dominicans and the Franciscans) with their zeal for papal orthodoxy, learning and missionary preaching seem to have played the most prominent part in the analysis of the suspected Jewish writings. About the same time a formal disputation was held in 1240 in Paris between Donin and a local Rabbi, Yehiel ben Joseph, at which Donin's detailed charges were aired publicly and an eminent Jewish leader given the opportunity to reply. The result of such proceedings was to give credibility to Donin's position. By 1242 the King of France had twenty or twenty-four waggonloads of Jewish manuscripts burnt in Paris over a period of one and a half days. Throughout the later medieval period there followed regular calls for the Talmud (and other Jewish liturgical works) to be burnt in the interests of evangelizing the Jews and of protecting Christendom from perverse religious influences.

At this juncture, therefore, the church had discovered a further reason to be suspicious of contemporary Judaism. One result would be to promote an aggressive missionary effort toward the Jews which was unknown in previous centuries.[36] It never entirely supplanted the sort of passive religious toleration associated with Augustine's legacy. But a change was noticeable. Whereas earlier generations of Christians had from time to time noted rabbinic distortion of the Scriptures and recognized this as a serious handicap to Jewish belief in Jesus as their Messiah, they had never suggested that this was tantamount to a new religion.[37] Donin, however, and those who followed him argued that such was the place given to the Talmud in Jewish life that it had effectively replaced the Old Testament Scriptures. This had serious implications for Augustine's understanding of the place of the Jews. No longer could the Jews remain within Christian society as living

---

[35] Cohen, *Friars*, 60–69.

[36] *ibid.*, 168–9. There is some scholarly debate as to whether these initiatives came mainly from the friars or were directed from the papacy itself. Jeremy Cohen thinks the papacy must have fully supported the aggressive policy of the friars, but Stow in Almog, *Antisemitism*, 71–89 argues that there is no reason to see a fundamental shift in papal policy in the late medieval period.

[37] Cohen, *Friars*, 74–6.

witnesses to the truths of their own Scriptures. Now that they had promoted the Talmud in preference to these Scriptures, they were the advocates of a rival holy book and of a rival religious system. In the eyes of some Christians, at least, they had become representatives of heretical perversion. No longer were they guilty simply of being blind to the true meaning of their Scriptures; but their leaders had wilfully supplanted these Scriptures with documents which took them further from the truth of the gospel. In a climate where heresy was considered virtually as treason against the church and the state, this changing attitude of the church toward Judaism was bad news.[38] It gave Christians a double motive for interference in Jewish religious life. Christians could parade as rescuers of ordinary Jews from the pitfalls into which their spiritual leaders had taken them. They could also take violent action against Jewish books as a way of protecting Christendom. This action against the Talmud, therefore, 'struck at the very foundation of European Jewry's existence', since an attack on the Talmud was an attack on the central plank of Jewish religious life.[39]

In addition to being a rival to the Old Testament Scriptures, the Talmud was thought both to contain blasphemies against the Christian religion and to advocate deceit and even violence against individual Christians.[40] On the level of blasphemy Donin alleged that the Rabbis had called Jesus' mother an adulteress and had spoken obscenely of Jesus, the Pope and Christianity. Moreover, they cursed Christians daily in their prayers, and held that Christians were subject to everlasting damnation, whereas sinful Jews were to suffer a maximum of only a year in purgatory. When it came to Jewish ethics, Donin and his followers ascribed to contemporary Christians passages in the Talmud which avowed hostility toward particular gentiles. Some Rabbis had allegedly instructed the Jews to kill the best of the gentiles, while others were supposed to have allowed considerable freedom for Jews to violate their oaths to gentiles. As such interpretations of the Talmud gained currency, many Christians began to see the Jews as an undesirable and potentially dangerous presence within society. The accusations against the Talmud gave theoretical confirmation to the charges of host profanation, ritual murder and well-poisoning which were regularly to be lodged against specific groups of Jews. It also encouraged a vigorous

---

[38] *ibid.*, 44–5.
[39] *ibid.*, 74.
[40] *ibid.*, 68–9. cf. the comments made by Pope Gregory IX and included in Edwards, *TJIWE*, 30–1.

response to the Jewish presence in society — either they should be converted or they should be expelled. There could be much less room for the sort of toleration advocated by Innocent III on the proviso of Jewish subservience and respect for Christianity, because Jews who followed the Talmud had clearly breached that condition.

Targeting Christ's enemies — the era of the Crusades

Some time before the discovery of the Talmud more traditional Christian objections toward the Jews had been brought into sharper focus by the Crusades. The First Crusade was originally proclaimed in 1095 by Pope Urban II with the twin aims of freeing the eastern churches from Muslim oppression and of liberating the holy city of Jerusalem from Muslim power.[41] It had nothing directly to do with the Jews. But the calling for a crusade proved more popular and had more wide-ranging consequences than the Pope had envisaged. He had, for example, sought to involve only the knights, but discovered a great interest in the Crusade from the lower strata in society. Moreover, the theological basis to the Crusade was the understanding that the Muslims (or Saracens as they were known) were the implacable enemies of Christ and the servants of the devil.[42] The Crusade was represented as a just act of vengeance for their insults to God, Christ and his church.[43]

In fact, popular preaching of the time put the Crusade on the level of a blood-feud or vendetta.[44] To modern ears this will appear shocking. But we must remember that this was a time when there was no national or international police force, still less an institution like the United Nations, to search out and to have punished those who abused the rights of racial or religious minorities. That responsibility often fell to the kinsmen of the injured parties. It was, therefore, incumbent on the Christians as Christ's kinsmen to avenge the wrongs he had suffered. This sort of argument was unashamedly used to justify violent action against the Muslims — 'I address fathers and sons and brothers and nephews. If an outsider were to strike any of your kin down, would you not avenge your blood-relative? How much more ought you to avenge your God, your father, your brother, whom you see reproached, banished from his estates, crucified; whom you hear calling, desolate,

41 Riley-Smith, *Crusade*, 18.
42 *ibid.*, 111.
43 *ibid.*, 143.
44 *ibid.*, 48.

and begging for aid.'[45] In short, the call for a crusade involved the authorization of violence against the perceived enemies of God.

Though this was never the intention of the ecclesiastical or the civil authorities of the day, there were repercussions for the Jews living in Christian Europe seeing that they too were recognized as enemies of God. It is hardly surprising that some crusaders highlighted the anomaly in proceeding against distant enemies of Christ when other enemies were being tolerated in the midst. Thus, in France crusaders were reported as saying, 'It was unjust for those who took up arms against rebels against Christ to allow enemies of Christ to live in their own land.'[46] At this point the main offences of the Jews were the traditional charges of the murder of Christ and persistent unbelief. A Jewish writer stated that crusaders would say to Jews, 'You are the children of those who killed the object of our veneration, hanging him on a tree; and he himself had said: "There will yet come a day when my children will come and avenge my blood." We are his children and it is therefore obligatory for us to avenge him since you are the ones who rebel and disbelieve in him.'[47]

That is not to say that in the First Crusade the attitude of the crusaders to the Jews was uniform. There was in this respect a marked contrast between the official contingents of crusaders, whose only slaughter of the Jews occurred during the seizure of Jerusalem itself in 1099, and the peasant or popular crusaders.[48] The latter, who sometimes ignored the Pope's instructions, even delayed their trip to the Holy Land in order to attack Jews in Europe. In particular, a group led by a Rhineland count, Emicho of Leiningen, murdered large numbers of Jews in Mainz, Cologne, Speyer, Worms and several other places in Germany in spite of opposition from local clergy and sometimes local princes. The motives of these popular crusaders may have been partly economic; Jewish money might help to finance the Crusade. But a more fundamental reason must have been religious since they faced the Jewish communities with a stark choice between baptism and death.[49] Many of the Jews preferred death, often by their own hands,

---

[45]   recorded from the history of Baldric of Bourgueil in Riley-Smith, *Crusade*, 48–9.
[46]   *ibid.*, 53–4. Even before this French knights who had gone to fight the Saracens in Spain had been responsible for sacking some of the rich Jewish communities in Spain — Poliakov, *History*, 2:114.
[47]   Bar Simson as quoted in Riley-Smith, *Crusade*, 56.
[48]   Langmuir, *TDAS*, 93–6.
[49]   Chazan, *European*, 72–5.

to such forcible conversion. (In later Jewish history these martyrs of the Rhineland were to be celebrated as models of steadfastness.) It has been suggested that some of the crusaders were influenced by millenarian expectations which led them to suppose the end of the world was at hand and the conversion of the Jews was imminent.[50] But the evidence does not permit a definite conclusion on this point.

The church authorities were in principle opposed to forced conversion, and even more to the indiscriminate killing of Jews. In accord with this, they tried after the lawlessness of the First Crusade to ensure that subsequent Crusades adhered more strictly to ecclesiastical guidelines. Thus, Jewish communities did receive a measure of protection.[51] In fact, after the horrors of 1096 the Jewish communities in Western Europe made a good recovery.[52] In the longer term, however, a sinister legacy was left. The Crusades had established a precedent of sanctified violence which could be turned against Jews, Muslims and heretics alike as recognized enemies of God. Jews would no longer be automatically preserved within Christendom as living witnesses to Christian truth. An alternative policy of obliterating everything Jewish had gained acceptance. Whenever there was a future call for a Crusade, the Jews felt the danger of further massacres.[53]

An increasingly negative image

The traditional theological objections to the Jews highlighted by the Crusades were augmented by further negative stereotypes. The perception of the Jews in wider society was affected by social changes as well as purely religious factors. Until about the year 1000, Jews were represented in a wide number of occupations. Their religion was their only distinctive feature. Landowning Jews, however, were adversely affected by changes in rural Europe during the eleventh century which saw the displacement of those who owned too little land or possessed insufficient patronage to protect their property against the encroachments of the greater lords. Being driven from the land, these Jews found it difficult to become established in traditional guilds, which were frequently in their origins religious associations.[54] These Jews, like the

---

[50]   Edwards, *TJICE*, 18–19.
[51]   Chazan, *European*, 169–79.
[52]   *ibid.*, 197–210.
[53]   Cohn-Sherbok, *Crucified*, 40–1.
[54]   Moore in Wood, *Christianity*, 37–40.

merchants I have mentioned earlier, were thus forced into less desirable occupations like money-lending where they were bound to incur even more odium.[55] The point is well made by the Jew in Peter Abelard's *Dialogue between a Christian, a Philosopher and a Jew* —

> Confined and constricted in this way as if the world had conspired against us alone it is a wonder that we are allowed to live. We are allowed to possess neither fields nor vineyards nor any landed estates because there is no one who can protect us from open or covert attack. Consequently the principal gain that is left for us is that we sustain our hateful lives here by lending money at interest to strangers. But this only makes us more hateful to those who think they are being oppressed by it.[56]

Evidently, Jewish money-lending was a result rather than a cause of the hounding of the Jews. So universal was this phenomenon that James Parkes could comment, 'It is only after the first Crusade that the word Jew comes to have any connection with money-lender, but within a century (i.e. about 1200) the two words became almost synonymous.'[57] That is not to say that money-lending was ever a Jewish monopoly; Christian money-lenders, however, never attracted the animosity reserved for the Jews even though the former often charged more interest.[58]

The Jews may have been stereotyped as excessively interested in and greedy for money, as they had earlier been stereotyped as obstinate, carnal and spiritually undiscerning. But, as Gavin Langmuir points out, there was at least a kernel of truth in these caricatures which was altogether absent in a host of new accusations with which the Jews were associated.[59] Horrendous deeds began to be attributed to Jews through the imagination of certain Christians who could never have seen such outrages being perpetrated. These included ritual murder, then ritual cannibalism, the profanation of the host and the deliberate poisoning of wells.[60] As a result, by the fourteenth century the Jews were viewed

---

[55] Cohen, *Friars*, 82–8.
[56] Abelard, *Dialogus inter Philosophum, Iudaeum et Christianum*, ed. R. Thompson (Stuttgart 1970) 51. It is interesting that this unusually sympathetic insight should have been shown by Abelard, who was often regarded as the enfant terrible among medieval Christian writers.
[57] Parkes, *Jew*, 83.
[58] Hay, *Europe*, 95–8.
[59] Langmuir, *TDAS*, 306–8.
[60] The well-poisoning accusations were particularly prominent as an explanation for the Black Death (1347–1350), but had already been made as early as the time of the First Crusade — see Mordechai Breuer in (ed.) Almog, *Antisemitism*, 140.

not as a strange religious sect, but as inhuman beings who carried out assaults on defenceless hosts and children and schemed to subvert Christendom. Needless to say, the Jews were left in a precarious position in a society where such charges abounded.

The accusations against the Jews did not emerge all at once. The first charge of ritual murder in the medieval period was made in England about 1150. It surfaced in circles where there was no knowledge of any such previous accusations.[61] The context was the murder of William, a twelve-year-old apprentice skinner, whose body was found outside Norwich on Easter Sunday 1144.[62] The only aspect of religious significance concerned the date. Moreover, the murder would probably soon have been forgotten had it not been for the work of Thomas of Monmouth, a monk who arrived in Norwich four years after William's death. Subsequently, Thomas saw it as his life's work to investigate and write up an account of who had murdered William, and how and why they had done so. This was to provide a basis for William to secure martyr status and in effect to become the patron saint for the city.

As a result of his investigations, which relied heavily on a Jew who had recently converted to Christianity, Thomas concluded that William's death was the result of an agreement by the Jews in Spain each year to sacrifice a Christian child as a way of insulting Christ and as a sacrifice to regain their political liberty. In 1144 the lot had fallen on Norwich, and in due course this information had been passed to all the synagogues in England.

Thomas also believed that the Jews had deliberately crucified William in a grotesque parody of Jesus' own death. Though this explanation for William's death did meet some sceptical reaction, not least among other monks at Norwich, it suited local interests to have their own martyr shrine and it fitted fears about the strange Jews (who were at that time new to Norwich) to have them associated with such a macabre crime.

Strangely, Thomas seems to have had no personal axe to grind against the Jews, but the spread of the tale he largely created does

---

[61]   Only two previous accusations of ritual murder of by Jews are found — one concerning Antiochus Epiphanes' entry into the Temple at Jerusalem, and the other an incident at Inmestar (Syria) about 415 AD. Langmuir, *TDAS*, 211–16 argues that neither of these incidents could have been known to folk in Norwich in the 1140s. Moreover, the paucity of earlier examples of such an accusation indicates how distinctive this charge was of the late medieval period.

[62]   for more detail see Langmuir, *TDAS*, 209–236.

presuppose a growing animosity towards them. Again, the implication that Jews regularly looked for Christian children to crucify meant that they automatically became objects of suspicion whenever a child mysteriously disappeared or was killed.[63] A number of such cases are recorded (especially from England and France) which ended in the brutal execution of Jews. The most famous or notorious such incident concerned 'Little Saint Hugh of Lincoln' in 1255.[64] Though no evidence linked the Jews with his death, which may well have occurred as a result of his accidentally falling down a well, Jews were accused of crucifying him. On the orders of King Henry III nineteen Jews were executed, while many more were placed under arrest, though later released. The story has attained prominence because it was highly unusual for a monarch to intervene in favour of a charge of ritual murder, and because Geoffrey Chaucer was to allude to it in the Prioress's Tale. It was to exercise a profound and sinister influence on subsequent English history. The lack of any real evidence against the Jews was overlooked.

The charge of ritual murder was unknown in Germany until 1235, when it appeared not in association with a crucifixion, but with an alleged act of ritual cannibalism.[65] On Christmas Day of 1235 a miller from the town of Fulda had gone with his wife to church, but returned to find his mill burnt down and his five sons dead in the ruins. The local Jews were immediately accused of killing the boys. They were supposed to have confessed that two of their number had killed the boys and drawn off their blood into waxed bags for use in their own religious rites. As a result on 28th December thirty-four Jews were cruelly executed. The story quickly became widely known and was accepted at face value, even though the Emperor Frederick II carefully looked into these events and dismissed the charge. For one thing he ascertained that such a use of blood was quite contrary to the Jewish religion. But his own public declaration of Jewish innocence was of little avail to prevent such charges being repeated and Jews being victimized.[66]

At the end of the same century a new charge was levelled against the Jews — that of stealing the consecrated host in order to assault it and

---

[63] *ibid.*, 240–2.

[64] *ibid.*, 237–262.

[65] Again, my account owes much to Langmuir, *TDAS*, 263–281.

[66] The papacy in 1242 and 1253 also disavowed such accusations, but with little practical consequence — Moore, *Formation*, 38.

thereby torture Christ himself.[67] Again this resulted in thousands of Jews being executed and new shrines being erected for the hosts which had supposedly been profaned. The charges, of course, were quite fanciful, and reflected more of the mentality of those who made them than they did of the conduct of the Jews. Indeed, Gavin Langmuir has suggested that it is no accident that the charges of ritual cannibalism and of assaulting the consecrated host emerged after the Fourth Lateran Council of 1215 had made transubstantiation into an ecclesiastical dogma.[68] The Council thereby tied the truth of the Christian faith closely to this controversial doctrine. Doubts within the Christian camp could be allayed if it were known that the Jews, as prime examples of public unbelievers in transubstantiation, were thought secretly to endorse its reality through their own perverse rituals. The ecclesiastical authorities, who would be alert to any doubts among their own flock, were unenthusiastic about quashing stories which seemed directly or otherwise to vindicate official church doctrine. Moreover, it was a vital part of the story that the host which was being tortured began to ooze blood — conclusive proof, it seemed, that it had indeed become the body of Christ.

Whenever charges such as these were made, Jewish lives were endangered. A society which held that the most serious offences against which it had to proceed were blasphemy and heresy would have little mercy to offer to Jews who were suspected of ritual murder, well-poisoning or the like. Generally suspicion would be enough to warrant condemnation, for Christian society had already been taught in visual art as well as both the written and the spoken word to view Jews as agents of Satan.[69] The connection between the Jews and Satan was even taken so far that the Jews were thought to possess physical characteristics which set them apart from other men and aligned them with the devil. Most commonly, they were thought to possess horns. They might be equipped with a tail and the beard of goat, and be recognized by a noxious smell — the *foetor judaicus*.[70] They were also thought to be subject to distinct medical complaints. Their men, for example, were believed to be affected by a menstrual flow of blood like their women. So deeply ingrained was this extraordinary notion that it even formed the subject of academic debates at

---

[67]   for more detail see Miri Rubin in Wood, *Christianity*, 169–185.
[68]   Langmuir, *TDAS*, 307–8.
[69]   Trachtenberg, *Devil*, 11–31.
[70]   *ibid.*, 44–52.

certain medieval universities.[71] By the late medieval period, therefore, the Jews were seen to be different from the rest of Christendom
not only in their religion but also in their physical characteristics.
Thus, the ground was prepared for the Nazi racial anti-Semites who
wanted to deny the special religious character of the Jew but corre-
spondingly to exaggerate almost every other type of difference from
the rest of humankind.[72] Adolf Hitler was reflecting the late medieval
concept of the Jew when he combined the language of disease (a
parasite, or a malignant germ or a bloodsucking leech) with that of
the demonic ('personification of the devil' and 'symbol of all evil') in
his description of the Jews.[73]

Harassment and mission among the Jews

In a climate where the Jews were not only recognized as enemies of
Christ and so of the church, but were also pictured as demonic or
subhuman, not surprisingly the Papal Inquisition found reasons to
interfere with the Jews. Like the legitimized violence of the Crusades,
the systematic repression of the Inquisition did not represent an
official response to the issue of unbelieving Jews within Christendom.
This Inquisition had been set up in the early thirteenth century
(significantly toward the outset of 'Christendom') to counter heretical movements like the Cathars and Waldensians within the Christian
fold.[74] Technically, it had no jurisdiction over those who had never
in any sense been Christians. But this position was modified with the
discovery of Talmudic Judaism, since the latter could be regarded as
a heresy and recognized as a danger to the Christian church. Moreover, it was suspected that Christian heretical groups were inspired
by Jews or at least had Jewish links.[75]

Other circumstances could bring Jews to the attention of the Inquisition. If Judaism *per se* was not the concern of the Inquisition, Jewish

---

[71]   Peter Biller in Wood, *Christianity*, 187–207.

[72]   Poliakov, *History*, 1:142 points out that in the 20th century some German scholars
projected a scientific investigation of the *foetor judaicus*.

[73]   Adolf Hitler, *Mein Kampf*, 294.

[74]   Edwards, *TJICE*, 21.

[75]   Cohen, *Friars, op. cit.* 48. It is worth noting, however, that the identification of
Jews as a class of heretics was not universal. In the subtle analysis of Thomas Aquinas,
Jews form a category intermediate between heretics and pagans — *Summa Theologica*,
32:10:5–6.

converts who lapsed, even if they had been forcibly baptized as children, did engage its efforts. In such circumstances the malign influence of other Jews in the vicinity was suspected, and they too could come within the scope of the Inquisition. As one eminent French Inquisitor, Bernard Gui, expressed it in a manual for fellow-inquisitors —

> The perfidious Jews try, when and where they can, secretly to pervert Christians and drag them to the Jewish perfidy, especially those who were previously Jews and converted and accepted baptism and the Christian faith, especially those who are of special concern or related to them. It has therefore been decreed that just as one should proceed against Christians who go over or return to the Jewish rite . . . as against heretics, so should one proceed against those who aid them as against those who aid heretics.[76]

This would entail at the very least public penance for the guilty party; and where their repentance was deemed inadequate, they could be handed over to the secular authority to be burnt.

According to canon law, prompting Christians to lapse or to fall for the first time into Judaism was the most justifiable reason for inquisitorial interference with the Jews. But this was not the only warrant Inquisitors found for trying unbaptized Jews. Relying on the idea of a shared Judaeo-Christian inheritance in the Scriptures of the Old Testament, some Inquisitors believed they were entitled to punish those Jews who rejected certain common beliefs like the creation, the unity of God and the Ten Commandments.[77] The same might apply if Jews were guilty of some sin (e.g. homosexuality) which was generally regarded as unnatural or of an offence against their own law (usury) which affected Christians.[78] Indeed, if the responsibility of the Inquisition was defined in the most general terms as 'the defence of the Christian faith', the Jews could be arraigned before it on fairly tenuous grounds. Such at least was the rationale allowing the Inquisition to proceed against Jews. But in practice direct attacks from the Inquisition ought not to be exaggerated. They seem to have been targeted against individuals rather than communities. Even Bernard Gui, whose words about the snares set by the Jews are quoted above, prosecuted only

---

[76] Bernard Gui, *Manuel de l'inquisiteur* (ed. G. Mollat, Paris 1964) 2:6–7. The translation is taken from Cohen, *Friars*, 91. A similar extract from the work of another Inquisitor, Nicolau Eymerich, makes the point about the Jew baptized in infancy — Edwards, *TJIWE*, 32–3.

[77] Nicolau Eyernerich, *Directorium*, 2:46:3–4. The relevant Latin is quoted by Cohen, *Friars*, 98.

[78] cf. the detailed analysis given by the Spanish Inquisitorial manual translated by Edwards, *TJIWE*, 36–9.

two cases of judaizing in his entire career.[79] The commonest form of action against the Jewish communities in western Europe was mass expulsion, not demoralization through the Inquisition. Besides, the Inquisition posed more of a threat to a converted Jew than to one who had remained resolute in the faith in which he had been born. The same pattern was to be repeated in the distinct Spanish Inquisition in the late fifteenth century.

In its early days the ranks of the Inquisitors were filled by the Dominican and Franciscan friars who were themselves creations of the early thirteenth century church with its obsession for purity and order within society. If their original mandate had been to reform the church from within, it was not long before they had added a Jewish dimension to their work. The main catalyst herein was the concern that Jewish literature, particularly the Talmud, was a threat to the integrity of Christendom. Bernard Gui was worried about potential damage to Christians in France from the Talmud even after the Jews had been expelled.[80]

But the friars were not content to remain on the defensive; they believed in taking the battle for Christian truth into enemy territory. After all, Dominic and Francis had both preached among heretics and infidels, and it was only proper that their disciples should imitate their example. Thus, certain friars entered on a novel strategy of promoting public debates with the Jews. More commonly they sought opportunities to preach to the Jews either by securing a legal obligation that Jews should listen to their sermons or even by going into synagogues — actions that might prove controversial and injurious to public peace.[81] Sometimes the friars had to be restrained, since their enthusiasm was not always tempered by wisdom, as far as the ecclesiastical authorities were concerned. But the importance of their work among the Jews obtained official recognition in 1278 when Pope Nicholas III made preaching and missionary work among the Jews part of the apostolate of both the Dominican and Franciscan orders.[82] This was fully in accord with the papal stance that Jewish conversion remained on the church's agenda.

At that time, however, missionary work among unbelievers of one sort or another was more of an aggressive enterprise than Christians

---

[79] Such is admitted by Cohen, *Friars*, 91 despite his desire to establish that the friars embarked on a novel aggressive strategy toward the Jews

[80] *ibid.*, 92–3.

[81] *ibid.*, 82–5.

[82] Simonsohn (note 15) 249–252 (docs 243–5).

today could easily contemplate. With a triumphalist understanding of Christianity it was inevitable that the late medieval church had problems with persistent unbelief. The best it could do was to marginalize it. This is well illustrated by the career of Ramon Lull, the Franciscan tertiary, who is regarded with justification as an outstanding missionary figure from the medieval period.[83] Indeed, he has been described as the first to develop a theory of missions.[84]

He is best known as a missionary to the Muslims. He took the unusual step of learning Arabic and of visiting the Muslim strongholds of North Africa. Here he suffered imprisonment and flogging, and on his final visit was so roughly treated that he died of his injuries. But his missionary endeavour also embraced the Jews. He would early have encountered Jews in his native island of Majorca as well as in the kingdom of Aragon, which had captured Majorca from the Muslims shortly before Lull's birth sometime in the period 1231 to 1235. The Spanish kingdoms at this period were known to shelter three religions — Jewish and Muslim as well as Christian.

Lull became devoted to the evangelism of infidels, who to him included the Muslims and the Jews alike. All of his prolific literary output, which involved some 280 books and treatises, touched on the conversion of the infidel.[85] Lull's main weapon was reasoned argument, whether in a literary form or preferably in face-to-face debate.[86] Since Lull wrote much in which he sang the praises of reasoned argument in preference to the use of coercion, it has sometimes been concluded that Lull set himself against the tenor of his age by opposing force altogether. But such would be a misleading conclusion. For coercion was involved in getting the Jews to listen to Lull. In 1299 he obtained from King James II of Aragon permission to enter Jewish synagogues on sabbaths and other festivals and compel the Jews to hear him preach. Moreover, it is clear that Lull was not impressed by the Jews' ability to engage in rational argument. He therefore proposed that the Pope set up a special college for Jews to learn Latin, logic and philosophy. This was not intended as an altruistic contribution to a liberal education for the Jews,

---

[83] Since Lull had been married before his conversion, he could go no higher among the Franciscans than a tertiary.

[84] Stephen Neill, *A History of Christian Missions*, (Penguin, Harmondsworth 1964) 134–5.

[85] Cohen, *Friars*, 200. Lull's works are listed by Anthony Bonner in *Selected Works of Ramon Lull* (Princeton University Press, 1985) 1257–1304.

[86] *ibid.*, 201–5.

but as a means whereby they could debate with Christian preachers on familiar Christian ground.[87] Lull at first was relatively confident that such exposure to reasoned arguments, as he saw them, would bring conversions among those Jews who attended his training college. Unsurprisingly, this ingenious scheme failed to get off the ground.[88] Lull emerges not as an advocate of personal liberty in religion, but as a zealous missionary who will allow no cultural or other barrier to stand in the way of his presenting the gospel to the infidel. Where it was impossible or undesirable for Christians to take on the culture of the infidel, then the culture of the infidel had to be altered, by force if necessary.[89]

Lull, of course, had to reckon with Jewish rejection of his message. He did not treat this with indifference, but typically for his age saw Jewish unbelievers as an insidious threat to Christendom which merited sharp and decisive action —

> they are more opposed to the law of the Christians than others, since they assuredly say that Christ is a rather evil man and that he never was nor will be. And daily they blaspheme him in the synagogues, and they say many terrible things, both concerning the blessed Mary and concerning the Apostles — for which reason wisdom, authority and charity affirm: if they do not convert, let them be ejected from Christendom.[90]

Thus Lull stood firmly in the tradition of Nicholas Donin and of the friars. The Jews were guilty of serious blasphemy. In Lull's mind this demanded from the sincere Christian energetic missionary endeavour. The Jews could not be left freely to practise their religion. They had to be subjected to Christian sermons. They even had to undergo courses in Christian academic disciplines so that they could understand Christian scholarship. Their religion and their culture could not remain unaffected. And if all this failed to impress them of the truth of Christianity, they were to be expelled from Christendom.

The case of Lull demonstrates that a harsher line toward the Jews was

---

[87]   Cohen, *Friars, op. cit.* 204–5 and 223–5 gives fuller detail on Lull's educational proposals and other devices for coercing the Jews to listen to Christian preaching and arguments.

[88]   Neill (note 84) 136 points out that Lull lacked 'executive effectiveness' as far as his numerous schemes were concerned.

[89]   Bonner (note 85) 54–5 points out that Lull shrewdly estimated the audience he was addressing, and thus could appear more or less tolerant as the occasion required.

[90]   R. Lull, *'Le Liber de acquisitione Terrae Santae'* 2, 3 p 274 from *Criterion* 3 (1927), as quoted by Cohen, *Friars*, 204

not confined either to individual converts from Judaism who may have had an axe to grind against their former co- religionists or to the ranks of the Inquisitors, whose very business it was to unearth threats to Christian orthodoxy. It might go hand in hand with a zealous missionary concern which was largely motivated by the good of the church (or of Christendom, which at this period was thought to be the same cause).

Lull may have been unusual in the depth of his missionary concern, but he was a man of his time in his acceptance of the notion of Christendom. This very notion was a threat to the Jewish presence in society. While Lull may have been content to suffer for the gospel at an individual level, he did not want the Christian society of which he was a member to suffer. His efforts to convert both Muslims and Jews may have been motivated as much by the security of Christendom as by a concern for the souls of lost individuals. A precise analysis of Lull's motives is in the nature of things impossible; probably Lull himself would not have discerned any difference between them. Since the Jews with whom Lull was concerned lay within Christendom, they became an enemy within if they refused to convert. Love, then, for Christendom, which was too often confused with love for Christ, demanded that the Jews had to go elsewhere.

In effect, the Christian outlook toward the Jews in the later Middle Ages oscillated between two conflicting obligations.[91] According to one of these, the Jews were to be protected as they were a standing witness to the truth of Christianity and were to be converted to their Messiah before the end of the age. This was the legacy of the old Augustinian viewpoint. Sometimes this might engender missionary endeavour toward the Jews especially if the end of the age was thought to be drawing close.[92] Where such endeavours were to have any lasting result, they had to be accompanied by some degree of compulsion. Even Lull recognized this. But at the same time there was a need to protect the Christian church from the Jews, understandably enough if the Jews began to be identified as a sort of incarnation of the devil. This also promoted the use of force, notably in the expulsion of the Jews from various territories.

Ironically, a greater interest in and acquaintance with the Jews in this period among Christians did not lead to more understanding and tolerance but the very opposite. It did not matter whether that interest

---

[91]   Oberman, *Roots*, 34.

[92]   Pope Paul IV (1555–1559) adopted a repressive policy toward the Jews in order to ensure conversions, largely because he believed the end of the world to be at hand — Edwards, *TJICE*, 66–74.

was prompted by the discovery of the Talmud or by some prophetic insight that the end of the world was at hand. Either way Christians discovered that the Jews thought and acted in a radically different way from themselves — a phenomenon which disturbed Christians precisely because they shared the same religious roots. Unless the Jews would convert (and only a few individuals would do that voluntarily), their very different religious life was felt to threaten Christian orthodoxy, and so the Jews were frequently faced with two violent choices — conversion or expulsion.

The case of Spain — from a golden age to expulsion for the Jews

When the Jews were expelled from Spain under a decree of King Ferdinand and Queen Isabella in 1492, Spanish Jews were shocked. Indeed, this event is still considered by many Jews as the most devastating in their history prior to the Holocaust because it signalled such a sharp change in their fortunes.[93] In the thirteenth century the Jews had flourished in Spain at a time when the lot of their co-religionists elsewhere in Europe was sharply declining. In part this was due to the Muslim presence in the Iberian peninsula which ensured that the Jews were not the only significant religious minority as they were elsewhere in Europe. Though the laws of the state and the official policy of the church in Spain toward the Jews were restrictive and unexceptional, local factors allowed the Jews more scope for economic and social interaction in Spanish society.[94] Yet, the potential was always there for a harsher line to be adopted toward the Jews.[95] For its part, the church had not forgotten the severe restrictions it had managed to arrange with the Visigothic rulers against the Jews in the seventh century.[96]

The Jewish situation began to deteriorate with the Black Death in the middle of the fourteenth century. Of particular significance were first an outbreak of pogroms in 1391 in the south of Spain which the

---

[93] Some modern historians feel that earlier Jewish and Spanish writers have exaggerated the significance of the decree of expulsion in itself — see Henry Kamen in Kedourie, *Spain*, 74–91. Interestingly, another contributor to this collection of essays, Haim Beinart, disagrees on a central question — the number of Jews who had to flee from Spain at this time — page 114.

[94] Edwards, *TJICE*, 26–27. This coincided with a time when Spanish Christians were optimistic about the conversion of Jews to Christianity — see Angus Mackay in Kedourie, *Spain*, 42–4

[95] Mackay, Kedourie, *Spain*, 34–5.

[96] The gist of these are conveniently summarized in Falk, *Jew*, 33–4.

authorities did little to check, and then the preaching of a Dominican friar, Vincent Ferrer, in the period 1411–1416 which induced many Jews to convert to Christianity.[97] As a result in the fifteenth century Spain had a considerable number of 'new Christians' (or conversos) whose social and economic significance greatly outweighed that of the remaining Jews. At the same time such earlier hostility as had been directed against Spanish Jews was largely redirected against the conversos. It was felt that many of these had become Christian in name only, since they retained their links with Jewish neighbours, Jewish practices and even in some cases with a synagogue.[98] From the middle of the fifteenth century a lively debate emerged on the place of these conversos[99]. While supporters of the conversos could appeal to the traditional doctrine of baptism and could point to conversos like Paul of Burgos and his son Alonso de Cartagena who had given outstanding service to the church, they were fighting a losing battle against an opposition which resorted to increasingly scurrilous and dishonest tactics.[100] For example, these opponents of the 'new Christians' circulated a fictitious correspondence between a certain Chamoro, purportedly the head of the Jewish community in Toledo, and Yussuf, his counterpart in Constantinople. Chamoro asked Yussuf for his advice in evil days, and received the reply that the Jews should become lawyers in order to penetrate Christian society and destroy it from within.[101]

As an example of the more scurrilous material, a noted poet from a converso family from Toledo, Rodrigo de Cota, received a satirical poem on the occasion of his wedding in which it was stated that his wife would give birth to a son as big as Goliath the Philistine who would inherit his parents' trade and become a tax-collector.

Amid suspicion, innuendo and worse it was natural that many conversos should undergo a severe identity crisis and find themselves more at home with their former Jewish brethren than with the 'old Christians'. And this could only aggravate the problem of disunity within the church in Spain. Thus, when the thrones of Castile and

---

[97] Edwards, *TJICE*, 27–30.

[98] for a summary of the activities of conversos see John Edwards in Wood, *Christianity*, 225–6.

[99] for more detail see Haim Beinart in Kedourie, *Spain*, 94–6 and 105.

[100] cf. Poliakov's comment at *History*, 2:181–2 — 'What power did theologians have against passions?'

[101] Significanlty, this occurred in the wake of the fall of Constantinople to the Turks. It could, therefore, be construed as evidence of an international Jewish plot.

Aragon were united in 1474 with the marriage of Ferdinand and Isabella, they as zealous Catholics turned their attention to this problem. They did not at first resort to a full-scale expulsion, but tried to resolve the problem and allow the conversos full integration into Christian society by segregating the Jews into ghettos. They also ordered the removal of the Jews from selected regions, beginning with Seville, where they seemed too influential. But their most important device was the establishment (with permission from Pope Sixtius IV) of a new Spanish Inquisition, whose task it would be to hunt down offending parties within the church.[102] In effect, this Inquisition devoted itself in its early years almost entirely to the prosecution of conversos, a policy it pursued with a ruthlessness that has become legendary.[103] The Inquisition, however, was relatively popular in Spain itself because 'it expressed the prejudices of most Spaniards about religion and race, and their resentment of successful conversos.'[104]

The combination of Jewish segregation and the prosecution of judaizing conversos did not solve the problem as far as either the monarchs or the Inquisition were concerned. Hence the decree of expulsion was published as a last resort. A continuing Jewish presence had proved too dangerous to be allowed. Ferdinand and Isabella explained —

> We are informed by the Inquisitors and by many religious people, ecclesiastical and secular, a great danger to Christians has clearly emerged, this having followed, and still continuing, from the activity, conversation and communication which these Christians have maintained with Jews. These Jews demonstrate that they always work, by whatever ways and means they can, to subvert and remove faithful Christians from our holy Catholic faith, to separate them from it, and attract and pervert them to their wicked belief and opinion, instructing them in the ceremonies and observances of their Law.[105]

The Catholic Monarchs, as Ferdinand and Isabella were pleased to be known, followed the example of the sovereigns of England, of France and of various Germanic states in exiling the Jews.[106] They were undoubtedly motivated in this by a desire for the well-being of the church with its long-standing anti-Judaism.

---

[102]   Henry Kamen in Kedourie, *Spain*, 76–7.
[103]   for the tactics of the Inquisition see Beinart in Kedourie, *Spain*, 106–7.
[104]   John Lynch in Kedourie, *Spain*, 141.
[105]   quoted from Edwards' translation in *TJIWE*, 49–50.
[106]   Edwards, *TJIWE*, 4 provides a summary of the various Jewish expulsions.

They did not nourish anti-Semitism in the sense of animosity against those of Jewish blood because it seems that their decree of expulsion was intended to induce the Jews to convert rather than to get rid of them.[107] Besides, they had no compunction about granting important positions to conversos. In effect, they had pursued a middle course between those Spaniards who remained hostile to the conversos and those for whom the conversos were to be fully welcomed into Christian society. Their main aim, as Kamen puts it, was to 'deprive the converso judaisers of an active religious choice'; there would now be no temptation for them to relapse into Judaism.[108]

The expulsion of the Jews did not end the Jewish question as far as Spain was concerned. This merely took on a new twist. The Inquisition, which had developed a momentum of its own, did not cease its efforts to find secret judaizers, and in a sense now had a larger field of jurisdiction including the former Jews who had converted at the time of Ferdinand and Isabella's decree of expulsion. These new conversos were to discover that the change in their religion which allowed them to remain in Spain did not bring lasting security. Not only were they liable to accusations of secret judaizing, but even the most enthusiastic Christians among them were subject in Spanish society to severe restrictions on the ground that their blood was contaminated. In fact, after 1492 new Christians of Jewish origin were regarded as a caste, different in its essence from the old and 'pure' Christian population.[109] They were, for example, increasingly denied entrance to universities and religious orders and to the possibility of holding public office. Rules concerning 'purity of blood' (*limpieza de sangre*) had been applied in specific situations before 1492, but the decisive impetus to such legislation on a national level was given by the cathedral chapter of Toledo, the ecclesiastical capital, in 1547.[110] When the last regulations in this sphere were removed as late as 1865, they had exercised a significant impact on Spanish history over three centuries.[111]

The new Christians of Jewish stock, it was believed, were tainted by a curse which had befallen them as a result of 'that despicable murder' (of Jesus), because then 'they lost their claim to their noble lineage, and

---

[107] Kamen in Kedourie, *Spain*, 80–2. Kamen goes on to conclude that as such the policy was largely a failure.
[108] *ibid.*, 90–1.
[109] Joseph Kaplan in Almog, *Antisemitism*, 153–6.
[110] Lynch in Kedourie, *144–5*.
[111] *ibid.*, 145–56.

the blood of the murderers of Jesus was so polluted that their children, their nieces and nephews, and all their descendants, all of them are as if born with polluted blood, and therefore they are denied all honours, offices, and titles . . . the abomination of their ancestors will cling to them for ever.'[112] This may largely explain why those of Jewish descent in general fared worse than those in Spain who were Muslims or at least of Muslim extraction, even though Muslims had been more numerous than Jews and might constitute a political threat because of their international connections.[113] Muslims never posed the same religious threat.[114] The Spanish establishment, for its part, justified its 'purity of blood' regulations on religious grounds, and associated these with ideas of a hereditary, immutable trait reminiscent of later Nazi propaganda.[115] No doubt the Nazi racial approach to the Jewish question differed from its Spanish predecessor in that it was designed to diminish the religious image of the Jewish people. But we should note the similarity in the belief that definite moral as well as physical characteristics were passed on by 'Jewish blood'.

It is doubtful whether all Spaniards who took pride in their 'purity of blood' regulations were exclusively motivated by religious zeal. Apparently, a variety of motives were at work — 'a mixture of religious fanaticism, race prejudice, social ambition, exclusivism and political monopoly' as John Lynch describes it.[116] Certainly, these racist statutes were founded on the religious belief of the medieval church that Judaism was one of the most sinister and threatening heresies it had had to face. Without such a belief there could have been no expulsion of Jews from Spain and no converso problem. But equally they went far beyond religion in their ramifications.

Such a course of events, however, was far from inevitable. At one stage it did look as if conversos might be happily integrated into the mainstream of Spanish Christian society.[117] Opponents of the 'new

---

[112] J. Arce de Otalora *Summa nobilitatis Hispanicae, etc.* (Salamanca 1559) 187f. The translation is that of Kaplan in Almog, *Antisemitism*.

[113] for a brief survey of Spanish attitudes and policy toward the Moriscos (Spaniards who remained faithful to the law of Muhammad) see Poliakov, *History*, 2:328–357.

[114] The inquisitorial manual translated by Edwards in *TJIWE*, 38 declares that Jews who became Muslims should not be punished because they had exchanged the worst of sects for a bad one!

[115] Poliakov, *History*, 2:226 alludes to Escobar del Corro, who argued in these terms.

[116] Lynch in Kedourie, *Spain*, 142.

[117] Edwards, *TJICE*, 30.

Christians' resorted to dishonest propaganda to win their point. Even prior to the Expulsion in 1492 the Inquisition thought it worthwhile to concoct a lurid case involving Jews and conversos so that its strategy of expulsion might go ahead unhindered.

This case concerning the 'Holy Child of La Guardia' is worth study in its own right as it must surely rank as one of the most notorious and influential charges of ritual murder ever lodged against the Jews.

Proceedings began in a relatively insignificant way with the arrest in 1490 of a pilgrim called Benito Garcia on his return from the shrine of St James at Campostela.[118] This man, who was an itinerant labourer and wool-washer, happened to be a converso. Among his baggage was found a piece of consecrated host, which Garcia confessed, probably under torture, to have taken for purposes of sorcery. Later on, more startling revelations emerged. Some three years previously Garcia, along with other conversos and Jews, had conspired to abduct a child from Toledo and take him to a cave near La Guardia, Garcia's home town. There the child had been abused and crucified in deliberate mockery of Christ. Then the child's heart had been extracted and mixed with a host (i.e. unleavened bread) as part of a magic ritual designed to murder all Christians in Spain by infecting them with rabies. This was all part of a wider plot to promote Judaism at the expense of Christianity. The protracted legal proceedings, which went on for well over a year, ended in most of the accused, Jews and conversos alike, being burnt alive at an *auto-da-fé* in Avila.

This sinister story went far beyond the usual range of charges against conversos which consisted in suggestions that they still adhered secretly or otherwise to prescriptions of the Mosaic Law or other Jewish customs. The Inquisition certainly made sure that details of the La Guardia case were circulated to all their regional tribunals, no doubt to influence attitudes both among the general population and among high political circles. It was no coincidence that the edict for the expulsion of the Jews followed some four months later.[119]

There is, however, good reason to think that the more lurid details of the case were all fabricated by the Inquisition.[120] Even by the procedures of the day the Inquisitors acted quite irregularly.[121] First,

---

[118] For an accessible detailed account see Baer, *History*, 2: 398–423.
[119] Edwards, *TJICE*, 34.
[120] Perhaps the only true charge that might have been brought against Garcia, if it could be called a crime at all, was a disillusionment with the Christianity he had espoused and a hankering after some Jewish practices.
[121] Edwards, *TJICE*, 33.

they themselves tried those Jews who were accused of complicity in the plot. This was outside their province. They could examine conversos, but not Jews who had never made any profession of conversion to Christianity. Such confessions as were given were mainly extracted under torture. Then, all the defendants were found guilty although the testimony of the witnesses did not tally even after they had been brought face to face with one another, a practice which was strictly improper. Moreover, the Inquisitors showed little interest in the identity of the child who had been abducted. No attempt was made to find the parents who had lost the child or to locate the place where the child had been buried. (Later legends quickly supplied such details.) In all probability no such child existed. Then, as now, there was great emotive power in the story of a child who had been ritually abused. The tale was carefully designed to give substance to an underlying suspicion in many minds — that most conversos remained at heart Jews and retained close relations with the Jews, who would leave no stone unturned to encourage them to commit violence against the Christians.[122]

If indeed this legal process and conviction was a fabrication by the Inquisition, it almost immediately had the desired impact. The expulsion edict issued on 31st March 1492 by the rulers, Ferdinand and Isabella, clearly acknowledged the advice of the Inquisition.[123] As we have seen, this measure took Spanish Jews by surprise. Modern historians may detect subtle moves against the Jews in the 1480's with an increasing number of horror stories about Spanish Jews, including the stoning of crosses and ritual murder.[124] But the significance of these moves probably remained hidden from the Jews at the time because Ferdinand and Isabella showed no sign of departing from the traditional policy of rulers in Spain of protecting the Jews in a sort of limited freedom.[125] Besides, on the surface at least the Spanish Inquisition threatened only conversos, and was even willing in certain places to accept evidence from Jews against their former co-religionists who had professed to go over to Christianity.[126] The Jews failed to reckon with the skilful and determined strategy of the Inquisition. They also failed

---

[122]   Beatrice Leroy, *L'Expulsion des Juifs d'Espagne* (Berg International, Paris 1990), 107.

[123]   Baer, *History*, 2:433–4; Edwards, *TJICE*, 33.

[124]   Edwards, *TJICE*, 33.

[125]   *ibid.*, 31–2.

[126]   Leroy, (note 122) 91.

to reckon with the insidious power of lies disseminated at a crucial juncture in history. Thus they found themselves represented before the general public through the case of the Holy Child of La Guardia as inveterate and almost demonic enemies of Christianity.

Conclusion

The medieval stereotype of the Jew may, as R.I. Moore has argued, have been largely the creation of the clerks in their bid first to acquire and then to hold on to power in the emerging European bureaucratic regimes. It is, however, remarkable how tenaciously the stereotype persisted long after the historical circumstances which engendered it had receded. Indeed, elements of the stereotype have persisted to the present day. It seems as if Christendom required a belief in a rival religion which it had clearly vanquished and at the same time a recognition of a devil (or devils) incarnate, whose wiles threatened its order and security. The Jews provided the best candidates for both these roles. The church, after all, had a long tradition of anti-Judaism, manifested especially in the conviction that the Jews as a whole and not simply the Jews of Jesus' own day were Christ-killers. Medieval stories about the Jews could build on this foundation.[127] But the fascination for the Jews in the medieval period also resulted from the strength of the Jewish communities in northern Europe up to about 1200.

This is reflected in several medieval cathedrals, which are adorned with parallel statues of the Church and Synagogue in the form of young maidens. While the Church, resplendent with truth and light, exhibits her triumph in the wearing of a crown, the Synagogue is represented as blinded and forlorn, and often carries a broken staff and tablets of the Law.[128] Interestingly, the Synagogue is not portrayed as a wizened hag who is clearly near to death, but as a lady in the bloom of youth with charms of her own. Implicitly, the attraction and so the threat of Judaism are recognized.

The medieval stereotype may have been the work essentially of an élite. But it was successfully implanted in the ordinary people. No doubt they perceived ways in which to exploit the social inferiority of the Jews, to which church teaching pointed. The Jews fulfilled a useful

---

[127] Langmuir, *TDAS*, 57–62.

[128] Wistrich, *Anti-Semitism*, plate 2b shows the two maidens from Strasbourg Cathedral.

function for those who wished to have at least some inferiors on the social ladder. They were also convenient scapegoats if there was an unexplained child murder in the locality or a disaster of some magnitude, like the Black Death. The very presence of such evils would have posed a threat to the validity of Christendom; now they could be explained by the activities of marginalized or hostile groups within society.

But perhaps the most significant point is obvious. If clergymen maintained that it was a Christian duty to fear and to hate the Jews (as with the devil), there would be those who would respond with relish to such sanctification of our baser instincts. It is plain that there were those who hated the Jews because they had been taught that God hated them. As one religious work put it —

> More bestial than naked beasts
> Are all Jews, without a doubt . . .
> Many hate them, as do I
> And God hates them, as well I wist,
> And everyone must hate them indeed.[129]

No less a person than the Renaissance humanist, Erasmus, stood four-square in this medieval tradition. 'If it is Christian to hate the Jews,' he once wrote to an Inquisitor, 'here we are all Christian in profusion.'[130]

It is, however, worth stressing that though general Christian attitudes and policies toward the Jews worsened in the later Middle Ages, the official line of the church did not alter. The Augustinian framework enshrined in the papal documents remained unchanged. And this did play a vital role in ensuring that the church did not try systematically to massacre the Jews.[131] But equally such a rationale had its limitations; it could do little to stop the demonization of the Jews at a popular level. These limitations, I suggest, involved the character of the Jew, who was now consigned to a special and sinister category of unbeliever. They also embraced the readiness to tie the proof of Christianity to its political supremacy in society.

---

[129] Cohn-Sherbok, *Crucified*, 42.
[130] Oberman, *Roots*, 75 — '*Si Christianum est odisse Iudaeos, hic abunde Christiani sumus.*'
[131] Haynes, *Jews*, 14–15 and 21–2.

Seven

Luther and the Jews

At the Reformation the traditions of the medieval church were brought under careful scrutiny. Many of the Protestant Reformers happily adapted the humanist slogan of *ad fontes* (return to the original sources) and showed a renewed interest both in the text of Scripture (including the Hebrew Old Testament) and in the patristic writers.[1] Here it was felt lay the church's true wisdom. By contrast, the church in the late medieval period had desperately lost its way. Since the same medieval church, especially from the thirteenth century, had presided over the burgeoning of 'classic anti-Semitism', Protestants might have been expected to diagnose this as an unworthy development in church history and at least to sketch out a healthier attitude toward the Jews.[2]

Several Jews for their part welcomed the initial stages of the Reformation with enthusiasm, and had every reason to sympathize with Luther's attack on the tyranny of the Roman Church. Some even suggested that possibly these events presaged the coming of the Messiah. They were further heartened by the publication in 1523 of a distinctly positive tract by Luther, *That Jesus Christ was Born a Jew*.[3] Were they at last to escape the demonization which had hounded them in the late medieval period and to enjoy an element of political security?

Such a change, however, was slow in coming. Indeed, any improvement in the lot of the Jews was more an indirect than a direct result of the Reformation. The Jews did benefit from a divided Christendom

---

[1] Timothy George, *Theology of the Reformers* (Nashville, Tennessee 1988) 47 and 324.

[2] The phrase 'classic anti-Semitism' derives from Poliakov, *History*, 1:123. Langmuir uses the comparable expression 'socially significant Antisemitism' in his *HRAS*, 305.

[3] Stern, *Josel*, 158. For detailed Jewish responses to the Reformation see Ben-Sasson, 'Reformation.'

which provided plenty of new scapegoats to blame whenever things went wrong. They benefited even more from the emergence of policies of toleration after people were exhausted by numerous and lengthy religious wars. But in the first generation of the Reformation anti-Semitism was further consolidated. As Heiko Oberman has put it, 'this same age which so consciously scrutinized the medieval tradition simultaneously passed on, with new strength, whatever withstood the test of inspection.'[4]

The hardened attitude toward the Jews is best exemplified in the two men whose public debate at Leipzig in 1519 transformed the Luther affair from a localized German dispute to a controversy affecting the whole of western Christendom — Martin Luther and Johannes Eck. Until his death in 1543 Eck was to prove the most tenacious and able of Luther's Catholic opponents.[5] Curiously, in the 1540s both men were to launch vicious attacks against the Jews. The reasons for their attacks may have been widely different, but it is significant that both were connected with the Reformation debates. The Catholic side accused the Jews of secret plots to incite the Reformation, while for Luther the Jews exemplified both the same reliance on religious works and the same preference for human traditions over the Scriptures as he had encountered in his Catholic opponents.

The diatribes of the later Luther against the Jews have become notorious. In this respect he showed himself a child both of the medieval period and of his own day. Eck's outbursts are less well known. He alone among Christian writers of the period exceeded Luther in venom.[6] Perhaps both men were temperamentally controversialists, but I doubt if this alone can explain their embittered attacks. May we not see in this strange meeting of opposites a recurrence of a familiar phenomenon? In the early medieval period the calling of a Crusade (or even the talk of such a thing) had threatened reprisals against the Jews living within Christendom, even though the Crusades were officially directed not against Jews but against the Muslim occupants of the holy sites. Any public religious controversy or crusade can only be ignited if there is some tinderbox of intense religious feeling. Such feeling is often further fuelled by the controversy itself. The passions roused and

---

[4] Oberman, *Roots*, xi.
[5] Preserved Smith, *The Life and Letters of Martin Luther* (Hodder and Stoughton, London 1993 edition) 80.
[6] *Luther's Works* (Concordia Publishing House and Fortress Press edition 1971) 47:129.

the consequent enormities suggest to many a demonic or at least an evil influence at work. Here the Jews living in the midst of Christendom have often taken the blame. Thus the Jews have suffered as a result of disputes which originally have little to do with them. Neither Luther nor Eck recognized such trends at work. Their failure to see this shows that both men were seriously handicapped by their medieval mindset.

Luther's writings on the Jews

Within the widespread movement of the Reformation Martin Luther, by any standard emerges as a towering colossus, whose personal influence was unrivalled, at least during his own lifetime. This was recognized by his colleague, Philip Melanchthon, who at the time when he learnt of Luther's death echoed the anguished cry of Elisha as he saw the prophet Elijah leaving this world. 'The charioteer of Israel has fallen.'[7] Melanchthon, however, was not insensitive to some of Luther's weaknesses and described him a little later in a funeral speech as a 'strict healer' of the church. He had in mind Luther's outbursts, including the exaggerations characteristic of his polemic. Indeed, Luther was a strongly emotional man; 'his temperament was like a volcano, liable to erupt in any situation, especially when he felt exuberant.'[8]

We might wonder whether this goes much of the way toward explaining Luther's outlook on the Jews. Was he simply disappointed in his early hopes for the conversion of the Jews and reacted accordingly? Or was something deeper at work?

Luther's tract of 1523 *That Jesus Christ was Born a Jew* may have been a short and relatively insignificant work within his literary corpus, but its implications were revolutionary. It indicated the church's policy toward the Jews over many centuries. It was addressed both to gentiles to urge them to a brotherly respect for the Jews, since they were kinsmen of Christ, and to Jews in the hope that some of them might be converted to Christ. His watchword to his fellow-gentiles was to 'deal gently with them and instruct them from Scripture.'[9] For the Jews had been mistreated by the leaders within the church. 'They have dealt with the Jews as if they were dogs rather than human beings; they have done

---

[7]   Oberman, *Luther*, 8.
[8]   *ibid.*, 326.
[9]   *Luther's Works* (Concordia Publishing House 1962) 45:229. Hans Hillerbrand collects other friendly comments about the Jews from the early Luther in, '*Martin Luther and the Jews*' Charlesworth, *Jews*, 1:129–30.

little else than deride them and seize their property. When they baptize them they show them nothing of Christian doctrine or life, but only subject them to popishness or mockery.'[10] By contrast, Luther could feel optimistic about a Jewish presence in the midst of a truly Christian community.

> If we really want to help them, we must be guided in our dealings with them not
> by the papal law but by the law of Christian love. We must receive them cordially,
> and permit them to trade and work with us, that they may have occasion and
> opportunity to associate with us, hear our Christian teaching, and witness our
> Christian life. If some of them should prove stiff-necked, what of it? After all,
> we ourselves are not all good Christians either.[11]

Luther plainly recognized that not all would be converted. This accorded with his acceptance of traditional church teaching about a future conversion of the Jews, but only at a time just prior to the return of Christ.[12] The prospect of continued Jewish unbelief, however, did not worry him. The Jews at this stage were not viewed as a threat to the gospel. Perhaps, most surprisingly of all, Luther made positive assertions about Judaism. He spoke of the Jews seeing that 'Judaism has such strong appeal in Scripture, and that Christianity has become a mere babble without reliance on Scripture.'[13] The later Luther would be much less optimistic about Judaism as a religious system. His emphasis on Scripture gives the only clue as to what was to come. If the Jews heeded Scripture, all would be well for them. But what if they did not?

Scholars have keenly debated the question of the change in the later Luther. Some, including the eminent Dutch scholar Heiko Oberman, have suggested that there was no basic change, since all the fundamental components of Luther's diatribes were present in his early works.[14] While there is some truth in this, it seems to me that at the very least Luther's perception of the religious scene changed. The open mind which he had kept in 1523 about the conversion of numbers of the Jews

---

[10]   *Luther's Works*, 45:200.

[11]   *ibid.*, 229.

[12]   In his early (1515/6) *Lectures on Romans* Luther takes the view that Romans 11 (esp 25, 26) does refer to a future conversion of Israel at the end of the world. He does, however, modify this by saying that the passage is so unclear that such an interpretation cannot be derived from that passage alone. He believes it is supported by a whole range of passages — Lk. 21:23, 24; Dt.4:30–1; Ho3:4, 5 and 5:12 and 15; Mt. 23:38, 39. Luther also believes that this was figuratively set forth in the story of Joseph and his brothers.

[13]   *ibid.*, 200.

[14]   Oberman, *Roots*, 107–117.

had vanished by the 1540's, if not considerably earlier. Oberman has pointed out that by that time Luther thought the church was living in the last days and his priority was to ensure the gospel witness was maintained amid all the assaults made upon it by Satan in a sort of final fling.[15] Luther envisaged Satan's unholy coalition embracing the Pope, heretics and Turks as well as the Jews. Thus Luther had little room for kind thoughts or practical toleration of the Jews. Though Luther's attitude to the Jews was indirectly affected by this apocalyptic view, we should not underestimate the more direct impact of Luther's personal experience of the Jews. He believed he could discern the pernicious influence of their own religious traditions and even some successful proselytism. Significantly, his 1543 tracts — unlike that of 1523 — were addressed exclusively to Christians to warn them against the Jews. He made no attempt to speak directly to Jews.

The change in Luther's outlook became public knowledge in 1537 when Josel of Rosheim (in Alsace), the recognized spokesman for the Jews in Germany, tried in vain to secure an audience with Luther though he came with a recommendation from Wolfgang Capito, one of the Reformers from Strasbourg.[16] Josel felt that Luther might use his influence with the Elector John Frederick of Saxony to reverse an edict of the previous year threatening the Jews with expulsion from Electoral Saxony. Luther, however, refused to see Josel, and explained his reasons in a letter.[17] In theory he would have been pleased to intercede on behalf of the Jews, but he believed that his previous services had been so abused that any further practical help he tried to give would be unavailing. The same ambivalence characterized the whole letter. His desire to see the Jews kindly treated and won for Christ was counterbalanced by a fear that efforts to assist them might simply harden them in unbelief — 'For my opinion was, and still is, that one should treat the Jews in a kindly manner, that God may perhaps look graciously upon them and bring them to their Messiah — but not so that through my good will and influence they might be strengthened in their error and become still more bothersome.' In 1523 it had not worried Luther that some Jews should be hardened further in unbelief. By 1537 this had become more of a worry, but not to the extent that

---

[15] *ibid.*, 117ff.

[16] for Josel's position see Stern, *Josel*, 52–4.

[17] This letter is found in the Weimar edition of *Martin Luthers Werke – Briefwechsel*, 8:89ff. The translation I have used below derives from the Concordia Publishing House and the Fortress Press edition of *Luther's Works*, 47:62.

Luther altogether despaired of conversions among the Jews. For he indicated to Josel that it was his intention to write a pamphlet to the Jews to win some of them over.

Such a pamphlet, however, was never written. Instead, in the next year (1538) Luther received confirmation and elaboration of earlier rumours that throughout large tracts of Christendom, from Bohemia and Moravia to Poland, Christians were having themselves circumcised and were thronging to accept Jewish ritual.[18] Some had even been induced to believe that the Messiah was still to come. It is unclear how accurate Luther's information was or to what extent these Sabbatarians, as the new groups were called, were influenced by Jews. More likely, they were extreme groups of Anabaptists who came to their own conclusions on reading Scripture.[19] But Luther assumed a Jewish influence.

Nor was Luther alone in suspecting increased Jewish influence on outsiders at this time. In 1539 Martin Bucer published in Strasbourg a treatise *On the Jews*, in which he advocated strict political and financial controls on the Jews as well as the demand that they attend Christian sermons. (In many respects Bucer was paving the way for the even more rigorous injunctions of Luther in 1543.) Along with other Protestant clergy, Bucer suspected that Jews were beginning to have influence with Philip of Hesse, the most vigorous Protestant champion among the German princes.[20] Bucer's work came as a shock to the Jews, who for a time considered him their greatest enemy in the Protestant fold. It is probably no accident that Eck on the Catholic side should write in even more venomous terms against the Jews in 1541, decrying the security and freedom they had been granted and recommending new and more stringent anti-Jewish laws.[21] Clearly suspicion of Jewish political and religious activity was in the air for whatever reason. Luther was not immune to these influences. On the contrary, he was predisposed to accept derogatory reports about the Jews because of his own disillusionment with them. While Luther may not be charged with insincerity, he cannot be absolved of gullibility and prejudice. He failed to recognize the tendency to make scapegoats of the Jews for many contemporary problems — for the age-old problems of indebtedness and social

---

[18]   The details come from Luther's letter, 'Against the Sabbatarians', which is found in *Luther's Work*, 45:65–98.
[19]   Such is the view of Brecht in *Luther*, 338.
[20]   For the background to this see Stern, *Josel*, 162–175.
[21]   *ibid.*, 183.

unrest and for the more recent problem of vast religious divides within Christendom.

From 1538 to 1543 Luther vacillated on the question of writing about the Jews. When he did eventually put pen to paper and produce three separate treatises in quick succession, it was with some reluctance, since he admitted he had resolved at one time to write nothing either about the Jews or against them. He changed his mind because he became convinced of persistent and sometimes successful Jewish efforts to win over Christians.[22] It was his duty to warn the church at large of this danger. Even so, he testified that he found the writing of the first and most important of these treatises *On the Jews and their Lies* a painful process.[23] To him the Jews presented a most distressing picture not only because of their exile and temporal misfortunes, but also because of the curse of God which condemned them 'to blaspheme, curse and vilify God himself and what is God's, for their eternal damnation.'[24] He was faced with the stark reality not only of Jewish unbelief but of God's punishment which consigned them to mock the true religion and to practise for themselves a religion which was a mockery of the truth.

Shocked by further 'revelations' of Jewish lies about Jesus, which made him out to be a cabbalistic magician, Luther wasted no time in penning another work *On the Tetragrammaton and the Genealogy of Christ*, which descended into scatological language to describe the Rabbis and their exegesis.[25] This must rank as the nadir of Luther's productions on the Jews. It even caused embarrassment among leading supporters of the Reformation of that day, the Zurich theologian, who declared, 'if it had been written by a swineherd, rather than a celebrated shepherd of souls, it might have some — but very little — justification'.[26] By contrast, Luther's other work, *Treatise on the Last Words of David*, was relatively moderate and was devoted to biblical exegesis.[27]

---

[22] Modern scholars have been unable to find due grounds for such fears of Jewish proselytising — see Hillerbrand in Charlesworth, *Jews*, 147.

[23] This work, *Von den Juden und ihren Lügen*, is translated in *Luther's Works*, 47:137–306.

[24] *ibid.*, 291–2.

[25] In German known as *Vom Schem Hamphoras*, available in the Weimar edition *W A* 53.579–648. This work has recently been translated into English by Gerhard Falk, *Jew*. For some suggestive comments on Luther's use of scatological language see Oberman, *Luther*, 107–9.

[26] cited in *Luther's Works*, 47:123.

[27] In German *Von den Letzten Worten Davids*, which is translated into English in *Luther's Works*, 15:267–352.

Right to the end of his life in 1546, Luther persisted in his determination to warn Christendom of the dangers of the Jews to the church and to Christian society. In fact, he appended to what was probably his penultimate sermon an *Admonition* against the Jews in which he highlighted their 'lies' against the Christian faith. This anti-Jewish mindset was apparent not only in his writing but in his wider work. On his final journey away from home Luther wrote to his wife, 'Dear Katie, I was weak on the road to Eisleben, but that was my own fault. For we had to pass through a village hard by Eisleben where many Jews live; perhaps they blew on me too hard . . . When the chief matters are settled, I must devote myself to driving out the Jews. Count Albert is hostile to them and has given them their deserts, but no one else has. God willing, I will help Count Albert from the pulpit.'[28] Warning against the Jews had become an obsession with Luther in his latter years.

This was in part due to a conviction that the Jews vilified Jesus and his mother Mary and in part due to his conviction that the Jews of his own day (apart from a few exceptions) were incapable of being converted.

> From their youth they have been so nurtured with venom and rancour against our Lord that there is no hope until they reach the point where their misery finally makes them pliable and they are forced to confess that the Messiah has come, and that he is our Jesus. Until such a time it is much too early, yes, it is useless to argue with them about how God is triune, how he became man, and how Mary is the mother of God. No human reason nor any human heart will ever grant these things, much less the embittered, venomous blind heart of the Jews.

This was a very far cry from the gentle approach of 1523!

Luther's disillusionment

Luther was influenced by personal experience of the Jews, both from a few direct personal encounters but even more from exposure to Jewish commentaries on the Old Testament. Luther tells us of one visit from three Jewish Rabbis early in his career as a Reformer when they were enthusiastic that some Christians were beginning to study Hebrew writings.[29] The subsequent discussion evidently turned to the consideration of what in Luther's view were Messianic passages in the Old Testament. The Rabbis remained unconvinced and resorted to the Talmud for alternative exegesis. This was in Luther's mind an evasion of the true meaning. In spite of this, Luther was prepared to give the

---

[28]   cited and translated in Preserved Smith (note 5) 252.
[29]   recorded in *Luther's Works*, 47:191–2.

Rabbis a letter of recommendation to the authorities, asking that for Christ's sake they be given free passage. Later on, however, Luther was horrified that they would not use these letters because of their mention of Christ. In fact, the Rabbis had described Christ as a *tola* (= a hanged highwayman). This was not to be the only occasion when Luther reacted violently to any suggestion of blasphemy against Jesus.

Luther also delved on his own initiative into rabbinical commentaries. He could even claim to have derived some initial benefit from these, not least as background to the *Lectures on Genesis*, which he began to deliver in 1535. In time, however, he became increasingly sceptical and even polemical about them.[30] Thus, in his *New Preface to the Prophet Ezekiel* of 1541 he accused the Rabbis of 'tearing the Scripture apart and tormenting it with their commentaries, like filthy sows rooting up and overturning a pleasure garden.'[31] It was part of the duty of the Christian scholar to rescue the true meaning of the Old Testament from those who had perverted it.[32]

Though Luther did not shy away from discussing detailed points of grammar or of philology, the issues at stake were far from minor or purely academic. They concerned the heart of true religion, which for him was the gospel of the grace of the Lord Jesus Christ.[33] It was vital to him to establish that Jesus was the Messiah and that he was God. Hence in his treatise *On the Jews and their Lies*, which is today best known for its political programme against the Jews, almost the first half of the work is devoted to a detailed analysis of four texts which clearly proved for him that Jesus was the Messiah. That was the vital issue in the church's quarrel with the Jews, as far as Luther was concerned. And if the Jews with their own special possession of the Old Testament rejected this, that was proof of their spiritual blindness.

Luther may have had some justification for his criticism of rabbinic exegesis. But undoubtedly he was moved by two important principles of his own hermeneutic — first, that the Scriptures were a clear and plain revelation, and second, that Christ was the key to unlock the whole of Scripture, the Old as well as the New Testament. With both principles Luther had a vital insight, but carried it to an extreme.

Luther reacted strongly to a saying of the medieval schoolmen that

---

[30] Brecht, 335–6.
[31] *ibid.*, 340.
[32] cf. *Luther's Works*, 15:344.
[33] see Brecht's comments at *Luther*, 336.

the Scriptures are obscure and equivocal, which he describes as a 'pestilential dictum'.[34] This was a slur on God, suggesting that God was inferior to human legislators — 'If laws need to be luminous and definite in secular societies, where only temporal issues are concerned, and such laws have been bestowed by divine bounty on all the world, how should he not give to Christians, his own people and his elect, laws and rules of much greater clarity and certainty by which to adjust and settle themselves and all issues between them?'[35] Luther followed this with extensive references to Scripture itself.

If Luther had argued that the main doctrines of Scripture were clear to all who read them with believing eyes, then his position would be incontestable. But he went further and argued much more controversially that no part of Scripture could be called obscure.[36] 'There stands within Scripture the statement . . . that the word of God is to us a lamp shining in a dark place. If part of the lamp does not shine, then it is part of the dark place rather than of the lamp.'[37] If, then, people did not agree with Luther's exegesis, whether they be Jews or anyone else, he was inclined to dismiss them as spiritually blind.[38] Hans Hillerbrand has appositely commented that Luther 'was so convinced, so profoundly convinced, that his premise on the simplicity and clarity of Scripture was correct that anything he perceived as a challenge to that premise sent him into an emotional tailspin.'[39] Luther, then, was a victim of an inflated view of the perspicuity of Scripture. The Jews, for their part, as the custodians of the Hebrew Scriptures, were bound to fall foul of such a viewpoint. And in this they were not alone.

Alongside this, Luther took the view that 'in the whole Scripture there is nothing but Christ, either in plain words or involved words.'[40] If he had confined himself to Augustine's perspective that what is patent in the New Testament is latent in the Old Testament, all would have been well; for then he could have agreed that certain passages of

---

[34] Luther, *The Bondage of the Will*, 125. All my references are to the translation by J.I. Packer and O.R. Johnston (James Clarke, London 1957).
[35] *ibid.*, 126.
[36] Later Protestants would modify this position — cf. the much more nuanced position of the *Westminster Confession*, 1:7.
[37] *ibid.*, 129. The biblical reference is to 2 Pet. 1:19.
[38] Luther was keenly aware of the reality of spiritual blindness. It was the only reason why many failed to see the plain meaning of Scripture — see *ibid.*, 132–4.
[39] Hillerbrand in Charlesworth, *Jews*, 147
[40] quoted in A. Skevington Wood, *Captive to the Word* (Paternoster, 1969) 173–4. The whole section from p171 to p174 is relevant here.

the Old Testament permitted more than one interpretation. But Luther went further and boldly argued that the Old Testament can have no meaning in its own right except one warranted by the New — 'We Christians have the meaning and import of the Bible because we have the New Testament, that is, Jesus Christ, who was promised in the Old Testament and who later appeared and brought with Him the light and true meaning of Scripture.'[41] The implications of this are clarified a little later when he wrote, 'Whoever does not have or want to have this Man properly and truly who is called Jesus Christ, who is called God's Son, whom we Christians proclaim, must keep his hands off the Bible — that I advise. He will surely come to nought. The more he studies, the blinder and more stupid he will grow, be he Jew, Tartar, Turk, Christian or whatever he wants to call himself.'[42] With such an hermeneutical principle it was inevitable that Luther would have no time for Jews (amongst others) who did not find Jesus as Messiah written large over every page of the Old Testament.

Even sterner corollaries were to follow seeing that the Jews had been made the custodians of the Hebrew Scriptures. If the Jews could not be trusted in their treatment of these, they could not be trusted on any lesser matter — and that, of course, in Luther's eyes meant they could not be trusted on anything —

> Dear Christian, be on your guard against the Jews, who . . . are consigned by the wrath of God to the devil, who has not only robbed them of a proper under-standing of Scripture, but also of ordinary human reason, shame, and sense, and only works mischief with Holy Scripture through them. Therefore, they cannot be trusted and believed in any other matter either, even though a truthful word may drop from their lips occasionally. For anyone who dares to juggle the awesome word of God so frivolously and shamefully . . . cannot have a good spirit dwelling in him. Therefore, wherever you see a genuine Jew, you may with a good conscience cross yourself and bluntly say: 'There goes the devil incarnate.'[43]

In the light of this, Luther did not dismiss the traditional medieval jibes against the Jews — that they were guilty of well-poisoning, kidnapping, piercing children and the like.[44] It is true that Luther gave these no emphasis in their own right. His main reason for hostility toward the Jews lay elsewhere — in their attitude to Scripture.

Luther believed he had personal experience and a theological war-

---

[41] *Luther's Works*, 15:268.
[42] *ibid.*,
[43] *Luther's Works*, 47:213–4.
[44] cf. *ibid.*, 217 and 277.

rant to justify total distrust of all Jews who had not become professing Christians. But how would his plea sound in the ears of those who lacked his biblical understanding or his sorrow at the degree of unbelief he believed he had encountered?

Exposure to some rabbinical exegesis was not the only reason why Luther developed an increasingly hostile picture of the Jewish religion. Luther also made it his business to consult available literature on the Jewish religion. In particular, he was able to utilize the work of a man from an eminent Jewish family, Anthony Margaritha, who had converted to Christianity in 1522 and had subsequently written a book entitled *The Whole Jewish Faith*.[45] Herein he rendered into German many of the commonest Jewish prayers, and appended his own controversial commentary. He wished to establish, amongst other things, that in their thrice-daily prayers the Jews asked God to tear out the Roman Empire by its roots, destroy all Christian authorities and 'spatter the blood of the Christians upon the walls.'[46]

He also contended that by a cabbalistic manipulation of the alphabet the Jews contrived regularly to curse Christ. Thus, they mentioned in their prayers that Christians worshipped before Hebel Vorik (= folly and vanity), the letters of which in Hebrew had the same value as Christ's own name.[47] A sinister underlying meaning was also attached to a familiar greeting which Jews used in everyday encounters with Christians. Mary, the mother of Jesus, was according to Margaritha a further target for Jewish opprobrium; she was a mere whore who had conceived Jesus in adultery with a blacksmith. It is little wonder that such a book roused anxieties among the Jews.[48] Josel of Rosheim argued before the Emperor that it was misleading and dangerous; he managed to secure a ban on Margaritha from Augsburg.[49] But one lasting result was to drive Margaritha into the Protestant camp. Luther

---

[45] for details of Margaritha's background see Stern, *Josel*, 98. The full title of his book was *The Whole Jewish Faith, Together with a Thorough and Truthful Account of all the Regulations, Ceremonies, and Prayers Both for Family and Public Worship, as Observed by the Jews throughout the Year, with Excellent and Well-founded Arguments against Their Faith.*
[46] Stern, *Josel*, 99.
[47] see *Luther's Works*, 47:256–7.
[48] To have a fuller perspective on the specific blasphemies of the Jews which Luther details see *ibid.*, 256–264. His treatise *On the Tetragrammaton and the Genealogy of Christ* is again devoted largely to refutation of what Luther saw as a further blasphemy against Christ. For a brief summary see Brecht *Luther*, 346–7.
[49] Stern, *Josel*, 99–103.

first read his book in 1539, and was so impressed with its contents that he reread it just prior to his three fateful anti-Jewish works of 1543.[50] He seems to have accepted all of its contentions virtually at face value.[51]

Thus Luther came through his reading to the conclusion that the Jews were guilty of blasphemy. Their lies were no ordinary lies. He regarded them as slanders against the very things which Christians held most precious — 'the lies, the blasphemy, the defamation, and the curses which the mad Jews indulge in so freely and wantonly against the person of our Lord Jesus Christ, his dear mother, all Christians, all authority, and ourselves'.[52]

Luther believed he had made an important discovery which it was his responsibility to pass on to the general Christian public. He urged Christians when they encountered a Jew to think along the following lines —

> Alas, that mouth which I there behold has cursed and execrated and maligned every Saturday my dear Lord Jesus Christ, who has redeemed me with his precious blood; in addition, it prayed and pleaded before God that I, my wife and children, and all Christians might be stabbed to death and perish miserably. And he himself would gladly do this if he were able, in order to appropriate our goods. Perhaps he has spat on the ground many times this very day over the name of Jesus, as is their custom, so that the spittle still clings to his mouth and beard, if he had a chance to spit.[53]

This perception of the Jew may be startling to an age such as ours which may be unused to such blunt language, but Luther at least cannot be accused of spreading deliberate lies about the Jews. He really did believe these were the Jewish practices.[54] He cannot, however, be so readily freed from the charge of gullibility. The Emperor of the day, after all, had been convinced that Margaritha was a troublemaker. And Luther may not have realized that the very extent of the divide between Jews and Christians at this time will have meant that any Jew who did change allegiance would very likely have a soured and imbalanced relationship to his former religion. About half a century after Luther one of the most noted scholars of the day, Joseph Justus Scaliger, was to admit, 'Rarely can you find a Jew converted to Christianity who is a respectable

---

[50] Brecht, *Luther*, 339–341.
[51] It was by no means the only work Luther consulted. For a more detailed list of his sources see *Luther's Works*, 47:130–1.
[52] *ibid.*, 274.
[53] *ibid.*, 274–5.
[54] From *ibid.*, 228 it is evident that he found similar accusations about Jewish worship in another converted Jew, Paul of Burgos.

person; the converts are generally bad types.'[55]

The implications of Luther's disillusionment

Luther's view had political ramifications. If Christians now knew that
the Jews were guilty of such blasphemies, it was inconceivable that they
should allow the situation to continue unchecked. Otherwise, he believed, they would be as guilty before God as those who had actually
perpetrated the blasphemies. It was a pastor's duty to warn his flock
against the Jews, though he was to be careful not to curse them or to
harm their persons.[56] He should also urge the secular ruler to take
appropriate action.[57] Then Luther spelt out in detail the measures he
advised. Significantly, he began with proposals to curtail, if not obliterate, the Jewish religion.[58] Synagogues were to be burnt to the ground,
and if anything survived the flames, it was to be buried so that no trace
remained of that place which to him had been unmasked as a breed-
ing-ground of blasphemy. Then, recognizing the importance of the
home in the Jewish religion, Luther urged that their houses be destroyed; if necessary, they could be assigned rough shelters like the
gypsies. Next, Luther wanted the confiscation of their prayerbooks and
the Talmud. The Rabbis, for their part, were to be forbidden, on pain
on death, either to give religious instruction or to conduct public
worship.

Luther's last three proposals concerned the social position of the
Jews. They were no longer to be allowed the right to travel on the
highways of the Empire or to practise usury. Finally, all able-bodied
Jews of either sex were to be required to undertake hard manual labour.
Realizing that these measures would not be popular with many of the
princes in Germany, Luther offered total expulsion of the Jews from
their domains as an alternative.[59] He declared somewhat flippantly that
he did not mind if the Jews returned to Jerusalem and their own country
in order to practise their religion there — a move he well knew was
virtually impossible at that time.[60]

Since some of Luther's suggestions were to be taken up in this

---

[55] '*Rarement un juif converti au Christianisme est homme de bien; les convertis sont
généralement mauvaises gens*' — quoted by Israel, *European*, 55.
[56] *Luther's Works*, 47:274.
[57] *ibid.*, 275–6.
[58] These are detailed at *ibid.*, 268–72, and repeated in brief at 285–7.
[59] *ibid.*, 276.
[60] *ibid.*, 79–80.

century in the Third Reich, it is well to highlight the differences both in motivation and in scale. Luther never envisaged attacks on the persons of the Jews. He did not want to exterminate the Jews, and in fact never entirely gave up hope that a few might be converted to Christianity. His primary motives were first to free the church (and the state) of a major source of corruption and so potentially of divine wrath and then, if possible, to do the Jews some good by bringing home to them their parlous condition. He argued,

> Since they live among us, we dare not tolerate their conduct, now that we are aware of their lying and reviling and blaspheming. If we do, we become sharers in their lies, cursing and blasphemy. Thus we cannot extinguish the unquenchable fire of divine wrath, of which the prophets speak, nor can we convert the Jews. With prayer and the fear of God we must practise a sharp mercy to see whether we might save at least a few from the glowing flames. We dare not avenge ourselves. Vengeance a thousand times worse than we could wish them already has them by the throat.[61]

To modern ears Luther's talk of not exercising vengeance and of practising a sharp mercy may appear incongruous or even hypocritical. But he lived at a time when people had no experience of a pluralistic society and no desire for such. Indeed, they believed that God exacted from each society a corporate responsibility to ensure that no public opposition was tolerated to his worship. If religious dissent was covert and the rest of society did not know of it, God would not require it of them.[62] But it became a different matter once that dissent became public knowledge. Luther believed that from various sources he had acquired new knowledge about contemporary Jewish religious worship. It was his duty to pass on that knowledge and to recommend an appropriate response. However misinformed Luther may have been and however flawed his judgments on the social role of the Jews, he undoubtedly saw himself as prophetically warning society of a great danger.

Luther disclaimed any desire for human vengeance on the Jews.[63] He did so partly because it was always a Christian's duty to bless and not to curse, but even more because he believed that Jewish history showed that this people were under God's special judgment. The latter he held to be self-evident to all but the Jews themselves. After all, the

---

[61] *ibid.*, 268.
[62] cf. Luther's permission that people could refuse to believe accepted orthodoxy *omissive et privatim* — *ibid.*, 279.
[63] It is also noteworthy that Luther's anti-Jewish proposals were less severe than those

Jews had been living away from Jerusalem for 1500 years in a dismal exile 'bereft of temple, divine service, priesthood and kingdom' and since it was only possible for their religion to function in Jerusalem, something fundamental had to be wrong.[64] Luther could declare bluntly,

> Such ruthless wrath of God is sufficient evidence that they have assuredly erred and gone astray. Even a child can comprehend this. For one dare not regard God as so cruel that he would punish his own people so long, so terribly, so unmercifully, and in addition keep silent, comforting them neither with words nor with deeds, and fixing no time limit and no end to it. Who would have faith, hope, or love toward such a God? Therefore this work of wrath is proof that the Jews, surely rejected by God, are no longer his people, and neither is he any longer their God. This is in accord with Hosea 1 [:9], 'Call his name Not my people, for you are not my people and I am not your God.' Yes, unfortunately, this is their lot, truly a terrible one. They may interpret this as they will; we see the facts before our eyes, and these do not deceive us.[65]

If the Jews failed to see this, that was a further mark of the spiritual blindness which was the severest divine judgment on them of all.

Some scholars have found here a contradiction with Luther's theology of the cross which he formulated in direct contrast to the scholastic theology of glory.[66] Briefly, Luther contended that God revealed himself most clearly to men not in a blaze of divine glory but in the paradox of the cross and of suffering.[67] From this demonstration of power in weakness, of glory in suffering and of life in the midst of death it emerges how mysterious is the working of God. We dare not lean on our own understanding if we are to recognize the ways of God. We can only submit to his revelation. If human reasoning could not unravel the cross, we might wonder why should it be any more successful in discerning God's ways in the historical process. How could Luther be so sure that the suffering of the Jewish people was a mark of the divine judgment?

I grant that there is something of a problem here, and it is noteworthy that the Reformed tradition did lay much more stress than Luther on the suffering and downtrodden condition of the church both before and after Christ.[68] (Hence it would be much more sympathetic to the Jews' plight in their Dispersion.) It would certainly be hazardous to

---

[64] *Luther's Works*, 47:68–9.
[65] *ibid.*, 138–9.
[66] cf. Hillerbrand in Charlesworth, *Jews*, 135–6.
[67] cf. Skevington Wood (note 40) 170–2.
[68] cf. Oberman, *Roots*, 140–1.

argue straightforwardly from suffering, even from prolonged suffering, to a divine judgment. Luther's remarks do, however, carry weight in their context because he was disputing the Jewish claim that they remained in special covenant relationship to God, who had bestowed on them a country, a city and a Temple.[69] Luther pointed out that their Dispersion and exile from the land of Israel meant that it was impossible for them properly to practise their religion. Besides, their unparalleled suffering over so many years — without any word of comfort from God or without any indication of an end in sight — could only be interpreted as a manifestation of divine anger for exceptional sin, which in Luther's mind was the rejection of the true Messiah. It was against the character of God to torment any people so long without good reason.

While the theology of the cross and the hiddenness of God was a vital insight for Luther, he did not in practice take the extreme view that because God's ways are not man's ways, it is impossible ever to see the hand of God in human history. He believed that only someone who was spiritually blind or perverse could fail to recognize it in the destiny of the Jews over the last 1500 years. In this he was following a Christian apologetic tradition going back at least to Nicolas of Lyra (c. 1270–1349).[70]

The appeal to history, therefore, was a traditional anti-Jewish theme to which Luther gave a new lease of life. So too with his hostility towards rabbinic exegesis. Shortly before Luther burst upon the European stage, there had been a preliminary drama within Christendom when a converted Jew called Johannes Pfefferkorn had urged rulers to destroy all Hebrew writings other than the Bible since these writings had persistently led the Jews astray. This effectively revived the mission of Nicholas Donin from the thirteenth century. In spite of a generally more enlightened attitude to scholarship in the Renaissance, leading Christian scholars were hard pressed to argue the case against Pfefferkorn.[71] Moreover, Luther himself in his *On the Tetragrammaton and the Genealogy of Christ* could allude to a scene depicted on a sandstone relief on the choir of the Wittenberg city church — 'Here at Wittenberg on our parish church is a sow carved in stone, and lying under her are young piglets and Jews who suckle there. Behind the sow stands a rabbi,

---

[69] for this and the subsequent arguments in detail see *Luther's Works*, 47:66–78 and 138–174.

[70] *ibid.*, 66.

[71] for a brief account of this controversy see Poliakov, *History*, 1: 214–6.

who lifts up the sow's right leg and with his left hand pulls the sow's rump toward him, bends down, and with great interest looks at the Talmud under the sow's rump, as if to read and learn something difficult and special.'[72] It was, therefore, commonplace to ridicule rabbinic interpretations, particularly those of a cabbalistic nature.

Luther could add further depths to this contempt by enlarging on his own experience. In 1523 he had been prepared to give Jews the benefit of the doubt; they had been victimized and so prejudiced against Christianity by the medieval church. Perhaps the opening up of gospel light would benefit them. On the contrary, he found that they exhibited exactly the same spiritual blindness as he had found in the Pope and other ecclesiastical leaders —

> If I had not had the experience with my papists, it would have seemed incredible to me that the earth should harbour such base people who knowingly fly in the face of open and manifest truth, that is, of God himself. For I never expected to encounter such hardened minds in any human breast, but only in that of the devil. However, I am no longer amazed by either the Turks' or the Jews' blindness, obduracy and malice, since I have to witness the same thing in the most holy fathers of the church, in pope, cardinals and bishops. O you terrible wrath and incomprehensible judgment of the sublime Divine Majesty! How can you be so despised by the children of men that we do not forthwith tremble to death before you? What an unbearable sight you are, also to the hearts and eyes of the holiest men, as we see in Moses and the prophets. Yet these stony hearts and iron souls mock you defiantly.[73]

When Luther took such an outlook towards the Jewish approach to the Scriptures, it is little wonder that he was inclined to believe assertions like those of Margaritha which indicated that Jews in their own worship directly insulted or cursed Christians.

In the above passage Luther manifested his strong convictions about the wrath of God — convictions not shared by many in our century. He saw the judgment of God at work not only in outward calamities such as a plague (which almost everyone at that time attributed to the hand of God), but in inward states of mind. When men preferred darkness to light, when men refused to accept the plain truth of Scripture and rushed into some other religion of their own devising, that was in itself a sign that they had come under God's judgment. Luther found this doctrine in the Apostle Paul and was not slow to apply it to many who disagreed with him, including the

---

[72] Translation from Brecht, *Luther*, 346–7. This relief is dated from the early 14th century.
[73] *Luther's Works*, 47:177.

Jews.[74] Those who cannot understand this perspective on God's wrath will find difficulties with Luther's position on the Jews, but they should recognize that it did exercise some restraint on Luther. There was no need, he declared, to add to the vengeance of God on the Jews. That was already bad enough and made them into pitiful creatures. Such action as Luther urged against the Jews was to avert contamination and to avoid the sort of guilt by association which would itself have triggered the judgment of God against conniving Christians.

At the same time Luther never denied the possibility of the conversion of at least some Jews; he alluded to this possibility in his final *Admonition* and urged Christians to treat converted Jews as full brothers.[75] Nor is there any reason to suppose he entirely abandoned his early acceptance of the church's traditional view that toward the end of the world the Jews would be converted to Christ.[76] Certainly he became increasingly pessimistic about the conversion of the Jews of his own day. That was a fruit of his own experience. But Luther did not generalize from the Jews of his own day to the Jews of all time. Indeed, the very measures he advocated against them were intended eventually to impress upon them a lesson they were ignoring — that they were in a wretched condition because they were under God's judgment. Only when they realized this and forsook their quite unjustified pride in some special status they thought they enjoyed would there be hope for them. This was the sense in which Luther's proposals were intended as a 'severe mercy'.[77]

That is not to deny that there were ambiguities and inconsistencies in Luther's position.[78] But Luther faced the same dilemma as the medieval church and did not entirely resolve it. Was the major aim to convert the Jews or to protect Christian society from contamination by the Jews? For all the severities imposed on the Jews in that period, the

---

[74] The *locus classicus* is Rom 1:18–32 while Eph 4:18, 19 and 2 Thes 2:10–12 are also relevant.

[75] *Martin Luthers Werke*, WA 51: 195, 39ff.

[76] Oberman has noted that in his later years Luther became convinced that he was living in the last days — *Roots*, 104ff — but that does not seem to have influenced Luther's perspective on the Jews.

[77] This idea had a long history within the church — cf. the parallel idea of *instantia* in Augustine of Hippo — Peter Brown, *Augustine of Hippo* (Faber, London 1967) 226–232.

[78] cf. the careful remarks of Brecht, *Luther*, 340.

medieval church remained at least in theory committed to their conver-
sion. This was implicit in the great controversy roused by Johannes
Pfefferkorn in Luther's younger days. In the resultant debate both sides
were arguing, amongst other things, over the best strategy to convert
the Jews. But alongside this went a concern over the effect of Jews, even
Jewish converts, on Christendom. It had been as recently as 1492 that
Ferdinand and Isabella had ordered the expulsion of the Jews from
Spain for this very reason.

Luther in 1523 had not been convinced that the Jews constituted any
danger to the church. He was too keenly aware of the faults within the
church, particularly the ecclesiastical hierarchy, to suppose that some
external group posed a real threat to the church. But as time went on
his perception changed. The Jews did threaten Christians by their
proselytising, by their distortion of Scripture and above all by the
blasphemies which they included in their worship. Thus, Luther's
emphasis changed from a tentative exploration that Jews might be ripe
for conversion to a determination in the 1540s to see that the church
was warned against the Jews as its deadliest foes. Luther altered none
of his fundamental convictions; the new emphasis in his later years
resulted from a more accurate knowledge (as he saw it) of the situation.
Even so, Luther's desire not to abandon outright the conversion of Jews
led to some strange statements. Thus, his major work of 1543, *On the
Jews and Their Lies*, ends with a summary of his reasons for writing —
'My essay, I hope, will furnish a Christian . . . with enough material not
only to defend himself against the blind venomous Jews, but also to
become the foe of the Jews' malice, lying, and cursing, and to understand not only that their belief is false but that they are surely possessed
by all devils.' But Luther does not end there; he proceeds immediately
to a brief prayer, 'May Christ, our dear Lord, convert them mercifully
and preserve us steadfastly and immovably in the knowledge of him,
which is eternal life. Amen.'[79] By any account it is an extraordinary
combination. The idea of the Jews being possessed by all devils is
juxtaposed with a prayer for their conversion.

Luther's influence

Whatever Luther's motives, it was ironic that he should propose one
of the most extensive and humiliating sets of anti-Jewish measures ever

---

[79] *Luther's Works*, 47:305–6. This is not the only point in the work where Luther prays
for the conversion of the Jews — cf. 291–2.

suggested up to this time. As Josel of Rosheim commented, 'Never before has a Gelehrter, a scholar advocated such tyrannical and outrageous treatment of our poor people.'[80]

It may be true that Luther's 1543 tracts were reprinted relatively seldom — certainly far less frequently than *That Jesus Christ Was Born a Jew*.[81] It may also be true that Luther's stance in *On the Jews and Their Lies* did not win universal approval among leading Reformers. Thus, Heinrich Bullinger (of Zurich) wrote privately to Bucer telling him that Luther's proposals reminded him of the methods of the Inquisition.[82] But any published work by as eminent a figure as Luther could scarcely go unnoticed. Besides, Luther was determined that the rulers should heed his message.

Some anti-Jewish measures did result from Luther's activity, but not on the scale he envisaged.[83] At most the Jews suffered expulsion from a few centres. In some places Luther even suffered a rebuff. The Magistrate of Strasbourg, who received a detailed critique from Josel, prohibited the printing of Luther's works in his own territory.[84] In Berlin an old Protestant adversary of Luther, Julius Agricola, spoke in defence of the Jews when the local dean began urging the Elector to take action against them. Perhaps the greatest immediate danger from Luther's proposals came not from princes, who would not allow their policies to be dictated by clergy, but from the populace, which was already heavily prejudiced against the Jews and was fired by the belief that it was possible to obtain forgiveness by destroying a Jew or his property.[85]

Perhaps the worst of Luther's legacy was left until this century when the Nazis were able to make capital out of the popular perception of Luther as an anti-Semite and German nationalist. Yet, the treatment of Luther's anti-Jewish sentiments even within the confines of the Lutheran Church was far from uniform.[86] Moreover, some Nazi spokesmen actually lamented that Luther's works were not as widely read as they ought to be — 'It is an intolerable state of affairs that this manifesto of the great Reformer [On The Jews and their Lies], which is both an important outburst of national religious sentiment and utterly relevant to the present day, is known among all Germans, but

---

[80]   citied in *ibid.*, 135
[81]   Poliakov, *History*, 225 n 9.
[82]   *ibid.*, 123.
[83]   for details see Brecht, *Luther*, 349–50.
[84]   Stern *Josel*, 196–9.
[85]   *ibid.*, 196.
[86]   Hillerbrand, in Charlesworth, *Jews*, 137–145 and 148–150.

by name alone, and read only by very few.'[87] Thus the Nazis could not build on a precise knowledge of Luther; they brought in Luther or rather a particular image of Luther to rationalize a stance they had taken up on other grounds.

Luther, in fact, would have been diametrically opposed to the Nazi idea of racial superiority or inferiority. Ironically, in his day he perceived a spiritual danger in Jewish claims to be privileged before God on purely racial grounds — 'The blind Jews are truly stupid fools, much more absurd than the gentiles, to boast so before God of their physical birth, though they are by reason of it no better than the gentiles, since we both partake of one birth, one flesh and blood, from the very first, best, and holiest ancestors.'[88] Luther's objections to the Jews were exclusively religious; and where he believed a Jew had sincerely converted to Christianity, he had no doubt that he should be regarded as a full brother in Christ. He himself gave considerable financial support to a baptized Jew called Bernard (Jacob Gipher) though this strained his finances.[89] This was a world of difference from Nazi ideology.

Hans Hillerbrand has observed that Luther exercised more influence over Nazi ideology in the role of 'the German' speaking against foreigners than he did as an anti-Semite.[90] Here the Nazis were drawing upon the perception of Luther which had become current in Germany from the latter part of the nineteenth century. And yet Luther did not see himself as a nationalist. On the eve of the Peasants' War in 1525 he had the opportunity to become a sort of German national figure in the mould of a William Tell or a Joan of Arc, but he eschewed such a role.[91] His life's work was to expound the Scriptures and thereby to edify the church. That work would have been hindered and the gospel would have been implicated if it were attached to some political or nationalistic cause, however appealing. As Oberman neatly puts it, 'He refused to become a folk hero, and by refusing became himself a German event.'[92] But it was precisely because he had become a national event that nationalists of a later era could capitalize upon him and mould him in their own image.

Few leading churchmen have been as sensitive as Luther to the

---

[87]   ed. W. Linden *Luthers Kampfscriften gegen das Judentum* (Berlin 1936), 7 cited by Oberman, *Roots*, 94.
[88]   *Luther's Works*, 47:148.
[89]   Brecht, *Luther*, 335.
[90]   Hillerbrand in Charlesworth, *Jews*, 150.
[91]   Oberman, *Luther*, 47.
[92]   *ibid.*, 49.

dangers of political or ideological entanglements. It was sad and ironic that the churches in Germany were not more outspoken in protest in the 1930s against the blending of religious and political programmes which marked the Nazi platform. Luther certainly cannot be blamed for this — except to the extent that he himself looked to the powers that be of his own day to undergird the Reformation. He did not foresee a day when these very powers might themselves begin to embody one of those ideologies of whose marriage with Christianity he was very wary. Rulers in his day, after all, tended to represent personal rather than ideological interests.

That is not to exonerate Luther entirely from the anti-Semitism which lingered over much of Europe. Luther professed to have obtained new insights into contemporary Jews and Judaism — insights which were not the least part of his legacy. But we might well ask about the accuracy of these insights.

Here, ironically, we have to begin with one of the strengths of Luther's approach. He was ready to look into rabbinical commentaries and into recent works about Judaism. He did not rehash complaints made about Jews in the time of Christ; thus he had little to say about the charge of deicide however popular it had been in the medieval period.[93] He was not guilty of automatically assuming that the Jews of the New Testament could be equated with the Jews of his own day. He may have come to the conclusion that the Apostle Paul's criticism of his fellow-Jews — 'they are zealous for God, but their zeal is not based on knowledge' — still applied to the Jews, but that was only as a result of personal investigation.[94]

Indeed, Luther showed a distinct historical perspective in his thoughts about the Jews.[95] Not long after the time of the New Testament, the Temple at Jerusalem had been destroyed and the Jews banished from the land of Israel — both intensely significant events for the people and for their religion. Since then they had experienced untold misery, while Christian apologists like Nicolas of Lyra and Paul of Burgos had tried to present to the Jews the meaning of these events and to reveal the hollowness of rabbinic explanations.[96] But, in Luther's view, the Jews had failed to heed the voice of God speaking

---

[93] Hillerbrand in Charlesworth, *Jews*, 144.
[94] Rom. 10:2 quoted in *Luther's Works*, 47:175.
[95] But Luther was unaware of how poorly developed among the Jews was any sense of their own history outside of their Scriptures — Kochan, *The Jew*, 1–34.
[96] *ibid.*, 138–140.

through their own history and through the helpful works of these Christian apologists. It was also futile for them to argue that they had no business to read the New Testament. The latter had been publicly available for almost 1500 years, during which time the Jews had received plenty of evidence that the Christian message was of God since they had beheld all sorts of miracles and 'heard how this doctrine has survived, by nothing but divine strength, against all devils and the whole world.'[97] The longer this process of deliberate spiritual blindness persisted, the worse their condition became. By the logic of this argument the Jews could be reckoned among the worst of sinners — certainly worse even than the unbelieving Jews of Christ's time.

Thus the way was paved for Luther to discover through Margaritha and others the horrendous blasphemies which were supposed to be part of regular Jewish worship. But Luther underestimated the effect of centuries of antipathy between Jews and Christians. It is little wonder that some Jews would have allowed this hatred to enter their worship, though doubtless Margaritha touched on some extreme or rare instances of Jewish venom, if there was any truth in them at all. Jews may even have cried out to God for vengeance on certain Christians who were guilty of atrocities or of injustices against them. This, however, was not the same as saying they hated God. Nor would converts from Judaism have necessarily been the most reliable witnesses about their former co-religionists.[98] They faced recriminations from those who continued in Judaism, and at the same time they had to establish their new Christian credentials before a sceptical Christian public. What better way to do this than by derogatory 'revelations' about the Jewish faith? Even so, sometimes the Jewish converts continued to arouse suspicion. Erasmus had written of the convert, Pfefferkorn, 'If one were to operate, on him, six hundred Jews would spring out.'[99]

In short, Luther was naive about the time and effort needed to offset years of Jewish-Christian antipathy. He showed some measure of understanding in 1523, but sadly he allowed this to be undermined by his unfortunate experiences of Jewish attitudes to Scripture. He was naive too in his supposition that all that was really necessary to convince the Jews of Jesus' Messiahship was to highlight some key

---

[97]   ibid, 280–5.
[98]   cf. Josel's comments on the bad influence of Margaritha and other Jewish converts — Stern, *Josel*, 228.
[99]   Oberman, *Roots*, 38.

passages from the Old Testament. It was foolish of him to write off the Jews just because they had some traditional alternative interpretations. A much more demanding missionary effort was required for Jews to be won over to Christianity than simply to issue *That Jesus Christ was Born a Jew*. The latter treatise would have made a good first step. It was a pity it proved to be virtually Luther's last public gesture to promote a more positive attitude toward the Jews.

Instead, the polemical works of Luther's later years inevitably hindered the possibility of rapprochement between Protestants and Jews, though by the end of the century individual Jews were generous enough to give Luther some praise.[100] Luther had examined contemporary Judaism after his own fashion, and found it desperately wanting. In some respects he had told the general public what they already wanted to believe for perhaps rather different reasons.[101] Luther simply added a theological rationale for anti-Jewish sentiment.

Some conclusions

If we weigh up the two parts of the Apostle Paul's perception of the Jewish people at Rom 11:28, we find Luther showing something of the imbalance which has plagued the church in the matter of the Jews. By the latter part of Luther's career he had fastened singlemindedly on that element which distinguished the Jews as the enemies of the gospel. At the same time he had lost sight of the idea of the Jews still being loved by God on account of their election, if indeed he had ever grasped that idea at all.[102] This may be understandable, given Luther's interest in the spread of the gospel. It may also reflect Luther's mindset, which was such that he liked to view everyone as friend or foe. More subtle analyses like that of the Apostle Paul eluded him.

Ironically, some of Luther's own Reformation insights, carried to extremes, proved a handicap. I have in mind his attitude to Scripture and its exegesis. Luther had an unequivocal confidence in the perspicuity of the Scriptures. Yet, it was a confidence which failed to allow

---

[100] cf. Josel's disillusionment with the Reformation as outlined in Ben-Sasson,'Reformation', 286–293. But the German-Jewish chronicler-historian, David Gans, spoke highly of Luther as a scholar amongst other things — Kochan, *The Jew*, 35.
[101] Luther encouraged a tradition of incendiary anti-Jewish pamphlets — Poliakov, *History*, 1:240–1.
[102] Haynes, *Jews*, 49 points out that Luther came to deny that the Jews of his day were descended from the patriarchs. This, however, had not been Luther's view in 1523.

for difficulties arising not only from Scripture itself but even more from alternative religious traditions. It was perhaps too easy for Luther to see in other religious traditions like Judaism the same man-made regulations as had angered Christ in the Phariseeism of his own day.[103] But the Judaism of Luther's time was a more complex entity than Phariseeism. After all, it had had to adjust to centuries of hounding and degradation at the hands of representatives of the Christian church. Nor did it straightforwardly regard the Old Testament as its only holy book. Moreover, the Jews maintained a vigorous cultural, social and even judicial life of their own. A more wide-ranging and sympathetic scholarship was required if Christians were ever to begin to commend their faith to Jews. Thankfully, later developments in the Reformation were to point in a different direction from Luther.

---

[103] cf. Mt. 15:1–9; Mk. 7:1–13.

Eight

The Reformation after Luther

Some Protestant contemporaries of Luther

Luther's own development on the Jewish question, whereby a cautious optimism gave way steadily to a perception of a Jewish threat and so to feelings of disgust toward unconverted Jews, had a notable parallel in at least one other leading Reformer — Martin Bucer. The parallel is surprising given that the two men were temperamentally very different. Perhaps it comes as no surprise that the volatile Luther, alongside whom colleagues sometimes found it difficult to work, should incline towards an extreme position on the Jewish question.[1] It is much more surprising in the case of Bucer, who had a reputation in Protestant circles for being conciliatory and was not averse to playing a leading role in exploratory discussions with Catholic representatives.[2] Yet in 1539, before Luther's outbursts of 1543, Bucer was regarded by Jews as their leading enemy in Protestant ranks.

Elaborating on these parallels will provide some indication as to how Jews were viewed about twenty years into the Reformation when theological positions for good or for ill were becoming increasingly fixed. The measures proposed by Bucer and his colleagues to deal with the Jews in Hesse were those of Luther in embryo.[3] They endeavoured to restrict the Jews in both religious and commercial activities. Luther simply went a few steps further. For example, whereas Bucer wanted no new synagogues to be built, Luther wanted all existing synagogues to be burnt down. But the underlying rationale was the same. Christian

---

[1] Oberman, *Luther*, 298–304.
[2] Stern, *Josel*, 165.
[3] for details see *ibid.*, 167–8.

society could not tolerate a threat from an alternative and economically prosperous religious group. Toleration could be extended only to a group which were obviously depressed and living witnesses to the inferiority of their own religion. Luther and Bucer had no hesitation in appealing to the state authorities to take requisite action against the Jews. They did not believe this was inconsistent with the gentleness of Christ. Indeed, they believed that any Christian ruler who neglected his duty here was liable to God's judgment.

Both Bucer and Luther (initially at least) recognized the Jews as descendants of the patriarchs and members of the race from which Jesus Christ had come. Both accepted the traditional church teaching of a conversion of the Jews to Christianity toward the end of the age. And yet both discovered in contemporary Jews the same sort of legalistic religion as they had found in the 'Papists'. Thus, if Jews were to be won over at all, it could only be through the exercise of a 'rigorous mercy.' In Bucer's own words they were to be 'considered enemies and combated as friends' — a somewhat paradoxical expression with obvious affinities to the Apostle Paul's perception in Romans 11:28.[4]

In the first generation of the Reformation Luther and Bucer were representative of a hardening in attitudes toward the Jews which probably affected many Protestants. But theirs was not the only reaction. Justus Jonas, who was for years a close companion of Luther and who delivered the sermon at his graveside, stressed the church's indebtedness to the Jews and took a more optimistic view of the possibility of Jewish conversions.[5] In his function as translator of Luther's German works into Latin to serve a wider public, Jonas often added a distinct, personal thrust. In his preface, for example, to his translation of Luther's *Against the Sabbatarians*, he avowed a missionary intent behind Luther's work; it was a Christian responsibility to lead Jews out of their errors and show them the right way.[6] It is difficult, however, to locate an evangelistic or even much of an apologetic thrust in Luther's original; his sole concern was to guard the church against error. Luther was not unaware of Jonas' different emphasis. He neither criticized it nor toned down his anti-Jewish tone in consequence. But Jonas' independence of mind illustrates that

---

[4]   *ibid.*, 165–6 and 174–5.
[5]   for a brief sketch of Jonas' life see Oberman, *Roots*, 7–8. For his independent line in translation see *ibid.*, 48–9.
[6]   Brecht, *Luther*, 339.

even early Lutheranism was not uniform in outlook toward the Jews.

Another Lutheran who made a vital contribution to a more positive perspective on the Jews was Andreas Osiander, the preacher at the Church of St Lorenz at Nuremberg.[7] In 1529 he produced a work which refuted in considerable detail the charge of blood-libel which had been levelled against the Jews for almost four centuries. Osiander used general principles to point out how preposterous it was that the Jews should murder children and then make use of their blood. After all, by their own law, which came to them with the authority of God, they were forbidden not only to kill any human being but even to make use of the blood of animals, still less of a human child. It is surely a mark of widespread (and possibly wilful) ignorance in society about Jewish practices that Osiander should have to stress such an obvious point. He corroborated it with the observation that no converted Jew had ever accused his fellow-Jews of ritual murder. He then went on to suggest a number of reasons why such charges should ever have been made — e.g. parents whose children had died of neglect or of unknown causes may have wanted to shift the blame to the Jews.[8]

A decade later Osiander's work was to fall foul of certain Catholic authorities and to attract the recriminations of Eck, who suspected a Lutheran hand behind this anonymous and unwelcome attempt to vindicate the Jews from one of the most serious slurs on their character.[9] This indicates that many had a vested interest in remaining in the dark about the Jews and their practices. Others like Luther himself may not have been so prejudiced, but they did underestimate the consequent difficulties in attaining the truth about them. True knowledge of the Jews was restricted to very few outsiders in this period and they risked suspicion for their efforts. It was no accident that Osiander's work was published anonymously!

Osiander probably was the only person to write directly to Luther to protest about his anti-Jewish tracts of 1543. This shows his independence of mind, but it does seem to have left him with rather a sullied reputation among later protagonists of Lutheran orthodoxy.[10]

---

[7] Stern, *Josel*, 181–2.
[8] for a summary of his position see *ibid.*, 182–3.
[9] Oberman, *Roots*, 37.
[10] *ibid.*, 10.

The Reformed tradition — the sixteenth century

Within ten years of Luther's death in 1546 those churches which had
aligned themselves with him fossilized into Lutheranism; they were
content to operate within the parameters of those doctrines Luther
himself had stressed. This, of course, was bad news for the Jews. The
Lutherans showed little desire to explore new areas of Scripture. As a
result, the impetus in theology and in other concerns passed to the
Reformed or Calvinist tradition, which even outside observers have
noted to be markedly more sympathetic toward the Jews.[11] This change
in outlook took time to develop. Initially, Calvinists were too concerned to establish their own brand of a Christian state to have much
practical concern for the Jews. But a change did emerge in time.

The reasons for this are complex. For one thing, this tradition began
to flower in the second generation of the Reformation, when medieval
prejudices and stereotypes were losing their force with the passage of
time. Then, Oberman has pointed out that many of the protagonists of
this tradition were refugees from the southern German, French and
then the Dutch cities.[12] They had undergone a sort of diaspora experience similar to that of the Jews. Hence they could sympathize with the
Jews as strangers in a foreign land and were not inclined to see exile
and diaspora automatically as signs of God's anger.

Theological factors were also at work. Reformed teachers insisted
on the 'total depravity' of mankind. All humans, Jews and gentiles
alike, stood guilty before God and without excuse.[13] It would, therefore, be inappropriate to assign the Jews to some category of specially
heinous sinners, as medieval Christendom had effectively done. This
smacked of a pretext by gentiles to evade the seriousness of their own
sin. Moreover, some Reformed writers began to examine in detail areas
of uncharted biblical prophecy and discovered there a future for the
Jewish race which was still to be fulfilled.

Ironically, John Calvin, the Genevan Reformer who is generally seen
as the founder figure in this tradition, 'seemed to remain silent' on the
Jewish question — at least in its political dimension.[14] He had little, if

---

[11] e.g. Poliakov, *History*, 1: 204–5 and Wistrich, *Anti-Semitism*, 38–42.
[12] Oberman, *Roots*, 140–1.
[13] for a typical statement see *The Westminster Confession*, chapter 6, especially section
4. The *locus classicus* in the Bible would be Rom. 1:18–3:20.
[14] The phrase is that of Poliakov, *History*, 1:198.

any, direct experience of Jews.[15] Yet, Calvin, a careful biblical exegete who generally adhered much more closely to the text than Luther, did through his exposition contribute toward a more positive outlook on the Jews. He insisted that when Scripture talked of the Jews and their sins, it did so as a mirror of all mankind everywhere.[16] Thus, when Jesus highlighted the hypocrisy of the Jews in building the sepulchres for the very prophets they themselves had killed, Calvin could find a parallel from the gentile world of his own day, 'The world, in general, while not daring to scorn God utterly or at least rise up against Him to His face, devises a means of worshipping God's shadow in place of God: just so it plays a game over the prophets.'[17] Contemporaries might erect beautiful statues of Peter and other saints, and adorn them with incense, candles, flowers and pomp of all sorts; but their treatment of the faithful in their own day showed how they would really react if they had Peter in their midst. They would 'tear him to ribbons'.

Unlike Luther, for whom God's special arrangement with the Jews was ended, Calvin insisted that however often God had to act in judgment against the Jewish people, this did not mean that God's covenant with them was broken because God always preserved an elect remnant. This emerges, for example, from Calvin's treatment of the imprecation of the Jerusalem crowd — in Mt. 27:25 'his blood be on us and on our children'. While he acknowledged that God had avenged this 'with fearful and unparalleled means', God had left a remnant so that his covenant might not be ended. 'God in their very treachery displays the constancy of His faith, and to show that His covenant was not struck with Abraham to no effect He rescues those he freely elected from the general destruction. Thus His truth ever arises superior to all obstacles of human incredulity.'[18]

Calvin believed that the Apostle Paul implied in Romans 11 that it was improper to despair of the salvation of the Jews. Commenting on verse 28, he was bold enough to say, 'Paul shows that the very worst feature in the Jews does not mean that they are on that account to be despised by the gentiles.' On both counts, intentionally or otherwise, he had rebuked the attitude of the later Luther. Calvin, however, would not go along with some who were teaching that Rom. 11:25, 26 implied a restoration of true religion to the whole Jewish people as before. He

---

[15] Edwards, *TJICE*, 61.
[16] cf. Calvin, *Commentary on St John*, 1:11.
[17] Calvin *Harmony of the Gospels*, 3:61 (St Andrew Press, Edinburgh, 1972)
[18] *ibid.*, 3:188.

rejected this interpretation because he took Israel in verse 26 to denote the people of God generally, both Jew and gentile —

> When the gentiles have come in, the Jews will at some time return from their defection to the obedience of faith. The salvation of the whole Israel of God, which must be drawn from both, will thus be completed, and yet in such a way that the Jews, as the first born in the family of God, may obtain the first place.[19]

Calvin thus demonstrated that it was possible to take a positive outlook on the Jews theologically without being committed to a future restoration of Israel or indeed any prophetic theory which gave them a significant place. That is not to say that there was an immediate improvement in the lot of the Jews in those areas where Calvin's teaching held sway. He did tend to concentrate on the Jews as they were portrayed on the pages of the Bible with only fleeting remarks on the treatment of Jews by others in subsequent generations.[20]

Calvin will have been aware of the traditional view (to which we have seen Luther inclined) that the conversion of the Jews was to be one of the events at the end of the age. Though Calvin remained unimpressed by this, in his own time at Geneva a new interest was emerging in a future mass conversion of the Jews. This was inspired by detailed exegesis of Romans 11. Thus, when the Geneva Bible was translated into English by Protestant exiles from the persecution of Mary Tudor, it contained among the notes to the 1557 and 1560 editions at Romans 11:26 this explanation — 'He sheweth that the time shall come that the whole nation of the Jews, though not every one particularly, shall be joined to the church of Christ'.[21] Through this Bible, which was very popular in Puritan circles in England, Scotland and New England, the doctrine of a future large-scale conversion of the Jews gained wide dissemination.[22]

The same view was held by the man commonly regarded as Calvin's successor at Geneva — Theodore Beza. In fact, he revealed a spiritual burden for the Jews which did not derive simply from his extensive biblical studies. He revived Luther's early view that Christian churches bore much

---

[19] Calvin explains that his understanding of Israel is based on Gal. 6:16.
[20] Edwards, *TJICE*, 61–3.
[21] Murray, *Puritan*, 41. The New Testament section of the Geneva Bible was first published in 1557, while the complete Bible became available in 1560.
[22] The first detailed exposition of this doctrine in English was by Peter Martyr in a commentary published in 1568. Martyr assigned the conversion of the Jews to near the end of the world — Murray, *Puritan*, 42–5.

of the blame for the current unbelief of the Jews —

> those who today call themselves Christians . . . are very certainly punished and will be in the future, because, solely under the guidance of wickedness and perversity, they have mistreated in every way these people, so holy in their forefathers, actually hardening them further [against Christianity] by setting before their eyes the example of an odious idolatry. As for myself, I gladly pray every day for the Jews.[23]

He then recorded the terms of his prayer which went far deeper than the perfunctory petitions of Luther in his work *On the Jews and their Lies*. Beza acknowledged the justice of divine anger against Jewish ingratitude and unbelief, but pleaded that Christ would remember his covenant towards them. Then, most unusually for his time, Beza recognized a responsibility of gentile Christians toward the unbelieving Jews —

> grant that we [= gentiles] may advance in thy grace, so that we may not be for them [= Jews] instruments of thy wrath, but that we may rather become capable, through the knowledge of thy words and the example of a holy life, of bringing them back into the true way by virtue of thy Holy Spirit, so that all nations and all peoples together may glorify thee for eternity.

If even a significant section of the Christian church had made Beza's burden their own, relations between Christians and Jews could have been transformed. But it is not easy to disseminate a personal burden of this nature widely.

In fact, in the sixteenth century, countries where the Reformed religion was established did not have a good practical record toward Jews. In the cases of Geneva and Lausanne, from which the Jews had been expelled in the 1490s, their request for readmission in 1582 was turned down by the unanimous agreement of the city council, clergy and general populace. In the leading Reformed state in Germany, the Palatinate, the Jews were expelled 'for all time' by Elector Frederick III, though in the event this proved to be only temporary.[24]

The limits of Reformation influence

The Reformation represented a protest against carelessness or ignorance about gospel truths. Little, if any, objection was raised in the mainstream of the Reformation to the idea of Christendom. The early Reformers (Lutheran and Calvinist alike) were concerned that secular as well as ecclesiastical authorities — in their own different ways —

---

[23] Poliakov, *History*, 1: 198 n 11. He alludes to a marginal note at the text of Romans 11:18 in *Nouveau Testament Grec*. (4th edition, 1589).
[24] Israel, *European*, 13.

should ensure the spread of the pure word of the gospel. They would have been horrified at the notion which has become acceptable in our pluralistic society that even the exponents of false doctrines have rights. It was inevitable, therefore, that these Reformers should not have encouraged the cause of unbelieving Jews. In their minds that would have been a wilful step toward the tearing down of Christendom.

Moreover, the beginnings of the Reformation fell in the middle of a period of intense anti-Jewish activity. From the latter part of the fifteenth century a series of expulsions had hit Jewish communities in western Europe, and were ultimately to shift the focus of European Jewish life to the dual commonwealth of Poland-Lithuania and to the Ottoman Balkans. This anti-Jewish agitation did not diminish after the Reformation. In fact, senior clergy and secular rulers became involved in what had hitherto been largely a movement among the towns and among the lower clergy, especially the friars. These expulsions were to continue roughly to the 1570s.[25]

The Jews were welcomed into Poland-Lithuania because vast expanses of these territories were underpopulated and underdeveloped commercially. The Jews were valued for the crafts, skills and wealth they brought from the west.[26] Moreover, Poland had even before the Reformation sheltered various dissenting religious groups like the Czech Brethren and the Armenian Monophysites. Yet more found refuge there in the aftermath of the Reformation.[27] In this relatively tolerant atmosphere little pressure of a religious kind was put on the Jews. In fact, they were given considerable freedom to run their own affairs.[28] As, however, the Roman Catholic Church began to reassert itself from the middle of the sixteenth century, the Jews became liable to the same sort of hostility as had been generated elsewhere in medieval Europe.[29] But the leading enemy of the Catholic Counter-Reformation was the various Protestant, not the Jewish, groups. While Protestantism was virtually eradicated from Poland, Jews remained a significant part of the Polish population until the Nazi era.[30]

---

[25] *ibid.*, 6–23.
[26] *ibid.*, 26.
[27] Edwards, *TJICE*, 131.
[28] Israel, *European*, 184–191.
[29] Edwards, *TJICE*, 132.
[30] On the eve of the Nazi invasion there were 3,460,000 Jews in Poland, the largest European community of Jews — Wistrich, *Anti-Semitism*, 157.

As at first in Poland, Jews did eventually benefit from the disappearance of the formal unity which had been at one time recognized in Christian Europe. By 1570 or so it had become clear that no one expression of Christianity would ever reign supreme throughout Europe. At various points conflicting Protestant and Catholic forces had fought themselves to a standstill. Amid the consequent exhaustion and the abating of religious militancy there was a place for the Jews to gain a foothold. Some Jews started to move back into areas of western Europe toward the end of the seventeenth century from which they had been removed in the past century or so. Often it was their skill or their contacts in trade which paved the way for Jewish acceptance. This was notably true in the city of Amsterdam, which in the seventeenth century became the leading Jewish community in western Europe and was known as the 'Dutch Jerusalem'.[31]

While the prospect of economic gain was an important factor in the readmission of the Jews to areas of western Europe, the Jews could not be disassociated from their religious connotations. The Jews were also to benefit from a more positive appraisal in the Protestant academic world of their learning. A key figure here was the Huguenot scholar, Joseph Justus Scaliger, who became Professor at the University of Leiden in 1593. Scaliger was noted for his critical attitudes to traditional scholarship, especially that concerning the text of the Bible. He thought that it was only possible to establish the true text and meaning of Scripture by engaging in fields unknown to earlier scholars. He valued access to Jewish scholars and said that Christians needed to grasp the significance of the Talmud and other post-biblical literature if they were ever to persuade Jews of the truth of Christianity. Thus, he argued that the Jews were to be allowed to return to western Europe not simply because 'they bring wealth' but because 'we need to learn from them.'[32] Scaliger, therefore, encouraged a trend of philo-Semitic scholarship. While it never became universal in the Protestant world, it was a corrective to earlier scholastic theology. By contrast, the Roman Catholic Church from the time of Pope Paul IV (1555–1559) set itself firmly against Jewish scholarship as a danger to Christian minds.[33]

---

[31] Edwards, *TJICE*, 144. For a brief account of the beginnings of Jewish economic activity in Amsterdam see Israel, *European*, 62–3.

[32] Israel, *European*, 54–55.

[33] *ibid.*, 18–21.

The Reformed tradition — the seventeenth century

The seventeenth century saw not only a new openness to Jewish learning but a lively interest among Reformed circles in unfulfilled prophecy. The general tenor of such investigations was to paint an optimistic view of the church's future and to link this in some way or another with the conversion of the Jews. Some even suggested that the conversion of the Jews was not necessarily an event toward the end of the age, but in fact foreshadowed a more extensive time of blessing for the church on earth.[34] These ideas sprang in the main out of intense Bible study. People began to gain confidence that the book of Revelation in particular offered a detailed account of church history from Pentecost to the Day of Judgment. This historicist approach was itself a fruit of the Reformation with its stress on the plain, literal sense of Scripture as against the allegorical. Both Luther and Calvin, however, refrained from detailed exposition of the book of Revelation. Their spiritual successors in the seventeenth century felt fewer inhibitions. That is not to say that exegetical considerations worked in isolation from wider events in the Christian world. To some extent this perspective was unconsciously adopted to provide optimism in the face of considerable opposition. After all, at first sight it was discouraging that a century after Martin Luther had fastened his Ninety-Five Theses to the door of the church at Wittenberg, the Papacy seemed as strong as ever, while the Ottoman Turks, embodying the power of Islam, continued to threaten Christendom at the heart of Europe. It is, for example, no accident that the first man to revive and adapt discredited millenarianism at this time was a German Calvinist, Johann Heinrich Alsted, who wrote out of the traumatic events of the Thirty Years War in which the very existence of continental Protestantism came under threat.[35] In England also, during the horrendous years of the Civil War the New Model Army was encouraged to military success by the preaching of millenarian chaplains who told their troops they were fighting against the armies of Antichrist and so were destined ultimately to secure success.[36]

---

[34]   Murray, *Puritan*, 46 ascribes the first hints of this view in the English-speaking world to Thomas Brightman.

[35]   Toon, *Puritans*, 42–56. To put this into wider perspective, it is worth noting that around this time messianic hopes were excited among the Jews — Israel, *European*, 207–216.

[36]   Toon, *Puritans*, 127.

In fact, the England of the 1640s saw the high-water mark of millenarian hopes, which in turn began to decline as soon as it was realized that the expected paradise for the church had not materialized after the overthrow of the Church of England and the defeat of King Charles I. Millenarianism (or premillennialism as we would call it) had been introduced to England by a Cambridge scholar, Joseph Mede, who closely followed Alsted.[37] Amongst his views, he held that the future millennium would be inaugurated or at least shortly followed by the return of the Jews both in a spiritual sense to their true Messiah and in a physical sense to the land once promised to Abraham by God. At the same time Mede believed that the Jewish nation would be converted in as spectacular and as supernatural a manner as the Apostle Paul was converted.[38]

Not everyone who was concerned to understand the details of Revelation concentrated on such a controversial passage as the millennium of Ch. 20. Some preferred to emphasize Ch. 13–19 as a divine promise of the overthrow of the enemies of the gospel (identified as the Papacy and the Turks). This was a necessary preliminary to a period of 'latter-day glory' for the church which would see the conversion of the Jews as part of a wider movement of the Spirit of God whereby earthly kingdoms would so submit to the gospel that they could be said to have become 'the kingdoms of our God and of his Christ'. In fact, these believers were the postmillennialists of the day.[39]

Belief in the conversion of the Jews was retained even by those critical of millenarianism. Into this category fell one of the Scottish Commissioners to the Westminster Assembly, Robert Baillie, who dubbed millenarianism as the old error of Chiliasm and who would today be labelled as an amillennialist.[40] Baillie and those like him held to this view of the Jewish people because they interpreted Romans 11:25f. in the tradition of Beza and of the annotators of the Geneva Bible.[41] In fact, it would be fair to say that the majority of Puritans in England and Scotland, whatever their differences on points of detail, agreed on this understanding of the future of the Jews.

---

[37] *ibid*, 56–65.
[38] Mede's ingenious but essentially speculative arguments are set out in detail in *ibid.*, 61 n 21.
[39] *ibid.*, 23–41. They would not have used the term 'postmillennialist' of their position.
[40] *ibid.*, 104–108 and 127 and Murray, *Puritan*, 50–1 for Baillie. Toon, *Puritans*, 108–114 for others who basically shared Baillie's position.
[41] They would be cautious about linking this passage to any section of the book of Revelation, which of itself gives no hint of any special dealing of God with the Jews.

This situation can be paralleled among the Protestant churches of the Netherlands. In their marginal notes on Romans 11, the orthodox Reformed translators of the 1637 Dutch version of the Bible followed Beza's lead.[42] They took 'the whole of Israel' as implying the fullness of the people of Israel 'according to the flesh'. Hence they had a biblical foundation for the expectation of the future conversion of the Jewish people. Almost every section of Dutch Protestant thought, including the Arminians who were generally considered to be rather lax in doctrine, took this viewpoint.[43]

This might seem very impressive. But an interest in the Jewish people for the fulfilment of prophecy need not entail an interest in the Jewish people for their own sake. The Jewish historian, Barbara Tuchman, has made this criticism of the leader of a nineteenth century English society for promoting the gospel among the Jews —

> To him, as to all the Israel-for-prophecy's-sake school, the Jews were simply the instrument through which biblical prophecy could be fulfilled. They were not a people but a mass error that must be brought to a belief in Christ in order that the whole chain reaction leading to the Second Coming and the redemption of mankind might be set in motion.[44]

Perhaps a similar criticism might be levelled against seventeenth century prophetic interest. After all, for many the restoration of the Jews was but one of a whole package of future events which could be deduced from Scripture.[45] Moreover, there was little agreement about the circumstances of Israel's restoration.[46] Would it involve a return to their ancient homeland?[47] Could it be promoted in any way or would it be such a supernatural event that no human hand would be involved in it? Those who followed Joseph Mede in the latter view would be disinclined to any active Jewish evangelism.

No doubt there were some Reformed churchmen in the seventeenth century to whom Tuchman's criticism would apply. But this is not the whole story. There is evidence from both England and the Netherlands

---

[42] Toon, *Puritans*, 139–40.

[43] *ibid.*, 137–153.

[44] Barbara Tuchman, *Bible and Sword: How the British came to Palestine* (London, 1956) 178.

[45] There were, however, some works devoted exclusively to the conversion of the Jews — notably by Sir Henry Finch in 1621 and by Thomas Brightman in 1635 — Toon, *Puritans*, 30–2.

[46] Toon, *Puritans*, 126–7.

[47] for an account of Christian Restorationism, a movement with a modern legacy see the essay of Margaret Brearley in Walker, *Jerusalem*, 99–124.

of improved and more positive attitudes toward the Jews. Since these improvements seem to begin in the second decade of the seventeenth century at the very time when there was heightened interest in what the Bible had to say about the future, a link, however intangible, is very likely.

Robert Healey has pointed out that in both England and the Netherlands the position of and attitudes toward the Jews improved significantly in the century from 1600 to 1700.[48] Though Jews had been expelled from England as far back as 1290, there were lingering memories of what they had been like and of what outrages they were supposed to have perpetrated. Thus, in the Book of Common Prayer of 1549 and thereafter, collects for Good Friday classed the Jews alongside Turks, infidels and heretics who were to be delivered from 'all ignorance, hardness of heart and contempt of thy word.' While this might be seen as purely a theological anti-Judaism, more sinister undercurrents were in operation. This emerged in 1594 in the context of the trial and execution of Rodrigo Lopez, a distinguished Portuguese physician of Jewish descent who was convicted of trying to poison Queen Elizabeth I. One further manifestation of these anti-Jewish feelings was the production in London of plays containing crude medieval stereotypes of the Jew — including Marlowe's *The Jew of Malta* and Shakespeare's *The Merchant of Venice*.[49] At the beginning of the seventeenth century Jews were regularly numbered alongside 'dogs', 'Turks', 'brute beasts' and 'filthy villains' in religious polemic.[50]

Given this unpromising background, it is surprising to find a movement early in the next century for the readmission of the Jews to England. As early as 1614 individual Englishmen began proposing that the Jews be allowed back into England.[51] The first such proposals, which emanated from Baptist circles, may have been prompted in part at least by a more general interest in toleration as well as by an interest in biblical prophecy. By the 1640s when this movement was gaining some momentum, and when the country was suffering under the upheavals of the Civil War, it could be boldly suggested that the

---

[48] Robert Healey, *Jew*, 63–79.
[49] for a more positive appraisal of *The Merchant of Venice* see Brett Usher in Wood, *Christianity*, 279–298.
[50] Katz, *Philosemitism*, 163.
[51] for more detail on these proposals see Toon, *Puritans*, 116–7. Even earlier in 1607 Sir Thomas Sherley had sent to King James I a project for the admission of Jews to Ireland — Katz, *Philosemitism*, 163–5.

country was suffering God's judgment for its previous cruelty and indifference toward the Jews. Whether deliberately or not, these philo-Semites were appealing to God's judgment in a way similar to Beza. They were not content to confine God's wrath, as Luther had done, to those who tolerated the contamination and blasphemy of the Jews. God's anger might equally fall on those who showed unjustified cruelty to his ancient people whom he had not entirely cast off.

Those who pleaded for Jewish readmission were not only content to dispel old prejudices. Positive considerations were also advanced. Notably, it was argued that if the Jews were allowed back into Britain, there they would encounter some of the best gospel preaching and some of the godliest men on earth. Their conversion to Christ would be hastened with a resulting golden age for the church.[52] To these were added more pragmatic arguments like the potential economic contribution to the wealth of England from Jewish merchants.[53]

Hopes for the readmission of the Jews were raised in the winter of 1648/9 when proposals for a new constitution were being drawn up.[54] In their final form, however, these proposals proved a disappointment; toleration was reserved for those who professed 'faith in God by Jesus Christ'. The agitation, however, for the readmission of the Jews continued with the support of no less a person than Oliver Cromwell. As part of a concerted campaign, an Amsterdam Rabbi and scholar, Menasseh ben Israel, was invited over in 1655 as the personal guest of Cromwell.[55] From Menasseh's viewpoint this provided the ideal platform both by word and by pamphlet to argue the case for further Jewish Dispersion and so readmission to England. His visit, however, with the attendant publicity, served mainly to stir up opposition from a motley group of people, including the gifted but vitriolic pamphleteer William Prynne, who wrote an influential tract *A Short Demurrer to the Jewes long-discontinued Remitter in England*. From this it emerged that Prynne was one of a number within the wider Puritan circle who were sceptical about a future mass conversion of the Jews and adopted Calvin's interpretation that 'Israel' in Rom. 11:25f. referred to the whole New Testament church of gentile and Jew. Not all the means

---

[52] Toon, *Puritans*, 117. This seems to have corresponded to Cromwell's mature view on the subject — Katz, *Philosemitism*, 224.

[53] Katz, *Philosemitism*, 189 summarizes the various motives which were operative at this time.

[54] for more detail on what follows see Toon, *Puritans*, 116–125.

[55] Katz, *Philosemitism*, 190–231.

used to discredit the readmission policy were so carefully argued. Many wild rumours were circulated, including one to the effect that the Jews were to be given two synagogues in London, of which St Paul's was to be one.[56] Thus, the readmission movement foundered for lack of popular goodwill.[57] It was too easy for traditional suspicions of the Jews and their religion to be reawakened. Besides, some were afraid that far from helping English mercantile interests, the Jews would actually enrich themselves at the expense of their English counterparts.

Curiously, by private and personal action Cromwell was able to secure on a small scale what he had failed to do by encouraging a public debate.[58] Shortly afterwards, war between England and Spain confronted Marranos then resident in England with a choice. They could continue as Christians of Spanish nationality and so fall into the category of resident aliens or else take the opportunity to declare that they were really Jews. They chose the latter course and threw themselves on the mercy of Cromwell as Lord Protector. They petitioned him for the right to establish a synagogue and cemetery and to live in London, unmolested, as Jews. Cromwell allowed their request, giving privileges which were to be reaffirmed by the government of Charles II.[59]

The Jewish community in England may have had these unlikely beginnings and may for a long time have remained a very small group, but the very fact that a community could be established at all represented a decisive change from attitudes at the end of the sixteenth century.[60] Menasseh ben Israel painted an over-optimistic picture of English attitudes when he wrote to representatives of European Jewry shortly before his trip to England — 'I have been informed by letter, and by faithful correspondents that today this English nation is no longer our ancient enemy, but has changed the papisticall religion and become excellently affected to our nation.'[61] The last sentiments did not apply to the whole nation but at least they did apply to a significant group among English Puritans. Per-

---

[56] Poliakov, *History*, 1:206.
[57] Healey, 'Jew', 77–8.
[58] Katz, *Philosemitism*, 235–8.
[59] This sort of informal toleration was found elsewhere in Europe — David S. Katz in Wood, *Christianity*, 335 points out that it was Cromwell's original device of admitting the Jews to England by a public conference that was 'eccentric in the extreme.'.
[60] Healey has some useful remarks about Jewish numbers in Britain — 'Jew' 78.
[61] quoted in Toon, *Puritans*, 122.

haps some indication of the change these Puritan writers and preachers sought to produce emerges from these remarks of Edward Elton, who directly challenged undercurrents of anti-Semitism. He contended that Christians ought

> not to hate the Jews (as many do) only because they are Jews, which name among many is so odious that they think they cannot call a man worse than to call him a Jew; but, beloved, this ought not to be so, for we are bound to love and to honour the Jews, as being the ancient people of God, to wish them well, and to be in earnest in prayer for their conversion.[62]

In Menasseh's own adopted country of the Netherlands the seventeenth century also saw significant improvements for the Jews, considering that the sixteenth century had seen Jews virtually disappear from the country.[63] By 1605 three Dutch towns had granted Jews charters with limited privileges. Beginning in 1619 the various provinces of the Netherlands allowed each city to adopt its own policy toward the Jews. A paper given in that year by the distinguished jurist Hugo Grotius to the States-General had proposed various restrictions on the Jewish community along largely medieval papal lines; but lack of agreement among the component provinces meant in effect that more tolerant policies were able to take root.[64] Even so, it was a remarkable and generous decision of the United Netherlands in 1657 to insist that their Jews abroad be recognized as citizens of the state, a measure which would never be repealed.[65] Undoubtedly, Jews benefited from a general climate of toleration which encouraged religious sects and inspirations of every sort to flock for refuge to the Netherlands. Thus, Amsterdam came to have the largest Marrano community in Europe numbering around 4,000 in 1700.[66] The inspiration for such toleration was varied; political and mercantile interests played their part alongside religious concerns. John McManners has written, 'In this least homogeneous state of Europe, which so soon had to fight for existence against the

---

[62] Edward Elton, *The Great Mystery of Godliness Opened, Being an Exposition upon Romans 9* (1653) 36.
[63] Healey, 'Jew', 64.
[64] Edwards, *TJICE*, 102–3 gives further details. The only exceptions which Grotius allowed to papal policy were the lack of insistence on distinctive Jewish ghettos, and the permission for Jews to be employed as shopkeepers and artisans on the same basis as the majority population.
[65] Oberman, *Roots*, 141.
[66] Healey, 'Jew', 78.

territorial ambitions of Louis XIV of France, ideological quarrels were too dangerous a luxury, while booming trade brought all classes into a co-operative venture in prosperity.'[67]

The Dutch Reformed churches soon reacted to the new Jewish presence. Their first response was traditional and largely negative. At the national synod of Dort (1618–9), a petition was made to the States-General that they pay attention to 'Jewish blasphemies' and they seek means to convert the Jews.[68] Initially regional synods stressed the more negative or coercive aspects of this programme; such was in keeping with the prevailing theocratic ideal which made the official Reformed church intolerant of the 'boldness' of Roman Catholics, Mennonites, Arminians and Jews alike. But the second part of the century saw an increasingly positive tone, with more concern to discuss spiritual means to attract the Jews and the necessary steps to remove obstacles which might prevent Jews coming to faith in Christ. Such a preoccupation tallies well with the consensus among Dutch Reformed theologians on a future conversion of the Jews.[69] It also shows that this theological concern was not motivated simply by a desire to establish or hasten some prophetic scheme.

In fact, these Dutch theologians cross-fertilized with the English Puritans, and revealed many of the same divergencies of opinion over whether the Jews would return to their homeland and what meaning was to be attached to the millennium. The one major difference was the detailed treatment in some writers of the means whereby the Jews were to be converted. But this difference was only to be expected since Jews were resident in the Netherlands and not in England.

This, however, did not necessarily imply close links between church and synagogue in the Netherlands. A stigma was attached to those Christians whose conduct or ideas were thought to have brought them into close contact with Jews. Thus, one Dutch theologian called Pierre Jurieu, who took a high view of the Jews and believed with Joseph Mede that the Jews would be supernaturally converted and then share with Christ in a millennial reign over the nations of the earth, received a letter ostensibly from some Amsterdam Rabbis, inviting him to join their synagogue. But the letter was not genuine; it had been penned by

---

[67] ed. John McManners, *The Oxford Illustrated History of Christianity* (Oxford, 1990) 269.

[68] Toon, *Puritans*, 138.

[69] for some exceptions to this consensus see P. T. van Rooden in van den Berg and van der Wall, *Relations*, 61.

one of his opponents in an attempt to discredit him because of his Jewish sympathies.[70]

Even more significantly, the most prominent Dutch philo-Semite, Petrus Serrarius, had to operate outside the main churches.[71] Though at one time a probationer in the Reformed Church, he had been deposed in 1628, presumably because of his mystical leanings. He aligned himself with an informal millenarian group which enjoyed many English contacts. These engaged not only in literary and scholarly endeavours to further understanding between Jews and Christians, but in practical charity toward Jews. Notably, they organized a collection which was sent to destitute Jews in Palestine. Many people in Amsterdam, however, took offence at the 'religious as well as civil intercourse' of Serrarius with the Jews.[72] Evidently an interest in the conversion of the Jews among many Dutch theologians co-existed with a certain tension or reserve about relations at a practical level. On the other side of the divide, Menasseh ben Israel experienced many difficulties with the synagogue hierarchy in Amsterdam because of his friendship with certain Christians.[73] Given the hostility generally between Christianity and Judaism over many centuries, it is hardly surprising that even in the relatively tolerant world of the Netherlands in the latter half of the seventeenth century we should find a considerable gulf between the world of the synagogue and that of the church.

In this context the rather isolated stance of Samuel Maresius proved perceptive.[74] Though in many respects a traditional Reformed theologian, he tried to play down the expectation of mass conversions in a plea for missionary effort among the Jews. While not rejecting this prospect entirely, he thought that only individual conversions were to be expected in his day. His ideas serve as a reminder that intense eschatological convictions, especially about the nearness of some sudden change, can in their own subtle way serve as a disincentive to careful, sustained missionary effort.

In retrospect, I would suggest that both in England and in the Netherlands there was probably too much concentration on the detail of prophetic schemes. It is one thing to have an optimistic view of the

---

[70] *ibid.*, 151–2.
[71] see Ernestine G.E. van der Wall's article in van den Berg and van der Wall, *Relations*, 73–94.
[72] *ibid.*, 152–3.
[73] R.H. Popkin in van den Berg and van der Wall, *Relations*, 11–12.
[74] *ibid.*, 140.

church's future; quite another to tie that optimism to recent or forth-coming events in church or even secular history more generally. But this is not to say that interest in the Jews was purely academic. It was the genuine fruit of a desire to do justice to the whole of Scripture, and inevitably it altered attitudes toward the Jews. The friendship and charity of Serrarius and his circle toward the Jewish community were revolutionary. Though heavily criticized at the time, they did not pass unnoticed.

Probably the greatest contribution of the Reformed tradition was to question the longstanding suspicion which surrounded both the presence of Jews in a Christian society and the conversion of individual Jews. No doubt, John Edwards has a point in his contention that on the whole popular gentile opinion remained unimpressed about the Jews.[75] But I would also endorse Healey's observation that there is a marked contrast with Spain and Portugal and their dominions where the suspicion about the authen-ticity of Jewish conversions and the persistent influence of Judaism was such that the Inquisition continued on its relentless way right into the nineteenth century.[76] Reformed theology, by contrast, provided a ration-ale for the church to look with confidence at present and future Jewish conversions as an enrichment of the church. Even where Jews did not convert immediately (and that was true of the vast majority), their presence was not felt to constitute any threat to the church or society. Did not the very Jewish Scriptures, which were shared by the church, promise a blessing on those who showed special regard to the resident alien? And conversely, was not divine judgment threatened against those who with-held kind regard from the alien?

Conclusion

It would be foolish to deny there were weaknesses in the attitudes of Reformed Churches towards the Jews. Sometimes interest was attached to prophetic schemes whose very detail would prompt the ruin of the whole fabric if a few threads appeared to be out of place. In particular, some hopes of an imminent mass conversion among the Jews proved unfounded. Moreover, these prophetic schemes did not of themselves encourage missionary endeavour among the Jews or even efforts to understand Jewish beliefs and practices.

---

[75] Edwards, *TCIJE*, 175.
[76] Healey, 'Jew', 77.

Perhaps too Léon Poliakov is right to hint that one reason why philo-Semitism took root in countries where Reformed religion flourished was the lack of indigenous Jews.[77] He might have added that in the Netherlands, where pluralism considerably anticipated developments elsewhere in Europe, Jews profited from a climate of toleration which owed more to political and economic than to religious factors.

But in spite of these caveats, the Reformed tradition profoundly differed from the later Luther at this point. No longer were the Jews placed in the category of exceptional sinners. Nor had God broken his covenant with them because of their unbelief. Their conversion was to be sought by spiritual means. Talk of a 'rigorous mercy' was forgotten. And where Reformed religion remained strong, with its insistence that the faithlessness of man cannot annul the faithfulness of God to his own covenant, there persisted a lively interest in the spiritual fate of the Jewish people.

---

[77]　Poliakov, *History*, 1:205.

Nine

From the Reformation to the French Revolution

Doubt about the Jews as a chosen people

In the Netherlands from the middle to the end of the seventeenth century the Jews flourished commercially and culturally amid the remarkably tolerant conditions for that time. Interestingly, it was to be in this open climate that the most serious challenge was to be made to the concept of the Jewish people as the Israel of God, the holy people set apart for God's own purposes from the rest of mankind.[1] This challenge derived not from outsiders but from an insider, Spinoza.

'In the dawn of the modern era the titanic figure of Baruch Spinoza dominates the horizon of Western Jewry.' Such is the claim of one Jewish scholar.[2] Spinoza was a man ahead of his time. He fell foul of the synagogue authorities in Amsterdam, where he had grown up, and was excommunicated in 1656.[3] He was also seen as a sinister threat by most mainline Christians. In fact, he was dubbed an atheist in many quarters, though he resented such a description of himself.[4] Essentially he brought a rationalist approach to Scripture, dismissing the supernatural elements in religion and reducing the concept of divine revelation to a bare minimum. But perhaps he was influenced most by his aversion to religious

---

[1] for the adjustment to the traditional view of Israel see Neusner, *Judaism*, 2.

[2] Agus, *Meaning*, 2:3–5

[3] Spinoza's parents were descendants of Portuguese Marranos, Jews from the Iberian Peninsula who had made an outward profession of Catholicism under pressure from the Spanish Inquisition but had continued secretly to observe Jewish rites. In the relatively free atmosphere of Amsterdam they were able to observe Judaism unhindered — Brad S. Gregory in the introduction to Baruch Spinoza, *Tractatus Theologico-Politicus* (E. J. Brill, Leiden 1989) 2–3. Agus, *Meaning*, 2:315–6 plays down the significance of the ban.

[4] Gregory (note 3) 25–30.

exclusivism, whether of the sort which would enforce its own brand of orthodoxy on others or of the rather different type which would take a perverse pride simply in being more blessed and fortunate than others.

This led Spinoza to challenge the Jewish claim to be the chosen people of God in anything but a limited sense, notably 'by reason of its social organisation and the good fortune whereby it achieved supremacy and retained it for so many years'.[5] That part of the law which was revealed uniquely to Moses and not to other nations applied to the Hebrew state alone. It was, therefore, relevant only to the Hebrews, and not even to them except when their state was an independent entity. At the same time Spinoza was adamant that Israel's election had nothing to do with its understanding or supposed spiritual qualities.[6]

God, he argued, was no more and no less committed to the Hebrews than to the Canaanites of old. They were chosen neither absolutely nor eternally.[7] Spinoza did leave open the possibility that the Jews might one day re-establish their own state where these laws might have a renewed significance.[8] But this had little to do with a special providence of God. In fact, Spinoza's main concern was to argue that the special Jewish laws and ceremonies had no meaning for his day. Their persistence blocked and imprisoned Jewish minds. In the Diaspora the Jews should pursue, along with the gentiles, those morals which corresponded with the universally recognized laws of the universe, which in Spinoza's mind were the same as the laws of God. The Jews should not claim to be more privileged than other nations.

Spinoza was certainly no anti-Semite, but he may be classed as a Jew who opposed Judaism.[9] His critical views derived in part from a liberal wing within the Jewish community and perhaps even more from certain figures on the margins of the Christian church who put forth ideas critical of the inerrancy of Scripture.[10] Moreover, Spinoza was bitterly opposed to intolerance, especially on the part of the state. Yet Spinoza

---

[5] Spinoza (note 3) 91–94.
[6] Here Spinoza was combating the view held by the synagogue leaders in Amsterdam — cf. Y. Kaphlan in (ed.) C. De Deugd, *Spinoza's Political and Theological Thought* (North-Holland Publishing Company, Amsterdam/Oxford/New York 1984) 89–92.
[7] Spinoza (note 3) 98–99.
[8] *ibid.*, 100.
[9] Even after his expulsion from the synagogue Spinoza felt no qualms about describing himself as a 'Hebrew'.
[10] for further details see Gregory (note 3) 32–36. It remains true, however, that Spinoza was echoing criticisms already made in Jewish circles in Amsterdam.

did in the longer term give some leverage to anti-Semitic ideas when he questioned Jewish credentials as a chosen race and offered his own alternative interpretation why the Jews had persisted so long as a distinct group with their own peculiar rites.[11] His explanation was far from flattering. Their persistence was hardly surprising 'since they have separated themselves from other nations to such a degree as to incur the hatred of all, and this not only through external rites alien to the rites of other nations but also through the mark of circumcision, which they most religiously observe.'[12] As if this was not enough, he proceeded to assert that the discipline of observing their ceremonies made it second nature for them to hate other nations.

> For their daily worship was not merely quite different . . . but also utterly opposed to others. Hence this daily invective, as it were, was bound to engender a lasting hatred of a most deep-rooted kind, since it was a hatred that had its source in strong devotion or piety and was believed to be a religious duty — for that is the bitterest and most persistent of all kinds of hatred. And this was reinforced by the universal cause of the continuous growth of hatred, to wit, the reciprocation of hatred; for the other nations inevitably held them in bitter hatred in return.[13]

Some of Spinoza's observations were hardly new; they reflect, consciously or otherwise, the criticisms of Tacitus. But his interpretation was novel in that he made the Jewish religion and ceremonies the source of Jewish perversity. This was effectively to invert the position of Tacitus, who had suggested that it was because the Jews were perverse that they had practices different from those of other nations. With Spinoza, on the other hand, their perversity resulted from the practices. In other words, he showed an awareness, unusual for his day, of sociological factors in the determination of the Jewish character and outlook. Perhaps he exaggerated these factors, and was not challenged at an academic level because of the novelty of his explanation. Certainly, others would soon recognize its attractions.

Though Spinoza's critical and selective approach to the Scriptures in theory affected Christianity as well as Judaism, his most immediate legacy concerned his highly negative concept of Judaism and of the Jews who continued to observe it.[14] This proved a potent image because it was in tune with the sort of rationalist thinking that was soon to come

---

[11] Poliakov, *History*, 2:277–8.
[12] Spinoza (note 3) 99.
[13] *ibid.*, 264.
[14] Israel, *European*, 219 points out that almost the entire output of the European Enlightenment was affected by this concept of Judaism.

of age.[15] This no longer looked to stories of ritual murder or the desecration of the host, which had something of a medieval and so outmoded ring to them, but to criteria of rationality, including sociological observation. Spinoza made the telling point that religious standpoints are more often dictated by considerations of power or of tradition than of truth.[16] He thus paved the way for a powerful picture of the Jews as a body of religious zealots locked into the observance of inappropriate and enervating religious ceremonies. It was an influential image because it was propagated at a time when men were disillusioned by the fruits of intense religious controversy. It was an image which could appeal to many Christians because superficially it resembled the criticisms of the Apostle Paul (and of others in the early church). It was also an image which could attract sceptics and outsiders who were presented with a way of demythologizing Judaism and so (if they desired) of attacking the Jews on a non-religious basis. No less a figure than Adolf Hitler was profiting from this legacy when he could argue that Judaism was not an authentic religion but simply a front for Jewish collective identity. Wherever the Jews' special vocation from God is rejected, it is inevitable that some other explanation be given of their distinctiveness. More often than not this will take a sociological form, and that in turn will commonly be unfavourable. Hitler's view that the Jews always stirred up hatred wherever they went and could never be assimilated to the native population was simply an extreme version of this approach.

Clearly, it does not follow that if the Jews are freed from religious criticisms like spiritual blindness, unbelief, deicide or whatever, they will be immune from odium in wider society. The fact of their distinctiveness remains. And some atheists have devised as sinister explanations for this as those medieval Christians who sought to identify a special bond between the devil and the Jews. Indeed, it is arguable that where the religious vocation of the Jewish people is denied, then the Jews are liable to a worse fate at the hands of their enemies than before. For in a religious setting the enemies of the Jews, in theory at least, are restrained by the thought of God's ultimate judgment to which the Jews as God's special people are liable first and to which all other peoples are then accountable. But where the Jews are considered to have no

---

[15]   *ibid.*, 217–8 observes that in 1678 the French edition of Spinoza's *Tractatus Theologico-Politicus* was greeted with enthusiasm 'though it was not considered decent to express approval openly.'

[16]   Edwards, *TJICE*, 166.

genuine religious distinction from other nations their enemies may assume greater freedom in dealing with them.

Doubts about the messianic hope

During Spinoza's life another vital element in traditional Judaism received a body-blow. In reacting to the challenge of Christianity, Jews had disclaimed the right of Jesus of Nazareth to be considered their Messiah. But they had not given up their messianic hope. Indeed, this hope encouraged the people to persist in Rabbinic Judaism, because they were taught that it was only when they had kept God's will as revealed in the Torah (and interpreted by their own experts) that the Messiah would come.[17] The upheavals to which many Jewish communities had been subject from the late fifteenth and sixteenth centuries gave some colour to the idea that the Messiah must be at hand to relieve the Jews of their sufferings.

A Jew from Smyrna, Sabbatai Sevi (1626–1676), proclaimed himself to be Messiah in May 1665. Despite scepticism among certain Rabbis, Sabbatai's claims were relayed throughout the Jewish Diaspora, along with a call for individual repentance and inner renewal as the vital preparation for the salvation the Messiah would bring.[18] Very soon, it was claimed, Sabbatai would take the Sultan's crown, bring back the lost tribes, and inaugurate the period of messianic redemption.

These claims were met with acclaim and with progressively greater excitement among the Jewish communities everywhere, though a minority remained adamantly antagonistic.[19] The majority were bolstered in their belief by stories of prophecies, visions and miracles from this Messiah. He proved to be the most influential messianic claimant since the first two centuries of the Christian era. But the high expectations were shattered almost as suddenly as they had been aroused. In September 1666 Sabbatai was summoned before the Sultan in Istanbul where he was given the choice of being tortured to death or of converting to Islam. He chose the latter. Though he continued to practise his mystic brand of Judaism under a Muslim exterior and retained certain disciples, most Jews were understandably disillusioned.[20] Some converted to Christianity, more out of disenchantment with Judaism than

---

[17]   Neusner, *Judaism*, 10–11.
[18]   for detailed background on Sabbatai's career see Scholem, *Sevi*, 103–223.
[19]   *ibid.*, 461–76.
[20]   *ibid.*, 695–9.

out of genuine conviction. Others retained their attachment to the Jewish community but became less observant about their religion — a trend which Sabbatai had encouraged himself by his claims to set aside traditional Jewish rules.[21] These Jews were now more inclined to embrace the practices of the society around them.

Thus, the dashing of the hopes surrounding Sabbatai damaged Jewish communal life.[22] The divisions which the movement had opened up in the Jewish communities were never fully healed. Ironically, the messianism of Sabbatai and the rationalism of Spinoza, seemingly at opposite poles of the religious spectrum, had combined to undermine traditional Judaism and thereby to remove one vital prop for Jewish distinctiveness.[23] Thus, by 1700 the Jewish communities had seen the removal of some of the strongest spiritual barriers to their integration into wider society.

Toward the eighteenth century — signs of a new era

The freedom allowed to the Jews in Amsterdam in the latter part of the seventeenth century did not go unnoticed and uncriticized in the wider Christian world. A great furore was raised by a voluminous work *Entdecktes Judenthum* (Judaism Unmasked) of Johann Andreas Eisenmenger (1654–1704). Eisenmenger was Professor of Hebrew at Heidelberg who had been dismayed on a visit to Amsterdam (in 1680–1) by the freedom the local Jews had to follow their own religion, to set up lavish synagogues and even to attack Christianity.[24] Eisenmenger believed that the best way to defend Christianity was to amass all the charges of medieval Christendom against Jews — including ritual murder, well-poisoning, and the evil and blasphemous nature of the Talmud. To achieve this, Eisenmenger quoted the Talmud out of context and sometimes mistranslated it. His work was 'the culmination of medieval anti-Judaism in its "learned" form'.[25] This is clear evidence that after almost two centuries of religious upheaval engendered by the Reformation anti-Jewish feeling remained powerful (though not all-powerful) among the more learned as well as the unlearned in society.

---

[21] Poliakov, *History*, 3:261–2.
[22] Israel, *European*, 254.
[23] The messianic hope in Judaism persisted. Much greater damage was done to it through the later process of emancipation — Kochan, *The Jew*, 59–68.
[24] Israel, *European*, 234–5
[25] Edwards, *TJICE*, 169.

A similar picture had emerged in England in the public debate initiated by Oliver Cromwell in 1655 over the readmission of the Jews.

Yet it would be wrong to see the situation as reverting to the medieval pattern. The Jews felt confident enough to take vigorous, political action. They believed they had the means to stop the distribution of Eisenmenger's book. By enlisting the support of a leading 'Court-Jew', Samson Wertheimer, and various German princes they were able to win the support of the Emperor Leopold. Eventually the book was only published after Eisenmenger's death by permission of the King of Prussia; but when it finally appeared, the title-page of the book wrongly gave Koenigsberg (which was outside the jurisdiction of the Empire) as the place of publication. The Emperors retained their ban on the work since it was 'prejudicial to the public and to the Christian religion, and especially to the unlearned'. Interestingly, they did not appeal to considerations of justice or toleration. They maintained that the well-being of the Christian religion was affected by the popular picture of Judaism. Perhaps they sensed that in the new climate of the eighteenth century traditional Christian smears on Judaism would merge with the rather different attacks of Spinoza and others with the result that Christianity would be discredited alongside Judaism.

Although old Christian objections to the Jews would retain some impact right up to the nineteenth century, especially in countries influenced by the Counter-Reformation, they were no longer accepted as a matter of course.[26] At the beginning of the eighteenth century Christian theologians were finding themselves on the defensive in many areas. The controversy over Eisenmenger's work thus marked the passing of an era, at least as far as Christian anti-Semitism was concerned. Sadly, it did not mark an end to Christian anti-Semitism as such. But this had to find new support in modern 'rationalistic' ideas if it was to make a serious impression on wider society.

The Enlightenment and emancipation

The eighteenth century in Europe is generally known as the period of the Enlightenment. It has often been considered a time of prosperity for the Jews which paved the way for their emancipation in many countries in the next century. The detailed study, however, of

---

[26]   *ibid.*, 176.

Jonathan Israel has revealed that this picture is highly misleading. This century in fact saw stagnation and decline across the various Jewish communities not only in economic and demographic terms but even more significantly in cultural life.[27] The cause was the mindset of the Enlightenment, by which Jewish learning and observance were dismissed as obsolete and superstitious. Every acceptable idea and practice had now to conform to the criterion of reason. This was in marked contrast to the seventeenth century which had seen from the time of Scaliger a flourishing philo-Semitic scholarship, at least among certain Protestants.

The dismissive attitude to Jewish learning, which became virtually uniform among European intellectuals in the eighteenth century, filtered through to the ordinary western Jew. Spinoza had left a lasting legacy.[28] The shattering of messianic hopes with Sabbatai Sevi also left Jewish religion at a low ebb; Jewish minds now tended to look for an improved future by integrating into the society around them rather than by looking for a Saviour from outside. Such messianic hopes as persisted in Jewish sectarian groups were reserved for a mystical realm where they would no longer impinge on outward, political circumstances.[29]

Jews became increasingly estranged from their own Rabbis and their own traditions of wisdom. If now the accepted wisdom of the Enlightenment, and later of the French Revolution, found barriers to progress in Jewish tradition and Jewish separateness, many Jews were inclined to agree. It would, however, be wrong to suggest that Jews flung overboard all their traditions. For whatever reason, perhaps force of habit more than anything else, they did retain some distinctive practices. Thus, Ashkenazai middle-class Jews frequently combined a loyal adherence to Jewish dietary and ritual observance with a sarcastic contempt for Rabbis and traditional Jewish learning.[30] The Jew who perhaps more than anyone combined Jewish learning with immersion in Enlightenment culture, the German, Moses Mendelssohn (1729–1786), did follow the essentials of Judaism in his personal life.[31] Yet, at the same time he contended that

---

[27] Israel, *European*, 237–251.
[28] Poliakov, *History*, 3:59–69 outlines the influence of the English deists on the changing climate of opinion toward Jews, the Old Testament and the whole of Jewish religion.
[29] cf. the comments of Scholem, *Sevi*, 792–802.
[30] Israel, *European*, 249.
[31] *ibid.*, 253.

there was no distinctive dogma in the Jewish religion. Such dogma as there was could be recognized by anyone on the basis of reason.[32] But the Jews had been given a distinctive legal code in order to fulfil their priestly calling before all the nations of the world. Thus, while Mendelssohn wanted to take his fellow-Jews out of a ghetto mentality and into the mainstream of cultural life, he did not see this as inconsistent with traditional Jewish observance — 'Adopt the mores and constitution of the country in which you find yourself, but be steadfast in upholding the religion of your fathers too . . . I cannot see how those who were born into the household of Jacob can in good conscience exempt themselves from the observance of the law.'[33]

Mendelssohn and a group of Prussian followers called the Haskalah formed what was in effect a sort of Jewish Enlightenment. They not only constituted a think-tank; they were primarily an active group who aimed to open up to the Jews patterns of thought in wider society. Thus, they translated the Pentateuch into German so that Jews would be better able to learn the language in the country where they lived. They also produced a commentary on Scripture to which they brought some of the principles of secular thought. They established Jewish schools at which a much broader curriculum was set forth than had traditionally been the case for Jews.[34] However, if Mendelssohn had aimed first and foremost to preserve a form of traditional Judaism consistent with Enlightenment thought, he largely failed. Shortly after his own death, among his own family and friends, there was an inexorable drift into complete assimilation and conversion to Christianity.[35] After all, once the distinctively religious reasons for Judaism had been removed, what remained to stop a complete adoption of the beliefs and practices of the predominant group in society? But Mendelssohn and his followers were unusual in their commitment to the worlds of both Judaism and of the Enlightenment. Many other Jews had imbibed Enlightenment values and done little to resist those currents which were sweeping them away from Judaism.[36]

Most Jews welcomed the political and social emancipation they were given in most parts of Europe (apart from Russia) in the aftermath of the

---

[32] Isidore Epstein, *Judaism*, (Penguin, Harmondsworth 1959) 287–8.
[33] quoted by Cohn-Sherbok, *Heritage*, 135.
[34] for more detail see *ibid.*, 135–6.
[35] Cohn-Sherbok, *Crucified*, 136–7 gives some examples.
[36] Israel, *European*, 253–4.

French Revolution.[37] Its ideals of 'liberty, equality, fraternity' were applied to the Jews, who were included among the victims of the *ancien régime*. Indeed, most intellectuals of the Enlightenment had vented their anger on the vicious intolerance which had been shown to the Jews in Christian countries. This was more because of their hatred for religious intolerance than out of any admiration for Jews as such. Indeed, they tended to dislike both Jewish religion and Jewish distinctiveness. The influential Voltaire crystallized the mood of the anti-Jewish element in the Enlightenment, which proved to be predominant. In his *Dictionnaire Philosophique* he included thirty or more articles attacking Jews. The article 'Jew' is the longest in the *Dictionnaire* and concludes, 'You will find them an ignorant and barbarous people, who for a long time have combined the most sordid greed with the most detestable superstition and the most invincible hatred for all the peoples who tolerate and enrich them.'[38] Voltaire was ready to accept that the Jews had suffered as a result of the wickedness of Christian leaders, but the Jews were at heart no better — 'The only difference is that our priests have had you burned by laymen, and that your priests have always sacrificed human victims with their sacred hands.'[39] Toward the end of his life Voltaire would even take up the Christian cause, as he saw it, against the Jews.[40]

Without actually espousing racist ideology, Voltaire did take a step in that direction when he envisaged contemporary European culture as rigidly divided into a good and a bad element. The good derived from classical Greece and had been mediated through the Roman Empire. The Jewish or oriental strain provided a contrary evil influence. Voltaire saw it as the task of the Enlightenment to return Europe to the golden age of Graeco-Roman culture and philosophy.[41] Needless to say, his picture of classical antiquity was highly selective, as though the religion of the Greeks and Romans was governed by reason and as though there was nothing pernicious about the slavery which played a vital part in these civilizations. At the same time Voltaire gave prominence to anti-Semitic sentiments in classical literature — particularly

---

[37]   Revolutionary France was the first country to emancipate the Jews in 1791. For a useful European perspective on emancipation see Martin Gilbert, *The Dent Atlas of Jewish History*, (Dent, London 1993) 59.

[38]   The translation is that of Poliakov, *History*, 3:88. This was included in the 1769 edition of the *Dictionnaire*, but removed from later editions.

[39]   Poliakov, *History*, 3:88–89.

[40]   *ibid.*, 3:90.

[41]   Hertzberg, *French*, 299–308.

the charges of superstition and misanthropy. Like Tacitus he implied there was a link between their religion and their character. It was because of their own nature that they allowed themselves to be governed by antisocial laws, and in a cycle of wickedness their misanthropic tendencies were in turn increased by these laws. Voltaire went so far as to give this ominous prophecy — 'They are, all of them, born with raging fanaticism in their hearts, just as the Bretons and the Germans are born with blond hair. I would not in the least be surprised if these people would not some day become deadly to the human race.'[42] There are sinister echoes of later Nazi propaganda. Voltaire had deliberately redrafted the Roman Catholic view of the Jews as enemies of Christendom. In his revised perspective the Jews had become enemies of the whole human race. The remedy, however, for the problem had a familiar ring from the medieval period. Voltaire admired the Emperor Tiberius for expelling all Jewish and Egyptian cults, as well as all other foreign religions, from Rome. Society should act likewise in dealing with the Jewish contagion.

There were some Enlightenment writers like Montesquieu who did not share Voltaire's antipathy to everything Jewish and wanted to establish the right of Jews to be Jews, but they were the exception rather than the rule.[43] In the French Revolution the Jews were emancipated in order primarily that they might become good citizens of France. Emancipation was given on the understanding that the Jews would somehow be regenerated, though the precise terms of this regeneration were never spelt out. Thus, the emancipation was accompanied with this slogan, 'To the Jews as citizens, everything: to the Jews as a nation, nothing'. And the same would apply in principle to emancipation elsewhere in Europe around this time. As yet the idea of a multi-cultural society carried little attraction. On the contrary, the nineteenth century was to experience a vogue for nationalism. Any group that threatened the national identity by preserving its own practices would become suspect. The authors of the American Constitution did take a different line, and were happy to allow the Jews their own distinctive religion and practices provided they fulfilled their obligations under the civil code of the state. The more liberal American line has doubtless played

---

[42]   Voltaire *Oeuvres Complêtes* XXVIII:439–40 cited by Hertzberg, *French*, 300.
[43]   Hertzberg, *French*, 273–80.
[44]   *ibid.*, 364.
[45]   Metz contained the leading Jewish community in eastern France, with 2,000 Jews out of a total population of 30,000 — Hertzberg, *French*, 121–32.

its part in the happier Jewish experience in the USA than in Europe.[44]

The French concern to improve the Jews is evident from a competition organized by the Academy in Metz in 1785, when the emancipation of the Jews was already in the air.[45] Significantly, the theme was given as 'Are there ways of making the Jews happier and more useful in France?' Evidently it could be assumed that the Jews in their present predicament were neither happy nor useful.[46] In publishing its results, the Academy agreed with most of the ten treatises it received to the extent that they had cited prejudice against the Jews as the main cause of their vices, especially their dishonesty which was considered particularly nauseating. The hope was that if French society removed its prejudice and dealt honestly and justly with the Jews, the latter would also become fair in their dealings with outsiders. The Academy, however, was less satisfied that the contributors had grasped how difficult it would be to integrate the Jews into wider society. Among the problems foreseen by the Academy was 'the fear of seeing the Jews, whose population is growing with stupendous speed, forming inside the kingdom a nation which would always be foreign and which, after taking advantage of the freedom of the trades and professions to increase its assets, and from the freedom of purchase to sell its shares, would end up by invading almost all landed property.' Thus the Academy was cautious, even pessimistic, about the full integration of the Jews. Most intellectual elements were agreed about the desirability of such integration. Debate centred on how easily it would be achieved.[47] In effect, the emancipation of the Jews was seen as an exercise in social engineering. It was designed to facilitate and accelerate the process whereby Jews became Frenchmen; it was not intended to give them rights to preserve their distinctive Jewish way of life.

The ambiguities of emancipation

As it was, it took over two years of sometimes bitter controversy before 'the Declaration of the Rights of Man and the Citizen' passed by the new French Revolutionary government was applied to all Jews.[48] The key principle (Article X) which eventually benefited the Jews stated, 'No person shall be molested for his opinions even such as are religious,

---

[46]   Poliakov, *History*, 3:150–6.
[47]   Agus, *Meaning*, 2:328–9 collects some of the more sceptical comments made around this time.
[48]   On the debate see Muller, *History*, 25–47.

provided the manifestation of their opinions does not disturb the public order as established by the law.' The biggest obstacle in the public debate to the immediate emancipation of the Jews was the character of the Jewish religion. Was it simply a private opinion with few ramifications for the social or civic life of the Jews or was it a whole way of life which must impinge on their conduct in wider society? Put another way, were the Jews in a similar position to French Protestants, whose loyalty to France was unquestioned, or were they analogous to Englishmen being offered French citizenship without having to give up their Englishness?

A similar concern motivated Napoleon, who is popularly considered one of the greatest benefactors of the Jews in the modern era. Certainly, by his conquests Napoleon brought the influence of French Revolutionary ideas to many other parts of Europe, and this did benefit the Jews. But Napoleon himself had a contemptuous outlook on the Jews. For example, he described them as 'an objectionable people, chicken-hearted and cruel.' Léon Poliakov has suggested that if all his opinions on the Jews were placed end to end, they would provide the material for an anti-Semitic catechism.[49] He was concerned about the Jewish potential for evil in wider society, and ideally looked for the abolition of the Jewish race by dissolving it into the Christian race. But he was under no illusions as to the difficulty of the task.

In order to satisfy himself of the loyalty of the Jews, Napoleon summoned to Paris in 1806 a General Assembly of Jewish Notables and then in the following year a 'Great Sanhedrin' to give official backing to the assurances given by the General Assembly. Despite the grandiose names, this was not an attempt to stimulate independent Jewish life. One of Napoleon's own representatives at the General Assembly expressed the Emperor's wishes in these terms, 'It is His Majesty's wish that you become Frenchmen, and it is for you to decide whether you accept this title or to reflect that you renounce it if you do not make yourselves worthy of it.'[50] As a test of its 'worthiness' the Assembly had to answer twelve questions.[51] The first three questions concerned marriage and divorce, covering issues like the compatibility of Jewish marriage and divorce procedures with the civil laws of France and the permissibility of inter-marriage between Christians and Jews. The next set of questions dealt with whether

---

[49] Poliakov, *History*, 3:228.
[50] Muller, *History*, 64.
[51] for more detail see *ibid.*, 62–72.

French Jews considered French citizens their compatriots and whether they regarded France as their country. The final sets of questions dealt with the authority of the Rabbis (envisaged as possible rivals to the state authorities) and the Jewish attitude to usury (a longstanding bone of contention). The Jewish representatives gave unequivocal assurances on their patriotism and their obedience to French civil laws. Their answers on the marriage question were interesting. They affirmed that Jewish marriages and divorces were valid only if they were preceded by a civil ceremony. Whereas their religion discouraged inter-marriage, they agreed that no discipline should be exercised against any Jew who did inter-marry.

Both the General Assembly and the Great Sanhedrin took pains to assure Napoleon of their loyalty to France. The former even introduced each of their replies to the twelve questions with a preamble stating 'in the name of those Frenchmen who believe in the Mosaic religion'. The significance of this is plain from their insistence that the idea of a distinct Jewish nation was obsolete. Not only realism but even faithfulness to their religion now dictated that they should 'regard the law of the land as the law of Israel'.

However satisfactory these replies may have been to Napoleon, they did not represent the views of all the Jews in his domain.[52] In the first place care had been taken to ensure that both bodies were composed almost entirely of 'enlightened' and wealthy Jews who were understandably among the most enthusiastic about the prospect of assimilation. Besides, even from their hesitation about mixed marriages it should have been clear that while many Jews welcomed political integration, the time had not yet come for the disappearance of the Jewish religion. But this consideration was not given the weight it warranted. Napoleon, as with the Metz Academy before him, was anxious to foresee and guard against any political danger from the Jews. They overlooked the power of religion in retaining a distinct Jewish identity. No doubt they imagined that as the Jewish religion had become outmoded, it would in the course of time die out. They underestimated the inner potential of a religious tradition to adapt to changing circumstances. But the Jews in the main reacted to the slogan that they were to be given everything as men and nothing as Jews with a principle of their own — 'A Jew at home, a man outside.'[53] This entailed a more

---

[52] for the earlier reluctance of the Ashkenazai Jews to give up their communal organizations even if they were to be given new rights — Hertzberg, *French*, 344–7.
[53] Neusner, *Judaism*, 3.

privatized or even secularized view of Judaism than had been hitherto the practice. Moreover, it meant dispute among Jews themselves, notably between the Reform Jews, the Orthodox Jews and the Conservative Jews, as to the most appropriate way of adapting Judaism to the nineteenth century situation. But though this debate was often tense and agonizing to the participants, it did not spell the end to Judaism as a religious tradition (or traditions).[54] And that was an outcome which few of those in France who were responsible for the emancipation expected, still less wanted.

Even where Jews were anxious to distance themselves from their traditional religion, integration into gentile society proved problematic. As Arthur Hertzberg put it, 'This "new Jew" had been born into a society which asked him to keep proving he was worthy of belonging to it. Unfortunately, this "new Jew" was never quite told exactly what he had to prove and before which tribunal.'[55]

Thus, the seeds were sown for a new sort of anti-Semitism, different from the Christian anti-Semitism of the late Middle Ages or even the early Reformation period. If gentiles deemed the experiment in social engineering had failed and they discounted Jewish religion as the reason, then the only explanation must be something distinctive (or even perverse) in the character of the Jew. The ground was prepared for the racial theory of the latter part of the nineteenth century which ascribed to Jews an unalterable character. The upsurge, therefore, in anti-Semitism at that later date is in large measure a result of disappointed hopes in Jewish emancipation. Not only had the Jews remained a separate group; but they had seemingly taken disproportionate advantage of opportunities to advance themselves amid the social changes of the Industrial Revolution. Ironically, the Jews came to symbolize not an archaic, fossilized religion, but everything that people felt was wrong with modernity. If animosity was felt against newly powerful institutions in society like the press or the financial markets, they were said to be controlled by the Jews. If the target of popular outrage was the moral decline consequent on modernity, rampant materialism or secularism were traits of the Jew. The image of the Jew thus shows some flexibility, but one important feature remains constant — the Jew will not integrate with the rest of his fellow-countrymen.

---

[54] *ibid.*, 30–35.
[55] Hertzberg, *French*, 365–6.

The Enlightenment, therefore, proved a mixed blessing to the Jews. It did bring political emancipation, but at a price. It began to sever the Gordian knot which bound civic privileges to religious affiliation. But in their concept of the Jews as a useless and alien group in society, the Enlightenment leaders were propounding a secularized adaptation of the medieval picture of the Jews as a threat to Christendom. Medieval Christendom had wanted the Jews baptized (or failing that, expelled). Enlightened European society now desired the more intangible goal of the reformation or regeneration of the Jews. They had not stopped to consider what alternatives should be employed if the desired goal failed to materialize. The Enlightenment thus failed to remove hostility to the Jewish independent way of life; it had simply found a new rationale for it.

Many Enlightenment figures professed indignation about religious intolerance. They, however, were not entirely free of their own brand of intolerance.[56] They hoped to create their own society of *philosophes*, a society where people thought exactly like themselves. And the Jews were expected to become a full part of this new society. As one supporter of Jewish emancipation put it shortly before the emancipation was carried out in 1791, 'your mission is not to use men as you would find them but to make of them what you require them to be.'[57] The Jews would be welcomed into the new revolutionary society provided they imbibed its values and relinquished their traditional ways.

Anti-Semitism in its Christian form may have been marginalized by the Enlightenment, but at the same time new channels were created for its expression.

---

[56]   *ibid.*, 312–3.
[57]   quoted at *ibid.*, 363.

Ten

Modern European Anti-Semitism

A largely German phenomenon?

The late twentieth century is so inclined to associate anti-Semitism with Auschwitz and the Nazi Holocaust that it is easy to forget that modern anti-Semitism is not a purely German phenomenon. Indeed, toward the end of last century the origin of any Holocaust might have been more readily predicted for Russia or for France than for Germany. We must, therefore, not underestimate political developments in playing their part in the Holocaust alongside national ideologies and the general undercurrents of popular opinion.

In Germany by 1900 the Jews seemed secure. They had found a place within most major avenues of German society. In greater proportion to their own numbers they had contributed to and benefited from the outstanding material, political and intellectual successes of the Second Reich.[1] As a result the German Empire was a popular destination for Jewish émigrés from the less prosperous and politically more insecure states of Eastern Europe.[2] At this stage anti-Semitism had not established an extensive political foothold.[3]

France, by contrast, in the 1890s saw a great flurry of anti-Semitic activity triggered by the writings and agitation of Edouard Drumont, whose work *La France Juive* became a best seller after it was published in 1886. Drumont, whose anti-Semitism combined Catholic and racist motifs, was able to tap much anti-Republican feeling with his

---

[1] Graml, *Antisemitism*, 40–42.
[2] *ibid.*, 37.
[3] This was not so true of Hitler's native Austria (then centre of the Austro-Hungarian Empire) — Wistrich, *Anti-Semitism*, 61–5.

contention that since the Revolution of 1789 the Jews had seized power in France and systematically undermined French traditions and culture. Anti-Semitic agitation, closely linked as it was to disaffection with the French Republic, was to provoke a national crisis in the long-running Dreyfus saga. Captain Dreyfus, a Jew on the French General Staff, had in 1894 been sentenced to imprisonment for life in Cayenne, supposedly because he had sold military secrets to the Germans. The matter, however, did not rest there as it was suspected that the judgment of the military court had been clouded by anti-Semitic feelings. Leading intellectuals and politicians were brought into the debate on either side. Virtually the whole French nation was divided on the issue. At the height of the crisis in 1898 there were even small-scale anti-Semitic riots in most of the larger French towns, with the cry 'Death to the Jews' a popular slogan among those who hoped to overthrow the Republic. The crisis was resolved only in 1906 when a general election signalled the defeat of the anti-republicans and the way was open for Dreyfus to be completely rehabilitated and in fact elevated to the rank of major.[4]

French political anti-Semitism had been nipped in the bud. Though it was to remain an undercurrent in French life, anti-Semitism would never regain respectability, except briefly during the Nazi period.[5] Resolute and timely opposition had secured its defeat. But a different outcome to the political struggles of the 1890s might well have resulted in a very different future for French anti-Semitism.

It was remarkable that such widespread agitation over the Jews should have surfaced in France at this time when the Jewish population was comparatively small — around 80,000. By contrast, it is perhaps not surprising that Russia which had the largest Jewish population in the world numbering around five million, roughly a third of world Jewry, exhibited a great level of anti-Semitism. While the Jewish element amounted to just over four per cent of the whole Russian population, it was much more heavily represented in the area known as the Pale of Settlement, a group of provinces extending from the Baltic to the Black Sea and embracing much of what is now Poland. Here Jews lived in poverty, subject to severe economic and educational restrictions.[6]

The Jews were victims both of the sort of religious hatred characteristic of medieval Christendom and of that generated by fear of

---

[4]   *ibid.*, 127–8.
[5]   Graml, *Antisemitism*, 36.
[6]   Cohn, *Warrant*, 51–2.

outsiders.[7] The latter resulted from the fact that unlike in western Europe the Jews had had very little opportunity to assimilate to wider society in Russia. They lived separately from Russians, dressed differently and spoke and wrote in Yiddish in preference to Russian. The religious hatred was due to the influence of the Orthodox Church, whose authority was closely bound up with that of the Tsars. The last two Tsars (Alexander III and Nicholas II) followed a decidedly anti-Jewish policy — not only for religious reasons but most of all to divert attention from revolutionary movements among the Russian population. If the Jews could be blamed for this agitation, so much the better. Their anti-Jewish policies took the form of economic restrictions, which were designed to keep Jews from prominent positions in society but in fact encouraged many Jews to emigrate. Also, even if the Tsars did not directly organize pogroms, they did nothing to stop them and readily subsidized groups like the Union of the Russian People and the proto-fascist gangs of Black Hundreds which did make pogroms their business.[8] As a further indication that anti-Semitism was more deeply rooted in the political system in Russia than elsewhere, this was the only country at this time to give its official blessing to propaganda about Jewish world conspiracies.[9]

The bad fruits from such policy lingered on after the Bolshevik Revolution. For this revolution was followed by a period of over two years of civil war in which the counter-revolutionary forces known as the White Russians endeavoured to overthrow the Bolshevik regime. Many of these troops were nurtured on the myth that the Revolution was the result of a Jewish-Masonic Conspiracy and essentially the work of the Antichrist. Hence they massacred Jews indiscriminately, and are reckoned brutally to have killed approximately 100,000 of them, mainly in the Ukraine.[10] It is true that several Jews were involved in the Revolution, and the leader of the Bolshevik armies against the White Russians was a Jew — Leon Trotsky. But talk of a Jewish conspiracy was quite inappropriate. Those Jews who were involved were the most cosmopolitan and the least attached to their Jewish roots. Understandably, they saw in revolution a chance at last to get rid of the burdens which had been imposed on Jews in Russia for decades.[11]

---

[7] Wistrich, *Anti-Semitism*, 171–2.

[8] Cohn, *Warrant*, 110–3.

[9] Tsar Nicholas II, however, would not use *The Protocols of the Elders of Zion*, when it was shown to him that they were a forgery — Cohn, *Warrant*, 114–5.

[10] Cohn, *Warrant*, 117–125.

[11] Cohn, *Warrant*, 121–2 shows the limits of Jewish involvement with the Bolshevik cause.

Though the Jews experienced chequered fortunes under Stalin and his Communist successors, there can be no doubt that their treatment was infinitely preferable to what it would have been had the White Russians triumphed.[12] Once again, the practical outcome of anti-Semitism in society was closely linked to political events, including those with little direct connection to the Jews.

The roots of modern German anti-Semitism

It would be foolish to deny that in Germany there was not potential around 1900 for serious anti-Semitic developments. Germany had a long historical tradition of hostility to the Jews, going back to the Rhineland massacres at the time of the First Crusade. Though medieval Catholic hostility was not well represented in Germany as such, it did enjoy fertile soil in neighbouring Austria. Protestants, for their part, were a stronger force in Germany and could tap the polemics of the later Luther against the Jews.[13] Moreover, in the realm of political ideology Germans had not altogether welcomed the egalitarian philosophy of the French Revolution since it was associated with a period of French domination.[14] More recently, the political unification of Germany in 1871 had not solved the vexed question of German national identity.[15] The strident affirmations of nationalist philosophy in Germany in subsequent decades reflected the weakness, not the strength, of national unity. This was not good news for a group like the Jews who wished to maintain a distinct identity within Germany.

The German anti-Semitism which was to reach its nadir in Hitler's Reich was influenced by both anti-Christian and Christian sources.[16] The latter maintained the traditional objections that the Jews were spiritually blind and as such had forfeited their privileges as God's chosen people. As long as they remained Jews, they were unable to be full members of German society, which was essentially Christian. At the same time there were more radical opponents of the Jews who saw Christianity itself as one of the Jews' most unfortunate legacies to the German character. They emphasized racial considerations as para-

---

[12]   cf. Wistrich, *Anti-Semitism*, 174–191.

[13]   for the comparative strengths of Protestantism and Catholicism see Langmuir, *HRAS*, 325–8.

[14]   Graml, *Anti-Semitism*, 43.

[15]   Langmuir, *HRAS*, 216–7.

[16]   Tal, *Christians*, 223–289.

mount. Anything tainted with Jewish blood (Christianity included) was irredeemable. Thus, no Jew could ever be improved by baptism, they claimed, contrary to much traditional church teaching.

Although during the Second Reich (1870–1914) Christian anti-Semites were aware of this darker form of anti-Semitism and sometimes tried to warn against it, there was no hard and fast distinction between representatives of these two approaches.[17] Sometimes they would co-operate for political purposes. Moreover, both groups agreed on certain key observations. Traditional German character was being eroded by the presence and the power of the Jews, who were happy to achieve equal civil rights, but insisted that they would not lose their separate identity and be absorbed into German society. They preferred to retain a distinct religious character, even though that normally entailed a liberalized form of Judaism.[18] This was difficult for Christians to stomach who might otherwise have been disposed to follow the Apostle Paul in his belief in the future conversion of Israel. These Christians had to admit that far from the Jews embracing true Christianity, they were much more likely to contribute to the growth of atheistic materialism. Where the Jews did accept baptism, they did so generally in bad faith — more for social and professional advancement than for reasons of genuine conviction.[19] In practice, then, Christian anti-Semites inclined like their non-Christian counterparts to believe that nothing could be done to change the Jewish character.

Merging racial and religious anti-Semitism

Besides, race was not necessarily a concept confined to those anti-Semites with anti-Christian leanings. At a time shortly after German unification when national identity was important and when German identity was thought in many quarters to be essentially Christian, it is hardly surprising that attempts were made to blend racial theories with more traditional forms of Christianity. In the 1870s, for example, Otto Glagau had contrasted the Jews as a homeless tribe without a native country and so the embodiment of instability and alienation, with the Germans as a Christian Volk, a noble race that sought to be rooted in a stable Reich.[20] Because of their racial character there was nothing to

---

[17] *ibid.*, 223–234 and 301–5. For a fascinating example from this period of an attempt to delimit Christian from racial anti-Semitism see Agus, *Meaning*, 2:402.

[18] *ibid.*, 163–5.

[19] *ibid.*, 159.

[20] *ibid.*, 260–2.

be gained if the Jews changed their religion and became Christians. For they would retain their obnoxious racial traits, including their desire for mastery, their parasitical nature and their hereditary arrogance. Clearly, in Glagau's scheme race had become a leading concept but it was not used to attack Christianity.

Other, more sophisticated, attempts followed to form links between religious anti-Semitism and racial anti-Semitism. It was even contended that Jesus was not of Semitic or Jewish origin but an offspring of the Nordic Germans.[21] However incredible this hypothesis may appear to us, it was backed by claims (for example) that Galilee had an Aryan population since it had been settled by blond, blue-eyed immigrants fifteen hundred years before the birth of Jesus. In Jesus and the Jewish leaders the struggle between Aryan and Semitic blood had been enacted, and the former had triumphed. If such an interpretation seems light years away from the gospel texts, we must reckon that Protestantism had been recently faced with challenges to many of its traditional beliefs. 'In the long run, the result was a watering-down of dogma and theology to a point where the Protestant religion threatened to become nothing but a bundle of ethical rules, inspired not by divine authority but by social utility.'[22] In such a climate people from Protestant churches were open to new ideas, especially where these encouraged them to equate their traditional German way of life with authentic Christianity. In short, with a loss of their hold on the principle of the authority of *sola Scriptura* these churches ceased to have any effective rule by which to assess contemporary ideas and culture.

Thus, we find in the forefront of the anti-Semitic crusade a figure like Paul de Lagarde, a philological scholar, who sought radical changes in Christianity.[23] He felt that the traditional Protestantism of the Reformation lacked spiritual dynamic for his day. He proposed, therefore, a 'cleansed version of Christianity . . . appropriate for the German character'. By this he intended the removal of everything Jewish. 'Every Jew', he claimed, 'is proof of the enfeeblement of our national life and of the worthlessness of what we call the Christian religion.'[24] If the extinction of the German race were to be averted,

---

[21] e.g. by Max Bewer, a poet, publicist and an active member of the anti-intellectualist Rembrandt movement — *ibid.*, 276–9. Poliakov, *History*, 3:180–1 makes Johann Gottlieb Fichte (writing around 1808) the first protagonist of an Aryan Christ.
[22] Craig, *Germany*, 182–3.
[23] Gutteridge, *Open*, 19–21.
[24] quoted in Fritz Stern, *The Politics of Cultural Despair: A Study in the Rise of Germanic Ideology* (Berkeley and Los Angeles 1961) 61

Christianity would have to be swallowed up in Germanism. Nonetheless, he did retain a place for Jesus in his scheme of things, but this was simply a Jesus divorced from all his Jewish roots and whose claim to prominence rested upon his genius in the perception of eternal truths.

But perhaps the most influential of these highly modified versions of Christianity was advocated by the Englishman Houston Stewart Chamberlain, who imbibed German culture particularly in its Wagnerian form, settled in Germany and became a confidant of Kaiser Wilhelm II.[25] He was in his own way a deeply religious man, with conservative instincts and anxieties over secularist and materialist influences on German society. In his most important book, *Foundations of the Nineteenth Century*, Chamberlain announced, 'I see the danger for the future of the Teuton in the lack of a true religion springing from and appropriate to our nature.'[26] Though he was well read, not least in liberal Protestant scholarship, his concept of true religion was an individualistic and undogmatic Christianity. Like Lagarde, he looked for a second Reformation that would carry further the process of uncovering the gospel of Christ beneath layers of theological dogma. Above all, he considered that Christianity had to be understood within the categories of race. It was not a message of love for fallen humanity, but of national fervour and devotion to race. Moreover, religion could not ignore the existence of glaring racial inequalities, notably between the superior Aryan race (the embodiment of virtue and of every positive cultural influence) and the inferior Jewish race (the embodiment of degradation and of every negative cultural influence). His Jesus, therefore, could not be a Jew, but had presumably to be reckoned among the Aryans because he pre-eminently displayed their moral virtues.[27]

While Chamberlain did work with the moral categories of good and evil, his was a dangerous variation on the biblical theme, not least because the Aryan (in effect, the German) race was automatically guaranteed divine blessing. Every German was assured that he merited divine favour not because of Jesus' self-sacrifice but because of the pure Aryan blood that flowed in his veins. It was his responsibility to awaken to the realization of his true destiny in ruling the world. Such beliefs in

---

[25]   Tal, *Christians*, 280–9. There is an excellent work on Chamberlain's life, writings and legacy — Field, *Evangelist*. Teuton was Chamberlain's most common way of describing the Aryan race.

[26]   *Foundations* 2:390.

[27]   Chamberlain never stated in as many words that Christ was an Aryan. He was content to offer substantial hints in that direction — Field, *Evangelist*, 182–3.

the writings of a professed disciple of Christ did encourage many
brought up within the Christian tradition to think that such views were
valid, however far removed they may have been from the world of the
Bible. Indeed, they were more acceptable to the wider public than the
atheistic notions of Dühring precisely because Chamberlain reserved
his criticisms for contemporary Christian churches but did not attack
Christianity as such.[28] While certain aspects of the *Foundations* were
subjected to criticism in Germany, his anti-Semitic remarks were left
unquestioned, much to the alarm of the Jews.[29]

　　Chamberlain survived into the 1920's when he met the aspiring
Adolf Hitler, who regarded him as the sort of high priest of the racist
movement.[30] In turn, Chamberlain's recognition encouraged Hitler
with his sense of mission. It also gave a sort of Christian veneer to
Hitler's own movement. Though Hitler's own convictions were decidedly more anti-Christian, his instincts in the years of his rise to power
was to give priority to political over ideological considerations. He was
happy to use Christian sentiments in his early propaganda. Thus, in
Mein Kampf he could parade as a sort of *Christus militans* when he
wrote, 'By keeping the Jews at bay, I fight for the good Lord's way.'

Christian anti-Semitism

Some Christians who were well aware of the emerging racial bias in the
attacks against the Jews preferred to distance themselves from this
particular line of attack as sub-Christian and dangerous. The most
notable figure here was an eminent Lutheran, Adolf Stoecker, who
from 1874 held the position of Court and Cathedral Preacher in
Berlin.[31] With his reputation for orthodoxy and for his oratory, he has
been described as 'the greatest popular missionary of Germany'.[32]
While he kept politics scrupulously out of the pulpit, he was concerned
that Christianity should not be restricted to the private realm. Hence
his anxieties about atheistic and materialistic trends in wider German
society induced him to try to establish a political party of his own. His
political activity, however, met with little success until he started

[28] *ibid.*, 311–2.
[29] *ibid.*, 225–248.
[30] Graml, *Anti-Semitism*, 75.
[31] for Stoecker I am indebted to the accounts of Tal, *Christians*, 248–259 and of
Gutteridge, *Open*, 4–12.
[32] by Theodor Heuss as quoted in Craig, *Germany*, 152–3.

emphasizing the results of the new Jewish freedoms in German society. In fact, he would later boast that he had turned the Jewish question from one of purely literary interest into a subject for debate in public meetings. He was justified in his boast; he was the first to politicize anti-Semitism.

On his part this was the result of genuine convictions. He saw the recent Jewish emancipation as a threat to the traditional character of Germany, which he assumed to be essentially Christian.[33] The Jews had not been content with basic political rights. They had assumed control of the press and the stock exchange, while their influence was increasing in the spheres of education and of higher government. Hence he proposed various measures, of a relatively mild sort, to restrict Jewish influence.[34] Stoecker, like many Christians in the medieval period, feared contamination. But he did not directly fear Judaism as such. He could describe Orthodox Judaism as 'a form of religion which is dead at its very core', and was equally scathing about Reform Judaism, which he felt was nothing more than 'a pitiful remnant of the Age of Enlightenment'.[35] He did, however, see a serious risk of contamination in the secular and materialistic attitude prevalent among the Jews of his day. As he wrote to the Kaiser in 1880, 'In all my talks against Judaism I have openly proclaimed that I do not attack the Jews but only that light-minded Judaism that is without fear of Heaven, that pursues material gain and practises deceit, that Judaism which is the real misfortune of our people.'[36]

Without perhaps realizing it, Stoecker encountered the same dilemma as confronted the states of medieval Christendom. He wanted to see the Jews converted, and yet he desired to protect the Christian character of society as he saw it. He believed in Pauline terms that the Jews would one day repent and that subsequently they would bring blessing to the church as a whole. (He rejected the notion that the restoration of the Jews would be reserved to the end of the age.) Their conversion was the true solution to the problems of a continuing Jewish presence in Germany. Only then could they be expected to take on the mores of the German Christian community. In short, he looked for them to lose their Jewish identity, and was optimistic about the prospects of their so doing. That is probably why he did not face squarely the implications of persistent Jewish unbelief in a

---

[33] It was as recently as 1869 that the Jews had attained full rights as citizens in Germany.
[34] summarized in Dawidowicz, *War*, 64.
[35] quoted at *ibid.*.
[36] quoted in Tal, *Christians*, 250.

Christian society. But what if the expected Jewish conversion and assimilation did not occur or seemed indefinitely postponed? Then the logic of
Stoecker's position would demand more vigorous political action against
the Jews — their eradication from society whether by expulsion or by more
drastic means.

Stoecker's anti-Jewish agitation at first roused considerable disquiet
among theologians, pastors and Christian politicians. One theologian,
Hermann Baumgarten, with unusual foresight warned of a blood bath;
for the anti-Semitic movement 'is called Germanic but is also Christian;
former murderers of Jews also wore the cross, if not in their hearts, at least
on their outer garment. We have been brought so low by these wild
outbreaks of anti-Semitism that our humane century reminds us of the
terror of medieval Jewish massacres.'[37] But Baumgarten's admonition was
never translated into concerted action publicly to censure or to stop the
anti-Jewish crusade.

Indeed, Stoecker's line received unexpected support from Heinrich
von Treitschke, who has been described as 'Wilhelmine Germany's
most influential historian, a veritable teacher of the nation both as
university professor and as historiographer'.[38] Though he was unsym-
pathetic to Stoecker's demagogic style, he did endorse the view that the
Jewish question was the key issue of the moment.[39] He felt that immi-
grant Jews in particular were bringing an alien element to German
society, and appealed to Jews to be more sympathetic to the faith,
customs and feelings of the German people. He disowned the title of
an anti-Semite; but it is understandable that many should see him in
that light when sentiments such as these are considered —

> Year after year over our Eastern frontier, from the inexhaustible Polish cradle
> there come, forcing their way in, a host of pushful, trouser-selling youths whose
> children and children's children are one day to dominate Germany's stock-ex-
> changes and newspapers; the invasion increases visibly, and ever more serious
> becomes the problem as to how we can ever merge their alien Volkstum with
> ours . . . . Right into the most highly educated circles among men who would
> reject with horror any thought of ecclesiastical intolerance or national arrogance,
> there sounds forth, as if from one mouth the cry, 'The Jews are our misfortune'.[40]

But an even more sinister step on Treitschke's part was to attribute
all the negative effects of Germany's economic and industrial

---

[37] quoted at ibid., 232.
[38] Graml, *Anti-Semitism*, 54.
[39] Gutteridge, *Open*, 12–17.
[40] cited by Gutteridge, *Open*, 14.

modernization to the Jews.[41] Since this process of modernization was irreversible, the Jews were saddled with continuing responsibility for all the evils it engendered.

Again, Treitschke's outburst provoked a series of replies, of which the most telling was that of Theodor Mommsen, the famous historian of Rome, who accused Treitschke of inventing his lurid tales of Jewish mass immigration and of strengthening the hand of a much more radical anti-Semitism.[42] Opposition, however, in academic circles was limited. Both Stoecker and Treitschke in their very different ways had put the Jewish question on the agenda of German politics. It was to have a profound effect in university circles, including theological students, in the 1880s.[43] But the debate could not be conducted exclusively in terms acceptable to Stoecker and Treitschke. They had in a way played into the hands of the racial anti-Semites, because they had seen the Jews as a threat more as a cultural or a social than a religious group. Moreover they overestimated the strength of Christianity in Germany. In 1882 Stoecker gave the assurance that if the German people were given the choice between expelling the Jews and expelling the anti-Christian anti-Semites, they would certainly choose the latter.[44] That may have been true for 1882, but the situation was to change for the worse.

General attitudes in the churches toward the Jews

From the 1880s attitudes within the churches were not uniformly anti-Semitic. The latter half of the nineteenth century saw the revival of the German Protestant Judenmission mainly through the efforts of the Old Testament scholar, Franz Delitzsch, whose work included practical missionary endeavour, especially in his production of a Hebrew translation of the New Testament.[45] He bitterly regretted first the apathy and then the outright hatred among certain Christian elements in Germany toward the Jews. He was bold enough to assert that 'those who do not show love to the People who gave birth to Him have no true love for Jesus himself.' He rejected the current view that the status

---

[41]   Graml, *Anti-Semitism*, 55–6.
[42]   In 1890 the Jews numbered only one per cent of the German population — Langmuir, *HRAS*, 323. Curiously, Mommsen called on the Jews to integrate into wider German society — Tal, *Christians*, 50–4.
[43]   Gutteridge, *Open*, 17–18.
[44]   Agus, *Meaning*, 2:405.
[45]   Gutteridge, *Open*, 327–8. The precise title of this mission was Mission unter Israel.

of the Jews as God's chosen people was a thing of the past, and held that without the conversion of the Jews the church would not attain her fulfilment. Delitzsch's work found a few successors, notably in Hermann Strack, the professor of theology and oriental studies at Berlin, who set up a theological seminar at which students could assess Jewish religion and culture with 'as objective as possible a judgment based upon Christianity and scholarly research unclouded by class, racial and mob hatred.'[46] Strack also took pains to expose some of the lies to which Jews were exposed. He wrote the first impressive refutation of the ritual murder accusation, while in later life he turned his energies to exposing the spurious *Protocols of the Elders of Zion*. But men like Delitzsch and Strack were swimming against the tide. The Judenmission was the Cinderella of the Evangelical Church, the preserve of a pious few.[47]

More typically, Christians in Germany did fear the Jews and see in them a threat to the German way of life. One champion of missionary endeavour among the Jews, Superintendent Richard Bieling of Soldin, revealed a complex set of feelings about the Jews when he wrote in 1913 —

> Am I able to love the Jew? Certainly not on the natural plane! All too much separates me from him. His characteristic ways are so different from mine. He has another spirit. Not that his manner is to be deemed worse than mine, for I am far from being racially arrogant, but it is different. It is in stark contrast to my sentiments as a German. The Jewish disposition has an ever-increasing influence upon the ways of thinking and manners of my people, and I regard this as perilous to German existence. For a German to give up his peculiar characteristics is tantamount to the abandonment of his express ego, and that is the beginning of the end for individual and nation alike. In whatever way I consider the situation I am aware of a gulf separating me from the Jew, and no argument on rational grounds will level it . . . As a human being the Jew remains a Jew, and I am German. There is honestly no way of getting over this. If I am to love the Jew, then I must have such love bestowed upon me. There is only one person who can give me this, and it is Jesus . . . In the love of Jesus I have learnt to love the Jew, and I think I will never lose that love.[48]

When such a seriously minded Christian admitted that it went against all his natural instincts and required a supernatural infusion of love to care for the Jews, what of those people in churches and outside

---

[46]   *ibid.*, 328–9.

[47]   *ibid.*, 328–31.

[48]   quoted in ibid., 26 from G.M. Lowen, *Die Juden und das Evangelium. Ausserungen hervorragender evangelischer Christen der Gegenwart* (Leipzig 1913) 11.

of them who were unprepared to examine their natural instincts or might even be taught that these instincts were to be treasured as the work of the Creator!

Most Christians in Germany associated their faith with a growing national consciousness. It was not simply that they desired to be patriotic. Patriotism was associated with the idea of Volk, which signified the union of a group of people with a transcendental 'essence', never specified but variously called 'nature', 'cosmos' or 'mythos'. This essence 'was fused to man's innermost nature, and represented the source of his creativity, his depth of feeling, his individuality, and his unity with other members of the Volk.'[49] National identity had in effect taken on a sacred character. Like marriage, it was to be carefully preserved and not polluted. Hence it was common to find Christians believing that though a Jew might genuinely be converted and become a Christian, he could not become a German Christian. This was based on the empirical observation (whether correct or otherwise) that the character of Germany was being influenced by the Jews, especially by their extensive immigration from the east. Race was not necessarily the exclusive or the primary consideration.[50]

But with the emergence of Nazism, racial doctrines could not be ignored. The churches were inevitably affected. There were varied reactions among Protestants. Some enthusiastically supported the New Order established by the Nazi government in 1933, and believed that it had been raised in the providence of God for the good of Germany.[51] These 'German Christians' as they came to be known followed the Guiding Principles issued in 1932 which affirmed race, Volkstum and nation as 'orders of life given and entrusted to us by God, to care for the preservation of which is for us God's Law.'[52] Perhaps without their realizing it, they were making Nazi ideology into a divine law above the Ten Commandments.

The 'German Christians' were opposed by the Confessing Church, who were concerned about the distortion of the Christian message and the erosion of ecclesiastical freedom.[53] Yet, the Confessing Church

---

[49] Mosse, *Crisis*, 4.

[50] Lagarde, for example, believed that the offence of the Jews lay in their state of mind, not in their race — Gutteridge, *Open*, 20.

[51] *ibid.*, 70–72. Gutteridge proceeds to point out that even a few Jews in 1933 welcomed the Nazi rise to power — *ibid.*, 73–74.

[52] A full English translation of these Guiding Principles is to be found in Conway, *Nazi*, 339–341.

[53] Its battle-cry was the Declaration of Barmen (1934) which was heavily influenced by Karl Barth.

limited its objections to the religious realm. It was careful not to attack the Nazi political order, which was regarded as a secular matter and outside its scope.[54] Hence they addressed the situation only of those Jews who had been baptized into the Christian faith and who now counted (in the church's eyes) as Christians and no longer as Jews. Those Protestants who wanted directly to take up the cause of unbaptized Jews or the whole racial question were exceptional.[55] That is not to deny that individual Protestant congregations, families or individuals did show kindness to Jews at great risk during the years of Nazi persecution.[56] Protestants were, however, paralysed when it came to a matter of a united public statement on the persecution of the Jews. They had other concerns on their agenda. Besides, they had little positive theology about the Jews. They were largely influenced by Luther's later outlook that the Jews were a people under severe judgment from God.[57] Besides, liberal theology had left them uncertain of their bearings within the Scriptures. At the same time, years of anti-Semitic talk in its milder as well as its extreme Nazi form had in many cases deadened the German Protestant church to the danger faced by the Jews and to their own responsibility to the Jewish neighbour in their midst.

Roman Catholics in Germany were not, of course, influenced by Martin Luther. But they had their own separate anti-Jewish legacy. Thus, Catholic reaction to the Jewish question proved in many ways similar to that of the Protestants. In part this can be explained by the restrictions imposed by the Nazi police-state and by the church's jealousy to preserve their limited ecclesiastical freedoms which might be jeopardized if they spoke publicly and consistently against Nazi racial theories and their implications. Even Pope Pius XII from the comparative safety of Rome did not venture to mention the Jews by name in any of his public statements during the Nazi regime. Most German bishops were indifferent and apathetic to the fate of the Jews.[58] They felt they had other priorities.

---

[54] Here the Protestant churches were affected by Luther's doctrine of the Two Kingdoms — see Gutteridge, *Open*, 280–5.

[55] *ibid.*, 125–131.

[56] *ibid.*, 206–218.

[57] *ibid.*, 268. Martin Niemoller, one of those Protestants most active in opposition to the 'German Christians', could speak of 'this manifest penal judgment which continues in force century after century'. He did, however, insist that this gave no reason why Christians should hate the Jews or should try to aggravate their punishment — *ibid.*, 103–4.

[58] Lewy, *Catholic*, 294–5.

Racial anti-Semitism

Many commentators have discerned a new phenomenon in the dis-tinctly racial ideology which was used from the 1870s to undergird certain attacks on the Jews.[59] Sometimes, as we have seen, this type of anti-Semitism worked alongside, sometimes in opposition to the more traditional forms of anti-Semitism. There is no doubting its novelty, though a case might be made that at heart it represented yet another protest against Jewish distinctiveness and attempted to replace the Jews as God's chosen people with an alternative, which it might style in more secular terms as the master race or whatever.

Indeed, some have seen the stress on race as a reflection of growing secularization. A society which experienced increased religious doubts might be expected to find non-religious and perhaps more scientific ways of expressing its antipathy toward the Jews.[60] There is some evidence to support this hypothesis. Many of the German racist anti-Semites accepted the critique of religion offered by Feuerbach.[61] According to this, religion was nothing more than a projection of human aspirations. Moreover, religion was a destructive influence, poisoning man's natural instincts and vital creative powers. Judaism, they believed, was particularly bad because it was inspired by a deep resentment against superior races such as the Germans whose thought and feeling were basically incompatible with those of Jewish or Christian origin.[62] In promoting the conscience, Judaism inhibited courage and true spontaneity, values central to the new German racial spirituality.

A further secular link may be found in the man who is accredited as the first to make race the source and determining factor of all that took place in history. This was a Frenchman, Count Artur de Gobineau. Writing in 1853, he declared, 'Race is a jealous god, it is everything.' Curiously, he had no axe to grind against the Jews. Indeed, he showed some respect for Jewish racial exclusiveness.[63] Thus, racist ideology did not always imply anti-Semitism.[64]

---

[59]   Tal collects a list of such commentators — *Christians*, 227 note 5.

[60]   for an interesting discussion of this question, which involves the complex areas of just what secularization is and whether it is a valid tool for understanding changes in outlook in the 19th and 20th centuries, see Langmuir, *HRAS*, 201–231.

[61]   *ibid.*, 260.

[62]   *ibid.*, 246.

[63]   Gutteridge, *Open*, 333–4.

[64]   Interestingly, the famous philosopher Freidrich Nietzsche used a racist framework to praise the Jews and assert their superiority over the Germans — Wistrich, *Anti-Semitism*, 60.

In a climate, however, of anti-Jewish feeling it was a small step for anti-Semites to appeal to racial theory as a sort of scientific basis for their political stance.[65] This was particularly true among atheists like Wilhelm Marr, the creator of the term 'anti-Semitism'. A much more influential figure than Marr in this connection was Eugen Dühring, a lecturer in philosophy and economics who had had to retire from his post at Berlin University. In 1881 he wrote the first thorough consideration of the Jewish question in Germany from a racial standpoint.[66] In many ways he paved the way for Hitler, though Hitler recognized no debt to him. He set forth the notion of the Jews as a sort of anti-race, who could neither form a society of their own nor be properly assimilated into another society because their basic nature was evil and immutable. This was the essence of the race-theory. If a particular group had certain identifiable racial traits, these were indelible. Baptism or any outward religious change made no difference whatsoever in the case of inferior races.

Dühring had little time for Christian objections to Judaism, since Christianity was 'itself Semitism' and the 'offspring of the Jewish oriental religious soul.' Christianity was responsible for the same personality defects as he had located in Judaism. 'For us,' he asserted,

> Christianity is nothing but neo-Judaism which, because of its characteristic Jewish features — we mention only the hypocrisy of loving your neighbour and your enemy — cannot be reconciled with the thought and feeling of more recent and better nations . . . Christianity impaired the understanding and the spirit; it unleashed wild fanaticism and engendered heinous crimes. Christianity has been, and is still today, the greatest obstacle to progress.[67]

For Dühring it was futile to gloss over the true nature of the hatred for the Jews. In essence it was hatred for religion in general, and this was simply obscured by use of traditional Christian objections to Judaism.

Dühring was both extreme and consistent in his opposition to religion (that is to Judaism and Christianity) where other racial anti-Semites were prepared to make compromises and to accommodate somewhat to Christianity.[68] He would talk as if it were better for the Germans if religion were superseded altogether.[69] And yet even he

---

[65] Tal, *Christians*, 259 lists several such figures.
[66] Dühring's work was entitled *Die Judenfrage als Rassen- Sitten- und Kulturfrage* (The Jewish Question as a Racial, Moral and Cultural Question).
[67] quoted in Tal, *Christians*, 234.
[68] Marr was one such example — Tal, *Christians*, 262–4.
[69] Dühring tended to ignore the existence of such religions as Islam, Hinduism and Buddhism.

might hint that he was replacing Judaism and Christianity not with atheism, but with a new religion. Thus he could say, 'The Nordic idols and the Nordic God contain a natural kernel and no thousand-year-old distraction can remove it from the world . . . Here has reigned an imaginative spirit incomparably superior to the Jewish slave imagination.'[70] We must make allowances for vivid imagery. We must also grant that there is nothing here which is inconsistent with the Feuerbachan concept of religion. Yet, it is significant that Dühring decks his positive concepts in religious language.

We can adduce further indications that these radical anti-Semites had in effect taken up a new religious stance of their own.[71] On close inspection the scientific status of their racial theories becomes suspect. At first racial ideology had indeed been intended to give scientific backing to anti-Semitic feeling and political programmes. Dühring had said as much.[72] This might be expected from someone with his academic credentials. Another figure in much the same mould, Theodor Fritsch, proclaimed in the 1890s that with their 'proof' of the depravity of the Jewish and the sublimity of the German race, German racists had not only advanced human knowledge but inaugurated a new epoch in human history.[73] But later writers like Houston Chamberlain took a different line. No doubt they felt they had to combat (however indirectly) scientific critics of race theory who made such inconvenient assertions as the denial of the existence of any Aryan race and as the claim that the Jews were more of a religious than a racial group. Chamberlain responded by rejecting scientific verifiability as the ultimate criterion in determining empirical facts.[74] Here he was probably being more honest or at least more accurate than the earlier racial anti-Semites.

Chamberlain preferred to rely on subjective intuition and direct sensation. The irrational impulses of our inner life gave a surer grasp of reality than scientific method, whose scope was limited to abstract, general laws. It hardly mattered to Chamberlain whether or not objective evidence could be found to verify or disprove what we feel in our hearts. What mattered when it came to the question of race was that we felt we belonged to such a grouping. 'I need not bother about

---

[70] quoted in Tal, *Christians*, 266.
[71] cf. the comments of Agus, *Meaning*, 2:451–3.
[72] Graml, *Anti-Semitism*, 58.
[73] Cohn, *Warrant*, 171.
[74] Tal, *Christians*, 281–2; Field *op. cit.* 215–8 and 295–6.

definitions,' he said, 'race is in my bosom.' Chamberlain did not intend this as a general rule; intuition was the key to absolute truth only in the case of the Aryans as the highest race.

Had Chamberlain left matters there, his contribution would have been unexceptional. But he used these inner intuitions to claim not only the existence of but also a great destiny for the Aryan race. 'Even if it were demonstrated that an Aryan race never existed in the past, we want one to exist in the future; for men of action this is the decisive point of departure.'[75] Surely this was a matter of almost religious faith, all the more remarkable in that it was blended into Chamberlain's own heterodox concept of Christianity. Chamberlain wanted the German people (or at least those who could identify themselves as Aryans) to live in the light of these unseen 'realities' and to work towards that great destiny they were guaranteed. Understandably such a flattering pros-pect appealed to many Germans. At the same time a political agenda was implied. The great destiny of the Aryan people could be attained only if they freed themselves from the pernicious influences of the Semites (i.e. the Jews).

It was not Chamberlain's work to spell out the details of this emanci-pation. That was more the task of Nazi ideologists who translated the sharp contrast between the Aryan and the Semite into an apocalyptic, life-and-death struggle. Herein they were helped by the discovery of a supposed Jewish plot to dominate the world, which was outlined in *The Protocols of the Elders of Zion*.[76] Thus, the struggle was not simply with Jewish culture or morality but with a sinister political force, which could be restrained only by political means. Hence for the leading Nazis their anti-Semitic activity took on the character of a holy war. One SS captain testified at his trial that the Nazi world-view included both pseudo-scien-tific biological theories and 'a mystical and religious view which sees the world as ruled by good and bad powers'.[77] He contended that it was impossible 'to make any impression on this outlook by means of logical or rational argument, it is a sort of religiosity, and it impels people to form themselves into a sect.' The SS captain dismissed the idea that Himmler (and he could have said the same of Hitler) was an ice-cold cynical politician. On the contrary, 'in his whole attitude Himmler was a mystic, who embraced this world-view with fanaticism.'

---

[75] *ibid.*, 284.
[76] On this see Cohn, *Warrant*, 179–193.
[77] The SS captain was Dieter Wisliceny, who was speaking at his trial in 1946 in Czechoslovakia. Cohn quotes extensively from one of his statements — *ibid.*, 179–80.

While we may demur at the assumption that all religious standpoints are necessarily irrational, there can be no doubt that the leading Nazis saw their racial and apocalyptic beliefs in more religious than scientific terms. We must, therefore, be wary of seeing modern racial anti-Semitism as an example of secularism. It was certainly anti-Christian, whatever temporary alliances its exponents may have forged with Christian anti-Semites. But it could not avoid religious concepts. It claimed a path to a knowledge of reality which was much more effective than scientific method. It claimed to be the instrument of destiny in a bitter conflict in the unseen realm.

Nor was this simply political rhetoric designed to win an immediate, emotional response. Hitler and at least the leading Nazis did come to believe it. Though Hitler and his associates were not successful in convincing their German countrymen of their apocalyptic beliefs, they did not need to be successful in this respect. With their incessant and varied propaganda against the Jews they did induce in most Germans a complete indifference to their fate.[78] And that was enough for Hitler's own devious purposes.

Politics in Germany before the Third Reich

Before World War I political and racial anti-Semitic parties made little public impact.[79] The reasons were in part political. Power in the Second Reich was not vested in political parties, but in the monarch, the princes and the governments appointed by these rulers. The ruling classes were anxious to avoid support from any cause like anti-Semitism which threatened turbulence in the social order.[80] There were also religious reasons. Uriel Tal has pointed out that the political development of racial anti-Semitism was inhibited by its non-Christian and even anti-Christian character.[81] By contrast, certain lobbies and interest groups with a strong nationalist and anti-Semitic nuance fared better. These ranged from Trade Unions to gymnastic clubs and student movements.[82] Such groups helped to carry over attitudes from the Second Reich to the Weimar Republic. Hermann Graml points out that there

---

[78] Cohn, *Warrant*, 210–11 quotes the results of two surveys carried out by Michael Müller-Claudius on certain Nazi party members first in 1938 and later in 1942.
[79] Tal, *Christians*, 298–301.
[80] Graml, *Anti-Semitism*, 67–8.
[81] Tal, *Christians*, 301.
[82] Wistrich, *Anti-Semitism*, 61.

was little originality in the racial ideas of the Nazi party in the Weimar period.[83] The new factors, however, consisted in the political conditions and the skills of Adolf Hitler.

After the end of the First World War and the collapse of the Hohenzollern monarchy, the Weimar Republic opened the door to party politics, but produced so much instability that many Germans were only too glad to escape from democracy to the shelter of an all-powerful national leader who was promising them renewed days of German greatness. As if the unexpected defeat in the First World War had not been a sufficient blow to German national pride, the Weimar Republic brought calamities of its own — notably massive inflation and a few years later an economic depression with huge unemployment.[84] The Nazis readily put the ultimate responsibility for all these misfortunes on the machinations of the Jews, both inside or outside of Germany. But this was not their only line of disinformation. They could picture the Bolshevik Revolution in Russia, which had already occasioned much suspicion in Germany, as a prelude to the future 'Bolshevization' of Germany and a key step in international Jewry's efforts to dominate the world. The linkage of anti-Semitism with anti-Communism ensured the Nazi movement much greater support than it would otherwise have secured.[85] Besides, Hitler made a speciality of attacking virtually everyone but his own party. As Cohn describes it, 'He attacked the Victorious Allies, especially the French, for enslaving the German people; and the German republican regime, for its failure to cope with the crisis; and the parties of the Left, for dividing the nation; and the parties of the Right, for their ineffectiveness; and the plutocrats and monopolists, for exploiting everyone else.'[86] In an immature and chaotic democracy there were plenty of targets for Hitler's vitriol.

Undeniably, the electoral triumph of Nazism was linked to Hitler's remarkable political skills. An exceptional orator and propagandist, he could inspire both individuals and mass audiences with his own imaginative vision of a Germany restored to greatness. At the same time he embodied that ruthless determination for supreme power which was the Nazi hallmark and which many thought to be sadly missing in the Weimar Republic.[87] His unscrupulousness and deviousness remained

---

[83] Graml, *Anti-Semitism*, 74–77.
[84] *ibid.*, 81–5
[85] Wistrich, *Anti-Semitism*, 70–1.
[86] Cohn, *Warrant*, 198.
[87] Graml, *Anti-Semitism*, 72–3.

unrecognized or were readily overlooked. While he and his Nazi associates made it plain that their anti-Semitism would be reflected in their policies once they attained power, at the same time they gave ordinary Germans many different reasons for voting on their behalf in order mainly to fulfil their economic interests and their social ambitions, to say nothing of their sense of national pride.

Hitler's own brand of anti-Semitism

Hitler was clearly a racial anti-Semite in the Dühring mould.[88] He expounded a type of racist creed in *Mein Kampf* and adhered closely to it for the rest of his life.[89] In fact, his final political testament drawn up on the last day of his life charged 'the leaders of the nation and those under them to scrupulous observance of the laws of race and to merciless opposition to the universal poisoner of all peoples, International Jewry.'[90] Thus, the burning issue for Hitler was that of race — not only for his own day but for any nation at any time which wanted to prosper. A nation would stand or fall by the extent to which it preserved the integrity of the race — 'What we must fight for is to safeguard the existence and reproduction of our race and our people, the sustenance of our children and the purity of our blood, the freedom and independence of the fatherland, so that our people may mature for the fulfilment of the mission allotted to it by the creator of the universe.'[91]

But it would be misleading to describe Hitler as a racist or a nationalist *tout court*. Alongside the above views and sometimes in tension with them, Hitler maintained his own version of the apocalyptic conflict between Aryans and Jews, two races struggling for domination on the world stage.[92] This was his equivalent of the struggle between God and the devil, or between good and evil. He could ape biblical language and assert, 'Two worlds face one another — the men of God and the men of Satan! The

---

[88] Hitler would not have seen things this way. In *Mein Kampf* he made out that he came to his anti-Semitic views almost by himself. In fact, Richard Wagner was the only predecessor whose influence he recognized.

[89] for the consistency of Hitler's views see Dawidowicz, *War*, 193–208. Gerald Fleming *Hitler and the Final Solution* (ET, Hamish Hamilton, London 1985) 1–16 argues that Hitler's anti-Semitism goes back to his schooldays.

[90] cited by Wistrich, *Anti-Semitism*, 77.

[91] Adolf Hitler *Mein Kampf*, (ET by Ralph Manheim — Hutchinson, London 1969) 195.

[92] for some interesting comments on how Hitler modified traditional Christian ideas about the Jews see Haynes, *Jews*, 60–1.

Jew is the anti-man, the creature of another god. He must have come from another root of the human race. I set the Aryan and the Jew over and against each other.'[93] If there was a chosen race, it was the Aryans and not the Jews. This mythical vision was more important to Hitler than any strictly scientific or sociological assessment of race.[94] In this respect Hitler mirrored Houston Chamberlain.

In fact, Hitler did have some problems in defining the 'Jewish race', though this was glossed over in *Mein Kampf*. Later he came to admit that he used the term Jewish race as a matter of convenience, 'for in reality and from the genetic point of view there is no such thing as the Jewish race'.[95] Supremely he saw the Jewish race as 'an abstract race of the mind', by which he meant that the Jews were impervious to processes of assimilation. At the same time he would not jettison the idea of Jewish blood as a sort of pseudo-biological basis for anti-Semitism.[96] This was too handy as a propaganda tool. And yet it was surely inconsistent with a race of the mind.

We meet a further contradiction in Hitler's descriptions of Jewish history and of Jewish influence on wider society. On the one hand, the Jews were the embodiment of all that hindered progress among a true race. Lacking the initiative and creative genius to construct a state of their own, they needed the work of other nations if they were to survive at all. Hence they were parasitical on the existence of other races. But, in a marked contrast to this indolent picture, they had shown amazing agility in weaving their way into the mainstream of a nation's life. Hitler claimed they had already seized the reins of financial power in Europe and were seeking to supplement this with political power. They tended to work covertly through ideological programmes such as Communism. They worked by deceit and their 'first and greatest lie' had been to parade as a religious group and not as the race which they really were. Hitler was emphatic that Judaism was nothing but a clever facade — 'The Mosaic religion is nothing other than a doctrine for the preservation of the Jewish race.'[97]

---

[93] Rauschning, *Hitler*, 238.
[94] The Nazis did promote religious rituals and creeds of their own which deliberately recast Christian equivalents. It remains, however, likely that among the leading Nazis the object of this exercise was more political than religious. They would use every means to secure the loyalty of the people to the Nazi regime and to the Führer — Conway, *Nazi*, 141–157.
[95] Hitler, *Testament*, 55. cf. Hitler's earlier admission to Rauschning that 'in the scientific sense there is no such thing as race' — *Hitler*, 229.
[96] *ibid.*, 55–6.
[97] Hitler, (note 91) 277–9.

Whatever the inconsistencies in Hitler's picture of the Jews, it was vital for him to argue against the possibility of change in the Jewish race, because this meant the Jews could never really be part of German (or rather of Aryan) society. Hitler had his explanation for Jewish assimilation into German society. This simply represented to his mind a sinister Jewish plot to endanger the Aryan race. Indeed, the more carefully integrated the Jews seemed to be, the greater the danger they posed. They would be working as a poisonous virus within the Aryan life-blood. 'As a matter of fact,' declared Hitler,

> the Jew can never become a German however often he may affirm that he can. If he wished to become a German, he must surrender the Jew in him. And that is not possible: He cannot, however much he try, become a German at heart, and that for several reasons: first because of his blood; second, because of his character; thirdly, because of his will; and fourthly, because of his actions.[98]

Hitler was engaging in rhetorical hyperbole. His four reasons amount to one; everything derived from Jewish blood.

Not all Germans ardently supported or even studied every detail of Hitler's creed. In fact, Nazi ideology was never fully articulated or codified.[99] Even its racial doctrines were not well defined, but were 'a confusion of often conflicting ideas.'[100] There remains, little doubt, however, that among the various appeals made by the Nazi Party to the German people before 1933 its racial implications proved the most attractive. And within their body of racial teachings their anti-Semitism struck the deepest chord. At early meetings of the Nazi party the audience responded most enthusiastically to attacks on the Jews.[101] Again, once the Nazis had attained power, one of their earliest anti-Jewish steps, a boycott of Jewish shops and businesses on 1st April 1933, which was sponsored only by the party and lacked the full authority of a law, received widespread support.[102] As the anti-Jewish policy gathered strength, scarcely a protest was raised among the Germans. This differed significantly from the Italians, who often shuddered at carrying out anti-Jewish orders or at turning Jews over to the Germans. Nearer to home, the silence over the Jews was in marked contrast to the German protests at the inception of Hitler's programme

---

[98]   ed. Norman H. Baynes *The Speeches of Adolf Hitler* (New York 1969) 1:59.
[99]   Conway, *Nazi*, 140.
[100] Field, *Evangelist*, 301.
[101] Dawidowicz, *War*, 209.
[102] Gutman and Schatzker, *Holocaust*, 39.

of 'euthanasia' for the mentally ill, where it is said that opposition reached such a pitch that it was able to prevent some of these killings.[103] But where the Jews were concerned, there was little opposition in Germany because anti-Semitism had firm roots among the people for varied reasons. Hitler himself believed that anti-Semitism was the most important weapon in his propagandist arsenal, and that almost everywhere it was of deadly efficiency.[104] That is not to deny that it also represented a genuine conviction in Hitler's mind; it was impossible, he declared, to underestimate the gravity of the struggle with the Jews. Not many Germans saw the issues in such a stark light. Nor would they have foreseen the terrible atrocities of the 'Final Solution', since anti-Semitism had been a feature of German politics for over 50 years without any such drastic repercussions.

Lucy Dawidowicz points out that Hitler and the Nazi party were able to take advantage of generations of German anti-Semitism, which had in turn been built on all manner of considerations, including 'Christian church teaching about the Jews, Volkist anti-Semitism, doctrines of racial superiority, economic theories about the role of Jews in capitalism and commerce, and a half century of political anti-Semitism'.[105] The variety of reasons for the anti-Semitism is significant. Hitler had admitted as early as 1922 that he judged that the Jews to be the group in German society against whom he could most readily incite popular hatred prior to the revolutionary upheaval which he hoped would sweep him to power.[106] Hitler was too politically shrewd to channel his anti-Semitic propaganda along one particular channel.[107] Anything suitable was grist to his mill. A composition written by a young girl called Erna Listing and printed in the anti-Semitic magazine *Der Stürmer* gives an insight into the range of anti-Jewish motifs which evidently percolated down to the mind of a German youngster of the 1930s —

> The Jew is a hybrid. He has inherited traits of Aryans, Asians, Negroes and Mongols. Evil controls the hybrid, and the only good thing he has is a white skin. A saying among the inhabitants of the southern islands claims: 'White is from God and black is from God. But hybrid is of the devil.' Jesus once said to them: 'Your father is not God but the devil.' The Jews have an evil book of laws. It is the Talmud. Furthermore the Jews consider us animals and behave accordingly. They take our money and property through trickery. Already the court of

---

[103] Gutman in Almog, *Anti-Semitism*, 374–6.
[104] Rauschning, *Hitler*, 233–5.
[105] Dawidowicz, *War*, 209.
[106] cf. Hitler's remarks to the journal Josef Hell recorded by Fleming, *Hitler*, 28–9.
[107] Fleming, *Hitler*, 30.

> Charlemagne was ruled by Jews, and therefore Roman law was established. But this did not suit the German farmer, nor was it law for the Roman farmer, but rather for the Jewish merchant. The Jews are even responsible for the death of Charlemagne . . . They instigated rebellions and war. They led Russia to sorrow and suffering. In Germany they supported the Communist Party and paid murderers. We were at the edge of the ditch. Then Adolf Hitler came . . .[108]

It is an extraordinary mixture of pseudo-biology, tendentious history, misinterpreted Scripture with something of an old wives' tale thrown in for good measure.

Erna Listing's composition reflects the fruits of sustained Nazi propaganda. But little of the traditional German hatred for the Jews had anything of the intensity of that shown by Hitler. Indeed, Hitler's animosity amounted to an overriding obsession; it was almost in a class of its own. Even Heinrich Himmler, Hitler's normally willing lieutenant to whom he particularly entrusted the execution of the Final Solution, admitted to initial hesitations about asking the SS to carry out 'such a horrid assignment' as the annihilation of whole communities of Jews.[109] But since it was the Führer's command, he proceeded to obey 'out of obedience and the fullest conviction'. As the Third Reich appeared doomed, Himmler was prepared to compromise and (behind Hitler's back) to renege on the Final Solution; but Hitler remained implacable on this score until his dying breath.[110] Hugh Trevor-Roper could write of the extermination policy — 'Even victory in war was decreed less essential than the completion of this macabre operation, to which essential resources, even in 1944, were still being diverted from the German armies now fighting desperate rearguard battles for the defence of the Reich.'[111]

Moreover, the political goals of ordinary Germans who were suspicious of the Jews were not nearly so radical as those of Hitler. Many Germans would have been content to stop with the Reich Citizenship Law of 1935, which deprived German Jews of the rights and protections of citizenship.[112] But for Hitler this was only a step along the road to a more drastic goal. A further sign that Hitler's own outlook and policies were far more extreme than that of the bulk of the German people emerges from reactions to the Kristallnacht pogrom in November 1938. That was the night when 119 synagogues were set on fire, 76 completely destroyed and

---

[108] cited in Gutman and Schatzker, *Holocaust*, 40–1.
[109] *ibid.*, 53–4.
[110] *ibid.*, 167–171 and 175–185.
[111] H. Trevor-Roper 'The Will to Exterminate' in *Times Literary Supplement*, January 28, 1983.
[112] Dawidowicz, *War*, 203.

20,000 arrests made. Subsequently the Jewish community were fined a billion marks. At the time it was estimated that only 20 per cent of the non-Jewish German community sympathized with these violent measures.[113] Henceforth the anti-Semitic programme of the Nazis had to be developed in a more secret and orderly fashion.[114] It is little wonder that when Hitler did have a free hand to implement the Final Solution, roughly at the time of Operation Barbarossa which he launched against the Soviet Union in June 1941, he went to considerable lengths to avoid personal association with the orders for the liquidation of the Jews which had undoubtedly originated with him.[115] Hitler was unconcerned about evidence being used against him at any future trial. He was more anxious to avoid resistance from his German people scandalized by the discovery that their beloved Führer had abused his position to engage in mass genocide.[116]

With his political skills Hitler was able to capitalize on earlier German political anti-Semitism. By propounding his own blend of pseudo-scientific and apocalyptic racial theories he extended a protest against the civil emancipation of the Jews in Germany into a campaign for their removal. And this in turn developed into the annihilation of the Jewish race when circumstances were right.

Was the Holocaust unique?

The uniqueness of the Holocaust has appeared self-evident to many. After all, never before in human history has a particular race lost six million of its members by a process of systematic annihilation. Whereas other racial massacres were generally prompted as a means to some other end, the Jews were dispatched to the gas chambers and the like as an end in itself, though they constituted no real threat to the German Reich. No exceptions were allowed.[117] It did not matter whether the Jews were observant or otherwise, whether they were children or adult, whether they retained or rejected cultural links with the Jewish

---

[113] Gutteridge, *Open*, 175–6.
[114] Wistrich, *Anti-Semitism*, 74.
[115] On Hitler and the art of concealment see Fleming, *Hitler*, 17–31 and 61–5. Fleming's book argues in detail that Hitler personally originated the idea of 'The Final Solution', even if its detailed execution was left to others. Saul Friedländer's introduction to this book gives an excellent summary of 'intentionalist' and 'functionalist' approaches to the Holocaust.
[116] *ibid.*, 173.
[117] cf. Dawidowicz, *War*, 18–19.

community.[118] Nor were they given a way of escape. At the time of the Crusades Jews could always escape death by submitting to baptism. In Nazi Germany some Jews might have made a useful contribution to the war effort. But such considerations were irrelevant to Nazi ideology.

In a notorious speech to SS leaders Himmler talked proudly of the very ruthlessness of the Final Solution —

> It's one of these things which is easy to say: every party comrade says, 'The Jewish people is to be exterminated.' Of course. It's in our party programme, elimination of the Jews, extermination. We'll do it. And then they come along, the eighty million good Germans, and every one of them knows a decent Jew. The others are swine, quite clearly, but this particular one is a splendid Jew. Not one of them who says that has seen what is happening, not one of them has been through it. Most of you will know what it means to see a hundred corpses lying side by side, or five hundred, or a thousand. To have lived through that, and apart from a few cases of human weakness, to have remained decent: that is what has made us hard. This is a glorious page in our history, but one which has never been written, and can never be written.[119]

In his own way Himmler was presenting this work as unparalleled. Indeed, the very code name employed by the Nazis, 'The Final Solution of the Jewish Question' illustrates that they felt dissatisfied with earlier restrictions on the Jews.[120]

The policy of exterminating the Jews was carefully planned. It was not the spontaneous eruption of mob violence. It was mainly carried out under the cover of a series of wars, while the motivation for these was explained in quite different terms to the German people. Moreover, the Final Solution could call on the technological and bureaucratic expertise of one of the most advanced nations on earth. There can be no doubt that in its scale the Holocaust proved to be the greatest onslaught on any single racial group.

And yet this is not the only possible perspective.[121] The Zionist movement would claim that the Holocaust was the fulfilment of the predictions it had made about the ubiquity of anti-Semitism and the impossibility of

---

[118] The Nazis were especially concerned to eliminate children. It is reckoned that only 1 in every 14 children of European Jews survived the Holocaust; whereas with adults the figure was 1 in 3. Himmler took pains to justify the execution of children on the ground that it was important not to leave a future generation who would avenge the policy of the Nazis — cf. his statements as cited in Graml, *Antisemitism*, 214–6.

[119] Himmler in *ibid.*, 213.

[120] Dawidowicz, *War*, 17–18.

[121] The Old Testament also sets forth catastrophic judgments of the Jewish people, notably at the time of the capture of Jerusalem by the Babylonians — Is. 1:9; 10:20–23. Je. 44:11–14 and 27–30. cf. Dt. 28:62.

full Jewish integration into other nations.[122] If it made this prediction, and
this met with general acceptance among Jews in the immediate aftermath
of 1945, clearly it saw the Holocaust as the logical development of earlier
treatment of the Jews. The Holocaust may have been different in magnitude from earlier exhibitions of anti-Semitism, but it was not intrinsically
different in kind.

Raul Hilberg has observed that since the fourth century 'there have
been three anti-Jewish policies: conversion, expulsion, and annihilation.
The second appeared as an alternative to the first, and the third as an
alternative to the second.' But they were not radically different alternatives. Each built on its predecessor. Hilberg continues, 'The missionaries
of Christianity had said in effect: You have no right to live amongst us as
Jews. The secular rulers who followed had proclaimed: You have no right
to live among us. The German Nazis at last decreed: You have no right
to live.'[123] Here there was a stage by stage development in antagonism
toward the Jews. The progression was perhaps inevitable as the earlier
measures seemed to have failed to eliminate the separate Jewish identity.

Furthermore, significant similarities can be drawn between the Nazis and earlier anti-Semites. Norman Cohn, for example, has pointed
out that there are parallels between Nazi ideology, especially the view
that the civilized world was threatened by a conspiracy of Jewish
Elders, and the concept of some in the medieval period that the Jews
were a group insidious to Christendom because they had formed a pact
with the devil.[124] Of course, there were differences allowing for the
different ages. The modern picture popular with the Nazis was a
secularized one. The Jews were not seen as seeking supernatural links
with the devil, but as forming a cabal of international conspirators
employing Machiavellian tactics to gain a stranglehold on power. In
the medieval period the evil Jewish 'activities' came to light sporadically
in instances of ritual murder and the like, whereas the Nazis pictured
a constant conspiracy seeking to infect all walks of life. Every unfortunate consequence of modern society could be ascribed to Jewish plotting. The medieval picture demanded a response only with the
'revelation' of another instance of ritual murder. The Nazi scenario,
however, demanded prompt action on a global scale, and insisted on
meeting Jewish 'terror' with terror of its own.

Though the Nazi and medieval myths were different, structurally

---

[122]   Neusner, *Judaism*, 172–3.
[123]   Hilberg, *Destruction*, 1–4.
[124]   Cohn, *Warrant*, 253–6.

they had considerable similarity. Both in effect saw the Jews as repre-
senting the stormtroops of the Antichrist against whom the righteous
would always have to struggle. At the same time the myths were
elaborated in such a way as to insinuate that the Jews were less than
human and so ought not to be accorded full human rights. In the
medieval period it was common for Jews to be assigned horns or other
physical features which somehow set them apart from normal men and
women. Under the Nazis the mental condition of the Jew was highlighted as sub-human —

> The sub-man — that creature which looks as though biologically it were abso-
> lutely the same kind, endowed by Nature with hands, feet and a sort of brain,
> with eyes and mouth — is nevertheless a totally different, a fearful creature, is
> only an attempt at a human being, with a quasi-human face, yet in mind and
> spirit lower than any animal. Inside this being a cruel chaos of wild, unchecked
> passions: a nameless will to destruction, the most primitive lusts, the most
> undisguised vileness. A sub-man — nothing else![125]

We cannot dismiss this as inflated rhetoric. Were not many of the Jews
piled into cattletrucks when they were sent to the concentration camps?
The Nazis, however, were not the first to see the Jews as less than human.

In the medieval period the demonic or sub-human pictures of the
Jews were never officially endorsed by the church, which preferred
more traditional objections like spiritual blindness and responsibility
for the murder of Christ. Moreover, the church insisted that like
Cain, the Jews were on no account to be killed just for being Jews.
But by the Nazi era the power of the church had so waned that these
safeguards counted for nothing. The anti-Semitism of the Nazis,
based as it was on racial considerations and a sort of biological
determinism, contained no inherent restraints. Its logical conclusion
was the elimination of the Jewish people from the human race, like
the amputation of an incurably diseased limb from an otherwise
healthy body.

Nazi anti-Semitism borrowed to some degree from earlier Christian anti-Semitism. It was not simply a matter of copying tactics from
an earlier Christian era, though the Nazis do seem to have been well
informed on the numerous devices employed in medieval Europe to
restrict the Jews.[126] At one stage Himmler was fascinated by the
potential of the ritual murder charge for planting the seeds of anti-
Semitism in lands where the Nazis did not yet exert an influence.[127]

---

[125] from a tract issued by SS Headquarters and quoted at *ibid.*, 188.
[126] Hilberg, *Destruction*, 4–6.
[127] Cohn, *Warrant*, 206.

That was bad enough. The Christian legacy, however, went deeper. Nazism depended for its success on the highly negative image of the Jews which had been implanted in Germany (and in many other places in Europe) by Christians among others.[128] Why, after all, was it the Jews and not some other race who were chosen as the antithesis of the Aryan master race?

It is cold comfort that Hitler was at heart as anti-Christian as he was anti-Jewish, and admitted privately his eventual intention of 'tearing up Christianity root and branch, and annihilating it in Germany'.[129] In practice, Hitler had to make accommodations with Christians in Germany if he was to have any success in prosecuting both his foreign wars and his policies against the Jews.[130] Nazi propaganda had surprisingly little success in turning Germans away from their church allegiances. In the 1939 German census only five per cent of the population regarded themselves as without any connection to the Christian churches.[131] Perhaps even a considerable number of the German Jews who perished under the Third Reich were converts to Christianity of some sort.

But this does not justify laying all the blame on the Christian church of Hitler's own day. Much damage had been done in earlier generations. Besides, the advent of the Nazi dictatorship put the churches in a series of moral dilemmas of which the Jewish question was not considered among the more serious. As Owen Chadwick has observed, 'the damning thing is less Christian anti-Semitism than Christian failure to do anything; or, if that is too strong, to do much.'[132] In the same vein Simon Wiesenthal has pointed out that since a stand was not made against the lesser injustices (as when the Jews were made to scrub the pavements in Vienna), it became impossible to resist the much greater injustices.[133] By endorsing the idea that there was a Jewish problem,

---

[128]   compare the speech of Julius Streicher to Hitler Youth in 1935 where he described Christ as 'the greatest anti-Semite of all times' and made various other religious allusions — Hilberg, *Destruction*, 12.

[129]   Rauschning, *Hitler*, 57–63 cf. 232. Gutteridge, *Open*, 295–6 points out that there were clear signs that the Nazis bracketed Jews and Christians together as joint enemies, but most Christians were too blind to notice.

[130]   Conway, *Nazi*, 166–7 and 328–9.

[131]   *ibid.*, 232. Of the remaining 5 per cent, 3.5 per cent declared themselves 'God believers', while only 1.5 per cent professed to be atheists.

[132]   Owen Chadwick in (ed.) Ernest-Wolfang Bøckenførde and Edward Shils, *Jews and Christians in a Pluralistic World* (Weidenfeld and Nicolson, London, 1991) 120.

[133]   Wiesenthal, *Justice*, 359.

the churches did not oppose the first comparatively mild anti-Jewish measures of the Third Reich. And so, by the time the trains started running to Auschwitz it was too late to do anything significant.[134]

But, to put things in perspective, European Jews themselves admit that they underestimated the threat posed by Hitler.[135] And that is witness enough that the Holocaust was quite unexpected, if not absolutely unique.

---

[134] for a detailed consideration as to why the German churches did so little see Gutteridge, *Open*, 267–305, and Conway, *Nazi*, 331–7.
[135] Wiesenthal, *Justice*, 354.

Eleven

Arab and Islamic anti-Semitism

Today the greatest cauldron for anti-Semitic propaganda and activity is the Islamic world, especially the Arab countries. Of course, this is closely tied to a complex political issue — the Palestinian question involving the right of Jews to occupy and control the state of Israel. But with this issue politics and religion overlap extensively. The state of Israel is a flashpoint for international tension because it has been established in the heart of what has been considered the Muslim world. It is not easy to say where an essentially political anti-Zionism has merged into anti-Semitism. Contemporary anti-Semites in the Middle East (and elsewhere) can camouflage their true feelings about Jews behind anti-Zionist rhetoric.[1] Equally, Israel and her supporters can deflect legitimate criticism by raising the spectre of anti-Semitism.[2]

We are often beguiled by a popular conception — that the Muslim religion has always been characterized by zealous fanatics who have not hesitated to resort to any tactic which will advance the cause of Allah. Yet, this picture applies to only a particular element in Islam which has attained prominence today because of novel political circumstances. It is particularly misleading when we turn to the question of Muslim attitudes toward the Jews. Violent hostility toward the Jews is a comparatively new phenomenon in the history of Islam.[3] It emerged

---

[1]   Wistrich, *Anti-Semitism*, 250–1. Equally it has been difficult for some western Christians to distinguish a sympathy for the Jewish plight and the state of Israel from support for political Zionism. Amid a vast literature see Chapman, *Whose*, esp. 268–282.

[2]   Ruether and Ruether, *Wrath*, 221–4.

[3]   Cohen, *Crescent*, sets out an extensive comparison of the Jewish situation under Christendom and under Islam during the medieval period. He documents the superiority of the Jews under Islam. He also points out at pages 3–14 how this academic issue has become embroiled in current political questions.

in earnest in the last century in the Islamic world, first among Christian groups and later spreading to Muslims themselves. Its growth this century, particularly in the aftermath of the formation of the Jewish state of Israel, has been one of the most remarkable and worrying trends in recent times. From being an alien import (largely from Christianity), it has taken on a life of its own, rather as anti-Semitism did in Nazi Germany.

The picture of the Jews in the early Muslim writings

A largely negative picture of the Jews is presented in the Quran and still more in the Hadith, the oral traditions concerning the life of Muhammad which carry weight in Muslim ethics.[4] While passages in the Quran show some respect for the Jews as a 'people of the book', it is made clear that they rest under a curse — 'Shame and misery were stamped upon them and they incurred the wrath of Allah; because they disbelieved His signs and slew His prophets unjustly; because they were rebels and transgressors.'[5] Their essential and persistent fault had been to reject the messengers or prophets God had sent them. The last straw had been to refuse to accept God's final and supreme prophet, Muhammad, a decision which was ascribed not to ignorance but to pique that this prophet should not have come from their own race. Thus the unbelieving and treacherous character of the Jews was unmasked. It was useless to look for any improvement because where God had decreed that their hearts should harden, so it would remain. Other passages in the Quran accuse the Jews of falsehood, especially in that most serious of all realms, the distortion of Scripture. They were tainted too with cowardice and greed. It comes as no surprise to read, 'the most implacable of men in their opposition to the faithful are the Jews and the pagans.'[6]

Muhammad's own career brought him into close contact with Jews, notably in the city of Medina where he encountered various Jewish clans and three major Jewish tribes.[7] He expelled two of the latter from

---

[4] for the Hadith see Harkabi, *Attitudes*, 222.

[5] *Sura* 2:62. The translation is that of N.J. Dawood in the Penguin edition (Harmondsworth 1974). There is an interesting account of the standard Muslim interpretation of this text by Haggai Ben-Shammai in Almog *Antisemitism, 164–5*.

[6] *Sura* 5:82 There is a more detailed account of the Quranic picture in Wistrich *Anti-Semitism*, 199–200 and in Ben-Shammai in Almog, *Antisemitism*, 161–9.

[7] for the importance of his experiences in Medina in Muhammad's formulation of his view on the Jews see Nettler, *Trials*, 4–6.

Medina, while he massacred all the males in the third tribe, the Banu Qurayza. Though at first he had sought to win the support of the Jews, in the main they derided his claims to be a prophet in the Jewish tradition. Muhammad accused them not only of unbelief but sometimes of outright treachery.[8] There was even a story that Muhammad died a slow, lingering death as a result of being poisoned by a Jewish woman, Zaynab.[9] Another Muslim tradition ascribed to Jewish machinations the first great dissension in the Muslim Community, before and after the assassination of the third caliph Uthman.[10] These should not be dismissed as of antiquarian interest, since Muslims regard actions and attitudes expressed by Muhammad during his lifetime as setting a pattern for future generations.[11] If Muhammad is believed to have been a man of the sword and have used his sword for the killing of Jews, amongst other peoples, a significant precedent has been established.

It is true that Muhammad also adopted the very different policy of imposing tribute on a conquered non-Muslim population in return for protection, and this is the policy which prevailed in the days of the early Muslim conquests.[12] But this century has witnessed renewed emphasis on some of the more violent sayings of Muhammad. Thus the modern militant Islamic organization Hamas (the Islamic Resistance Movement) has included in its constitution this hadith — 'The day will come when Muslims will fight the Jews and kill them to the degree that the Jew will hide behind the rocks and trees which will call out to the Muslim and tell him, "Servant of Allah, a Jew is hiding behind me. Come and kill me!" '[13] Or again, no less a person than King Feisal of Saudi Arabia, guardian of Islam's holiest shrines, has declared, 'Verily the word of God teaches us and we believe it, that for a Muslim to kill a Jew, or for him to be killed by a Jew, ensures him an immediate entry into heaven and into the august presence of God Almighty.'[14] In effect,

---

[8] for Muhammad and the Jews see W. Montgomery Watt, *Muhammad — Prophet and Statesman*, (Oxford, 1961) 112–8; 148–151; 171–5; 188–194.

[9] Wistrich, *Anti-Semitism*, 200.

[10] Nettler, *Trials*, 39.

[11] for the authority of the Hadith see Kenneth Cragg, *The Call of the Minaret* (Collins, 1985) 89–94.

[12] Cohen, *Crescent*, 56–7 and 163. This tribute was mentioned in the Quran — *Sura* 9:29.

[13] article 7 of the Hamas consitution as quoted by David Dolan, *Israel: The Struggle to Survive* (Hodder and Stoughton (London, 1992) 171. For the background to this hadith see Harkabi, *Attitudes*, 269.

[14] quoted by Wistrich 233.

the killing of Jews has become a religious duty. It is little wonder that we have seen suicide bombers at work against Israeli (and other related) targets.

Some have argued that the Quran lends less weight to strictures against the Jews than does the Christian New Testament.[15] After all, there is no suggestion of the charge of deicide, since in the Quran Jesus is not the Son of God and he does not die on the cross. Nor are the Jews assigned any special diabolical character (as some have wrongly found in the New Testament). Instead, the greatest condemnation is given to unbelievers or perhaps apostates, without further delineation. But this is to overlook the most significant point in the Quranic picture, which is its absolute fatalism.[16] If Allah wills that the Jews remain unbelievers for all time, so they will. There is no alternative prospect — a very different scenario from the New Testament. The Quranic picture was summarized by King Saud (the father of King Feisal) when he described the Jews as 'a race accursed by God according to His Holy Book, and destined to final destruction and everlasting damnation.'[17] To seek accommodation with Jews is pointless, if not sinful.[18] As we shall see, Islamic Fundamentalists go even further and make the Jews almost into the very incarnation of evil.

Besides, the Quran cannot be taken in isolation. It is not in practice the sole authority for Muslim conduct. It requires to be supplemented by commentaries and by the Hadith. And these, as we have seen, encourage, at least in certain circumstances, the killing of Jews, an action which neither the New Testament nor official church teaching has ever sanctioned. Indeed, the question arises why for so long in the Muslim world the practice was less austere than the theory, whereas in Christian Europe from the Middle Ages the reverse was true and official sanctions against the murder of the Jews were either ignored or circumvented.[19]

---

[15] e.g *ibid.*, 202.

[16] for the difference between the predestination found in the Christian Scriptures and the fatalism of the Quran see Samuel M. Zwerner, *The Moslem Doctrine of God* (American Tract Society, New York 1905) 93–106.

[17] Wistrich *Anti-Semitism* 232.

[18] This is exactly the point made in Article 13 of the Hamas Constitution.

[19] Lewis *TJOI* 24. Lewis also makes the point that though the Quran is more friendly toward Christians than to Jews, there was no appreciable difference in the way in which Christian and Jewish dhimmis were treated — *ibid.*, 61–2.

A subservient status for Jewish communities

The explanation lies partly in historical circumstances and partly in a different slant in the Quran to that which I have outlined above. Some sections of the Quran have been interpreted as endorsing a form of religious pluralism, though certainly not of the equality of all religions.[20] Besides, the Arabia where Muhammad lived was pluralistic. While Muhammad insisted in banishing all idolatry, he would tolerate monotheistic 'peoples of the book' where they acknowledged his political leadership.[21] In the lands which were subsequently conquered by Muslim armies, the ruling Muslim groups were at first a dominant minority among other minorities. It was convenient for them to tolerate most of these minorities, including Jews. Within the Muslim world for many centuries the Jews did not normally constitute a threat to the Muslim supremacy either theologically (since they represented a religion that had been superseded) or socially (since they remained an insignificant minority). Very few Muslim works were written against Judaism. Ironically, these derived mainly from Christian converts to Islam who brought with them strong anti-Jewish prejudices.[22]

In Muslim law and practice Jewish communities (along with Christians and Zoroastrians, all of whom were considered peoples of the book) were accorded better treatment than pagans by Muslim states. They became in effect a protected minority covered by a pact called dhimma. The peoples themselves were known as dhimmis and were allowed freedom to practise their religion provided they paid a poll tax and recognized the supremacy of Islam. Their social subservience, which was thought to be mandated by the Quran, was tangibly expressed in detailed restrictions in their dress, their mounts, their saddles and their headgear. They were not to bear arms, and were to refrain from noise and displays in their own ceremonies. On no account were their synagogues, churches or whatever to be higher than the local mosques. While walking in the streets, they had to show deference to the Muslims by walking on the left (or impure) side of the Muslim. Their gait had to be rapid and their eyes lowered. Again, if they were riding their donkey in the country and saw a Muslim, they had to dismount out of deference to their superior and only remount once their superior had passed out of sight. Thus, detailed measures were applied to ensure that Jews, in common with the other dhimmi groups, were

---

20   *ibid.*, 13–16.
21   Watt (note 8) 175.
22   Lewis, *TJOI*, 85–6.

aware of their social humiliation.[23] Where these rules were breached, they were sometimes noted in Muslim literature as rare and undesirable exceptions.[24] Since such breaches were unusual, the prevailing attitude of Muslims toward Jews remained that of a superior's contempt for his inferior. There was, however, little hatred of an adherent to a rival religion.[25] Where persecution did affect the Jews, they suffered because of their status as dhimmis rather than as Jews.[26]

Dhimmi status did not prevent Jews from engaging in lucrative vocations, especially in commerce, banking and brokerage (careers from which Muslims kept apart because they involved contact with infidels) or from participating in government.[27] Normally they were involved in the lower or middle ranks of state bureaucracy, but occasionally penetrated to higher circles. The prominence, however, associated with the latter did not tie in well with their supposed subordinate status. A backlash against the individual concerned or the Jewish community sometimes followed.[28] Moreover, the period from about 900 to 1200 saw a flourishing of Jewish cultural achievement to coincide with the renaissance of medieval Islam. Jews worked side by side with Muslims in medicine, the sciences and in philosophy at this period. It was a remarkable time for cultural and intellectual harmony.[29]

Since the Muslim authorities treated their obligations to dhimmis as a legally binding oath, outright persecution of the Jews was rare under this system. When it did occur, this was where Muslim hegemony was threatened. Thus we find accounts of massacres in Spain and in Morocco which significantly were near to the borders with Christendom.[30] We discover too that the challenge of the Crusades and later of the Mongol invasions were difficult times for the dhimmis.[31] Indeed, where Muslims perceived their power to be weakening, they were inclined to be less tolerant.[32] At the very least this meant the imposition of harsher

---

[23] The precise details varied somewhat from place to place, but the general principles were the same. For more details see Cohen, *Crescent*, 52–74 and Lewis, *TJOI*, 24–30.
[24] Nettler, *Trials*, 9–10.
[25] Lewis, *TJOI* 32–33. He also points out that Muslims on the whole were less concerned about heresy than were Christians in the medieval period.
[26] Cohen, *Crescent*, 163–4.
[27] *ibid.*, 28–9.
[28] for some examples see Cohen, *Crescent*, 164–6.
[29] Lewis, *TJOI* 56–7
[30] Wistrich *Anti-Semitism*, 196–7
[31] Lewis, *TJOI*, 54–5
[32] *ibid.*, 147.

dhimmi conditions. Sometimes it was argued that by undue prominence in society a dhimmi group had broken the terms of their covenant. Therefore, the ruling Muslims were no longer bound by their
promise to protect them. Thus, a Muslim poet, Abu Ishaq, is said in
1066 to have provoked a massacre in Granada of the entire Jewish
community (of about 4,000 souls) with a long poem including such
words as these —

> *Do not consider it a breach of faith to kill them,*
> *the breach of faith would be to let them carry on.*
> *They have violated our covenant with them,*
> *so how can you be held guilty against the violators?*
> *How can they have any pact*
> *when we are obscure and they are prominent?*[33]

While dhimmi status involved mutual obligations and in this respect
had parallels with the arrangements in Europe set out by Popes such
as Innocent III, the violation of the covenant was potentially more
serious in the Muslim world. In Christian society killing Jews was, at
least in theory, never an acceptable option.

Political changes in the nineteenth and twentieth centuries.

Dhimmi status began to crumble in the nineteenth century with the
inroads of the European colonial powers (especially France, Britain and
Russia) into the Muslim world. Even where Muslim rulers retained
power as in the Ottoman Empire, dhimmi groups, mainly Christians
but also some Jews, often prospered. For one thing, trading links with
the European and non-Muslim world were taken up much more readily
by dhimmis than by Muslims, who were still bound by scruples about
dealing with infidels.[34] Besides, the French and Russians regularly
intervened within the Ottoman Empire on behalf of Roman Catholics
and Orthodox Christians respectively.[35] Even the egalitarian ideals of
the French Revolution filtered through to the Muslim world. Though
they cut clean across the fundamental Muslim distinction between
believer and unbeliever, they were not without their influence. The
Ottoman Empire, for example, established equal citizen rights in 1856.[36]

It did not, however, follow that the collapse of the dhimmi system
was uniformly good news for the Jews. Christians benefited much

---

[33]   recorded in Lewis, *TJOI*, 45.
[34]   *ibid.*, 63–4
[35]   *ibid.*, 159–60. Britain tried with less success to become a patron of the Jews living
within the Ottoman Empire.
[36]   *ibid.*, 64–5

more. In fact, they could use their new-found power against the Jews. Where the Jews were beginning to enter a new phase of economic activity and prosperity, as in the Ottoman Empire, Christian merchants scented the possibility of unwelcome competition and sought to stifle it.[37] To this end they were assisted in the second half of the nineteenth century by an upsurge in anti-Semitism ideas emanating from Europe. They also gave a new lease of life to the blood libel, the idea that Jews were required by their religion to murder Christian children and use their blood to bake Passover bread. Though the notion was denounced by the Ottoman authorities, as they had traditionally done, it did not stop these accusations reaching epidemic proportions.[38] At first the Muslim population was largely unaffected by this overspill of the worst forms of Christian anti-Semitism. They recognized that both they and the Jews were victims of a changing political climate.[39]

But this situation did not last. Toward the end of the nineteenth century we find the first of a new-style Muslim polemic against the Jews. Most of it was directly translated from European anti-Semitism literature published around the time of the Dreyfus affair.[40] It is no coincidence that it appeared around the time of the emergence of political Zionism, and was to grow as Jewish interest and activity in Palestine intensified in the twentieth century.

In recent times, therefore, anti-Semitism has entered the Muslim world via Christian populations in its own midst. It was not the culmination of the Islamic tradition, but more the result of the breakdown of the dhimmi arrangement. Once anti-Semitism had re-entered into the Muslim world, it could quickly identify new sources of inspiration from within its own early history, notably from the Quran and the Hadith. In both of these there was plenty of fuel to light a conflagration of anti-Semitism hatred in the appropriate historical circumstances.

The increasing status of minority groups within the Islamic world was bound to provoke something of a crisis among Muslims, because Islam is in its essence a triumphalist religion. Moreover, its superiority must find expression in the political realm. 'For a Moslem, the will of Allah comes to realization in the political order. The arena wherein

---

[37]   ed. Norman A. Stillman, *The Jews of Arab Lands: A History and Source Book* (Philadelphia 1979) 107.

[38]   Lewis, *TJOI* 156–9. The most notorious of such incidents was the Damascus Affair of 1840 which led to intense diplomatic activity culminating in a declaration by the Ottoman Sultan that there was no basis in the blood libel. Nonetheless, the truth of the accusation is still maintained today in certain Muslim academic circles — *ibid.*, 186.

[39]   *ibid.*, 171.

[40]   *ibid.*, 184–5.

salvation is worked out and God's sovereignty made manifest is the state.'[41] Here there is a marked contrast with Christianity, whose truth is not dependent on its political success in this world — though within medieval Christendom this was wrongly assumed to be the case, with unfortunate results for the Jews. Muhammad's claims stand by virtue of his political success. Muhammad made out that he was the last and supreme prophet of God, and so superior to all predecessors. His religion was infinitely superior to all other forms of religion in existence. 'It was Allah who has sent forth His apostle with guidance and the true faith to make it triumphant over all religions, however much the idolaters may dislike it.'[42] Hence, if Muhammad's prophecies are ever universally rejected or simply marginalized, either God would be proving a failure in his revelation or Muhammad's credentials as a prophet would be undermined. And neither of these is acceptable to a Muslim.[43]

Muhammad's claims have been historically corroborated by his own success in forming a religious community, and not least in triumphing over his former enemies in Mecca and in purging the Kaaba of its idols.[44] The same applies with all other true prophets in earlier times. After meeting opposition, they are vindicated by eventually triumphing over their enemies. Thus, Muslims find it inconceivable that God should have allowed Jesus (in Islamic thought a true prophet) to die on the cross, and suggest that in one way or another God saved Jesus from such a humiliating experience.[45] The success of Muhammad as the supreme prophet was vital to Islam in the long term. Temporary reversals, like the Muslim defeat at the Battle of Uhud, could be accommodated, but not long-term political defeat or disgrace.[46] The same would apply to Muslim armies fighting in the cause of Allah. Abu Ishaq, the Spanish Muslim to whom I have referred above, put the point succinctly, 'God watches His own people and the people of God will prevail.'[47]

---

[41] Father John C. Haughey quoted in Nettler, *Trials*, 4.

[42] *Sura* 9:33.

[43] Muslim sensitivities at this point have been made plain through the Salman Rushdie affair. Rushdie raised doubts about Muhammad's claims to be a prophet when he highlighted the issue of the Satanic verses — for the background to this see Watt (note 8) 60–5.

[44] Nettler, *Trials, 6.*

[45] Cragg (note 11). 265-8

[46] for a somewhat less optimistic Muslim view of the future see Michael Cook *Muhammad* (Oxford 1983) 41.

[47] see note 24 above. At *Sura* 9:29, for example, Muslims are urged to holy war against unbelieving Jews and Christians 'until they pay tribute out of hand and are utterly subdued.' The implication is that they will ultimately be successful in their warfare.

But what if political circumstances arise which allow infidels to gain the upper hand over Muslims? Toward the end of the nineteenth century the Muslim world became conscious that it was largely under the cultural and economic domination of western powers which were non-Islamic. It seemed as if in the process of history God had perhaps forsaken his cause.[48] The result has been a determined attempt by Muslims in this century to reassert their religious identity and to meet the various challenges of modernity to their faith. In this they have been partly successful, though doubts remain about whether the new material prosperity of much of the Arab world has not been achieved at the expense of spiritual values, while divisions within the Muslim world remain as intractable as ever. In particular, minorities have been regarded with less toleration. Christian Armenians and Muslim Kurds have experienced massacres along with some of the Jewish populations which remained scattered throughout much of the Muslim world after many centuries.[49] Since the establishment of the state of Israel and even more after Israel's success in the Six Day War of 1967, Jews living in the North African countries, in Egypt, in Syria, in Iraq and in Iran have been so hounded that only a pitiful remnant remains from once extensive and thriving communities. Though such Jews were initially unenthusiastic about Zionism, which they perceived as a European movement, they have been forced by events into that standpoint. As Albert Memmi, a Tunisian-born Jew put it, 'We should have liked to be Arab Jews. If we abandoned the idea, it is because over the centuries the Muslim Arabs systematically prevented its realization by their contempt and cruelty.'[50] Today, the concept of an 'Arab Jew' sounds almost like a contradiction in terms. That is a measure of the hostility engendered among Muslims by the state of Israel.

The threat to Islam posed by the state of Israel

The very existence of a sovereign Jewish state in the Arab heartland, to say nothing of its successful resistance to Arab armies, represents a threat to the political triumphalism which is part of the Muslim identity. It is acceptable to have Jews living in Palestine under dhimmi status; even a militant organization like Hamas have indicated they would be satisfied to attain this.[51] But it is a very different matter when

---

48   Cragg (note 11) 189–90.
49   Wistrich *Anti-Semitism* 208–9
50   quoted in *ibid.*, 240.
51   cf. Article 6 of its Constitution.

the roles are reversed and Jews can treat Palestinian Arabs as their social inferiors. With the whole Islamic world identifying the Arab countries as her heartland, Palestine is irretrievably associated with Islam. Besides, Palestine contains several Islamic holy sites, notably the Abrahamic mosque in Hebron and the Dome of the Rock in Jerusalem, the spot from which Muhammad is said to have made a journey into heaven. Jerusalem was also the first place toward which Muslims were directed to pray. Even now it is ranked the third holiest city in the Muslim world.[52] But the religious concerns of Muslims about these holy sites ought not to be evaluated too highly. Their outrage about Jerusalem has surfaced only when it has fallen into the control of non-Muslims — first at the time of the medieval Crusades and then after 1967 when the Israelis captured east Jerusalem.[53]

Generally, Islam has not taken pride of place in the struggle against the state of Israel. The first attempts to stifle the state of Israel were fuelled more by Arab or Palestinian nationalism than by Islam. When the PLO was set up in 1964, it was largely under the direction of President Nasser of Egypt, a leader of a decidedly secular turn of mind, who thought he could combine the goals of Arab unity and the liberation of Palestine. The PLO even included some Christians and had a non-religious, socialist wing.[54] In more recent times Palestinian Christians have played a significant part in the intifada — out of all proportion to their small numbers.[55]

PLO ideals were expressed in terms of liberation and self-determination for the Palestinian peoples; they were the language of western political discourse and not the language of Islam.[56] Thus, the Palestinian National Covenant endorsed by the PLO in 1968 began with this statement, 'Palestine is the homeland of the Arab Palestinian people; it is an indivisible part of the Arab homeland, and the Palestinian people are an integral part of the Arab nation.' A later article explains the political implications of this nationalist creed — 'The liberation of Palestine, from an Arab viewpoint, is a national duty and it attempts to repel the Zionist and imperialist aggression against the Arab homeland, and aims at the elimination of Zionism in Palestine. Absolute responsibility for this falls upon

---

[52] Naim Ateek in Walker, *Jerusalem*, 127–9.
[53] Wistrich, *Anti-Semitism*, 231–2.
[54] Chapman, *Whose*, 93.
[55] for some background to these Palestinian Christians and some examples of their thinking see Ruether and Ruether, *Wrath*, 181–9.
[56] The idea, however, of a covenant comes from the Quran — Harkabi, *Palestinian*, 27. The original 1964 Covenant also contained a formal Islamic preamble — *ibid.*, 107.

the Arab nation — peoples and governments — with the Arab people of Palestine in the vanguard.'[57] The enemy is identified with Zionism, in effect the state of Israel, itself the creation of imperialist and racialist aggressors who have sought to rob the Arabs of their rights. Yasser Arafat's Fatah group, which became supreme within the PLO in 1968, even argued that a militarily powerful state like Israel could hardly have been the creation of the despised and subservient Jewish people acting on their own. They were, in fact, being used as a new front for the activities of western colonialists and imperialists. Thus they employed the sort of Marxist rhetoric common to liberation movements in many Third World countries in the 1960s.[58] Israel and international Zionism, therefore, were not the exclusive targets of the early PLO. Both Islamic and anti-Semitic themes were noticeably absent at this time when the PLO was canvassing for international support from 'all liberals' and 'all forces of good, peace and progress in the world' in their struggle against the imperialists.[59]

In the main the Covenant adheres to the sort of expressions we might expect in the charter of any independence movement. There is one point, however, where it does overstep these bounds and indulge in anti-Semitic rhetoric. In article 22 Zionism is not only dismissed as fanatical, racist and imperialist, but 'its methods are those of the Fascists and the Nazis'. This line of propaganda, by which the Jews are dubbed as being as bad as their Nazi persecutors, has proved very popular in the Muslim world and wider afield.[60] In November 1975 the United Nations even passed a resolution equating Zionism with racism.[61] This jibe is all the more ironic in a PLO document which affirms the rights of a different national group and talks of the necessity of 'armed struggle' and 'commando action' by that group to liberate Palestine.[62] Indeed, the National Covenant is an absolutist statement recognizing the rights of only one group in the Palestinian conflict and denying all possibility of compromise. As Yehoshafat Harkabi has put it, 'The conflict is presented as a zero-game and a deadly quarrel of survival without compromise. We say "yes" to Palestine, the Palestin-

---

[57] Articles 1 and 15 as translated in Harkabi, *Palestinian*. The 1968 Covenant represents a minor revision of an original 1964 covenant. This covenant has never been formally annulled or repealed — Rubin, *Revolution*, 20.
[58] Rubin, *Revolution* 8–9.
[59] Article 22 of the Palestinian National Covenant.
[60] Wistrich *Anti-Semitism*, 247.
[61] Rubin *Revolution*, 47. This resolution was repealed in 1991 — *ibid.*, 186.
[62] cf. Articles 9 and 10. the PLO did eventually renounce terrorism in a declaration from Algiers in 1988.

ian state, and therefore we say "no" to Israel.'[63] This need not be construed in an anti-Semitic light. After all, it is common in political controversy for one side to claim to be in the right and their opponents to be guilty of all the injustices; but clearly there is considerable potential for anti-Semitic developments.

Despite the relative political sophistication of the Palestinian National Covenant and the avoidance of the language of Islamic jihad, its original framers could not realistically hope to insist on an Arab identity without recourse to Islam. Robert Wistrich has highlighted the difficulties of establishing a purely political pan-Arabism, 'Although Arabism tried to identify what constitutes Arab identity through history, language and culture, the only social cohesion on which it seems able to build is that which has been instilled by Islam.'[64] In time, then, pan-Arabism had to rely more heavily on Islam, especially a militant Islam, if it was to be a major factor in attacks against the state of Israel. This was notably true after the debacle of the Six Day War of 1967 when the armies of Arab coalitions under the control of secular leaders failed to dislodge Israel. Moreover, the proportion of Christians among the Palestinians has declined substantially in recent decades.[65]

Going back further into the past, in the 1920's and 1930's Arab opposition to Jewish settlement in Palestine had ranged widely in the accusations it brought against the Jews. As well as asserting their right to self-determination, the Arabs complained that the Jewish settlers were part of a Communist plot for world domination. The Grand Mufti of Jerusalem, Haj Amin al-Husseini, who was later assiduously to court the support of Hitler, proclaimed that the Jews had designs on the Temple Mount area in order to rebuild Solomon's Temple on the ruins of the mosques. Thus he stirred up popular Islamic feeling in Palestine and, in a foretaste of the more recent conduct of Saddam Hussein, was to appeal to Muslim leaders throughout the world for concerted action in defence of the Muslim holy places against Zionist designs.[66] Shortly he was able to be instrumental in fomenting three days of pogroms in August 1929

---

[63]   Harkabi, *Palestinian*, 14. It remains to be seen how the National Covenant is affected by the Israeli–PLO peace agreement of September 1993.

[64]   Wistrich, *Anti-Semitism*, 307 note 14.

[65]   Patrick Johnstone, *Operation World* (OM Publications, Carlisle 1993) 315 estimates that Palestinian Christians have declined from 30 per cent in 1940 to 2.5 per cent in 1990, at least in the Middle East.

[66]   *ibid.*, 241–4.

which left 133 Jews dead and a further 339 wounded. The blatant anti-Semitism of the Grand Mufti, which made no distinction between anti-Zionism and opposition to Jews as such, was discredited for a while on the international stage once the details of the Holocaust became known. But it never entirely disappeared from the Muslim world.[67] It had already proved its power to incite the passions of ordinary Muslims. Besides, the Arab world has maintained an ambivalent attitude to the legacy of Hitler and his Nazi government. On the one hand, the founders of the PLO utilized the widespread condemnation of fascism and Nazism when they accused Israel in the context of their National Covenant of these very sins; but at the same time some Arabs have been sympathetic to Hitler.[68] His *Mein Kampf*, along with other Nazi anti-Semitic material, is regularly printed in the Arab world. The Saudi Arabian authorities have even used some of their extensive revenues to fund anti-Semitic Holocaust denial literature in the West.[69] Perhaps this betokens more their obsession with the Jewish question than any genuine admiration for Hitler, whose ideas of Aryan racial supremacy are unlikely to be congenial to Arabs. But it is simply because Arab passions on this question have reached such a pitch that they are so dangerous. Besides, most Arabs have little understanding of the Holocaust since it is not part of their immediate history.[70] An absence both of sympathy and of rational judgment toward the Jewish predicament could be a lethal combination.

A further example of this irrationality may be found in the reaction to the epoch-making statement from the Second Vatican Council in 1965 whereby the charge of deicide was removed from the Jewish people. Although the Muslim religion holds that Jesus did not die on the cross, Muslim leaders were horrified at this change and made public protest about it. The Council of the World Muslim League in Mecca, for example, dismissed it as 'a purely political move aimed at securing the Christian world's support for the Zionist concept and its devilish and wicked designs against Islam, the Arabs, and the whole human race.'[71] Many Muslims

---

[67] Lewis, *SAS*, 160–3.

[68] David K. Shipler, *Arab and Jew — Wounded Spirits in a Promised Land* (Bloomsbury, London 1987) 334–5. It is only fair to add that some Palestinians do deplore the Holocaust, and see themselves as lumbered with the guilt that really belongs to Europe.

[69] *ibid.*, 233–4.

[70] *ibid.*, 339.

[71] Wistrich *Anti-Semitism* 235–6.

evidently had a vested interest in ensuring the embers of anti-Semitism elsewhere in the world were kept alight, because this would affect the amount of international support the state of Israel would receive.

This does not mean that all anti-Semitism in the Muslim world is simply plagiarized from Europe or can be explained entirely by hostility to Israel. Certainly, there is little in previous traditions of anti-Semitism from which the Arab world has not drawn.[72] Only the racial theories current in Germany from the 1880's have been exempt.[73] This may be in part due to their secular bias, but even more because they formed the rationale for an independent state of Israel. Whereas Hitler and the racial anti-Semites said the Jews were a race and not a religion, the Arabs have reversed this. Thus, the Palestinian Covenant states, 'Judaism is a revealed religion; it is not a separate nationality nor are the Jews a single people with a separate identity; they are citizens of their respective countries.'[74] One extreme view of Jewish identity (that Jews are merely a race) has been replaced by another (that Jewishness is merely a religion). Neither view is helpful. The reality is more complex.

Islamic Fundamentalism and anti-Semitism

The Arabs have added a new and effective dimension to the history of anti-Semitism. They have created the image of Israel as a racist and fascist state. Thereby they have tapped general revulsion against the horrors of Nazi totalitarianism, and have exploited Israel's difficulties with the Palestinians. This picture may have been largely designed for external propaganda. But it is strengthened by the predominant image of the Jew within the Arab world itself — 'the portrait of the aggressive, brutal Jew who embraces violence without remorse.'[75] This has formed an explosive mixture with Palestinian aspirations after autonomy and Islamic concerns about a non-Islamic state in its heartland.

But perhaps the most significant development of all is what has been called 'the Islamization of anti-Semitism.'[76] It is manifest in a height-

---

[72] Lewis, *TJOI*, 185–8.

[73] But Harkabi, *Attitudes*, 300 argues that though Arabs would not directly cite a racial argument against the Jews, on close inspection there does turn out to be a racial element in their anti-Semitism since from the very first the Jews are said to have destroyed the element of truth their religion contained and to have preserved that error through their religious and cultural channels.

[74] Article 20 of the Palestinian National Covenant.

[75] Shipler (note 68), 199.

[76] Lewis, *SAS*, 196

ened sense of the evil represented by the Jew. No longer are Arabs content to describe Jews as rather pathetic pawns in the hands of the great western imperialist nations; it is the imperialist nations which are controlled by the sinister Jews.[77] In the Islamic world Fundamentalists have seized most of the intellectual high ground.[78] Effectively, they have promoted a novel but by no means eccentric interpretation of the Quran and other traditional Muslim authorities. These Fundamentalist groups have proved influential because it is plain that the Muslim world has a crisis of identity, prompted by the prominence of the supposedly humiliated Jews and by the influx of western values and traditions.[79] The Fundamentalist movement has rallied those who would utterly reject these new ways and would resist any attempt to accommodate Islam to modernity. The solution to the crisis, as they see it, is to return to the Muslim 'Creed', understood as the comprehensive wisdom of the Quran and related documents, to which the Muslim community adhered in its earlier successful days. It would be an insult to Allah's wise guidance to suggest his revelation is somehow insufficient for the twentieth century and requires to be supplemented by modern science, scholarship or whatever.[80] Instead, Muslims should pay renewed heed to the Quranic stress on jihad (holy war) which they understand in a physical sense and advocate should be applied to all enemies both inside and outside the Muslim world. Fundamentalists are well aware that other professing Muslims, including statesmen and even religious leaders, do not share their viewpoint. They are not, however, disturbed by this opposition. Far from it. It is to them evidence of the extent to which Muslims, wittingly or unwittingly, have become a prey to hostile Jewish influences.[81]

It is a characteristic of these fundamentalist groups to attack verbally and otherwise their own national leaders if they see them as compromisers or hypocrites. The late President Sadat of Egypt was assassinated by one such group, angered primarily by his peace agree-

---

[77] *ibid.*, 194.
[78] Here I base much of my account on the work of the Egyptian writer and Islamic Fundamentalist, Sayyid Qutb, whose main treatise on the Jews is translated by Nettler, *Trials*, 71–87. Much of the rest of Nettler's book is commentary on this fascinating and seminal text.
[79] Wistrich, *Anti-Semitism*, 224–6.
[80] Qutb as found in Nettler, *Trials*, 76–77.
[81] for the difference between Islamic traditionalists and Islamic Fundamentalists — Nettler, *Trials*, 16–19.

ment with Israel. More recently Hamas represents a disillusionment with the PLO, who they feel have compromised with Israel. They affirm, 'Initiatives, so-called peaceful solutions, and international conferences to solve the Palestinian problem contradict the principles of the Islamic Resistance Movement . . . There is no solution to the Palestinian problem except through jihad.'[82]

Islamic Fundamentalists believe that Allah in the Quran not only sets forth a picture of the character of the Jews for all time, but indicates that the Jews will always be the most relentless and dangerous enemies of the Muslim community. This is the point at which they employ novel exegesis.[83] The situation which Muhammad encountered in Medina, the first Muslim community, becomes a paradigm for all the later history of Islam.[84] There the Jews provided Muhammad with his most significant opposition on two different fronts. One was the outright opposition of battle and the reneging on treaty obligations; the other was clandestine activity to wean the Muslim faithful away from their Creed. 'The enemies of the Muslim Community would not always fight it only in the field, with sword and lance. For the enemies of Islam fought it first in the realm of Creed! And they fought it there through conspiring, sowing doubt and confusion, and hatching plots.'[85] Even after the Jews were subjugated, they did not cease to be relentless enemies of the Islamic religion. In fact, they would be satisfied only with the complete destruction of Islam. The current Zionist enterprise in the Middle East is simply the most intense and explicit of the Jewish devices to undermine Islam.[86]

By this exegesis, therefore, the Jews were not incidental to Muhammad's work as a prophet or to his activities as a leader. Through the record of Muhammad's encounters with them in the Quran and elsewhere, Allah had unmasked the character of the Jews as repeated repudiators and distorters of his message. This had been true long before the time of Muhammad when the Jews were the main recipients of Allah's message. But it was through Muhammad and through the community he established with its Creed that Allah showed the way to put the Jews in their proper place. Muslim Fundamentalists, however, are painfully aware that the contemporary scene in the Muslim world

---

[82]   Article 13 of the Hamas Covenant (note 13).
[83]   for a contrast with older Muslim positions see Lewis, *SAS*, 196–7.
[84]   Nettler, *Trials*, 34–44.
[85]   Qutb at Nettler, *Trials*, 73.
[86]   *ibid.*, 85.

is very different, with an ascendant Jewish state. This must imply that Muslims have lost their religious bearings and consequently the blessing of Allah. The way to regain that blessing is a return to the Creed advocated and embodied by Muhammad. As it is, 'the Muslim Community does not take advantage of the Islamic sources which its Ancestors used. Only in this way were the Ancestors able to overcome the Jewish conspiracy and double-dealing in Mecca.'[87] In practice, Muslims must revert to constant jihad against all the enemies of Islam, and especially against the Jews as the greatest enemy of all.

This may be a bleak and violent picture, but it is bound to be popular as an exegesis of the Quran because it does emphasize the paradigmatic quality of Muhammad's life and experiences, and because it re-emphasizes the idea of a Muslim state as distinct from the secularized regimes common in the Arab world, based on the western model.[88] At the same time it explains the current malaise in Islam and holds forth an attractive remedy.

Given their identification of the Jews with the epitome of evil, the Fundamentalists have not been slow to pinpoint specific evils resulting from Jewish influence. Thus, the spiritual leader of the Muslim Brothers in Egypt, Umar al-Tilmisani, in the early 1980s identified the Israeli embassy in Egypt as the control centre for destroying the economy, the values and the customs of the nation. Amongst other things the Jews would bring with them 'all manner of moral evils such as cabarets, drinking of liquor and white slavery'. They would promote economic exploitation and the taking of interest. They would take steps to spread deceitful propaganda. Above all, they would claim 'to be fighting backwardness which they allege is due to Islam; while they also in fact fight all varieties of Islamic tradition.'[89] Such sentiments are not confined to a lunatic fringe. They have been endorsed by academics, notably in Egypt and in Jordan.[90] They effectively became part of Ayatollah Khomeini's political creed.[91] Not all Arab intellectuals have taken this viewpoint. But those who would wish to espouse a more tolerant line toward the Jews are restricted by the lack of a genuinely free press anywhere in the Arab world.[92] At the same time there have been Muslims who have complained more generally about decadent, western influences without suggesting these are confined to the

---

[87] *ibid.*, 72.
[88] cf. the remarks of Bernard Lewis as quoted by Shipler (note 68) 141.
[89] quoted by Wistrich, *Anti-Semitism*, 227–8.
[90] *ibid.*, 254–6.
[91] Lewis, *SAS*, 219.
[92] *ibid.*, 256.

Jews. The latter, however, have proved the easiest targets for Muslim outrage
because they have been the most accessible, whether through the Jews who
lived in a sort of Diaspora in the Arab world or the Jews in the state of
Israel itself.

Many parallels can be adduced from the Arab world to anti-Semitism elsewhere. The most obvious are with Germany before and during
the Nazi period, where the Jews were made scapegoats for everything
evil. The same trend is apparent among the Islamic Fundamentalists.
Moreover, there is a clear similarity with the religious anti-Semitism
which emerged in Germany in the latter part of the nineteenth century
and saw the Jew as the embodiment of every corrupting and seculariz-
ing modern influence. But perhaps the most significant parallel of all
is with medieval Christendom, where it was insisted for theological
reasons that the Jews remain in a subservient and downtrodden condition. The situation in the contemporary Islamic world, however, is
potentially even more horrendous. There was nothing in medieval
Christendom to correspond to a successful Jewish state. And Christianity had no recognized doctrine of jihad against the infidel. Islam has
added this to the previous degradation and diabolization of the Jews.
Islamic anti-Semitism may be a hybrid, drawing promiscuously from
all sorts of sources. It may have come relatively late in human history.
But these are not good reasons to underestimate the threat it carries.

It would, however, be naive and unhelpful to suggest all opposition
to the state of Israel is essentially anti-Semitic. Some Jews — admittedly
a minority — are opposed in principle to the state of Israel.[93] Others
feel that in its present form the state of Israel repudiates the aspirations
of Zionism.[94] Much of the Palestinian opposition to the state of Israel
arises out of a concrete historical situation where they feel they have
been deprived of their rights. In its National Covenant the PLO reflects
this position. It is not intrinsically different from any other activist
liberation movement. Their tactics may have been questionable, but
the PLO can hardly be placed in the same league as the Nazis. It is the
genuine political problem posed by the Jewish state in the Middle East
which differentiates the Arab scene from both medieval Christendom
and Nazi Germany.[95] In the Middle East there is no doubt that the Jews
do hold corporate political power; so, there is no need to postulate

93   Chapman, *Whose*, 85–7.
94   Roberta Strauss Feuerlicht, *The Fate of the Jews* (Quartet Books, London, 1984)
246.
95   Harkabi, *Attitudes*, 299–300.

clandestine conspiracies. Real Jewish might has been faced by the Arabs in several wars; it is based on a formidable arsenal of weapons and on powerful international allegiances. The danger from the Jews to the Arabs is so self-evident that there is no place to speculate about some secret pact between the Jews and the devil. If, then, the Jews are seen to pose an essentially political threat, then the possibility remains that this situation may be resolved by political means.

The problems of the Middle East, however, have proved particularly intransigent. Inevitably, this has engendered frustrations through which strains of anti-Semitism have been given time to germinate alongside Arab nationalist sentiment. Moreover, the political failure of Arab nationalism has almost necessitated a new ideology if the struggle against the state of Israel is to be maintained. This has taken on an Islamic colouring because of the strong associations between the Arabs and the Muslim religion and because of the success of the Islamic revolution in Iran. The latter has illustrated that a Muslim regime in which church and state are effectively one need not be anachronistic. Islamic Fundamentalism has thereby received a great boost. To blend religious and political concerns as it does inevitably heightens anti-Semitic feeling. There is no longer a ready cure by some political compromise.

Long before Khomeini's revolution in Iran, Middle Eastern governments had been sponsoring anti-Semitic literature and publications all over the Arab world.[96] When some thirty or forty newspapers produce anti-Semitic articles and cartoons on a continuous basis, clearly many people are being indoctrinated against the Jewish people as the Germans were through productions like *Der Stürmer* under the Nazis. The Arab language, for example, today has the largest number of editions of *The Protocols of the Elders of Zion*.[97] This propaganda assault by governments can largely be explained by a desire to denigrate, even to dehumanize, Israel as its political and military enemy. At the same time links have been cultivated with anti-Semitic groups in the West and elsewhere, and attempts have been made to spread anti-Semitic sentiment to Africa and Asia, where hitherto it has been unknown.[98] Again, such activity can mainly be explained by its political end — international support for the Arab cause against Israel. But insofar as it

---

[96] Ehud Ya'ari, Arab Affairs correspondent for Israeli television, as quoted in the Thames Television booklet *The Longest Hatred*.
[97] Lewis, *SAS*, 208–211.
[98] Harkabi, *Attitudes*, 284–92.

promotes the notion of the Jews as a global threat or as a cancerous growth in the midst of humanity, it may leave an insidious legacy far beyond the present political crisis and beyond the bounds of the Islamic world.

It remains uncertain to what extent the persistent spread of anti-Semitic literature has affected the outlook of the ordinary Arab in the street. Observers of the Arab world have noted that the common people lack the deep-seated personal hostility to Jews that characterized much of Europe in the pre-Hitler era. Indeed, the new images of the Jew which are being promulgated in the Arab world run counter to the more traditional Arab stereotype of the Jew as weak and cowardly.[99] Arab anti-Semitic activity remains largely political and ideological.[100] Thus some have expressed the hope that with favourable political developments in the Middle East some of the sharpness of the current anti-Jewish invective may disappear.

There can be no doubt that the course of political events will affect the future prospects of Arab anti-Semitism. In this connection it is reassuring that the PLO, itself a loose coalition of groups, has steered a moderate line adhering to political issues and avoiding the complications of a distinctively religious anti-Semitism.[101] In this it has mirrored the outlook of Yasser Arafat, who has been in undisputed control of the PLO since 1969. Arafat is a pragmatic politician with contempt for ideology. 'We do not have any ideology,' he once declared, 'our goal is the liberation of our fatherland by any means necessary.'[102] But Arafat is not immortal, and the peace treaty he agreed with Israel in September 1993 has already met with severe, if not irreconcilable, difficulties at the hands of the Israeli public. As a result the credibility of the PLO and of Arafat has been impaired.

Arafat's main opposition derives from the Islamic Fundamentalists with their more deeply rooted antipathy to everything Jewish. It remains to be seen how strong these groups are within the Arab world. The political tide has steadily been flowing in their favour.[103] But they are unlikely to be supported by current Arab leaders since they constitute a challenge to them. It is, however, at the grass roots level that the

---

[99]   *ibid.*, 298.
[100]   Lewis, *SAS*, 258.
[101]   The rhetoric of PLO leaders, however, has been ambiguous — Rubin, *Revolution*, 178–80.
[102]   *ibid.*, 19.
[103]   Nettler, *Trials*, 69–70.

soul of the Muslim Arab world will be won. There can be no doubt that the Fundamentalists are well equipped emotionally and intellectually. Their appeal rests not simply in a new slant on the crisis posed by the state of Israel, but in their perspective on Islam itself. They can claim to be true radicals going back to the historical roots of their religion. Perhaps this also highlights their one weakness — their threat to the unity of the Islamic world itself. Their success would unquestionably mark the indigenization of anti-Semitism in the Islamic world. Even if theirs were to remain a respected minority view, they would have increased the profile of the Jews' historic opposition to Muhammad. Here there is a noticeable contrast with Christian forms of anti-Semitism, which have normally tried to distance themselves from the Old Testament or from the Jewish origins of the church. A return to the church's Jewish roots should lead to a modest form of philo-Semitism. But the opposite is the case with Islam. A return to the origins of the Muslim faith in the career of Muhammad and particularly the opposition he faced from the Jews in Medina has aggravated the Muslim sense of Jewish depravity and unbelief.

The Arab world would not be the first to see a steady intensification in what were originally quite reasonable feelings against the Jews. The early and medieval church may have had some justification in seeing a threat from the presence of Jews in the midst of Christendom, but they could do little to prevent their moderate opposition turning into the complete diabolization of the Jews. The religious concerns of many Christians in the Second Reich in Germany about the Jews unwittingly gave some respectability to the racial anti-Semites, whose position gradually strengthened until they were calling all the shots. While Arabs first became hostile to the Jews only because of their opposition to the state of Israel, this hostility has shown signs of overstepping its original bounds. It is no longer confined to a political entity, but has been extended to the Jewish people as the creators and rulers of Israel, no matter whether they live in Israel or not. Moreover, if the state of Israel is an evil, then its creators must be evil. The way is open for the Jews to be diabolized in Arab eyes. In short, anti-Zionism is steadily being overtaken by a virulent anti-Semitism. The question remains — has this process gone so far as to be irreversible?

Twelve

Conclusion

By any account, the Jews are an unusual people. Their persistence as a distinct group into modern times is amazing when we consider it is difficult to pinpoint a key element or elements in their distinctiveness. It is not clear, for example, that the Jews possess either a common physique, language, culture, religion or history which would form a unifying bond among them.[1] Perhaps the Hebrew language would be the best candidate for such a role, but there have been periods when the majority of Jews have neither spoken nor thought in Hebrew.

Ironically, the very persecutions from which Jews have suffered and which were intended to obliterate their distinct identity have tended to have the reverse effect. A halt has been put to those processes of assimilation which might otherwise have taken their inexorable course. This has particularly been the case in societies where Christianity or Islam has dominated; for these are religions which implicitly teach their adherents to look on Jews as a group apart. The expectations of Christian and Muslim societies have in various ways assisted Jews who relished their separate identity, and at the same time deterred those Jews who wanted to become indistinguishable from wider society. And this influence may continue even after Christian or Muslim beliefs have been largely discarded.

Thus, Jewish distinctiveness may in part have been encouraged by outsiders. But these outsiders will not often have seen matters in that light. Host nations have found it more convenient to explain the separation of the Jews in terms of Jewish peculiarities than in terms of gentile attitudes and policies. Some gentile societies have concluded

---

[1] Karl Barth, *Church Dogmatics* 3:3 (ET, T. and T. Clark, Edinburgh, 1961) 213–9 is especially good on this point.

that the Jews are, for whatever reason, a unique group, even a distinct species of humanity. As a result, the Jews have appeared at times contemptible and at times actually threatening. The precise reaction will depend on social and political changes in surrounding society. In contrast to the Christian or Muslim world, the Jews do not appear to have suffered significantly in places like India and China where they have had communities centred on Cochin and Kaifeng respectively.[2] Here Christian and Muslim influence has been limited and the Jews themselves have laid little store on their special relationship to God. So, it is not surprising that these communities have all but died out as result of assimilation.[3]

Karl Barth may be absolutely right in his observation that 'the Jew as a Jew is neither better nor worse than other men.'[4] But he is misguided in his suggestion that anti-Semitism originates from our general recognition of this fact and from our revulsion at the sinister picture this presents of ourselves, especially our natural hostility to God's gracious overtures.[5] Barth errs in assuming that everyone views the Jews with the same erudition as himself.[6] On the contrary, anti-Semitism has been most potent when Jewish distinctiveness has been associated with notions (or more accurately, fantasies) that the Jews are either subhuman or else exceptionally close to the devil. In other words, anti-Semitism thrives where the Jews are misrepresented as inherently different from their neighbours. Conversely, Haynes is right to detect a danger over the long term in forms of philo-Semitism which look up to the Jews as special beings somehow set above the rest of mankind; for such expectations are mythical and are bound to end in disillusionment.[7]

In sharp contrast to Barth's position, I believe it would represent a significant step away from anti-Semitism if it were recognized that intrinsically the Jews are no different from the rest of mankind. Such distinctiveness as they possess may then be entirely attributed to God's electing purposes. That election embraces both the formation of the Jews as a distinct people and the role they are to play in God's dealings

---

[2] Poliakov, *History*, 1:13–16.
[3] Currently Jewish leaders in Britain are worried by the effects of assimilation on the Jewish community. This process has largely accounted for the reduction by one-third in the number of British Jews since 1945.
[4] Barth (note 1) 221.
[5] *ibid.*, 221–6. In effect, Barth sets out his own rationale for an eternal anti-Semitism.
[6] for a more extensive critique of Barth's position on the Jews see Haynes, *Jews*, 64–81.
[7] Haynes, *Jews*, 182.

with the whole of mankind. But neither Jews nor gentiles should conclude that God's election of itself alters the Jewish character — or rather the character of individual Jews, since it is misleading to speak of some Jewish character in the abstract. Jews remain part of the human race which God created from the one source.[8] They reflect in themselves a whole variety of personality types and character traits. They are also deeply implicated, with all the other nations, in the consequences of Adam's disobedience.[9] While the Jews may have been given a privileged role in the purposes of God, the Jews are not entitled to lay claim to an exceptional character or some other merit. But on the other side of the same coin, anti-Semites have no justification for vilifying Jews as though they were outstanding sinners in their failure to fulfil much of their role as God's special people. The Apostle Paul, we have noted, was alert to this danger and warned gentiles about the possibility of priding themselves in being spiritually superior to the Jews. Thereby they would simply repeat the sins of many of the Jews.

The variety of anti-Semitic motifs

Anti-Semitism has found many pretexts over the course of history. This observation would apply particularly to the twentieth century which has not only seen the most virulent and successful assault of all time on the Jews, but has revealed a remarkable variety of perspectives culminating in anti-Semitic activity.[10] My own treatment has necessarily had to be selective.

Thus, anti-Semitism may usefully be envisaged not as a precise phenomenon dominated by one sinister image of the Jews but as a spectrum with a range of possibilities. At one end would lie religious antagonism building on the image of Jews as stubborn resisters of God's messages; while at the other would be found antipathy toward Jews as a race or at least as a significant political group. The latter would highlight the image of Jewish misanthropy and their consequent unwillingness to integrate into wider society.

Changes over time reflect movement along that spectrum. Thus, pagan anti-Semitism inclines towards the racial end of the spectrum, while the Christian outlook which replaced it represents a distinct move toward the religious end. It is possible to detect movement along that spectrum even in more restricted situations. In Spain, for example, the

---

[8]   cf. Acts 17:26.
[9]   Rom. 3:9–23; 5:12–21; and 7:7–25.
[10] cf. Lewis, *SAS*, 236–259.

emphasis on *limpieza de sangre* (purity of blood) was at first intended to make a religious point. Those baptized from a Jewish background could not be trusted as genuine converts.[11] In time, however, as the age of mass Jewish conversion receded into the past, this came to demarcate a racial or social distinction in Spanish society. The Arab world in this century has experienced a similar process in the reverse direction. Initially, Arabs objected to the political entity known as the state of Israel; but as that dispute has persisted, Muslims in the Arab world have added significant religious grounds for revulsion to the Jews anywhere in the world.

That is not to say that it is primarily the Jews' religion or their race which stimulates outbursts of anti-Semitism. These are, after all, the basic ways of classifying Jewish distinctiveness. The real trigger for anti-Semitism may be different; but if it is to carry weight, it must focus on one of the more traditional negative images of the Jews. It is clear, for example, that the growth of capitalism in the nineteenth century prompted antagonism toward the Jews in various guises.[12] Jews were accused by some of stimulating and of unduly profiting from capitalist activities, and at the same time by others of trying to undermine the whole process. Opponents of a religious cast of mind would tend to pick up the traditional picture of the Jews as addicted to usury and focus on their exploitative activities. More secularly minded opponents would fasten on either the evil characteristics of a race which kept to itself the means of production and money-making or on the quite different picture of a parasitic race which was incapable of anything constructive in its own right but sought to undermine the creditable efforts of others. Thus, quite different and even contradictory approaches to anti-Semitism were canvassed at the same time. The point on the spectrum at which criticisms were made reveals more about the critics themselves than about the Jews of the time. The modern western world with its pluralistic outlook on society is more likely to harbour a variety of forms of anti-Semitism than did a monolithic society like that of medieval Europe.

With these substantial differences in perspective, it is surely inappropriate to contend that anti-Semitism has exclusively Christian roots. Such would be a lop-sided viewpoint. It ignores the anti-Semitism which was found before the time of Jesus and was not entirely passed over by the early church. It also ignores the Muslim roots of anti-Semitism in the contemporary Arab world. (Yet, who would ever argue that

---

[11] *ibid.*, 84.
[12] *ibid.*, 110–5.

anti-Semitism originated with Islam or even that it is a predominantly Muslim phenomenon?)

The variety of forms of anti-Semitism also means that it is very difficult, if not impossible, to sustain a very different thesis popular among some Christians who have a high view both of the Christian Scriptures and of the Jewish people. They hold that anti-Semitism is invariably a manifestation of man's natural antipathy toward the living God.[13] No doubt, this view can be proposed with some sophistication as in these remarks of Professor Tom Torrance, 'Anti-Semitism is . . . a rebellion against the peculiar vocation and destiny of Israel, especially against its vicarious mission, but for that very reason it is also deep-seated rebellion against the vicarious mission of Jesus Christ himself.'[14] And I must concede that anti-Semitism has been manifest in those societies where the claims of the Jewish people to a unique destiny under God have been widely known.

But to focus attacks on the Jews because they are distinct in some way is not necessarily to express a deep-seated resentment against God himself. With some, like Haman or Hitler, this may well have been true.[15] It cannot, however, account for the cases of Christians who have claimed to love God and yet have been actively anti-Semitic. I would include here eminent Christians like John Chrysostom or Martin Luther, whose piety is unquestioned and whose opposition to the Jews clearly derived from their piety. (This indicates that even outstanding Christian leaders have great faults, which sadly may leave a worse legacy to the church than the views and behaviour of rogues.) Moreover, the high Middle Ages, which saw the greatest burgeoning of anti-Semitism before the Third Reich, were precisely the time when Christendom had developed and the kingdoms of the earth (or at least those in Europe) had reputedly become the kingdoms of Christ. Then whole societies of Christians were hostile to the Jews, and believed that in such an outlook they were pleasing God because not only had the Jews' ancestors murdered Christ but Jews of their own day had compounded those sins by contemptuous parodying of Christian rituals and worse.

There are those who would dismiss as outside the business of the historian the claim that anti-Semitism is always a manifestation of man's hostility to God. They would see this as 'meta-history', an arena for theological rather than historical comment.[16] And there is a sense

---

[13]   e.g. David W. Torrance in Torrance, *Witness*, 7 and 9. Similar ideas are found in the French writers, Jacques Maritain and Fadiey Lovsky — Langmuir, *HRAS*, 25–28.

[14]   Thomas F. Torrance in, Torrance, *Witness*, 87.

[15]   cf. Rauschning, *Beast*, 155–6.

[16]   cf. Langmuir's comments at *TDAS*, 51–4.

in which this comment is justified. An assumption is being made about the truth of the Christian Scriptures which professional historians would not wish to take for granted. But I believe that it is possible historically to refute the claim that anti-Semitism always reflects hostility to the covenant God of the Jewish people. We have the clear examples I mentioned that some Christians did see opposition to the Jews as an expression of their piety toward God. This outlook cannot be dismissed either as hypocrisy or as a rationalization because the Bible does refer to unbelieving Jews as enemies of God (although this is only part of its picture) and does include passages where believers are encouraged to see God's enemies as their own — 'Do I not hate those who hate you, O Lord, and abhor those who rise up against you? I have nothing but hatred for them; I count them my enemies.'[17] Since their position does have some biblical justification, I believe it is impossible to ascribe all hatred of Jews to hatred of God.

Besides, the same Scriptures give no warrant for assuming that all opposition to the Jews reflects hatred toward God. (They do assert that for the quite different case where true disciples of Jesus are persecuted for righteousness' sake.[18]) Not all opponents of the Jews were in the same league as Haman. Some were agents of God's judgment. Even King Nebuchadnezzar of Babylon, responsible for the sack of Jerusalem in 586 BC, receives modified praise for his attack on Judah.[19] He had the right from God to punish the king and people of Judah for breaking their oath of allegiance to him.[20]

A satanic element?

If Christians are to pursue a 'meta-historical' line on anti-Semitism, they might do better to explore the notion of anti-Semitism as satanic — perhaps a ploy to hinder the Jewish people from re-assessing their relationship to Jesus of Nazareth and his disciples as well as from bringing blessing to the other nations of the world.[21] The advantage of

---

[17] Ps. 139:21, 22. Again, the wider context is vital. It is surely significant that David immediately recognizes that his words must be applied to himself first before anyone else.

[18] Mt. 10:22; 24:9, Mk. 13:13; Lk. 21:17; Jn. 15:18–24; 1 Jn. 3:13. The passage at 1 Pet. 4:12–19 makes an important distinction between suffering for the name of Christ and suffering as a wrongdoer.

[19] 2 Ch. 36:17; Je. 43:10.

[20] 2 Ki. 24:20; 2 Ch. 36:13

[21] For an interesting example of this see Barry R. Leventhal in *Mishkan* 8/9 (1988), 113–117, though I would not accept his exegesis at several points and would not concur with his dispensationalism.

such an approach would be this: Christian anti-Semites could be included under this heading. No less a person than Simon Peter, Jesus' leading disciple, became a mouthpiece of Satan in his own ignorant devotion to Jesus and tried to deter Jesus from the cross.[22] I would suggest that Christian leaders may have performed a similar role in sanctioning an unduly severe and uncharitable line toward the Jewish people if they appeared to persist in stubborn unbelief and to question or ridicule cardinal Christian doctrines. The Apostle Paul was envisaging a real danger when he warned Christian ministers and evangelists against even verbal clashes and confrontation with opponents. How much more would his warning apply when Christian leaders have advocated or actually employed physical violence against Jews![23]

To resort to the devil as an explanation, however partial or tentative, might seem a step into the unknown or at least into an arena where assertions become unprovable. But in this case it is not inappropriate seeing that the Christian Scriptures, which were often used against the Jews, do present something of the character and activities of the devil. In fact, the passage from John's gospel where Jesus accuses a group of Jews of being children of the devil has acquired notoriety as the text with the most anti-Semitic potential in the whole of the New Testament, because its highly charged language has often been applied to the whole Jewish nation without qualification.

And yet the record of subsequent history would suggest a very different picture, if we are to take at face value the descriptions of the devil as 'a murderer from the beginning' and as 'a liar and the father of lies.'[24] For it would be difficult to imagine a group who have more persistently been victims of dangerous lies and of murder, commonly judicial murder, than the Jews. In the medieval period the Jews became subject to a whole battery of accusations involving blasphemous or inhuman acts — the practice of ritual murder, the use of human flesh and blood in their own rituals, the mutilation of the host, and the poisoning of wells. Some at that time even believed in a Jewish conspiracy to overthrow Christendom and its values. Such charges gained currency even though no one could have seen Jews performing such outrages.[25] When such charges surfaced, they were regularly accompanied by the execution of Jews. The case of the Holy

---

[22] Mt. 16:22, 23 (Mk. 8:32, 33).
[23] 2 Tim. 2:23–26.
[24] Jn. 8:44.
[25] Langmuir, *HRAS*, 264.

Child of La Guardia must rank as one of the most notorious of such instances. Its impact was considerable, as the expulsion of the Jews from Spain followed shortly afterwards.

But perhaps the best example to illustrate this theme of the Jews as victims of lies is the recent one of Adolf Hitler. He not only demeaned the Jews with lies, but projected on to the Jews the very deceptions of which he himself was guilty. Thus, he admitted that he did not care if that most potent of modern forgeries, *The Protocols of the Elders of Zion*, were a fiction or not.[26] When Hitler came to write *Mein Kampf*, these *Protocols* were his greatest source of 'information' about the Jews.[27] But that was by no means all. They provided Hitler with ideal tactics to pursue against the Jews and more widely. In particular, Hitler testified that he had learned 'political intrigue, the technique of conspiracy, revolutionary subversion; prevarication, deception, organisation.'[28] He sought to translate the fantasy-world of the *Protocols* into reality. 'The ruthless struggle of a band of conspirators to achieve world-domination — a world-empire based on a small but highly organized and regimented people — utter contempt for humanity at large — a glorying in destruction and mass misery — all these things are to be found in the *Protocols*, and they were of the essence of the Nazi regime.'[29] The *Protocols*, of course, had represented these conspirators as Jews. In real life they turned out to be the Nazis.

Hitler could wax eloquent on the dangers of International Jewry, but in 1922 he had admitted to the journalist Josef Hell that one reason why he targeted the Jews was their weakness — 'They are totally defenceless, and no one will stand up to protect them.'[30] Here Hitler showed an accurate perception of the true position of European Jews, but at the same time his talk of the Jewish menace is exposed as deliberate lies and scaremongering.

Curiously, it was a lie Hitler came at some point to believe. How else can we explain references in his last testament to International Jewry as 'the poisoners of all peoples'? Earlier that year Hitler had tried to rewrite history to suggest that in 1933 world Jewry had decided to wage war tacitly on the Third Reich, and the reason why the Reich was facing defeat in 1945 was that the Jews had managed to organize a coalition against it.[31]

---

[26] Rauschning, *Beast*, 235.
[27] Werner Maser, *Hitler's Mein Kampf — An Analysis* (ET, Faber and Faber, London 1970) 164.
[28] Rauschning, *Beast*, 238.
[29] Cohn, *Warrant*, 193.
[30] quoted in Fleming, *Hitler*, 29.
[31] Hitler, *Testament*, 77 and 89.

Hence, when Hitler described Jewish duplicity in these terms, 'Words are for the Jew not a means to expressing his thoughts, but rather a way of disguising what he is thinking. The lie is his source of strength, his weapon', he was really describing himself.[32]

On a wider scale, it is extraordinary that the Jews of all people should have been painted in the guise of a unified group, singlemindedly bent on the domination of the world.[33] Norman Cohn has seen a bitter irony in the intensification of this story at the very time when the Jews were more divided than ever and were in many cases integrating into the society around them. In fact, the Jews in the twentieth century lacked the sort of communal institutions which would have been necessary to make a corporate political impact.[34] Since the Diaspora there has been no central Jewish authority of any kind. The Great Sanhedrin of prominent French Jews which Napoleon summoned in 1807 was a purely temporary arrangement given a grandiose title by the Emperor, who was primarily concerned to ensure that the Jews were as submissive as the rest of France.[35] But it may have encouraged some to draw the erroneous conclusion that there had been a Jewish government in existence over the centuries, albeit in secret. Moreover, where countries have designated an individual as the Chief Rabbi, that is a modern device and largely an administrative convenience. In the context of the Final Solution some of the SS men did belatedly begin to realize that the Jews had little organization. How else could they explain how unprepared these Jews were to rescue one another from the death squads and the gas chambers!

Hitler may have been an outstanding example, but to some extent the same comment may apply to most of those who have originated lies against the Jews. Ironically, another German, Christian-Wilhelm Dohm, who was a forerunner of Jewish emancipation, had made a similar comment about those he saw as the unenlightened groups in society — 'It is only the mob which considers itself allowed to deceive a Jew, who accuses him of being allowed by his law to deceive members of another religion, and it is only intolerant priests who have collected myths of the prejudices of the Jews which serve simply to prove their own.'[36] I would simply query the restriction of this

---

[32]   as suggested by Fleming, *Hitler*, 62. Hitler's remarks were made in the Führer's Headquarters on 5th November 1941.

[33]   That did not begin either with Hitler or with the *Protocols*. Cohn, *Warrant*, 32–33 traces this back to 1862.

[34]   Cohn, *Warrant*, 252–6.

[35]   *ibid.*, 29.

[36]   quoted in Poliakov, *History*, 3:20.

observation to the unenlightened. Some Enlightenment figures, like Voltaire, were equally guilty.

The misrepresentations of the Jews had unanticipated implications for the credibility of the Christian faith. This was recognized by a rough contemporary of Dohm, the Polish Jew, Zalkind-Hourwitz, who had largely assimilated to Parisian society —

> The lies uttered about the Jews provide Pyrrhonism (= Scepticism) and irreligion with decisive weapons. In fact what belief does History in general deserve, and particularly Biblical History which is the history of the ancient Jews, if the government sanctions so many calumnies against that Bible and so many absurd falsehoods about even modern Jews, if it encourages effrontery to the point of depicting them as a people of Pygmies, who have cross eyes and narrow minds . . . ?[37]

These were salutary words on the eve of the French Revolution. But they are applicable at any time. The maligning of the Jewish character, from whatever motives, has a detrimental effect on the general acceptance of the Christian religion. The Christian church cannot and ought not so to lay aside her Jewish origins as to slander the character of the very people from whom her Lord came and by whom most of her Scriptures were written.

To return to John's gospel chapter 8, Jesus' words do apply more widely than the group of Jews he was then addressing. His words must be allowed their full significance in terms of those who have peddled lies against the Jews. That is why it is apposite to talk of a satanic element behind anti-Semitism, perhaps especially in the anti-Semitism which has blossomed on Christian soil.

The Jewish reaction to anti-Semitism

Fifty years on, it is clear that the state of Israel has not brought security to the Jews. In the words of Rosemary and Herman Ruether, 'In reality there is no place today where a Jew is more likely to be killed because he or she is a Jew than in Israel. Thousands of Jews have died in Israel in the last forty years, most of them soldiers who died in wars.'[38] Furthermore, with Israel now a nation in the international spotlight, we can extend beyond the Christian world these shrewd observations of Heiko Oberman —

> The concentration on Auschwitz and Holocaust studies is a danger because it suggests that anti-Semitism is a German phenomenon and a German evil . . . I

---

[37] quoted in *ibid.*, 3:152.
[38] Ruether and Ruether, *Wrath*, 229.

think that the historian of anti-Semitism has to warn and speak out quite loudly today . . . anti-Semitism is a snake that is so adjustable, that can throw off its skins and lives on in so many different forms. It is a poison that is present in the whole Christian world . . . given the right economic and social conditions, anti-Semitism can explode.[39]

The Holocaust has undoubtedly left an indelible mark on the consciousness of the Jews everywhere, even those living in places untouched by the Nazi inferno. In the short term it has served to vindicate Zionism, which had been a minority opinion among Jews before the Nazi atrocities became known. In the event the Nazi persecution turned out even worse than anything the Zionists had predicted. But at least Zionism had diagnosed the basic condition; its cure lay within grasp in the form of a separate Jewish state. History had proved Zionism right — or so it seemed to most Jews.[40]

At the same time the Holocaust has raised acute questions for the Jewish religious consciousness. These are eloquently expressed by Alexander Donat, a survivor of the Warsaw ghetto and the death camps, who wrote in a letter to his grandson —

> The Holocaust was for every survivor a crucial religious experience. Day-in and day-out we cried out for a sign of God's presence. In the ghettos and in the death camps, before gallows and the doors of the gas chambers, when confronted with the ultimate incredible evil, we cried: 'Lord, where are thou?' We sought Him, and we didn't find Him. The acute awareness of God's puzzling and humiliating absence was always with us. Memory of this experience is always with us . . .
>
> The far-reaching religious implications of the Holocaust have by no means been explored, nor has the process of coming to grips with its meaning been completed. It implies a profound revolution in the basic tenets of Judaism, and the rise of a new set of Judaic values.[41]

A staggering variety of explanations has been offered within different strands of Judaism to account for such a momentous event.[42] The variety indicates both the urgency of the question and the difficulty in attaining a uniformly satisfying answer. No doubt, debate will continue.

---

[39] cited on page 14 of the Thames Television booklet *The Longest Hatred*. Oberman's statement can be given a wider application since it is not only the Christian world that is affected by anti-Semitism.

[40] Neusner, *Judaism*, 172–3.

[41] quoted by Barry Leventhal in *Mishkan* 6/7 (1987), 15.

[42] Leventhal's article, which is entitled *Theological Perspectives on the Holocaust Part 1*, gives an excellent categorization and summary of the various positions which have been taken up.

But alongside this an even more fundamental question should be raised — that of Jewish identity. Zionism had answered the question as to what gives the Jewish people its unity by appealing to a common experience of anti-Semitism.[43] It was assumed that once an autonomous state was gained by the Jews and made their own, this would not only remove them from the sphere of anti-Semitism, but would need no deeper unifying ideology. It is true that some early Zionists were dissatisfied with what they saw as no more than a Jewish variant on the popular nationalisms of the day and proposed a state based on Jewish culture, which they assumed to be bound up in the heart of every Jew.[44] But mainstream Zionism contented itself with an exclusively political ideal. And where they looked for ideological support, they found it not in Jewish religion or in Jewish culture but in Jewish history. This was not, however, the history of the Jews as a distinctive people marked out by God for his own special purposes. Rather, it was the history of Israel conceived as a secular entity. One Zionist writer, Jacob Klatzkin, described it as a new Judaism, different from the old credal forms of Judaism. 'We are neither a denomination nor a school of thought,' he declared, 'but members of one family, bearers of a common history . . . The national definition too requires an act of will. It defines our nationalism by two criteria: partnership in the past and the conscious desire to continue such partnership into the future.'[45] Of course, the history on which Zionism was built was selective.[46] It tended to ignore the Jewish Diaspora, even with its times of great cultural achievement, as a blip between those periods which really mattered when Jews exercised political autonomy.

The modern state of Israel needs to appeal for its justification also to the recent past. Hence since the 1980s it has seen what Tom Segev describes as the worship of 'the heritage of the Holocaust' (*moreshet hashoah*).[47] Most Israeli Jews have appropriated the Holocaust and made it into their own experience, even when they have come from the Arab world and so had no first-hand experience of the Nazi terror. Inevitably, this reinforces the centrality of a common experience of

---

[43] Neusner, *Judaism*, 160–2.
[44] I have in mind the movement whose intellectual leader was Ahad Ha-Am: see Cohn-Sherbok, *Heritage*, 173.
[45] quoted in Neusner, *Judaism*, 167.
[46] *ibid.*, 163–6.
[47] Segev, *Seventh*, 513–7. Segev's book is full of warnings about how the legacy of the Holocaust may be wrongly used — e.g. his summary of an article by the columnist Boaz Evron on page 402.

anti-Semitism to Jewish (or at least Israeli) identity. Jews living in North America remained largely unaffected by the Holocaust until the crisis preceding the Six Day War of 1967 brought home to them the possibility that again a significant Jewish population stood at the verge of extinction. Subsequently they have incorporated the Holocaust experience into their self-image as Jews.[48]

But there are dangers whenever the special religious identity of the Jews is denied. It was Spinoza who first brought to public attention Jewish questioning of this identity. Though this was not Spinoza's intention or indeed his own solution to the question of distinct Jewish identity, inevitably he turned the spotlight on the racial characteristics of the Jews. Where religious experience, religious history or religious traditions are underplayed in the delineation of the Jews, something else has to be invoked to explain Jewish distinctiveness. The dangers of such a procedure are graphically described by a Jewish writer, Jacob Bernard Agus,

> To conceive of the Jews as a nation is to identify the primary motivation of their long struggle for existence as ethnic in character. Then the entire range of the Jewish faith, from the practice of circumcision to the anticipation of a Messiah, is flattened out along the one plane of ethnicism, appearing to be nothing more than a projection of the ethnic will for self-segregation from the rest of humanity. All the rituals of the Jewish faith, seen in this monochromatic light, seem to be only so many instances of Jewish separatism, attempts to erect an inner ghetto-wall against the outside world . . . In brief, if the Jews are viewed as a nation, then, by virtue of the ethnic-cultural aspects of their faith, their world-wide dispersion, and their age-long battle against the processes of assimilation, they take on the aspect of a *super-nation*, endowed with an excess of self-love and accursed by the fear of the friendship and fraternity of other peoples.[49]

Agus also points out that such a view would pander to a form of Christian anti-Semitism. The killing of Jesus and their resistance to the Christian message would seem a prime example of the Jewish refusal to share their own spiritual treasures with the rest of mankind.

The force of Agus' contention is illustrated by the case of Hitler with his dismissal of the claim that the Jews were a religious body. He explained this by the observation that the Jewish race 'accepts on equal

---

[48] Neusner, *Judaism*, 206–226.
[49] Agus, *Meanings*, 331–2. A Jewish Rabbi, Dan Cohn-Sherbok, has stated recently, 'the conviction that God has selected a particular people as his agent is nothing more than an expression of the Jewish people's sense of superiority and impulse to spread its religious message' — in his *Judaism and Other Faiths* (Macmillan, Basingstoke, 1994) 169. Evidently, the legacy of Spinoza is alive and well!

terms both the most determined atheists and the most sincere, practising believers.'[50] Interestingly, in the same context Hitler does admit that the Jewish race had its origins in the Hebrew religion, and the religion had some effect in moulding the Jewish character. So, strictly speaking, Hitler avoids the purely ethnic concept of the Jewish people of which Agus was talking. But, Hitler implies, religion is no longer relevant to Jewish identity. No doubt, some would want to argue that Hitler was operating with an unduly narrow concept of what constitutes a religion, and that he was unaware of the religious debates and tensions among Jews from the time of emancipation. Nonetheless, both Hitler and Agus have highlighted from their very different perspectives the dangers of regarding the Jews as nothing more than a race.

This was a danger Zionism ignored. Or rather, Zionism has worked with a concept of the Jews which is too close to that of the anti-Semites whose influence it has rightly feared. Here we see the limitations of the word 'anti-Semitism', embodying as it does racial connotations. The analysis of the causes of anti-Semitism given by the early Zionists was limited and superficial.[51] Hence their political remedy has proved inadequate. The Jews are not and have never been a race like other races; or even a nation like other nations. Already in its short history the modern state of Israel has proved in many ways isolated and unusual, dependent in large measure on help from outside.

Moreover, attacks on the Jews have not been restricted to the crude overt attacks of a Haman or a Hitler. There have been the more selective attacks on distinctive Jewish religion which we noted (for example) with Antiochus Epiphanes. In this case Antiochus enjoyed the support of sections of the Jewish community, who wished to see an end of a separate Jewish religious and cultural identity. Indeed, from early days not all Jews have found it congenial to live with their status as a special people. They would prefer to be like all the other nations. This was perhaps evident as early as their wilderness days when many longed to go back to Egypt and submerge their identity amid the comparative comforts of that civilization.[52] If we turn to more recent times and to the debates on Jewish emancipation at the end of the eighteenth century, Bernard Lewis points out certain defenders of the Jews argued that 'there are Jews who are not at all Jewish'. Some Jews responded to this kind of defence and the implied invitation with eager

50 Hitler, *Testament*, 55–56.
51 Neusner, *Judaism*, 178–9.
52 cf. T.F. Torrance, in Torrance, *Witness*, 86–7.

enthusiasm, while others were outraged. Lewis proceeds to observe that these opposite responses can also be found among Jews to this day.[53] It seems that the Jewish people remain caught in a tension between a ready acceptance of their distinctiveness, which involves a religious identity, and an outright rejection of any such thought.

Strange as it may seem, there are dangers for the Jewish people at the present time if they concentrate unduly on anti-Semitism, and the Holocaust in particular. This may seem paradoxical because anti-Semitism remains a real danger. Anti-Semitism has, however, become for many the leading badge of Jewish identity. Again, in its current form it is a decidedly secular badge. And yet all attempts at Jewish identity without a religious core have proved unavailing. Jews would do well to ponder the implications of the absence of religion in their identity. One theme to emerge from Holocaust survivors, including Alexander Donat, whom I quoted earlier, is the profound sense of the absence of God in the concentration camps — a very different thing from an assurance of atheism.[54] There may be a connection with the disturbing absence of God from modern Jewish identity.

Ironically in the light of its secular foundation, the state of Israel has found that it could not dispense with a religious core to Jewish identity. When its politicians were framing the Law of Return, which affirms that every Jew in the world has a right to immigrate to Israel and claim automatic citizenship, they had to turn to the Orthodox Rabbis for an answer to the legal question 'Who counts as a Jew?'[55] This does not mean that Israel is a religious, still less a theocratic state; but it does highlight the current ambivalence over Jewish religious and national identity.

Christian reactions to anti-Semitism

Since the Holocaust the churches, particularly in western Europe and North America, have attached renewed importance to their relations with the Jewish people. Some theologians have been bold enough to assign the Holocaust a revelatory significance from God.[56] But this rather extreme position, in my view, distracts from the more urgent task of detecting the roots of the anti-Semitism which formed the backcloth to the Holocaust.

---

[53] Lewis, *SAS*, 93.
[54] cf. Jacob Jocz in, *Witness*, Torrance, 60–3.
[55] Ruether and Ruether, *Wrath*, 230.
[56] Haynes, *Jews*, 126–9.

It is a good sign that most churches have acknowledged that Christians bear some responsibility for anti-Semitism, though it is unfortunate that they have not yet reached accord on the precise nature of that responsibility.[57] Again, there is welcome agreement that the Jewish people still stand in a special relationship to God. Due account is thus taken of the Apostle Paul's affirmation — 'As far as election is concerned, they are loved on account of the patriarchs, for God's gifts and his call are irrevocable.'[58] A general consensus, however, is harder to find on the ecclesiastical and missiological implications of this.[59]

At the same time the other strand of Paul's declaration — that the Jews are 'enemies' on account of the gentile believers — is underplayed. Effectively this brings contemporary churches to almost the polar opposite position from that of the medieval church, where it was held that the Jews were indeed enemies of God, but this was so interpreted as to put the Jews into a special class of unbelievers who were virtually beyond redemption. Today some churches veer to a position where the attitude of Jews to Jesus has almost become an irrelevance.

Unbelief of any sort and its serious consequences are not popular themes in most modern theology. Talk of Jewish unbelief, in particular, carries the additional problem that it raises the spectre of divine judgment — judgment that might in some eyes make the Holocaust justifiable. Yet, as I have argued, the Bible emphasizes spiritual blindness or hardness of heart as the primary element in such a judgment. I believe it is not inappropriate to give this judgment a contemporary focus. Perhaps it could be illustrated in the bewildering variety of Judaisms which now compete alongside atheism for the allegiance of ordinary Jews. Or if we dare to venture into the social and political spheres, what of the embittered conflicts Israeli Jews have experienced among themselves, never mind with their Arab neighbours?[60]

With liberal Christians the underplaying of Jewish unbelief is evident in a tendency altogether to replace mission, which makes its goal the recognition of Jesus as the Messiah, with dialogue, which emphasizes learning from one another and the identification of common moral

---

[57] World Council of Churches, *The Theology of the Churches and the Jewish People* (WCC Publications, Geneva 1988) 166–170 and 184–5.
[58] Rom. 11:28, 29.
[59] World Council of Churches (note 57) 153–6 and 184.
[60] It is noteworthy that a healing of old divisions among the Jewish people is included in Old Testament passages about the restoration of Israel — Ezk. 37:15–23 and Zc. 12:10–14, where repentance involves not only the house of David but that of one of his bitterest enemies, Shimei.

concerns.[61] It has also meant that Messianic Jews have been ignored, even though this is an increasing movement both in Israel and especially among the Jews of the Dispersion. These groups, which endeavour to wed Christian beliefs to an affirmation of Jewish identity, raise awkward questions. They remind the churches that there are Jews in this generation, as in previous generations, who believe Jesus of Nazareth is the fulfilment of authentic Judaism, and so the rest of their countrymen are in serious error at this point. They also raise for the first time since the patristic era the question of how gentile churches are to relate to Jewish churches. It is sad that the World Council of Churches and affiliated groups, as well surprisingly as some Christian fundamentalist bodies, have ignored this exciting development in the Jewish community and preferred to cultivate closer relationships with the mainstream of Jewish society.[62]

There has been a further complication for Christians in the emergence of the state of Israel very soon after the Holocaust. Church bodies immediately faced pressure to comment on the state of Israel as well as the Jewish people and religion. Some (like the Vatican and the World Council of Churches) have tried to distinguish statements about Judaism, which they have been happy to approach in theological terms, from statements about the state of Israel, where they have confined themselves to concepts of social justice.[63] By focusing on moral issues, they have sought to balance the rights of the Palestinians, some of whom are Christian, and those of Jews living in Israel.

Other Christians, however, have not hesitated to speak of the state of Israel in theological, even apocalyptic terms. I have in mind such American Christian Fundamentalists as Hal Lindsey, Jerry Falwell of the 'Moral Majority', and presidential contender Pat Robertson.[64] They have identified the emergence of a Jewish state as a fulfilment of biblical prophecy, a vital stage on the road to the establishment of the millennial kingdom of Christ. Though in some cases they were responding to dramatic events like

---

[61] *ibid.*, 173–6.

[62] It is alarming that in his part of the 'Final Reflections' to the World Council of Churches collection Allan Brockway mentions the growing number of Hebrew Christians, only to add a theological reflection that the way forward may be 'to proscribe all proselytism of Jews on the theological ground that it is rejection of Israel's valid covenant with God' — *ibid.*, 185–6.

[63] Ruether and Ruether, *Wrath*, 166–73.

[64] Haynes, *Jews*, 151–8. It is, however, unwise to say that all conservative Christians are pro-Israel while liberal Christians are more neutral or even against Israel. The reality is more complex, as Haynes goes on to point out — *ibid.*, 168–70.

the creation of the state of Israel in 1948 and especially the Israeli success in the Six Day War of 1967, their prophetic views have much longer roots. They extend back to the nineteenth century dispensationalism associated with the British pioneer of the Plymouth Brethren, John Nelson Darby, whose views quickly spread to American Evangelicals.[65] Today we find a broad movement known as Christian Zionism which is resolutely committed to the state of Israel as a sovereign Jewish state.[66] They have not only given Israel virtually uncritical moral support, but have amassed in the USA considerable political and military aid to bolster Israel's security.[67] While they do not reject the notion that unbelieving Jews need to repent and to believe in Jesus, in practice they downgrade this idea. They believe very few conversions are to be expected among Jews before the advent of Jesus in person. Moreover, if their main responsibility is to 'comfort Zion', that means avoiding any sort of activity like evangelism which meets with the disapproval of Israel's authorities.[68] Thus they ignore the Apostle Paul's strategy for winning the Jews to Jesus — verbal witness and rousing them to spiritual envy from signs of God's blessings among gentile believers.[69]

Christian Zionists cannot be accused of underestimating anti-Semitism. On the contrary, they exaggerate its significance and approximate to the view of an 'eternal anti-Semitism'. For they see anti-Semitism in an apocalyptic light. Satan, they point out, is continually trying to thwart God's blessing to the whole of mankind. This entails opposition not only to the Messiah and his followers (which would be uncontroversial among most Christians) but also the Jewish people as they too in their own way are destined to bring blessing to mankind. Such a struggle is bound to continue until Satan is destroyed. In practice this means that some Christian Zionists adopt a quiescent approach to anti-Semitism, because they see it as essentially a spiritual plague which cannot be eradicated by political or social action.[70]

---

[65] *ibid.*, 144–7.

[66] Haynes asserts that in 1990 the number of Christian Zionists in the USA was estimated to be as high as 40 million. Clearly they are an immensely powerful lobby — *ibid.*, 162.

[67] Ruether and Ruether, *Wrath*, 177.

[68] John S. Ross in *Mishkan* 12 (1990), 13–19 discusses the goals and strategy of a representative Christian Zionist body — the International Christian Embassy in Jerusalem.

[69] Chapman, *Whose*, 280 points out that Christian Zionism also frustrates Christian witness to Muslims in the Middle East.

[70] Haynes, *Jews*, 165–7.

At the same time they classify every attack on Jews as anti-Semitism. They interpret God's promise to Abram in Gn. 12:3 as applicable to all Jews, whether in Christian terms they would be described as believers or unbelievers. Thus, whoever blesses the Jew (and the Jewish state) will be blessed by God. Whoever curses the Jew (and the Jewish state) will be cursed by God.[71] Where Christians have in periods like the Middle Ages attacked the Jews, then that is a sure sign of their not being true Christians. Yet, this view, as we have seen, is highly questionable. It ignores the biblical evidence that unbelieving Jews, like unbelievers among the rest of mankind, are regarded by God as his enemies.[72] Besides, today it plays into the hands of those Jews who repel every criticism of the Jewish state or of any version of Judaism by raising the bogey of anti-Semitism. An incorrect diagnosis of anti-Semitism will lead to wrong strategies. For instance, unreserved support for the Jewish leadership in Israel will neither promote justice among the peoples of the Middle East nor further the claims of Jesus of Nazareth among the Jewish people.

It will also gloss over the harassment accorded groups of Messianic Jews by Jewish leaders who dislike their stance and their proselytism.[73] This is ironic because the emergence of a sovereign Jewish state has seemingly provided a context in which a distinctively Jewish church can re-emerge. We have seen that by the fifth century the (gentile) church had become very hostile to distinctively Jewish churches, and classed them as forms of Judaism rather than of Christianity. Thus, over the centuries Jews who have professed to become Christians have at best been expected to assimilate to a gentile church and to discard all their distinctively Jewish ways. At worst they have been regarded with such suspicion by both the Jewish and the Christian mainstream that they have found themselves in a religious no man's land.[74] Toward the end of the nineteenth century, however, the idea of a distinctively Hebrew Christianity was again raised as a possibility. (Perhaps this reflected the popularity of nationalist ideas around the time.) In a few instances Hebrew Christian communities were established without outside support, most notably by Joseph Rabinowitsch (1837–1899) in Kishinev in Bessarabia (now Moldova). His community did succeed in defusing initial criticism in the gentile Christian world, but it was never accepted

---

71   Ruether and Ruether, *Wrath*, 178.
72   Rom. 5:10; Eph. 2:3 and 12; Col. 1:21.
73   Ross (note 68) 24–5.
74   Jocz, *Jewish*, 233–4.

as authentically Jewish by the wider Jewish community. Moreover, it did not last long after the death of its leader.[75]

In fact, it has been wisely suggested that an independent national life is a vital precondition if a Jewish church is to develop roots. With no assimilationist pressures the church will be free to develop its own witness and ministry to the wider Jewish community.[76] This will pose a challenge not only to the mainstream of Jewish society but to Christian churches. What attitude are they to have to those Messianic Jews? Are they to align with them as examples of the believing Jewish remnant of which the Apostle Paul speaks?[77] Or are they to overlook them in preference for the main pillars of Jewish society in the fear that any other policy would be dismissed as anti-Semitic? If the latter policy is pursued, the gentile churches will be treating Jewish unbelief as somehow different from that of other men. They will be guilty of the reverse of the medieval position when Jewish unbelief was regarded as far more pernicious than that of others. The present danger is that it may be treated as innocuous.

Clearly it is as difficult today as at any time for the gentile churches to hold in balance the two elements of Paul's perspective in Rom. 11:28. Yet, they must strive to do so. If they forget that the Jewish people are beloved of God and their election is irrevocable, inevitably they will slip into anti-Semitic attitudes and practices. On the other side of the coin, to ignore the reality of Jewish unbelief and the fact that it makes them enemies of God means that the Jewish people will be deprived of the greatest service the gentile Christians can give them — the testimony to Jesus of Nazareth as the Saviour of Israel.

---

[75] *ibid.*, 235–8.
[76] *ibid.*, 239.
[77] Rom. 9:27–29; 11:7.

Select Bibliography

General works

Agus, Jacob B., *The Meaning of Jewish History* (Abelard-Schuman, London/New York/Toronto 1963)

Almog, Shmuel (ed.), *Antisemitism Through the Ages* (Pergamon, Oxford 1988)

Charlesworth, James H. (ed.), *Jews and Christians: Exploring the Past, Present and Future* (Crossroad, New York 1990)

Cohn-Sherbok, Dan, *The Jewish Heritage* (Blackwell, Oxford 1988)

Cohn-Sherbok, Dan, *The Crucified Jew* (Harper Collins, Glasgow 1992)

Falk, Gerhard, *The Jew in Christian Theology* (McFarland and Company, London 1992)

Haynes, Stephen R., *Jews and the Christian Imagination* (Macmillan, Basingstoke 1995)

Isaac, Jules, *Jesus and Israel* (ET, Holt, Rinehart and Winston, New York 1971)

Isaac, Jules, *The Teaching of Contempt: Christian Roots of Anti-Semitism* (ET, Holt, Rinehart and Winston, New York 1964)

Jocz, Jakob, *The Jewish People and Jesus Christ* (SPCK, London 1949)

Kochan, Lionel, *The Jew and his History* (Macmillan, London 1977)

Langmuir, Gavin I., *Towards a Definition of Antisemitism* (California U.P. 1990)

Langmuir, Gavin I., *History, Religion, and Antisemitism* (California U.P. 1990)

Lewis, Bernard, *Semites and Antisemites: an Inquiry into Conflict and Prejudice* (Weidenfeld and Nicolson, London 1986)

Parkes, James, *The Conflict of the Church and the Synagogue* (London 1934)

Parkes, James, *Antisemitism* (London 1963)

Poliakov, Léon, *The History of Antisemitism* 3 Vols (ET, Routledge and Kegan Paul, London 1974)

Ruether, Rosemary R., *Faith and Fratricide: The Theological Roots of Antisemitism* (Seabury, Minneapolis 1974)

Torrance, David W. (ed.), *The Witness of the Jews to God* (Handsel Press, Edinburgh 1982)

Walker, P. W. L. (ed.), *Jerusalem Past and Present in the Purposes of God* (Tyndale House, Cambridge 1992)

Wistrich, Robert S., *Anti-Semitism:The Longest Hatred* (Thames Methuen, London 1991)

Wood, Diana (ed.), *Christianity and Judaism* (Blackwell, Oxford, 1992)

World Council of Churches, *The Theology of the Churches and the Jewish People* (*WCC* Publications, Geneva 1988)

The earliest period down to New Testament times — theological works

Beck, Norman A., *Mature Christianity: The Recognition and Repudiation of the Anti-Jewish Polemic of the New Testament* (London and Toronto 1985)

Davies, Alan T. (ed.), *Anti-Semitism and the Foundations of Christianity* (New York 1979)

Dunn, James D. G., *The Partings of the Ways* (SCM, London 1988)

Dunn, James D. G., *Jesus, Paul and the Law* (SPCK, London 1990)

Evans Craig A. and Hagner, Donald A. (ed.), *Anti-Semitism and Early Christianity* (Fortress Press, Philadelphia 1993)

Gager, John G., *The Origins of Anti-Semitism: Attitudes Towards Judaism in Pagan and Christian Antiquity* (OUP, New York 1983)

Maccoby, Hyam, *Judas Iscariot and the Myth of Jewish Evil* (Peter Halban, London 1992)

Motyer, Steve, *Israel in the Plan of God* (IVP, Leicester 1989)

Murray, John, *The Epistle to the Romans — New London Commentaries* (Marshall, Morgan and Scott, London 1967)

Richardson, Peter and Granskou, David (ed.), *Anti-Judaism in Early Christianity Vol 1* (Wilfrid Laurier Press, Waterloo, Ontario 1986)

Ridderbos, Herman, *Paul: An Outline of His Theology* (SPCK, London 1977)

Sanders, Ernest P., *Paul and Palestinian Judaism: A Comparison of Patterns of Religion* (London, SCM 1977)

Sandmel, Samuel, *Anti-Semitism in the New Testament?* (Fortress Press, Philadelphia 1978)

Wright, Christopher J. H. *Living as the People of God* (IVP, Leicester 1983)

Wright, Nicholas T., *The Climax of the Covenant* (T and T Clark, Edinburgh 1991)

Wright, Nicholas T., *The New Testament and the People of God* (SPCK, London 1992)

The earliest period down to New Testament times — historical works

Bartlett, John R., *Edom and the Edomites* (Sheffield Academic Press 1989)

Bilde, Per, *Flavius Josephus between Jerusalem and Rome* (Sheffield Academic Press 1988)

Davies W. and Finkelstein Louis, (ed), *The Cambridge History of Judaism Vol 2* (Cambridge U.P. 1989)

Feldman, Louis H., *Jew and Gentile in the Ancient World* (Princeton U.P. 1993)

Hengel, Martin, *Judaism and Hellenism*, 2 Vols (ET, SCM, London 1974)

Sevenster, J.N., *The Roots of Pagan Anti-Semitism in the Ancient World* (E. J. Brill, Leiden 1975)

Stern, Menahem, *Greek and Latin Authors on Jews and Judaism*, 3 Vols (Israel Academy of Sciences and Humanities 1974–84)

Tcherikover, Victor, *Hellenistic Civilization and the Jews* (ET, The Jewish Publication Society of America, Philadelphia 1961)

Whittaker, Molly, *Jews and Christians: Graeco-Roman Views* (Cambridge U.P. 1984)

Early centuries of Christian era

De Lange, Nigel R. M., *Origen and the Jews* (Cambridge U.P. 1976)

Pritz, Ray A., *Nazarene Jewish Christianity* (E. J. Brill, Jerusalem/Leiden 1988)

Simon, Marcel, *Verus Israel* (ET, Oxford U.P. 1986)

Wilken, Robert L., *Judaism and the Early Christian Mind* (Yale U.P. 1971)

Wilken, Robert L., *John Chrysostom and the Jews* (California U.P. 1983)

Wilson, Stephen G. (ed.), *Anti-Judaism in Early Christianity Vol 2* (Wilfrid Laurier Press, Waterloo, Ontario 1986)

Medieval period

Baer, Yitzhak, *A History of the Jews in Christian Spain Vol 2* (ET, Jewish Publication Society of America, Philadelphia 1961)

Cohen, Jeremy, *The Friars and the Jews: The Evolution of Medieval Anti-Judaism* (Cornell U.P., Ithaca and London 1982)

Chazan, Robert, *European Jewry and the First Crusade* (California U.P. 1987)

Edwards John, *The Jews in Christian Europe 1400–1700* (Routledge, London 1988)

Edwards John, *The Jews in Western Europe 1400–1600* (Manchester U.P. 1994)

Hay, Malcolm, *Europe and the Jews: The Pressure of Christendom on the People over 1900 Years*, (Academy Publishers, Chicago 1992)

Kedourie, Elie (ed.), *Spain and the Jews* (Thames and Hudson, London 1992)

Moore, Robert I., *The Formation of a Persecuting Society* (Blackwell, Oxford 1987)

Parkes, James, *The Jew in the Medieval Community* (Hermon Press, 1976)

Riley-Smith, Jonathan, *The First Crusade and the Idea of Crusading* (Athlone Press, London 1986)

Synan, E., *The Popes and the Jews in the Middle Ages* (Macmillan, New York 1965)

Trachtenberg, Joshua, *The Devil and the Jews: The Medieval Conception of the Jew and its Relation to Modern Antisemitism* (Yale U.P. 1943)

The Sixteenth and Seventeenth centuries

Ben-Sasson, Haim Hillel, 'The Reformation in Contemporary Jewish Eyes' in *Proceedings of the Israel Academy of Sciences and Humanities 4* (1969–70) 239–329

Brecht, Martin, *Martin Luther — The Preservation of the Church 1532–1546* (ET, Fortress Press, Minneapolis 1993)

Healey, Robert M., 'The Jew in Seventeenth Century Protestant Thought' in *Church History 46* (1977) 63–79.

Israel, Jonathan, *European Jewry in the Age of Mercantilism 1550–1750* (Oxford U.P. 1985)

Katz, David S., *Philosemitism and the Readmission of the Jews to England 1603–1655* (Oxford U.P. 1982)

Murray, Iain, *The Puritan Hope* (Banner of Truth, London 1971)

Oberman, Heiko A., *The Roots of Anti-Semitism in the Age of Renaissance and Reformation* (ET, Fortress Press, Philadelphia 1984)

Oberman, Heiko A., *Luther — Man between God and the Devil* (Harper Collins, London 1993)

Scholem, Gershom, *Sabbatai Sevi: The Mystical Messiah 1626–1676* (ET, Princeton U.P. 1973)

Stern, Selma, *Josel of Rosheim: Commander of Jewry in the Holy Roman Empire of the German Nation* (ET, Jewish Publication Society, Philadelphia 1965)

Toon, Peter (ed.), *Puritans, the Millennium and the Future of Israel: Puritan Eschatology 1600–1660* (James Clarke, Cambridge 1970)

Van den Berg, J. and Van der Wall, Ernestine G. E. (ed.), *Jewish-Christian Relations in the Seventeenth Century: Studies and Documents* (Kluwer, Dordrecht 1988)

From the eighteenth century to modern times — the Jews in Europe

Cohn, Norman, *Warrant for Genocide* (Eyre and Spottiswoode, London 1967)

Conway, John, *The Nazi Persecution of the Churches, 1933–1945* (Weidenfeld and Nicolson, London 1968)

Craig, Gordon A., *Germany 1866–1945* (Oxford, 1981)

Dawidowicz, Lucy S., The War against the Jews 1933–1945 (Penguin, Harmondsworth 1990)

Field, Geoffrey C., *Evangelist of Race — The Germanic Vision of Houston Stewart Chamberlain* (Columbia University Press, 1981)

Fleming, Gerald, *Hitler and the Final Solution* (ET, Hamish Hamilton, London 1985)

Gilbert, Martin, *The Holocaust — The Jewish Tragedy* (Collins, London 1986)

Graml, Hermann, *Antisemitism in the Third Reich* (ET, Blackwell, Oxford 1992)

Gutman Istrael and Schatzker, Chaim, *The Holocaust and its Significance* (ET, The Zalman Shazar Centre, Jerusalem 1984)

Gutteridge, Richard, *Open Thy Mouth for the Dumb: The German Evangelical Church and the Jews 1879–1950* (Blackwell, Oxford 1976)

Hertzberg, Arthur, *The French Enlightenment and the Jews* (Columbia U.P., New York 1968)

Hilberg, Raul, *The Destruction of the European Jews* (Quadrange Books, Chicago 1961)

Hitler, Adolf, *The Testament of Adolf Hitler*, ET by Col. R. H. Stevens (Cassell, London 1961)

Lewy, Günther, *The Catholic Church and Nazi Germany* (Weidenfeld and Nicolson, London 1964)

Mosse, George, *The Crisis of German Ideology* (Weidenfeld and Nicolson, London 1964)

Muller, Raphael, *A History of Modern Jewry 1780–1815* (Vallentine, Mitchell, London 1971)

Neusner, Jacob, *Judaism in Modern Times* (Blackwell, Oxford 1995)

Rauschning , Hermann, *Hitler Speaks* (Thornton Butterworth, London 1939)

Rauschning, Hermann, *The Beast from the Abyss* (Thornton Butterworth, London 1939)

Tal, Uriel, *Christians and Jews in Germany: Religion, Politics, and Ideology in the Second Reich, 1870–1914* (ET, Cornell U.P., 1975)

Wiesenthal, Simon, *Justice not Vengeance* (ET, Weidenfeld and Nicolson, London 1989)

The Jews and the Muslim world (including the state of Israel)

Chapman, Colin, *Whose Promised Land?* (Lion, Oxford, 1992)

Cohen, Mark R., *Under Crescent and Cross* (Princeton U.P. 1994)

Harkabi, Yehoshafat, *Arab Attitudes to Israel* (Vallentine, Mitchell, London 1972)

Harkabi, Yehoshafat, *The Palestinian Covenant and its Meaning* (Vallentine, Mitchell, London 1979)

Lewis, Bernard, *The Jews of Islam* (Routledge and Kegan Paul, London 1984)

Nettler, Ronald L., *Past Trials and Present Tribulations: A Muslim Fundamentalist's View of the Jews* (Oxford U.P. 1987)

Rubin, Barry, *Revolution until Victory?* (Harvard University Press, 1994)

Ruether, Rosemary R and Ruether, Hermann J., *The Wrath of Jonah* (Harper and Row, San Francisco 1989)

Segev, Tom, *The Seventh Million — The Israelis and the Holocaust* (ET, Hill and Wang, New York 1993)

Index

List of Main Biblical References

Genesis

25:23 13, 98, 103
45:4–8 47
50:19–21 47

Exodus

19:5, 6 76

Numbers

21:14–21 11

Deuteronomy

23:7 13
27:26 70

1 Kings

19:10 53

2 Kings

24:20 269

2 Chronicles

36:13 269
36:17 269

Nehemiah

2:10 15

Esther

3:8 10

Psalms

59:11 99
69:22, 23 98
87 15
139:21, 22 269

Isaiah

11:10 82
42:18–22 77
43:8–13 83
59:20, 21 66

Jeremiah

27:3 12
31:34 85
31:35, 36 85
43:10 269

Ezekiel

16 54
25:8–11 12
25:15 12
26:2 12
35:5 12
36:3–5 17
36:20 17

Daniel

11:21 17